RING

OF THE

CABAL

By

Ella Cruz

The Secret Government of

The Royal Papal Banking Cabal

From the series

"Filthy Shades of Deception"

BOOK 1

3

Table of Contents:

How Did Post WW2 Agreements Take Place

-The Rothschilds

The Secret Government (The Deep State)

-The Axis of Evil and Its Connections To High Societies: Follow The Money

-The Vatican

-The Axis of Evil and Old Russia, The Bolshevik Revolution

The Formation of The Brigade

-World Wars

-The United Nations Charter

- Micro-Chipped "Citizens of The State"

5

-The Deep State

- *How Does The Ministry of Deception work*

-What we "act" is the extension of our beliefs

-The "Quick Acceptance Disorder"

-Our Death Rope

-Europe's National Sovereignty Destroyer

-The Grand Chessboard

-Eurasia, The Cold War, and The Middle East

-The "Osama" Lie

Primary Tools of Control

-The United Nations, Treaty of Rome and The European Economic Community, NATO

Secondary Tools of Control

-Surveillance, Gun Control, Global Warming

-9/11, The "Pass" To Control

-Regionalization of The World

-Was Hitler a Rothschild?

-Did Hitler Flee in Argentina?

-Who Is Angela Merkel?

-The Replacement of The Western Nations

-Refugees?

-The Proxy Army

-The False Flag And The Hoax

-CO2 Is A Good, Clean, And Ecologically Essential Gas. Why Should It Be Eliminated?

-The "Cash Pot" To Fund The World Government

The Crime Network

-George Soros Has A Nazi "ISSUE"

1- OCCUPY WALL STREET September17, 2011

-The Cult of Nihilism

-Communism = Anti Diversity

2- Antifa Anarchists Are Brainwashed By All Universities And Colleges And Trained By Soros

-"People's Republic of Berkeley"?

-The Religious Cult

-Generation "Me"

-Congressional Record–Appendix 1963, pp. A34-A35

3- Soros And White Supremacy

-The Biggest Lie In History of Humanity.

9

Saul Alinsky; Rules for Radicals

-Hillary Clinton, a Raving socialist

-Enemies Within

-Zombify The Nation

-The Road to Suppression

-Wolves Are Coming

-Wolves In Suits

-Alinsky In Action

The Divider In Chief

-I Am An Angry Young Man

-The White-Man Issue

-The Jackpot

-Master of Agitation

-The Chief of Mischief

-Workshop: How To bring down America?

-Who Is a Community Organizer?

-Legacy: Race Race Race Race

-The Angry Black Man Becomes The Authentic Black Man

-Vehicle of Destruction

-The Shadow President

-The Constitution Is Not Fluid!

Obama And Saudi Arabia

-Prince Al-Waleed Bin Talal

-Donald Warden A. K. A Khalid Al-Mansour

-Huma Abedin & Hassan Abedin

The Federal Reserve

-A Private Bank

- Woodrow Wilson And The Authorization of The Federal Reserve

-Titanic, The Unsinkable Ship

The Playboy Empire

-Hugh Hefner

-MKUltra Sex Slaves

-Bill Cosby

-Project Paperclip And Importing Nazi War Criminals

-CIA Becomes The New Third Reich

-Paperclip Treason

-Operation Porn

-Sadistic Porn

-Who Funded The Playboy?

-The Kinsey Case

-Pedo-Mania Becomes The Science

-Sexology or Rapology?

Obama – North Korea

-North Korea?

-Why North Korea?

-Project ARTICHOKE

-Alice And the Wonderland

-Treason Was The Reason for Obama's Season

Pope Francis

-The first Jesuit Pope

-Cardinal Jorge Mario Bergoglio and The Military Junta

-The Vatican Billions

-The "Nazi-Jesuit-CIA" Alliance

-Masons Congratulate Pope Francis

-The Final Destruction of Catholicism

-The International Tribunal into Crimes of Church and State

-Why Did Pope Benedict Resign?

-The Queen of England In a Lawsuit??

-Court Documents

-Lizards and Reptiles

-What Witnesses Say

-The Angel of Death

-RING OF THE CABAL Infiltrates Everywhere

-Hidden No More

-Bigger The Names, Bigger The Crimes

-We Eat The Babies

-RING OF THE CABAL Becomes Satanic

-The Hampstead Case

-Cathy O'Brien; The Presidential Sex Slave

The Royal Family

- Soros's New Political Boy Toy; Justin Trudeau

-Who Are The Windsors?

-Loyalty Is To The Monarchy, Not To The People.

-Germans Become British

15

-Close Nazi Relatives

-The "Dutroux Affair"

-Behind The Royal Doors

Drip Drop of Liberations

-Where Did It Come From? How Did Humanity Open Its Gates To a "Coup of Cruelty"?

-The End Justifies The Means

-There Is Nothing On The Internet You Can Delete

- Everything Is Registered Somewhere

-Obama DOJ To Legalize 12 Perversions

-Gird Up Your Loins!

How To Stop The Cabal And Prevent The Future Agendas

-There Is a Solution

-27 Steps

Disclaimer

This book is a reflection of Author's perspective, personal thoughts, assumptions and beliefs according to facts or her common sense depending on the issue. Other people's statements are properly quoted and the name of the author/speaker is cited and credited. In order to help readers in fast research, references are named immediately. The author should not be held liable or responsible for any misunderstanding, misuse, damage or misinterpretation that some readers may go through. Fortunately, we still live in a world that people can express their thoughts and ideas even though they may receive a conspirator label. Freedom of thought, speech, and expression is people's tool to investigate. To request any type of reproduction, please contact: info@ellacruz.org

Dedication

Presidents choose a former President as a role model

Teachers choose a model in historical figures

Spirituals look into Saints and Gurus

Warriors look into heroes

This book is dedicated to great heroes of my time:

Andrew Breitbart

Seth Rich

and

Julian Assange

■■■

My great love is a contribution in the memory of

Kim Clement

Introduction

It's coming. The freedomless, cashless, gunless, pornographic, pedophile society is coming. 250 smart city projects in progress, 800,000 children who are missing in the U.S. each year (meaning 2222 child per day), lawmakers and judges who push legalizing pedophilia, and Nazis in America who have established one of the most horrifying concentration camps which by no means look like the German concentration camps and call it "smart cities."

It's coming.

Smart cities are not beauties that I denigrate. There is nothing vital in them that I flatten. There is no universally defined vocabulary to describe the viciousness of smart cities.

The final product of the new world order,

and the mark of the beast

is coming.

Just as Twitter and Facebook shut down your account in a fraction of a second because they don't like you, your business and your bank account will be unauthorized – if they let you have any in the first place. You will be watched and traced to everything you do and everywhere you go. The highly technological city cannot be formed without the whole city being watched. We will be forced to integrate the system and saturated by the synthesis.

Our health will become a public concern as it may affect the "public good", so if they determine that we have a mental problem because we disagree with them, we will be given our medicine and will be watched to take them and will be kept in contempt if we don't as for the "public good" principle, we will be a threat to the "public." We will be so controlled to forget the sequence of what has happened to us. Basically, we will be catapulted to knowing our place. Intensity and clarity of our mind will be considered a threat.

They may consider an exact time for sleeping and to wake up. They may consider we are not allowed to eat meat or bread or whatever they don't consider it healthy, because if we are not healthy, it may affect the "public health."

They will severely obligate our kids what to read. They may even forbid us to have kids, or they may force us to conceal for them just to confiscate the child at the moment of birth.

The possibilities are unlimited, but as a free people, we are not able to paint a situation like this. Had you anybody in prison? Ask them how were the rules for taking a shower or taking their meals, talking to other inmates and reading books. Watch movies made in prisons. The information available to you will be limited because no historical prison will be like smart cities.

People will be completely dependent on the government for everything they get. Nothing in the world is free. If they shed a positive light on smart cities that everything will be free, and nobody will own nothing because the government will provide everything you need, that is a big lie. They have removed our biggest commodity in the world which is OUR freedom. Your freedom is gone, and they will have all the freedom they want.

We will be all the same.

Pain doesn't discriminate.

There will no longer be energy providers as the government will provide while tracking our fair share of energy. They will track whatever electronics and technology we have in our house. They will know what is and what is not in our refrigerators and if we are storing a forbidden food, they will know it.

We can no longer move without our microchipped ID verification on the public transportation system, and we will have a coupon to be able to move to a certain distance as more distance will consume more fuel and we will harm the global warming. What is or is not our "right" will be completely modified and determined by the government regulations according to the "public good."

Add to all that, Artificial Intelligence and robot superiority is the next to come. There will be no focus on what is authentic and appropriate for us, just total obedience. The mighty and smart will be bullied as unappreciative and uncooperative, and the lowlife will be promoted, toured, assigned recognition and installed in higher positions. There will be no tantrum or outrage, no plan or dream project for the future.

On top of that, we will have porn indoctrination hundred folds of what we have now. For now, they have been so successful to bring pornography in the streets. What we see in the streets, regardless of being about looks, behavior or bizarre sexual insanity are the reflections of porn movies. We are actually watching porn movies in offices, stores, national TV, cartoons, books, schools and wherever we might think. And now they are pushing the same in schools. They have actually done this without our knowledge. Parents don't know what their children are studying in the schools, and there have been incidents when parents found themselves shocked encountering pornographic sections or the promotion of pedophilia in their children's books.

According to the National Center For Missing and Exploited Children NCMEC, 800,000 children are missing in the U.S. each year. That makes almost 2222 children a DAY. It is huge. It is horrendous. Where do these children end up? What if there is a team in higher places that provide children for some people?

What is the biggest crime in our society? Pedophilia is certainly one of the biggest crimes and the rulers who run the rulers have been pedophile rulers. The black-mailing system demands this principle and is designed to do so. What is the moral result of sexualizing children at the age of kindergarten or right after? It desensitizes society and "pedophilia" as a crime will remain just in history books and pedophile criminals who we can't wait to see them behind bars will no longer be considered criminals, as the culture of sexualizing children will automatically decriminalize them. No crime, no criminal. All will be considered consensual. This is a systematic push and an organized movement by the establishment to gradually shift the parameters and decriminalize the criminals at the expense of degenerating our children. There is no mercy here for children. People who sexually educate children in kindergartens don't give a damn about children's sexuality which is actually nonexistent at their age. The only thing they care about is to pave the way for pedophiles and have fun publicly with no need to hide.

They don't care about the children's needs.

They care about children getting used to being touched.

The pedophilia shock is far beyond what we know. They have social conversations, books, and arguments that publicly praise pedophilia, picturing it as a very romantic, and enthusiastic attraction. This is ludicrous but what is more absurd is to ask us to compress our conscience to the extent to fit in their agenda.

This has been going for decades but was intensified since 2015.

They are silently shifting to create a new sexual "preference" called "pedo-sexuality". Mysterious accounts on Facebook & Twitter proclaim themselves as not-harming pedophiles argue that "being a pedophile and sexually attracted to children is a preference, not a crime". By insisting and repeating the "no harm" mantra, they aim to earn our pity and soften our vision toward pedophiles, resign from protecting our children, authorize them into the pain, and sacrifice them by glorifying the horrific act.

The partisan left is united with the pedophiles. We see how the media hide the pedophiles' arrests. Am I surprised? Not at all, but yes my jaw drops when I see the left debates pedophilia and calls it liberation. "A child has a sexual need" means I (the pedophile) need my prey and have to justify an excuse to get it.

If our laws were severe enough, and if once convicted as a pedophile, the predator could be sentenced to death by gas chambers or whatever the law determines, this horror show would have been ended way before. A pedophile will never be trusted with a child in a room again. That's my opinion; I do not agree with the death sentence in any other case except pedophilia as there is no cure for it and I am unapologetic about it. Our laws need to be changed and not having enough severe laws has been the reason to let this maniac pandemic overtake the world as we see today.

Children are not commodities. They are not mature enough to know what they want. Children at ten don't know who they want to be, what major they want to study, to whom they can trust. They can't drink alchohol, they can't drive; they can't stay out at night alone, they can't vote. Why should they have sex? Tell me how many children who are grown in safe and healthy homes wanted to have sex at the age of FOUR to TEN as the pedophiles claim. These people are sick!

They also have their pedophile-sympathizer psychologists and judges who spend hours using complex psychological and legal concepts to intimidate people, knowing normal people will not understand their terminology and discussions on the benefits of pedophilia and the right for children to have sex.

It is time to stop romanticizing pedophilia!

How do they use children as their satisfaction tool?

As revealed by CIA documents, the Nazis have never been eradicated but moved to America. They enjoyed a protected status in America and were accommodated to continue their Eugenics experiments to achieve a final result on how to exterminate the unwanted species and modify the species which are going to be born. They have franchised their Nazi ideology to the authoritarians in power and there was actually no distinction between German Nazi scientists and the CIA's eugenic mind controllers of the era. They should officially be considered as the 4th Reich. Eventually, they were, and those of them at the core of the deep state are in fact the fourth Reich as what they did is the evidence of this premise.

Except that the Nazis' enthusiasm and savageness indeed were intensified, nobody was after them anymore and, no one would call them war criminals or scientifically racist.

The co-operation and mind exchange between the Nazis and the high profile CIA ranks had several results which the continuation of German Eugenics, Project MKUltra, project Artichoke, space programs and numerous CIA operations were its results.

They used MKUltra technics on children to condition their minds.

With tools of mind manipulation and body control, the
fourth Reich engineered a new form of concentration
camps.

A non-physical camp where prisoners are not locked
behind walls and bars. They are not tied with chains.

They are not going to die in gas chambers.

They have manipulated people to the extent that today
after 80 years, the public vision of concentration camps
look like Auschwitz, surrounded by big grey walls and
fences, and distant in a location that nobody can reach.
Not considering the fact that that this is a super modern
world. Nothing is as it was 80 years ago. Concepts like
transportation, information, healthcare, and education

that you once knew, have all been changed.

The principles of life also have changed. People don't
receive their information and lessons from the hard work
and experiences of their parents or history books but
from the TV, movies, and schools. So if nothing looks
the same, why should concentration camps look the

same?

Where does the main information come from for most

people?

The information comes from the combination of how the
technocrats monitor their consumption, what the "bad

science" declares, what the media says, what the students learn in the school, what they see in the movies, what their hero celebrities and actors do and what the books of law tell them about what they can or cannot.

All these manipulative industries have been compromised for almost a century. People ARE in the prison of their minds. People ARE controlled by these corporations and industries which act as the front men for the elites in power, so people ARE in concentration camps. They are distracted, and they are very happy with it.

Aldous Huxley the English writer who was interested in parapsychology and philosophical mysticism in 1946 predicted:

"There will be in the next generation or so a pharmacological method of making people love their servitude and producing dictatorship without tears, so to speak, producing a kind of painless concentration camp for entire societies so that people will, in fact, have their liberties taken away from them but will rather enjoy it."

Had all this being said, how can we stop it?
That's why you need to read the book.

I was tired of frightening alarms, but no strategy and I was tired of addressing the issue but raising the sense of helplessness.

We feel helpless if we don't know "what who why when how" of an issue. But when we know, the monster becomes a puppy.

Simplifying the complication was the key. If we want to achieve victory over the CABAL, the path should be simple and practical. People should feel the problem. Otherwise, they won't engage.

If it's hard for them to collect the pieces of evidence, we do it for them. "Ring Of The Cabal," not only exposes the entire ring responsible and involved in the abuse of power and crimes against children and humanity, but it also prepares us with technics to fight for our lives.

This is our world, and we cannot let them eliminate us. We have to come together and fight the CABAL. We have to see humanity not race, praise humanity, not gender, gratify humanity not just being on your side. We have to act just like when we act after an earthquake, a tsunami or a disaster when we forget anything but humanity and God. Our children are in danger. Those who are not yet kidnapped or abused are sexualized in schools, and those who are gone are kept somewhere in cages. This is the only thing that may open the eyes of the asleep and the only subject that can unite us and the only goal to be commonly perused.

"Our Children."

Just think about children and anything else will vanish.

We must do whatever in our power to save the children.

No matter what.

Smart cities will be the beginning of the end, where our children will officially become a commodity and a currency.

Get yourself together. Put your pants on.

Find your tee shirt. Tear down that wall.

Move this mountain. Shake this ground.

This Is A War.

"All's fair in love and war."

Poet John Lyly's novel "Euphues

Chapter 1: The Axis of Evil and Ministry of Deception

How Post WW2 agreements took place

"Power Corrupts....and absolute power corrupts absolutely."

Lord Acton, in a letter to Bishop Mandell Creighton written in 1887.

The "Hunger Games", the fiction where the totalitarian elites of society control the public and gamble on their lives had a message. What if our future world becomes the same? But if we press our memories, The Hunger Games has a flashback in history: The Gladiator. Same concept, same style of living, different times, different outfits and locations.

People lie when money and power are involved.

We were not the real owners of our society after WW2. We were not living in our countries but in several corporations and the owners of these corporations are decision-makers. We are convinced to have freedom of choice, but we choose what they want, reinventing ourselves to fit their decisions. More programmed, more scheduled, more "them", less "us," less me. Someone was teaching our mind to be the servant. When we trusted our governments so much and preferred to sleep, we let them decide for us. It is a blueprint, a new way of being. The dissolution of the old good days. Our memories fade, and history is vanished and gone with the wind. "We" become less, "they" become more. A heroic scene or a phrase in a historical book flashbacks into our generational memory but the deception is more colorful. Was it the black and white of the war to push us toward a color? Any color but just a color?

They lobbied to cut our ties with our past, sang a new song, gave us a new name, dragged us elsewhere, somewhere called " future" and the mainstream media swept the road for them. Where is this promised land of the "future"?

The Hunger Games is the future.

The media cuts the synaptic connections between our rational mind and the truth and keeps us in the dark while feeding us with misinformation or distorted information. They do everything to prevent the public from critical thinking. That's why we should wake up and look beyond the illusion. During past years of deception, we have faced this issue repeatedly; people catch a big scoop of major news outlets, feel its falsehood but deceive themselves to believe it as they love their safe spaces and when they face the truth, for the very reason that it pulls them out of their comfort zone, they react aggressively and rush to come back in their safe zone again.

The idleness of mind is spiritual suicide. We prefer false hopes and a luxurious package of lies rather than bitter truth. But that way, we don't become better, we become bitter. A better gladiator slave.

Kaboom after kaboom and nothing happens. We are the silence inside the conch shell on the table. It's like having a ball filled with bitter insects inside; but smooth, perfumed and beautiful outside. Our professed ignorance knows what is inside, so we prefer to play cautiously with that ball in a way that it doesn't "remind" us what is inside. We can't face it as the functions of our brain including thinking, alertness and information processing are distorted by "Psychological Operations" constantly affecting the encoding procedure of information running on our minds.

The self-claimed owners tell us how to think, how to feel, what to buy and decide what they decide. Their menu (Agenda) is on the table but the choice is just within the options on "their" menu. We can become an extremely good servant, a good servant, or just a servant, the choice is ours but always a servant and nothing but the servant. Nobody wants to take a look at outside alternatives. If people just take a glance at possibilities and listen to other voices, it won't take more than a few days to overcome lifetime indoctrination.

"Diet, injections, and injunctions will combine, from a very early age, to produce the sort of character and the sort of beliefs that the authorities consider desirable, and any serious criticism of the powers that be will become psychologically impossible. Even if all are miserable, all will believe themselves happy, because the government will tell them that they are so."
Bertrand Russell

We have been programmed since we are born. No Trojan horse was better than the TV. Manipulation has told us who we are, where we are, and whoever had questioned was mocked and ridiculed by the corporate media. This is a "Scrutinized Design" to make us lose our cognitive abilities and be hopelessly dependent on the system so we cannot be able to fight back.

They gave us garbage with the beat, and we called it music. They gave us garbage so weird, but we called it art. Why did they consider this design? Because only this design matches their agenda and "they" want it. They want the world and they want it so bad. They want all its resources and work power. They want it all and try their all to get it. For them, the world is "their" property and we have occupied it, their chessboard and we are intruders and enemies, and we shouldn't know this; because when we do, we fight back and if we fight the good fight, someday it will have the domino effect.

It stuns me, when today, in 2016, people still accuse us of being a conspiracy theorist even though, after almost

70 years of plotting and running a hidden agenda since the end of WW2, nothing is in a theory phase anymore. It has come to pass, and you can see the outcome of the so-called "conspiracy theory" all around the world. So how can a "theory" have tangible and irrefutable proofs if it is just a theory? When a "theory" breaks through and leads to a result, it's not a theory anymore. It becomes FACT.

"Then ye shall know the truth, and the truth shall make you free."
John 8:32

Hollywood is known for being a one-party "system" in which you are either with them or against them. Movies and TV series condition our minds and normalize misbehavior to degenerate the society at its roots and make it OBEY. Society is stuck with a meaningless popular culture. The same Hollywood sometimes has been used as a pathway to truth. There are movies and TV series which are not just there to entertain but to tell the truth beneath the surface; mostly because big producers involved in the agenda are so in love with their iconography and symbolism that they just love to openly communicate it. The same symbolism which I believe someday, when everybody is enough informed, can trace them back and bring them down.

In some other incidents, however; some authors aim to reach out to people, while some others are probably so drowned in the corruption that they have fun revealing how they did it. House of Cards? How many movies did you watch in your childhood and the story unmasked the CIA plotting and killing whoever decided to serve the country and oppose their agenda? How many TV series and movies like *the Matrix, Person of Interest* and *Hunger Games* painted the vigorous-intensity of mind-controlling systems that self-claimed elites use on citizens to prevent them from asking and thinking critically? How many TV series like "House of Cards" and "Scandal" exposed the scale of corruption, deceit, and power-thirst inside the system and unmasked the truth behind the presidential campaigns and how they really run for office? Jason Bourne for example; a movie inspired by Edward Snowden, the American NSA- CIA contractor, pictures a young tech tycoon who in my opinion impersonates Mark Zuckerberg and Jack Dorsey, owners of Facebook and Twitter. The tech tycoon in the movie has built "Deep Dream," a social network that collected users' Metadata and information and passed them to the CIA.

Having our popcorn, we watch them and think *"Oh, this is a great movie."* No, this is not; this is a reality show and is not great. What we dictate to ourselves and what the media is architecting in our heads are lies. Our reality is fiction. We should wake up and help everybody to wake up and destroy the illusion. Had we not closed our eyes, we wouldn't have to fight for what we already were: A Free People.

We need to learn HOW to see and when we do, the proof is in plain sight. The mainstream media is tool number one to indoctrinate the mass and tool number two, is the education system.

The education system can program us to changes our "perception" of reality. So our brain will be prevented from "deciphering" and will produce electrical signals to our bodies based on distorted perceptions.

If our "perception" of what is going on changes, we can easily be manipulated to live in an illusionary dimension of the bitter reality. In this case, our minds will be able to fight against ourselves and in favor of mind-managers, who programmed us to continue to live in a dream world. The education system wants us to OBEY and teaches "How not to think". Their proof of evidence are links to their own titles on their totally owned media which are good excuses to stop any comfort-seeking mind. If students encounter an alternative article, the educations system labels them as "mental ghettos", forbidding students to go there. Why? Because If they can see the invisible, they can do the impossible. Once they start thinking, once they see the truth, there is no coming back. The genie will be out of the bottle and in a matter of hours; they will start to discover a mixture of compulsion and worms of lies that they have been told over the years. I know so many people who were the product of a long trajectory of manipulation and were sleeping for years who woke up to the truth in a matter of few months from the moment they realized the deceit. It's not that the self-claimed elites were so intelligent to deceit us, but it was just unbelievably easy to do so as we deactivated our common sense, unplugged our wisdom, over trusted our governments and sank into sleep.

When the only source of information is a combination of two monopolies; the education system and the mainstream media, both controlled by the government, then waking up and turning on the TV means to see, hear and feel what the government wants us to. If the elites who fancy themselves to control and own the world, both financially and politically, secretly run the government, then all we hear-see-feel is their words in your ears, their fictional world before our eyes and submission to their will is the only operative path in our minds. **We are obeying them by default.**

The world's richest and most powerful people are some philanthropists who donate their money and re-invest back into society. Why should they do that? Let's first see who is a philanthropist.

According to Wikipedia, a philanthropist by definition is:

"Someone who engages in philanthropy; that is, someone who donates his or her time, money, and/or reputation to charitable causes. The term may apply to any volunteer or to anyone who makes a donation, but the label is most often applied to those who donate large sums of money or who make a major impact through their volunteering, such as a trustee who manages a philanthropic organization."

Considering the definition, there are a large number of good philanthropists doing a magnificent job engaging in charities in favor of positive changes and humanitarian activities like homeless, AIDS, cancer, real education and many more. No doubt in their good intentions and they do so mostly through charities and sometimes by setting up a non-profit organization. But some people have hijacked the concept of philanthropy and mask their evil intentions behind euphemisms, and the patina of "public good's legitimacy" to donate monumental amounts of money to their evil causes and plague their intentions on the public. There is a natural antagonism between what they want and what is good for us but money is their vehicle of destruction and empowers these oligarchs, and the road is a non-profit organization that acts as a channel.

The pattern is as follows: They establish and finance a nonprofit organization which will be their "Crime Network". These organizations always have very appealing names and interesting and courageous mottos. These oligarchs camouflaged as philanthropists start to donate their "own" money to their "own" nonprofit organizations, then hire people with good intentions who are mad at or misinformed on some issues in society, and they start to work. Later, surprisingly and being a suspicious observer, we notice what that organization is doing is quite the opposite of their motto and their slogans. Some of them are so rich who can set up a series of non-profits to wash their fingerprints on the issues. How? They establish the main non-profits and those main non-profits establish sub-non-profits. The philanthropist funnels his money into the main ones. When they need to create a cause, it is a sub-non-profit to come forward and announce the case. So the name of the philanthropist has nothing to do with the created cause. Then the main non-profit (acting as the bank) pours the money into the cause of the sub-non-profit and the sub-non-profit pays armies of publicists, judges, lawyers, politicians, journalists, and academics into the cause. Therefore, the name of the philanthropist or his money is nowhere near the cause, and nobody thinks of any connection to condemn it. If the cause is criminal, we just can't put them in jail.

The substantial actor in this "seek and hide" field of philanthropy after the Rockefellers is George Soros, a Hungarian immigrant who was 14-year-old during the rise of Hitler. In his famous 60 minutes interview with

Steve Kroft on December 20, 1998, he admitted while he was a Jew, he presented himself to SS Nazi authorities as a Christian and cooperated with them in confiscating his fellow Jews' properties. He not only claims to feel no regret for this inhuman act but also recalls those years (helping Nazis), as: *"the happiest years of my life."*

I have dedicated two full chapters to this strategic game-changer and forced intruder of our lives. This planetary parasite is a man who changed the balance of post WW2's global power through his financial terrorism. His war machine and total control over major countries, his tactics, massive donations, and his austerity have dramatically modified the world and the fundamental structure of our families and consequently, our societies. He shook the main Pillars like social-sexual-religious beliefs, laws and sexual identity. All these concepts have been shaken up to prepare the population for the underground, unelected, unwritten, but dangerously pursuit and almost accomplished, NEW WORLD ORDER on the face of the earth.

"It is sort of a disease when you consider yourself some kind of god, the creator of everything, but I feel comfortable about it now since I began to live it out,"

George Soros interview with The Independent, June 3, 1993

But he is not alone. He is just the final bead. There is a RING that chains these "self-claimed owners" together. A destructive team with their own rules and currency whose tools and dogmas are presented to us as natural law and the mechanisms for social and economic matters of "do or die" and aim to extinguish what we know as life. I would rather start with the older protagonists of this chain who have been the greedy founders of the mortal machine during ages. Then I will break down three different blueprints of a desired technocrat World Government, which together became the manual for achieving their final goal and the official form of it. Having this accomplished, I will focus on new entries like Soros, who because of their un-natural devilish talents became even more powerful than the old mind-managers and replaced some of them. In the end, the connection between different leaders and masterminds will be revealed. We will find out how they are all part of the CABAL and how the RING works. You may have no idea of the names revealed here. Unimaginable people are part of the RING and run the CABAL. The fiber that keeps them together. their currency and the pathology to go up and become part of them will blow your mind. Become stronger and tougher and have the gut for the final chapters. It will not be easy, but it is a duty to know and help those in danger. Spread the awareness or they will continue to pillage. Awareness is our greates weapon. May God help you with His strength.

-The Rothschilds

There is no doubt that the Rothschilds are the wealthiest family in the history of the world. Their wealth started to build up back in the 1760s when Mayer Amschel Rothschild; a German, founded a bank to take care of the German Royals' wealth.

55 years later in 1815, Mayer and his five sons, had already owned several other banks across Europe which their official task appeared to be only portfolio management for the rich elite and wealthy politicians of those European countries. However, this was not their only mission and being the few noble families at the time and expert in doing financial management for long, they have mastered other capabilities, and auto qualified

themselves to other capacities and competencies and progressed at the speed of light. Right after a century, around 1910, the Rothschilds had owned all major banks across Europe and the world, and when the temptation of this surreal power, urged them to conquer the world, the conflict began, and this exact point connects the Rothschilds to today's World Order. Control the money and you own the power to control. Control the money and you control the source of information which is the substantial tool to paralyze the ability to think and the ability to making decisions.

During both WW1 and WW2, the Rothschilds had control of the money coming from all countries who were engaged in war in Europe. It was just simple. They were the only bankers even if with different names. They were the only money exchangers, the only loaners, and treasurers. Whatever should be bought or exchanged, whether arms, staff or safety, the Rothschilds were involved. They could easily manipulate strategies and policies governing both wars and lead them to the results they wanted to happen which means the results we see today. It's just more than easy to understand; if you are the only one who can do a job and if you are highly capable of it, then anybody in need of that service, needs you. Now if you are good enough to play the game, the winner is you. Because the "leverage" for being "the only one" is vigorous and can discipline whoever needs the service, under "your" control. Worldwide strategies and decisions have been manipulated by the Rothschilds up to that very moment in history around 1913, but there was still no serious plan to overtake countries and politicians and curbing all means, and there was still no trace of the so-called fantasy of a New World Order. But the experience of overseas manipulation gave them an idea.

In those years, the Rothschilds learned something: "The power of Radio and Newspapers".

For us living in 2016, it would be so difficult to imagine a world without all means of communication as we see today. In those ages instead, the greatest joy for people was listening to the radio. Reading headlines in newspapers was the only gateway to be informed about the events in their cities, their own country and abroad. A wealthy Rothschild who is clever enough to manipulate royals and politicians will soon feel the power of media as a channel to further their own interests. The Rothschilds had fully understood that "money and media" should be inseparable allies to stifle dissent. One word on newspapers or radios, which at those times would have been taken by people as the "holy truth," could miraculously create money. That was why they started to fund newspapers and radio stations, but as they were super-intelligent, they had never talked about themselves in news. That was how the media became the dance floor of their thoughts. The Rothschilds were always silent progressive policymakers behind closed doors. They create NEWS.

Back in the 1800s, Paul Reuter, the founder of Reuter, who in the late 1890s bought the rights to Reuter from the Rothschild family, and remained a partner in House of Rothschilds, was one of their banking partners. The Rothschilds had financed elites and politicians of all time.

As mentioned before, Reuter bought the "right" of Reuter not all of it, so the Rothschilds remained the partner. Today, Reuter is a worldwide agency that owns the Associated Press. The latter by itself owns 1700 newspapers; 243 news bureaus which employ more than 5000 broadcasters across 120 countries. Keep in mind that almost all newspapers and TV channels in the world use Reuters and Associated Press as sources. Reuters and Associated Press serve as international news corporations. To avoid going far from our main storyline here is a very brief explanation which is a key to understanding these news agencies:

NBC, CBS, Owned by GE = General Electric = JPMorgan = the Rothschilds

CNBC, MSNBC = Microsoft &Time Warner & General Electric = JP Morgan = the Rothschilds

ABC, ESPN = Disney = Very old ties to the Rothschilds

HBO = belonged to Time Warner. Time Warner now belongs to Ted Turner, and he is the Owner of CNN. Ted Turner founds CNN; then takes over the Time Warner and becomes its biggest shareholder. So Time Warner owns CNN too. Ted Turner = Very close ties to David Rockefeller = The Rothschilds

Turner and Rupert Murdoch; the owner of Fox News, are hostile enemies. The conflict between them goes back in 1983, when a Murdoch-sponsored yacht, crushed into the yacht skippered by Turner during a race. Turner's yacht run around 6.2 miles (10 km) from the finish line and at the post-race dinner, Turner verbally assaulted Murdoch and challenged him to a fistfight. Decades of a verbal fistfight between CNN and Fox News is an old wound.

In 1998, Ted Turner donated $1 billion to the United Nations. Considering the function of the United Nations, which we will cover in the next chapter, this is a very important fact to know why CNN acts as we see today. As you see, constructing the Ministry of Deception, and installing bricks of its foundation, is a result of a 360 degree scrutinized work and not an overnight agenda.

In 1913 Jacob Schiff, the plotter in chief in designing and financing the Bolshevik revolution, has set up the Anti Defamation League (ADL) in the United States (Does the surname look familiar? Do you recall Congressman Adam Schiff? Adam Schiff is the son of Edward Maurice Schiff and grandson of Frank E. Schiff; a notorious Khazar). (ADL) the organization is formed to slander anyone who questions or challenges the Rothschild global conspiracy as being anti-Semitic. Schiff's descendant Andrew Newman Schiff was married to Al Gore's daughter Karenna which is a matter to consider carefully. Al Gore was the former Vice President to Bill Clinton. He is the main Climate

Change's architect. He is one of the crucial figures of the Trilateral Commission.

-The Rockefellers

The Rockefeller family is the 24th wealthiest family in the United States' history. Today, their wealth would be estimated at 11 billion dollars. The origin of this wealth comes from oil.

In the late 1800s, gasoline was considered as an unnecessary and unwanted byproduct obtained from Kerosene Company productions. Regarding the company's policy, gasoline was a waste, therefore; the company poured it into the river. It was John Rockefeller who discovered a use for the wasted gasoline; a discovery that changed the destiny of the entire world.

From wasted gasoline to oil production and from oil production, the Rockefellers shifted from being inventors to orchestrators of greedy wars across the globe to attain more oil. The "Black Gold Power" was precedent to nothing ever before. The Rockefellers made their gigantic fortunes so they too, like the Rothschilds started to make huge investments back into the government and society to fulfill their own goals and became the forever bête noire of the coming generations.

Their targets were education and healthcare. What we see today as modern federal education and medical care is founded by the Rockefellers. A big part of the medical care system which was totally dominated by the Rockefellers was the vaccine industry. That's why we see a special confederacy between "Lords of Vaccine"; the Rockefellers and Bill Gates, which we will intensely investigate.

Up to here, we have four core industries owned by these families: the Media, Oil, Education, and Healthcare.

-J.P. Morgan

J.P. Morgan is not just a Wall Street's invest smart personage and investors' guru. Modern Americans know him as one of the wealthiest men in the United States and one of the most influentials in Wall Street, but the history of the name is considerably older than that.

1913, has great importance in the financial history of the United States. The bankers' monarchy; the "Federal Reserve" is born in 1913 and the same year, the US banking icon; J. Pierpont Morgan passed away, and the empire was inherited by son Jack Morgan, and again the same year, The Rockefeller Foundation was formed.

The House of Morgan sat on the cusp of the American financial system around 1838 and became the Rothschild's banking partner and "cover-up" front. The Rothschilds love for secrecy was the reason they used J.P. Morgan & Company to be their front agency. Perhaps the strategy of putting sub-non-profits at the front row to cover-up for the main non-profits comes from this principle.

Why do we focus on details about Morgan? Because he shaped General Electric and why is this important?

After inventing the electric lamp, Thomas Edison had business ties to many companies. Edison Electric Lamp and Edison Machine Work were some of them. Morgan financed Edison's products and research and merged with some of those companies which led to founding "Edison General Electric Company." This company was also heavily involved in railroads and Motor industries other than electricity. Morgan was the Lord of railroads and electricity. Later, "Edison General Electric Company" merged with another big company "Thomson-Huston Electric Company" and formed the legendary General Electric which J.P. Morgan later bought all its shares. To answer our prior question of *why J.P. Morgan is important*, the answer is here.

We have to add the monopoly of Electricity and Railroads to the three elite families. These industries are still in the hands of the same families.

We had the Media, Oil, Education, and Healthcare on our list and now we add Electricity and Railroads or transportation. Consider that trains were the only means of transportation and also consider that we are talking about the early 1900s. Whoever had these monopolies in hand, had a governmental power. The oligarchic state was unofficially formed but talking about it was the forbidden topic.

Today, General Electric is a multinational corporation headquartered in Boston; Massachusetts. Its main offices are located at 30, "Rockefeller" Plazas at "Rockefeller" Center in New York City, known as the Comcast Building.

Notice the connection here. The main headquarters of **GE** is located in "**Rockefeller** Plaza." Back in 1904 John Moody, the founder of Moody's Investor Services, said, *"It was impossible to talk of Rockefeller and Morgan interests as separate."*

The fact is, in 1893, The United States was down on the road of an economic collapse, and this depression took two years. The economy was in danger and threatening the country. It was the 1893's recession that empowered Morgan. That year on the surface, lending $62 million worth of gold to the government, Morgan saved the U.S.

Looking back at the time, the U.S government was 360 degrees different from today. Things were so much easier. The federal government and the military compared to what we see today were almost nonexistent. So the impact of that money was tremendous, and the power behind that impact is the influence we are tracking today.

What happened after that gold was lent to the government? Morgan's bank was one of the main managing partners of the Federal Reserve. America fell into the trap of owing the Federal Reserve Gang (a private bank), and also to The House of Morgan. Does owing always lead to bowing? Definitely yes but let's see what happens later.

In 2008, Wall Street faced another total disaster; the big collapse. When all those companies, who seemed too big to fail, crushed in the blink of an eye, to avoid panic and suicide, the Federal government dedicated trillions in loans to people to resist and survive. But the government didn't have the money and to avoid the collapse the money was necessary. Where to ask for help?

Who better than J.P. Morgan?

Again, the government is sinking more and more, and the lifesaver climbs higher and higher to the top. Since then, the government is nothing but a financial servitude to the Federal Reserve demagogues.

We are not going through the whole story of these three families as you can search online and there is tons of information concerning them. Besides, it takes us away and becomes distractive to our main story, but it's crucial to know how these three familial monopolies had and still have all the control over main banks, industries, education, and the press. For centuries, their tentacles of power owned every major industry, and that's how they consolidated their financial terrorism and pushed an agenda that affected every aspect of our lives.

In 1936, Senator Gerald Nye, launched a probe to investigate the Morgan family as he believed the House of Morgan pushed the U.S into WWI, just to create more loans. He wrote a documentary report titled "The Next War" or "the old goddess of democracy trick." He had pieces of evidence that have convinced him Japan will be used to push the U.S into WWII, and this is exactly what happened. So we start to notice that suspicious moves commencing to "creation" of major wars are not a modern instrument but have an old background.

Morgan had close relations with Japan's two wealthiest families: the Iwasaki and Dan families, owners of Mitsubishi and Mitsui. Morgan also had a close friendship with Italian fascist Benito Mussolini. During WW2, the German Nazi Dr. Hjalmer Schacht was

Morgan's Bank link. After the war, Morgan's people met with Schacht at the Bank of International Settlements in Basel; Switzerland to avoid a public appearance with Nazis and a direct meeting with them.

What was the reason for this meeting? Did Morgan fund anything related to Nazis? He was an investor, a moneylender, but he was also a railroad professional. Did Dr. Hjalmer have anything to do with Eugenics in Nazi camps? How the Rockefellers became so active in human experiments and Eugenic topics after the war? We know that Morgan and Rockefeller were inseparable.

We will see in other chapters that direct Nazi ties are strangely intertwined with these families.

-Bill Gates

Who doesn't know him? The Co-founder of Microsoft, Harvard's second-year dropped-out to work on a project that later became Microsoft. Gates says: *"I realized the error of my ways and decided I could make do with a high school diploma."*

Today, the wealthiest man in the United States has become another name on our philanthropists' list and uses his mega fortune to push a selective set of policies around the globe, and these policies have nothing to do with digital products. Bill Gates is one of the newcomers joining the old bloodlines who have always been watchful to expand and grasp the new superstars who could be aligned with their agenda.

Why do we talk about Bill Gates here in this chapter, which is dedicated to studying the older families of the secret societies? Because due to him being in bed with them for decades, he has become the prominent connection between the old families and the new "Soros and allies" group. Enough to say that Gates's father was the president of Planned Parenthood, and he has donated $20M to it. But there is somebody else who had a bigger donation to Planned Parenthood and that person is his best buddy, the silent Warren Buffet who only up to 2013 had donated **$231M** to killing babies; shameful.

Bill Gates is obsessed with over-population. He produces vaccines, and he has personally put forward 2.5 billion dollars to spread vaccines across the globe. The substantial part of his vaccine project includes most regions of Africa, and he is the man behind Monsanto as the largest shareholder of the company. A company that sells death by producing genetically modified crops for third world countries but effective all over America. Why genetically modified? Good question.

Monsanto has become the seed crop cartel in America. Each farmer should buy seeds and machinery from Monsanto, and all seeds bought from Monsanto are genetically modified. Are these seeds for construction or destruction? We will come back to this issue.

Gates's domination goes beyond vaccines and seeds. He wants our mind too. He is one of the major donors of Common Core operative through the federal education system and has established new guidelines for our educational system. So our kids go to school and learn the standards that the Common-Core dictates. Books have been changed accordingly as well as what our kids eat in school. It's not just about selective science but also selective mentality. Education and science have been perverted into selective ideologies. The "divine earth's" chosen people decide what fits their cultish Earthology and that is what is taught in schools. Is there anything else that can shape the children's perception of the world as schools and universities do? No.

Anything wrong here? Maybe not yet but if you listen to Gate's speeches in his different seminars around the world, you will notice what is wrong. He constantly lectures about DEPOPULATION trying to justify its legitimacy. He believes the population of the world is much more than the earth can bear which is immoral, and the government should implement procedures to REDUCE the population. He is a con artist, a charlatan, and a demagogue. A true imperialist who self assigns the right to purge the world of unnecessary breeds.

He says loud and clear: *"The world today has 6.8 billion people. That's heading up to about nine billion. Now if we do a great job on new vaccines, health care, reproductive health services, we could lower that by perhaps 10 or 15 percent."* Just Google the same sentence and the video stands out so you can see the exact words coming out of his mouth. Unfortunately, the google monopoly which has become worse than Nazi SS Gestapo in obstructing the information; drowns these links if not eliminate them completely, so although I cited the link in my references, by the time you click, it may not help.

Gates says this DEPOPULATION can be done via "vaccine programs." Do you get the irony? Depopulation through vaccines? Bill Gates expounds on how we must all consent to a "kill the humans" strategy: meaning a gradual kill-switch, to save the planet from the carbon dioxide we make.

So who will decide who shall live? Gates?

How about starting with you Mr. Depopulator?

Many parents do not want to vaccinate their kids anymore. Vaccine-injured children have received billions of dollars in recent years. Parents insist that injecting a virus into their children's body, is making them sick. On the other hand, a new study shows regardless of what virus the vaccine contains, the adjuvant "aluminum" is doing damage to our health.

In his interview with Doctor Sanjay Gupta broadcasted by CNN on February 2, 2011, Gates said:

"We could cut the number of children who die over a year from 9 million to half of that, we have succeeds on it, and we only need about six or seven vaccines more -- and then you would have all the tools to reduce childhood death, Reducing sickness, REDUCING THE POPULATION GROWTH Stability and the environment benefits from that."

In his other speech titled, "Innovating to Zero!" Which was held in Long Beach, California TED2010 Conference, approximately four and a half minutes into the talk, Gates, again clearly said:

*"First we got population. The world today has 6.8 billion people. That's headed up to about 9 billion. Now if we do a great job on new VACCINES, health care, reproductive health services, WE LOWER THAT by perhaps 10 or 15 percent."***(What?? We lower what? The population by use of vaccines??)**

The host of the speech was David Rockefeller and the King of CNN; Ted Turner. In 1996, in an interview for the Audubon nature magazine, Ted Turner said: *"A **95%***

reduction *of world population to between 225-300 million would be ideal".*

As we said in the previous section, CNBC and MSNBC, belong to Microsoft, Time Warner's and General Electrics which means: Bill Gates + Ted Turner + JP Morgan.

The invitation letters of TED2010 "Innovating to Zero! Conference" were signed by Gates, Rockefeller and Warren Buffet. They called themselves: "The Good Club."I am not sure if good ever can emerge from evil. These people detached from all morals. We are talking about the same Warren Buffett, Gates's closest friend, who in 2006, decided to merge his $30 billion Buffett Foundation into the Gates foundation to create a $60 billion tax-free private foundation. What can these people do together other than destruction? While some of them working on eliminating our rights, this cult-like Earth's chauvinism fiefdom works on our complete removal, and they don't even have the face of a criminal.

Who are these people? **Why should they have an "automatic existence by default" and decide who will**

live? How can we not expose the unfettered greed of these cockroaches? How can anybody with an epsilon unit of IQ listen to CNN- which its owner, Ted Turner, wants 95% of the world's population gone?

"If I were reincarnated I would wish to be returned to earth as a killer virus to lower human population levels."

Prince Phillip, the Duke of Edinburgh

Bill Gates, the philanthropist, the Microsoft giant said not only once, but on different occasions <u>with his authoritarian tone</u>, that vaccines do the destructive job of depopulation and who builds the vaccines? Bill Gates. Meaning? He produces "substances" that "reduce" the population. **What is the definition of an act that "reduces" the population? Depopulation.**

How are people reduced? They die.

So what is the exact legal interpretation of this reduction of people? Murder?

Bill Gates is a college dropped out. He has no degrees. Not any field but especially not in medicine or pharmacology. How does he produce vaccines?

Bill and Melinda Gates Foundation is a founding member of the (GAVI) Alliance or Global Alliance for Vaccinations and Immunization, in partnership with the World Bank, World Health Organization; (WHO) and the vaccine industry which was repeatedly caught dumping dangerous, unsafe, untested vaccines that were proven to be harmful.

After the H1N1 swine flu emergency in 2009, there were a hundred million doses of untested vaccines left. The flu was over, and they could just have destroyed the vaccines. But instead, the leftover drugs were handed over to the WHO to be sent to third world countries. During Sarkozy's government, France has given 91 million of the 94 million doses of leftover vaccines bought from the pharmaceutical death champions; Britain 55 million of its 60 million doses; Germany and Norway did the same. If the pandemic was over and people in third world countries statistically die due to heart attacks and circulatory diseases and not H1N1 swine flu, why these generous humanistic donations? And besides, pay attention that the H1N1 epidemic appeared in 2009, just after the big collapse in 2008 and the money it made went right into the pharmaceutical companies' pockets? Did this happen just by accident?

Many vaccines, especially multi-dose vaccines are less expensive which is why they go to the Third World. They contain the ingredient "Thimerosal" (sodium ethylmercurithiosalicylate) which contains 50% mercury and is used as a preservative.

In July 1999, the US National Vaccine Information Center declared: *"The cumulative effects of ingesting mercury can cause brain damage."* The same month, the American Academy of Pediatrics (AAP) and the Centers for Disease Control and Prevention (CDC) issued an alert on possible health effects associated with thimerosal-containing vaccines while the FDA ordered to remove it.

In 1920, the Rockefeller Foundation in co-operation with Kaiser-Wilhelm Institutes in Berlin and Munich chaired research called *Eugenics Research in Germany*. The research was focused on Sterilization methods during the Third Reich by Hitler. The research had praised methods and ideas of race purity. (Nazi ties Alert)

It was after that research that John Rockefeller started to present the idea of depopulation through his "Population Council" and his interest in vaccines later in 1950.

Who is the Nazi here? Why all these people have ties to Nazis not only through their personal connections but also mentally connected to their ideology and praise their research? Morgan, Rockefeller, Rothschild, all individuals push for global world order. CNN's Ted Turner or Bill Gates who push depopulation want the same thing. What did Nazis do in gas chambers? They depopulated the "UNWANTED" impure population. What do Ted Turner and Bill Gates want to achieve? The same thing that the Nazis wanted and did: "DEPOPULATION." Isn't this Earth's chauvinism religious intolerance, anger, and racism?

GMO or Genetically Modified Organism is a depopulation con-trick designed by Bill and Melinda Gates, David Rockefeller and WHO which has never been proven safe for humans or animals. They invade the seed's DNA and change its chain. Just as harmful as Herbicides, which are sold as a part of GMO contracts. Herbicides contain above the safe and highly toxic glyphosates which are proved to be damaging to human umbilical, embryonic and placental cells in a pregnant woman who drinks water even near GMO fields, let alone eating the main GMO product itself.

Vaccines and GMO are both designed to reduce the population. I saw some propagandists calling us anti-vaccine mongers and conspiracy theorists. Their reasoning focuses on the issue that Bill Gates said a reduction of population "Growth" and not the population by itself. Eventually, they call us not only deplorable but stupid too. If vaccines help people to have better health, how "the growth" of the population; as they claim Gates meant, will be reduced?

How with a better life, "The population growth will be reduced"? If the population is healthy and in good shape, how will its growth decrease? Healthy people live longer and better, and don't die from certain diseases so they have a longer time to produce and take care of their babies and their living conditions are stable due to their ability to work normally and longer. Just as our ancestors did. Hence, the population will "grow"; again, just as our ancestors did. The population OR its growth won't be reduced unless with vaccines and Monsanto poisoning the globe, Gates, and friends have other intentions that assure them the population will decrease.

Families named and mentioned here are not the only families deciding for the world. There are 13 families. But the first above mentioned three families, are the oldest engaged and effective in planting the seed of a world government and protected the project from the outsiders. In the course of time, with new technologies and new masterminds, whenever they found a new intelligently vile superstar, ambitious to conquer the world, they pulled him under their heretical wings. Gates and others are some of them, and this went on for long up to the moment they encountered George Soros, the second greatest evil strategist in the history of the world.

The first one was Zbigniew Brzezinski, the political monster who founded the strategy of Eurasia and the new world order and what the other great strategists did was just to find policies that can fit into Brzezinski's plans and guidelines. Brzezinski was discovered by David Rockefeller in the 70s through his book "Between Two Ages" and climbed the ladder of political rulership almost instantly after. He was National Security Advisor and President's Advisor to five US presidents including Barack Omaha. His daughter Mika Brzezinski is the host of the MSNBC'S Morning Joe and married to the co-host, Joe Scarborough.

It is my lifetime goal to write a book about Brzezinski.

George Soros, who called himself "god," "World's Conscious" and "Game Changer," almost controls everything in this modern age. His power has tripled since 2009, and he became the main running machine over the world since 2013. For such an evil intelligence, I had to dedicate full two chapters to cover one-tenth of all the damage he has done to the world, to humanity, and to the generations to come.

We became familiar with the main producers of the "our life" movie. We saw how newcomers got on board. In the next chapter, we will discuss how these powerful individuals and groups found each other, morphed the agenda together and how they shaped a secret deep state that is intertwined like a RING and hermetically sealed inside the main CABAL, worshipping it and thwarting everything on their way. A fascist beast with several heads, which from the moment it's heart started to beat, it never stopped but the monster grew larger and larger. A monster fed with the bloodshed, abomination, inherent cruelty, corruption, and exploitation.

Chapter 2: The Twilight Zone of the Axis of Evil

The Secret Government

"Word secrecy is repugnant in a free and open society; and we are as a people inherently and historically opposed to secret societies, to secret oaths, and to secret proceedings. We decided long ago that the dangers so excessive and unwarranted concealment of pertinent facts for outweighed the dangers of excessive and unwarranted concealment of pertinent facts far outweighed the dangers which are cited to justify it. Even today, there is little value in opposing the threat of a closed society by imitating its arbitrary restrictions. Even today, there is little value in insuring the survival of our nation if our traditions do not survive with it. And there is very grave danger that an announced need for increased security will be seized upon by those anxious to expand its meaning to the very limits of official censorship and concealment..."

John F. Kennedy, Presidential speech.

The Rothschilds, the wealthiest family in the world, believe in their legacy. Unity, the dynasty, and the bloodline were and still are the main core of their power. They never betrayed or competed, and always stood by the hierarchical priorities of the family. For the bankers' monarchy there exists another type of hierarchy. The "blue blood" is not the only blessing that sits kings on their throne. There is a "Secret Throne" hidden in such plain sight that we have been fooled to notice. "Real Kings" ascend to a real throne, and that is: "The Money Throne."

On June 24, 1814, Amschel Lord Rothschild, the founder of the Rothschild Empire, in a letter to his son, Nathan Rothschild, quotes from Sir Davidson's book, The Shadow of a Great Man. *"As long as a house is like yours, and as long as you work together with your brothers, not a house in the world will be able to compete with you, to cause you harm or to take advantage of you, for together you can undertake and perform more than any house in the world."*

Another example of this dynastic unity is in a letter written by Salomon Rothschild, one of Amschel Rothschild's five sons (Anselm, Nathan, Salomon, Karl,

James), to his brother Nathan on Feb. 28, 1815, which says: *"We are like the mechanism of a watch: Each part is essential"*.

Digging into their books, quotes, and beliefs, we learn for them, money is what makes the world go round and money buys anything. Greed is their god; money is the throne, money is the ideology and money is the lifeblood running in their veins. Great wealth breeds power for anybody but for them great greed is the running force.To worship and serve this god, to sit on this throne and to advance this ideology, obsessive "unity" among themselves is the key. The strategy is to keep all the crossroads under control and divide the enemy and the project is the ongoing seizure of our land and our resources by the Rothschild colonizers.

Heinrich Heine, poet and philosopher, who himself was the son of a banker, once said: *"Money is the God of our time, and Rothschild is his prophet"*. Amschel Rothschild's famous quote says: *"Give me control of the economics of a country, and I care not who makes her laws."*

The pathology of maintaining the influence of the Rothschilds among them is marriage. Like the royals in history, these marriages are pre-selected on a family tree map attached to a contemporary world map. The "who-where-how" is determined to shape new family units to serve the dynasty; to expand and to empower the kingdom. Unless there is no "must merge" with an influential outsider family at the time, Rothschild marriages are within the family, usually with first cousins. It can hardly come as a shock that perversion, occultism and the swinging lifestyle are the routine lifestyles in these elite families.

The Axis of Evil and its Connections to high societies: Follow the money

-The Vatican

As stated previously, every source of money leads to the Rothschilds, so it's not surprising that in the early 19th century the Pope asked the Rothschilds for a loan. The Rothschilds welcomed him with open arms. Visits and the flow of money continued to the point that, over time, the Rothschilds came to manage the entire wealth of the bank of Vatican, taking over all the financial operations of the worldwide Catholic Church in 1823. From that day until today, the Catholic Church's global financial system governance has been interlocked with the

Rothschilds and their colonial occupation. The Vatican accumulated an unprecedented treasury that the House of Rothschild continues to control to this day. Remember the famous quote said by Amschel Rothschild?

"Give me control of the economics of a country, and I care not who makes her laws."

Their god and their throne, their ideology, and their strategy, overtook Vatican City's bureaucracy and that influence spread through the Church's international veins. The Vatican has been steadily corrupted since the first loan. It does not advocate Christianity but the fake messiah of Churchianity. Today, the hierarchy is nothing but religious leaders wearing the right clerical garb while actually being wolves in sheep's clothing. Their goal is to eradicate Christianity.

Pope John Paul II

Why is the cross upside down?

A tragic historical error dangerously impacts our assessments. A mistake made by most scholars, authors, researchers, and bloggers divides truth-seeking people.

Rothschilds and the secret families are not Semitic (descendants of Abraham) Hebrews but charges of anti-Semitism and racism will be on whoever speaks against them. (They are Ashkenazim/Khazars. See Chapter 5.) They hate Semitic Jews. The Khazars call themselves Jews to deflect attention to the Semitic Jews. Once aware of the difference between the Ashkenazim/Khazars and Semites, one understands the entire establishment cannot be attacked effectively without understanding their Khazarian roots and extensive tentacles. Not being aware of this lifesaving difference, we will become separated, fractionated and divided, just as they have planned. Khazars and militaristic Jesuits, believe in Satanism. They call The Lucifer "Lord of Light", they practice the ancient customs related to Moloch, they are occultic oligarchs as seen in their leaked private meetings, communique, and statements. They believe in cultish brotherhood and bloody rituals obligatory in their in freemason units. Jews believe in God. Is that a "little" difference??

We will fully discuss "Khazars" in chapter 5. So wherever you see for example the Jewish Rothschilds or Jewish Jacob Schiff (another Khazar who joined the Rothschilds and produced at least 148 heirs), you have to substitute the word Jew with Khazarian as follows: The Jewish Khazarian Rothchilds or the JewishKhazarian Schiff and this simple substitution is fundamental.

-*The Axis of Evil, Old Russia, and the Bolshevik Revolution*

Living and dealing with money and politics, while always crunching the numbers and seeking profits, the Rothschild colonizers were acutely aware of any move from the start and could forecast events happening in countries where they were portfolio managing the wealth of its ruling class. Meticulously documenting the vulnerabilities of a particular economy and political system, the Rothschilds created causes to produce outcomes in their favor.

It was so tempting to the Rothschilds, with $35 million deposited in Rothschild's Bank of England and $80 million in the Rothschild's Bank of Paris all belonging to the Tsar (not to mention the entire wealth that belonged to the Russian aristocracy), almost all wealth of the Tsar was entrusted to them. The Rothschilds realized that if anything happens in Russia that can endanger the empire, they could hijack the wealth that they had already in possession and nobody will ever know.

When an idea is so simple and the solution so profitable, why not create a cause to sweep the aristocrats off their wealth? Now we start to see where the platitudes about equality, class wars, humanity and democratic rights came from. The concepts of "working class" and the dictatorship of Plotraria were instantly manufactured and supposed benefits of communism and ruling the working class was savagely advertised to the society that was about to be oppressed and a mendacious call for democracy was made while those poor men and women were just targeted for destruction. Leveraging wars and preparing circumstances, conflicts or illogical policies are simple for those who dynamite and scheme them. If people keep themselves alert to these plots and tricks they can defeat them but this was never a case in history. Ordinary people have been conditioned to look at the powers as "on top of the top," so their belief is that they are "untouchable."

Wrong. They are more vulnerable than they seem. Simple tricks defeat simple plots. If the self-proclaimed elites fancy themselves with the title of "owners", it is just because people didn't know and were not evil enough to plot to resist them. Now that we know, I'm *so sorry* for their loss, but the genies are out of bottles.

The Rothschilds and the Schiffs financed the Russian Revolution. If we go through the details, this book becomes exhaustingly long. The Bolshevik/ Communist Revolution, based on Marxist ideology, was an anti-religion and anti-class movement that targeted those two institutions simultaneously: The empire and the orthodox church. Class war targeted Tsar and aristocrats while religious war targeted the church's wealth. The Bolsheviks confiscated the Tsar's wealth in Russia and prevented him from withdrawing a single ruble of the millions deposited in various Rothschild's banks. The Communists looted the Orthodox Church's physical objects and furniture while the treasury of the church, its gold, lands, and bounds were managed by the Rothschilds and revolutionary guard and their miniature soldiers never known where they were or even existed. They closed the churches and slaughtered the clergy to eradicate Christianity and to establish the state as the new go-to god.

Russia was the Rothschilds first official, radical experiment of overthrowing a foreign government. This taught them two lessons. First:

1. Their greedy god and money as its tool make overthrowing a government as easy as playing a chess game where you own both players and their moves.

2. When a good strategy is tailored for a particular country with a lot of bizarre canards to play the emotions, the mass has no clue as to what is going on and will follow the crowd.

They just need to formulate a cause; pay someone of reasonable intelligence to fabricate an ideology and doctrine fashioned according to the mentality of that particular area; teach him to build a group (as of today's Community Organizers); then launch them into the streets. The mob will follow the trained leaders: they will scream in the streets, break windows and kill people. The misguided troop often endeavor more and go further and get themselves killed as their cognitive ability has been swept out with emotions created by the manipulative cause, waving the flags of the cause which promise everything but deliver nothing.

 Second: the money invested in the overthrowing process, will pay back double, triple or even more as hijacking the treasury and natural resources of that country are the goal. Any war and conflict is a wealth-creating machine. The "business" of overthrowing governments is not only a fun and playful challenge for them but also a huge investment that causes income. The exact wealth gained by the Rothschilds from the Bolshevik revolution is now worth over $50 Billion.

The Formation of the Brigade

Around the fall of Germany, John Rockefeller has already started his business with Morgan playing with the Rothschild's money. At this point, they were all tied together. John Rockefeller, who made his fortune selling narcotics and moved his capital later on oil, was rich but not powerful. His power comes from the crossing point with the Rothschilds' capital. Together, they founded an organization called "Co-Masters of the World" (notice the ambitious name), which its goal was to drain the influence in all Christian churches. This way, the secret government initials were about to shape. The young secret government needed an army, so they founded the "Salvation Army", which was a faithful mini army with a red shield flag, driven from the Rothschilds' surname Roth = red, Schild = shield. (Does the color "red" in Bolshevik revolution and communism flag ring your bells?)

In Europe, they were above the law ruling in the Twilight Zone. Nobody to respond to and nobody to need. They were auto-sufficient and independent. They started to fund moral organizations and inject their perverted mentality into the education system. The establishment loves the education system, and its vehicle is morality. The oligarchs subterranean force rides on wings of morality to institute cultish rituals, recycled communism sold as socialism and technocracy using the back-door "expression" of "liberalism".

Public Education never meant education to them but to camouflage the "knowledge." Knowledge is the key to freedom and "real liberation from mass ignorance", but they obstructed the knowledge and called it "liberalism". Their liberation means the manipulation of moral values which is fundamental to socialism. liberty and freedom canards were are used to weaken the moral concepts. So to eradicate each old value first soften it by sticking a liberation etiquette on it, then leave it to the popular culture to play with it and use it on bathroom doors and gradually vanish. Through numerous clubs and communities, the Rothschilds-Rockefeller-Morgan establishment was in close contact with churches and Methodists. They loved to penetrate the religion and degenerate it from within. Infiltration became their most powerful weapon. Eradication through infiltration lasts for good. Catholic leaders around the world, both in the U.S and Europe have had close ties to the Rothschilds.

From now on when we say, the Rothschilds, it means Rothschilds + Rockefeller + Morgan.

The octopus advanced for ages. The influential tentacles of the beast's network have rooted so deep in every social, political, economic, religious, medical, and industrial aspect of our lives that cutting their roots is impossible unless cutting all related organizations and their recipes for endless conflicts.

We talked about how the deep state owns the media in the previous chapter. We discussed how Rockefeller bought Reuter and Associated Press. CNN which at first was an independent news agency joined their club later. Intermarriages between people who work for these agencies never let a complete separation between companies happen. But how owning the media can architecture our minds? How could these people build such a morally bankrupt society?

What do Americans, Europeans or other people around the world do every day? The average people wake up in the morning, check their cell phone, turn on the radio or

TV to watch the news while drinking a coffee then go to work. That means they switch their car and turn on the radio. Some of them go to the metro station and watch the big screen in the terminal while waiting for their train. The story repeats on the way home, and they can't wait to open the door, take their clothes off, prepare some food to grab fast while laying back on the sofa and watching TV. This is our life, our beautiful modern life. It's amazing to be home after a hard working day and just thinking of nothing while watching the wicked screen and let our eyes and minds go with what is on it. TV is a big help not to focus on what we have to do tomorrow or the bills on the kitchen's table.

We think that we are not thinking. We think that our mind is chilling out, but there is something on the screen right? We are listening to the slogans that the screen is mouthing. The big screen takes us with itself wherever it wants. However, it wants. **We are absorbing whatever is being projected to us on the big screen and while becoming the toxic identity "they" give us, and receiving our designed "perspective" which becomes the reflection of our perception.**

But do we have the right perception? What if there is intelligence behind what we are watching? An intelligence to indoctrinate how to think, respond, accept or reject in a special way? What if somebody or some idea which comes from superior societies with superior authorities demand the TV personnel to follow a special policy while they produce movies, broadcast news, TV series, and documentaries, hold talk shows or even launch cartoons? In that case, a director who aims to produce a documentary and has to spend a lot of money and knows no network will broadcast his movie as he has crossed the redline, will he still produce the movie? If he doesn't follow the rules, no manager will work on his documentary.

A report published by Tom Secker and Matthew Alford of "Insurge Intelligence," and tweeted by the WikiLeaks on July 4, 2017, shows how Hollywood promotes war on behalf of the Pentagon, CIA, and NSA. Basically, the report proves US military intelligence agencies have influenced over 1,800 movies and TV shows. These documents for the first time demonstrate that the US government (the deep state establishment) has worked behind the scenes on over 800 major movies and more than 1,000 TV titles.

We previously stated how the Rothschilds were the first people to discover the power of the media and how all three major networks are under the Rothschild's control to protect their power.

Yet, I have another point here. If you are the only major news outlet, then every political or financial event ends up in your newspaper. To some degree, from the economic point of view, news reached to you firsthand, can act as an insider for all business fields. It's just like magically living in the future and knowing what has happened in the past. But it is still more magic if you are the closest person to a king, minister or a politician. In that case, those "insights" reached to you during your high profile friendly chats with your imperial benefactors are not simple gossip but alerts coming from the authorities. Will it lead you to invest early or sell early regarding those "friendly speculation" and make an empire? The answer is yes if you are a Rothschild.

Secrecy in language was essential to the Rothschilds. They exchanged letters written in codes on a daily basis. They have never faced official espionage and each time eyebrows were raised, and somebody put his nose into their business, the intruder was technically screwed as some highly placed person stepped in and stopped the investigation. Their personal system of intelligence and communication kept them quite out of reach in their Twilight Zone. The beast known as the deep state was formed, and a progressive long-term plan was in hand. The beast was in place, in purpose and in position. Dispersed interventions were not giving them satisfaction anymore. They were ready for wholesale executions and macro-bombardment of the society. They had a drafted goal. "Secular Humanism" as a single world government with single money and a single religion and to do that, they needed to rebrand themself as an anticolonial, anti-nationalism and inter-religious movement.

Unions and treaties were crucial tools to gradually put different countries under same authority and obligations and could perfectly work as the first steps to dissolve the power and sovereignty of each nation. Treaty here treaty there, obligation after obligation, free nations were creepily positioned under the authority of a trade union which instead of being an economic tool, morphed into a twentieth-century colonial authoritarian nanny state.

As for the moment, "create a cause and propose a solution" was the winning strategy. Somebody somewhere is guilty while the matchmakers search for a crime to fit the guilt. It worked awesome in Russia. The generated "result" was the initial GOAL in the first place. It was orchestrated BEFORE the "problem-solution" Vanity Club starts to work. However, one must consider the notion that during this global engineering process, not one hundred percent of the plan may go exactly as it was presumed. Unwanted events and people's meddling, or Geo-Political miscalculations could change the outcome but even proximity could be as desirable.

The premium member of this "problem-solution Club" is Chaos. Social engineering "cannot" happen without a "Class A celebrity" named: CHAOS. Let's imagine a vision. Imagine a barbaric anti-human group with a superstition to attack and harass people, then imagine the media mouthing slogans about the necessity of international meddling for "humanitarian help" as the solution. This "humanitarian help" normally takes place in its military form as the barbaric forces may prevent civil groups so, this help should be forced and military secured. Changing the geopolitics of a specific region by architecting big chaos is what the deep state has been doing for decades. Chaos is the fixer and the barbarians used are the proxy army. At the final step, the battle will be settled through a pre-determined settlement which was programmed well before the conflict starts, and the big lie of democracy will finally conquer while leading the region to its own decadence. The region is transformed. It will never be the same as it was before. What happened to the region? It is changed and reshaped. The new system of the region is rebranded as a new good but the reshaped region is what they were looking to create in the first place. What was first on "their" map on the table of their secret meetings, is now officially on the world's map. Mission accomplished. The "pre-designed result" is what the whole theater has been set up to attain it.

learning this mechanism changes our entire point of view about what happened in the world during the past 70 years. It's all about perception. **Our perception changes our means of expression and consequently, our minds and bodies. Our perception is like a zoom lens. We can open or close down our views. What makes us do it, is our perspective of the available territory. When you stop restricting your perspective**

and zoom out your lens, you see patterns, intentions, and knowledge of a wider view.

An evil Masonic slogan which is George Soros's motto says:

"Out of the battle of Chaos, would come a new order."

That's evil. Dictatorship is not order. A dictatorship with different manifestations under different false democratic labels is still a dictatorship. If they create chaos, what we need is to target the confusion, diagnose the separation of different entities of the chaos, put them in a frame by establishing a new connection and give them a shape being still. **You can't shape anything when everything is moving. And you can't create order by just shutting down everything in motion. That's called "death" not order. The crucial element in every society subject to chaos is DISCONNECTION. The order cannot come by silencing disconnected parts. That's "Oppression". The order comes by finding common grounds and CONNECTING again.**

-World Wars

Back to the secret society colonizers, the global subterranean plan of taking over the planet was cosmopolitan, subconscious and unspoken and included three world wars, which as the result of order after chaos, each of wars, would have fulfilled part of the plan and advanced them one step closer to the world government fantasy. Each time, prior to the reshaping process, the land which was subjected to "reshape", had to be monitored; a special PROBLEM just in alliance with the geopolitical needs of the zone should have been manufactured, and the solution should have been vowed through the bullhorns of the establishment media and humanistic canards.

The first land subjected to deconstruction was Russia. Global engineering in Russia took place in three phases. **First**; the manufactured "problem or cause" appeared to be the Tsars leading to class wars, and the presented solution was Communism leading to the Bolshevik revolution. The rewards were exquisite: Hijacking both Tsars and the Orthodox Church's wealth, the result was so promising, the first episode of the operation was successful. Mission accomplished.

This process took place before WW1. However, the first phase's outcome; that is "The Soviet Union," was going to occupy the land and stay in power as a new proxy to threaten the West and hence, to justify the **second** phase which was WW1 and the post WW1 era's militarization of the East. This way; founding organizations like NATO to militarize the west as a shield to protect the land, sea, and sky against the Soviet threat was justified. Finally, going through WW2 and the **third** phase later (Now this is beautiful) was to shake up the Soviet Union into pieces, and it was a piece of cake.

So after all the bloodshed on the streets, executions of the political prisoners and tortures by the heinous monster of the Soviet Union, the Soviet Bimbo was not useful anymore. NATO, WW1 Treaty, Treaty of Rome and Europe Economic Community, and the United Nations were all created. Time for the Soviet tool to disappear. What they have planned for Russia from the beginning, was several small countries with no power under the West's influence and control. Although the third phase of Russian deconstruction was accomplished decades later, it was part of the plan from the beginning and WW1-2 were Guest participants of the plan. Wars entered the game at their set time, played their role and exited accordingly. Without this plan, there was no other way to hijack the Russian countries from Tsar's hands and build up militarized organizations with international power in the West. Not in a million years. The subterranean government of the deep state didn't attack Russia. They managed that Russians themselves did the job for them and the Bolsheviks imprisoned, wounded, killed, or exiled whomever they wanted.

WW1 had the following results:

1-The "Cold War" between the Soviet Communism in the East and the "Democracy" in the West, the militarization of both East and West with weapons of mass destruction.

2- The "United Nations"

Each country that signed the United Nations' Charter agreed that the Privy Council is bound to put into operation, the provisions of the Charter. We the people didn't vote for that Charter. We didn't read it. The United Nations Charter is horrific and non-human. If you have followed the story of Charlie Gard, the eight-month-old British baby died in July 2017; then you already know his story happened because of the United Nations' Charter. The European court didn't allow his parents to take him home to die or take him to the US to cure and had ordered that the baby should die in the hospital while they terminate the cure and withdraw his life support. **What kept the baby detained in the hospital was the "United Nations horrendous Charter" which says the child doesn't belong to their parents but the government.** The United Nations and not his parents decided that the baby is better off dead. Despite the American Citizenship granted to the whole family Trump administration to dethrone the European authority upon the child and transfer him to the U.S for medications, the hospital didn't let the child out.

Charlie's parents launched a Go Fund Me page and rose $1.65M to cover the costs of taking the baby to the United States and for the treatments he needed, but the hospital didn't let them, claiming "this is not at the best interest of the child".

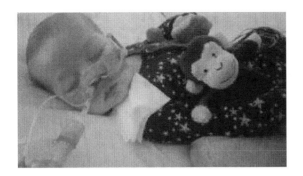

Charlie Gard in Great Ormond Street Hospital. London

Charlie died on July 28, 2017, at eleven months old.

This is the future of our babies.

United Nations, Once in power, was no longer responsible to the people who elected them but to their international cosmopolitan bosses.

The United Nations Charter

The United Nations Charter officially declares there will be a world government. A uniform population, a uniform educational system, and a one-world religion called: Humanism, one world police force and a one-world monetary system. Does it sound familiar today? Did you agree with this charter when it was formed? Was it you to vote for this? Everything was decided in secrecy.

Nobody told people that Socialism is behind the United Nations' Charter. The Charter was drafted in classified nature at Dumbarton Oaks by Alger Hiss the chief planner and executor of the project, who became United Nations' Secretary-General. Alger Hiss, a Khazarian, was a senior Soviet Communist spy convicted and imprisoned for perjury and sending secret material to the Soviet Union representatives in 1950.

Are you listening? The United Nations' Secretary-General was a Soviet's convicted felon and a jailed Khazarian spy. This is how the United Nations is formed. By Khazarians.

In "Time" magazine, on 16th August 1953, appeared the speech of Usher Burdick of the American House of Representatives in which he mentioned Alger Hiss as follows:

"Who were the principal movers at San Francisco for this United Nations Charter? Who wrote the Charter? And who had the most to do with shaping its provisions? The answer is that the Russian Communists Alger Hiss, a representative of our State Department, was the prime movers in arranging its provisions. That is the same

Alger Hiss who was convicted of Perjury. It's very beginning gave this document a bad odor."

The United Nations was designed to be the force, the hammer, and the army of the world's government. It would have needed years to shape and gradually took power. Today it has officially become the dominant acting power beyond the borders. Paying close attention, the similarities between the United Nations' emblem and the ex-Soviet Union's is quite noticeable.

Looking back in history, we see 90 percent of what was once their goals have now been fulfilled. The plan is advanced right as it has been programmed and today their final steps are almost at hand.

James P. Warburg, another Khazarian, a member of an influential banking family stated with an authoritarian tone on February 17, 1950, before the United States Senate:

"We shall have a world government whether we like it or not. The only question is whether world government will be achieved by conquest or consent."

The United Nations is designed to act as the icon of the world government. World Health Organization, World's Labor Organization, and the World's Educational Organization and so on will be its ministries and divisions. This will be the shape of their world government if we, let them have it. We can still be substantial role players with the remaining 10 percent chance that we've got. We will discuss later why even this 10 percent is a big block to their fantasies.

-The Microchipped Citizens of the State

Back to reviewing the rise of the deep state fascism and their big subconscious plan, the post WW2 era, which is our main focus in this book, was designed to act as a mini stage in which huge but gradual progressive changes should occur. These changes were both geopolitical and socio-psychological because the dynamics should well fit together. These Dynamics included the preparation of people's minds for a global disaster like WW3, a weather-related catastrophe or a dangerous pandemic which up to the present date in 2017, still failed because of "We The People".

This global disaster is the main stage and the final ACT which will shape the world in a completely new order and will establish a One World Government. Living in 2017, this era and its tensions are so tangible to us. We will break it up in the next chapter of how we are living this process, but before that, we have to finish what we were doing here, reviewing the plan of subjugating nations.

As stated, after the post WW2 reshaping process, there will be a WW3 (by their plan in 1952, not necessarily a must for us as the nations have been awakened and started to fight back). This WW3 fantasy should be big and biblical. Something staged that match the Bible's prophecy to ring the 2000 year generational unconscious of everyone including atheists. To have a WW3 like never before, the world should go afoul of chaos like never before. Riots, unrests, attacks, and massacres like never before until a point that governments declare a state of emergency. A situation that causes them to be incapable of controlling their countries like before and force them to ask for a universal board of governments with benign intentions to meddle and protect all countries. (Isn't it a situation similar to that of today's? Did you ever ask yourself why all the countries are dealing with chaos and riots at the same time? Where did it come from?) In this way, we will contribute to forming a world government to save ourselves from that chaos especially when the scene is biblical. At some point, a fake Messiah, who is already waiting to play his role, will be brought out of the closet and will be praised and worshiped by the media bullhorns and will give some relief to nations while we are well played and fooled by the New World Order's dictatorship copied from the ultimate George Orwellian control system which at that point, there will be no coming back. We will become "The Microchipped Citizens of the State." The expulsion of the majority and putting them behind the iron walls that the human race can't breach will be the state's priority. Total slavery in favor of imperial benefactors and owning our natural resources like food, water and social constructions like; labor, educational system, family, property, sexual behavior, customs, tradition, psychology and everything you can imagine is the plan.

Even our children will belong to the State; just as happened to Charlie Gard's parents. We will be a bad odor for the colonizers but not our children. They will be a commodity to the state. The colonizers who rebranded themselves as anti-colonizers coddled our demise. If this is hard to imagine then just remember "The Hunger Games", the Oscar winner movie. Stepping to a Hunger Games future dimension is as easy as stepping into the past Gladiator. Was it impossible to live like a Gladiator? No, because it existed and the Hunger Games is just a modern version of Gladiator in a modern technocrat world. That story, that madness, and sadness had nothing to do with winning an Oscar. It was just appealing and pleasing to the mind-managing oligarchs to have their plan pictured as a movie.

Yes, the Masters of Deception are the directors of the "madness", we are the players, and the world is their stage. Their ministry is a big party. A party in which you and I are their currency to spend and have fun with it.

-The Deep State

Now one may ask, why should the main deep state figures work for a plan older than themselves? An average human being's life is 60 years. For them, some longer as you might have noticed, they get really old. David Rockefeller just died in March 2017 at the age of 101. But yet at 101 years of age, he hasn't fully accomplished the plan. So why should they seed something they will not survive to harvest? Considering the original Rothschilds started their dynasty and hierarchy in 1800 and ruled generation after generation until they overlapped their brotherhood with Rockefeller and Morgan in 1900 and before WW1, why do they serve a plan that will live it partially?

Because they are part of the Jesuits-Khazarian network. The network existed long before them and will still live after them and they have to either be on top of it or somebody else will be on top and destroy them. Just like the Mafia system. Once they enter, there is no way out. They believe in the mission of their dynasty and brotherhood established in weird bloody ceremonies and rituals, sacrificing to dimensions and entities and worshipping the kingdom of darkness. According to their Jesuit-Khazarian beliefs they have to serve and be part of global governance so that's why they serve a plan that won't be able to live it. They need to maintain the position at the upper top of the network of power. If they won't be the head of the snake, somebody else will be and will crush them. They are not accustomed to being inferior or somebody else ruling them and invade their twilight zone. In their assembly, they should be at the top of the top and for remaining at the top; they have to fulfill the plan. It's a power grab game. A luxurious jungle not so familiar to us. Once the game is started, it can't be stopped. A Mafiosi system but on a world scale. This is how the deep state or the deep state has been born. A combination of these colonizer oligarchs is the enablers in chief strategic posts like CIA, NSA, media, entertainment industry, education system, the Police, international organizations and etc. Wherever they needed a seat, and the position didn't exist, they just created it.

Chapter 3

The Anatomy of the Formation Era

As we saw, WW1-2 gave the deep state (The Deep State), the design they needed. Consider a hammer, a nail, and a wall. Nobody starts with big strikes when nailing into the wall. We start with soft strikes continuously, and finally, the last shot will be a heavy strike on top of the nail. World wars are those final strikes that installed the deep state's plan (nail) right on the map of the world (wall) forevermore. The world's map was their painting, and they repainted it as they were pleased. Nobody was there to stop them. Chaos and humanitarian aids camouflaged as "Democracy" or the biggest modern lie were all the soft strikes of the hammer. This is the process in which the globalization, the new scam meaning the centralization of power in every area of our lives has begun. The wall is the world's map, the hammer is the globalization, and the nail is every single tactic to push their various strategies to achieve the final goal during decades.

"War is peace. Freedom is slavery. Ignorance is strength."

George Orwell

"The Cold War isn't thawing; it is burning with a deadly heat. Communism isn't sleeping; it is, as always, plotting, scheming, working, fighting"

President Richard Nixon

"The war is not meant to be won; it is meant to be continuous. Hierarchical society is only possible on the basis of poverty and ignorance".

George Orwell

- How Does The Ministry of Deception work

Post WW2 was a "Formation Era". Imagine two big screens broadcasting two movies at the same time in the same cinema.

One movie is a reflection of a civil socio-psychology and the other is a documentary on riots and chaos around the world. The colonizers are watching and having so much fun monitoring how their plan is folding and how the deplorable serve their plan as front-line soldiers. We contribute and accomplish their plan unconsciously. Some of us even beg, urge, protest and demand their design be fully actualized. The lunatic desire of self-destruction and foolish contributions advance the mind-manager's plan effortlessly. **This is cognitive dissonance through deception. Ignorance has always been humanity's biggest enemy, and it is always accompanied by intolerance.**

"Logic is an enemy and truth is a madness."

Rod Sterling in, "The Obsolete Man,"

We demean down ourselves and let them watch us in the broadcasting room, giving them an intense joy and satisfaction of our blood's taste.

On those two big screens, two different movies are playing and the story is always the same. One screen features the media condemning a savage dictator who is oppressing his people. Barbarian masked monsters appear from nowhere and start to flense, torture, rape, behead and attack unarmed civilians, all registered and filmed by some reporters on camera. Who knows how these so-called reporters got there? The United Nations and the barking media become obsessed with broadcasting the same clips, over and over to shove down our throats the scenario, while calling for an urgent "Humanitarian" response. The exportation of western democracy as an emergency pill overseas will be exercised, the dictator will be removed but the international army needs to stay in the region to fully demolish the barbaric group.

The "democracy" suddenly needs its troops and now we are talking about the "United Nations Troops" or in fact the "United Nations independent army". An army immediately deployed through the sea, land or the sky. An army which intends to FIGHT THERE, BE THERE, LIVE THERE, OCCUPY THERE AND NEVER COME BACK FROM THERE. Mission accomplished. The target is occupied.

The second screen on the other hand, which is in fact, the social and psychological screen, plays concerning changes in society's behavior. New ideas, confusions, concepts, terminologies injected into people's inner core brain. Deep injections programming their minds preparing them to absorb these new ideas. Concepts are well manipulated, thought and measured to be digested and accepted as modern ways of reflection and existence. The brainwashing machine creates an ecosystem that facing the isolation and being called old-fashioned and fanatic will be the punishment for those who don't integrate with the injected policies. **A social distortion through engineering and revolting morals based on undiluted ignorance in which everything becomes less important, less conservative, less clothing, less family, fewer fundamentals, less religious, less patriotism, less privacy, less creativity, less resistance but more and more obedience to authorities.**

We see swing becomes normal in couples' sexuality and we observe advertisements to end monogamy. We see gender confusion push. We see child abuse in high societies under pedophile rings; we hear rumors that you can have sex with the younger and age doesn't matter. Mysterious accounts and websites pop up citing children as young as four have the right to enjoy sex. Extreme feminism like "future is Female" and Extreme anti-women like "nothing exists as rape but forcing women to do what they have been born for", become the two sides of the same coin. We watch drugs and especially opium circulating and trading easily, we see Satanism as a new cool and cannibalism as new normalcy not in horror movies but in children's TV series, and nobody is raising red flags. In the past decade, we faced new attractions in pornography. Concepts like: "women are just there to be used" or "a sad boy is a sissy boy in pink panties" are the trendiest on the internet. We run into transgender sex change pushed in elementary schools, satanic groups and spirit cooking rituals held in art exhibitions as new forms of art, and a systematic pressure to spread violence and stone the debate. We see a series of vocabulary like kill, assassinate, white genocide, white supremacy, discrimination, racism used by the media like candies while minions and zombies of TV series' are promoting them.

-What we "act" is the extension of our beliefs

"The Mick" which was aired at 8:30 am eastern time (a traditionally family hour), shows Ben; a seven-year-old schoolboy talking about a girl's dress he is wearing, saying:*" Thanks but it's kind of breezes my vagina."* His aunt; Mick, who brags about her use of Planned Parenthood on-air, allows Ben to have his buddies over and approves the loud banging noise coming from the upper room, by vulgarly commenting before the seven-year-old: "Your sister is getting fu***." This is abusing Jack Stanton, the child actor playing Ben's role and it is outrageous.

In the same scene, Ben says proudly: *"I'm a Transformer!"* and as Mick; her aunt, fixes his dress's collar says: *"Well, ...you're a Trans - yeah, sure, close enough."* During the trailer, the F** bombs flew between 3 characters once in a second for 6 times.

New Netflix series, "The Santa Clarita Diet blatantly promotes cannibalism and assassination of white males labeled as "Nazis". Drew Barrymore grabs the bottle of blood and squeezes it into her mouth, pours it onto her chin and leaves it to drop down onto her clothes. She eats anything from raw chicken to cadaver's body parts, and this is not happening in a TV series like Game of Thrones full of sexual and cannibalistic scenes aired on nightly hours. The Santa Clarita Diet is a family comedy series that glorifies violence, spreads fear and decriminalizes abhorrent crimes to downplay it as something to laugh at. **This is an infantilization of the most fearsome issues of history and framing new normalcy and ignoring the consequences. Beliefs**

have extensions and what we "act" is the extension of our beliefs. Everything first occurs in our minds before it is materialized through actions so if these microwaves of invasion break the ground for new brutal beliefs, the macro results as macro cruelty and macro savageness will be inevitable.

All these Psychological Operations or "Psy-ops" act as the soft hammer strikes on the nail that we were speaking of and the "Deception Managers" are monitoring the progress step by step, on the screen of their Ministry of Deception.

When evil becomes good and good becomes evil, norms should be upside down to fit an evil society and what departments have dedicated their resources to officially accomplish the distortion? The Department of Education and the Department of Justice. The shameless 2007-2016 decade played a destructive role in our inner culture and therefore needs a closer investigation which we will fully cover in chapter 6.

-The "quick acceptance disorder"

We need to go back to our big screens.

The colonizers are watching. On one screen they have routine physical wars which lead to occupying and reshaping countries, and the other screen displays a constant ideological-war on the human mind, society's conscience, religion's power, spirituality, and the fundamental morals and traditions. These elements used to act as pillars reinforcing unity, strength, and faith in each other. **When people are bonded together, they have more in common to defend.** The deceivers knew this very well, and as they were preparing a new regional map of the world, they were also shaping a new map based on human's "perception" of themselves and each other, by dividing them. It is a hard definition so let's go deeper to have a better understanding.

If the regions need to be reshaped, the interconnections and bonds between the people of the same country should be cut off too. With these newly shaped regions, people will soon be dispersed between the regions and having traditions and memories in common will cause resistance against this distribution over the new map and is considered as an enemy to the globalist. The colonizers need a complete denial of an authentic, and independent national identity.

The "quick acceptance disorder" and inability to rationalize come through division. To accept a completely odd new ideology, formulating an opposite mindset in comparison to what one has had before is fundamental. The new odd ideology is based on completely different values and to have those completely different values, one has to change his "perception" of the current values he already believes in, and when he changes his perception, he loses the old ties to the community where he belonged once. Therefore, one will become a disconnected and detached single individual who has no one to consult with and reacts alone according to what has been projected on his mind. That's what the deep state did to us insinuating an egregious act of historical amnesia.

The result of the interaction between these two big screens is two matched products, groomed to be used in the final phase before their WW3 or colossal disaster fantasy. These products which will play a significant role side by side the United Nations are "The United

States of Europe" AKA The European Union and the phenomena of "Refugees" at one hand, and a wholly degraded, deranged, and disturbed human society across western countries, on the other hand. Both phenomena will be fully discussed in the next chapter.

*"We are grateful to The Washington Post, the New York Times, Time Magazine and other great publications ...It would have been impossible for us to develop our plan for the world if we had been subject to the bright lights of publicity during those years. But, the world is now much more sophisticated and prepared to march toward a world government. The supranational sovereignty (*That's why they fight National Sovereignty*) of an intellectual elite and world bankers (*Who are not elected) *is surely preferable to the national auto-determination practiced in past centuries."*

David Rockefeller, Bilderberg France.

(Parentheses hold my interpretations)

The deep state is using the American laws and the Constitution to devastate and uproot the United States and bring it down. They parallelly bring down any superpower strong enough economically to stand against the new world order. Without a good economy, the rest of you have doesn't matter because you don't have the means and the position to fulfill any plan that you may design.

How does the world see America?

Monitoring every comment section in all real and fake news networks to see what people say, I'm thrilled to see how people around the world are looking at America in an unprecedented negative way.

The Rt Channel's comments section is a declared "war zone" against America. They are not the same bots who work for MSM. They are real people who are well deceived to hate America. Some of them are from Arab countries who even can't speak English properly but just enough to attack America as they see it through a completely different lens.

They see America as the country which attacked and slaughtered people around the world having no idea about Eurasia. What is Eurasia?

-The Grand Chessboard

Zbigniew Brzezinski, the former adviser to all five ex U.S. presidents and the father of CFR: The Trilateral Commission, which is one of the most decisive global means of suppression after the United Nations Charter has authored several controversial books. Unfortunately, as usual, none of these rare books seemed appealing to ordinary people at their time. With the impeccable evidence in these books, if the intellectuals were enough committed to acting against it, they could without a doubt stop many traps that we find ourselves in right now. Such books and their influence came under public rigor, only after many operations successfully accomplished by the deep state. Just then a few scholars to some degree were able to see the evidence. It is literally like believing in the possibility of murder just after finding a slaughtered body: TOO late if it could have been prevented beforehand.

For Brzezinski, Eurasia was his grand chessboard and the game was designed to win. Eurasia is a region designed by Brzezinski which includes the whole Middle East together with Russia, China, and Africa. Basically, this was one of the inexistent regions that he had designed and inorder for this hypothesis to become reality, like any chess player, he Put the chessboard before him and started to focus on the center: Central Asia.

He designed peaceful economic agreements for this region. He needed China. He created a Trilateral Commission together with David Rockefeller to shape a *world state* in which Eurasia will merge into a coming North American Union. When he said America would govern the world, he didn't mean this existing America, but the Trilateral America they have been working to create it for years. On his chessboard, Russia will split into three republics in a loose confederation, and this Russian confederation SHOULD happen either by negotiations or by force of a big war, even a WW3 if required. It is fundamental to the plan. It doesn't matter how but it has to happen. This State (Eurasia merged into North American Union) will fully control the public's food, water, energy, jobs, immigration, politicians, governments, and religion and in this way, dominated Eurasia will control the world's three most productive regions.

Why the European Union and the Democrats insist in attacking Russia? Because it is the due time of the blueprint and should perform it at any price as it is written hence, need to find a crime to fit in.

In September/October 1997's American foreign reports we read his writings: *"US domination of Eurasia is a must. Therefore, US is now occupying the center of the chessboard, Central Asia – at any cost, even World War III. And he might have it soon in case Russia and China are unable to participate in a new armament race."* -- Zbigniew Brzezinski

So as you see when the writer is a National Security Advisor, the content of the book finds itself in American foreign reports that's why we should consider Brzezinski's books as America's foreign policy already in place and position.

-The "Osama" lie

When the Soviet Union occupied Afghanistan in 1979, Brzezinski was the head of the operation "Cyclone" one of the most expensive U.S operations to train, arm, and finance Afghan military Jihadists. That was when Brzezinski; the architect behind major catastrophes during five presidencies including Obama's, created Taliban and Al-Qaida. Islamic fundamentalism which later blew up the U.S on 9/11 was never an issue to him. He could just care about ending their orchestrated cold war to eradicate the Soviets and liberate the Russian territory and form the Russian Federation. Brzezinski's two-step-children: The Taliban and Al-Qaida were his proxy armies to blow the Soviet Union.

The pattern was to create new catastrophes to solve out-dated ex-catastrophes. It's so amusing watching Brzezinski in a video, raising his left hand towards the sky, and talking to Afghan militias in Afghanistan. It is amusing because he says:*" We support you because your cause is right and God is on your side. "*

Knowing him, this is just laughable.

You might not know that Osama Bin Laden was actually Tim Osman, a CIA asset who died in 2001, years before being ridiculously thrown into the sea. A fiction on a screen made by President Obama to credit himself for the prize. Nobody saw an operation where Bin Laden was captured or dead. Nobody saw his corpos either.

The only proof for such a historical event was a falsified photo which later, be emerging the original photo before the photoshop, proved to be a fraud. Osama was trained and backed by Brzezinski in the 1980s when Bin Laden was the head of the CIA's Arab Legionaries in Afghanistan. The strategy was trapping the Soviets into a war and keeping them busy until its breakdown. A strategy that history proves its success. But just 20 years later, the same Bin Laden ashes down the Twin Towers. When Brzezinski was criticized for creating Taliban and Al-Qaida, he became furious and said he did it as a geopolitical weapon to defeat Communism and he was so successful that would do it again. He didn't say that he was building his Eurasia and there was no need to regret it.

There are direct connections between Osama bin Laden's business interests, his brother Salem and the Bush family which starts with Bush the father, immediately after he becomes director of the CIA in 1976. If this alone is not enough, then what is?

David Ray Griffin, the political analyst, philosopher and an emeritus, former professor at California's Claremont School of Theology at the time, in his book "Osama Bin

Laden: Dead or Alive?" claims that Bin Laden died of kidney failure, or a linked complaint, on December 13, 2001 (And we know that it is true and he died in Tehran's hospital after a kidney surgery. He was in Iran and the CIA knew it). Griffin gives a bright analysis about Bin Laden; a man with a civil engineering degree, who had made his fortune from building constructions in the Middle East, and his death which we are not going through it in this book.

Brzezinski training Osama Bin Laden in Afghanistan

Photo from public domain

In January 1998, in an interview with Le Nouvel Observatour, Brzezinski admitted that it was United States policy for radical Islamists to undermine the Soviets and when the reporter asked if he regrets it or not he says: *"it had the effect of drawing Russians into the Afghan trap and you want me to regret it?"*

Question: *"Neither do you regret having supported Islamic fundamentalism, having given arms to future terrorism?"*

Brzezinski: *"what is more important to the history of the world? The Taliban or the collapse of Soviet Union?*

Some stirred-up Muslims or the liberation of Central Europe and the end of the cold war?"

I'm sure you remember how they created the cold war themselves...

To answer the question of why American expanded its military race in Iraq but let Osama Bin Laden live free for several years was the plan to occupy Eurasia and not hunting Bin Laden. Bin Laden was just the pass. It is vital to bear in mind that while researchers and thinkers see America as the authority in place, it was indeed the deep state's fascistic cult using the American office as their shield to destroy it from within. Eurasia doesn't exist on our world's map but it exists on their trilateral world map and when it exists on "their" map, they advance operations to reshape the region. However, that doesn't mean that we should be aware of these transformations. We will act upon if we know so they go forward on schedule but blame the invasion on already created causes and justifications to distract us from their true objectives.

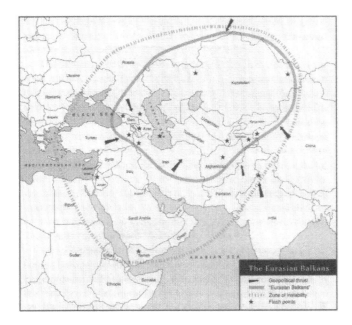

Brzezinski's Eurasia; The Grand Chessboard: American Primacy and Its
Geostrategic Imperatives (1997)

Quotes from "The Great Chessboard" by Zbigniew Brzezinski.(A must read.)

(Parenthesis holds my interpretations.)

"Ever since the continents started interacting politically, some five hundred years ago, Eurasia has been the center of world power." (Page 13)

"... But in the meantime, it is imperative that no Eurasian challenger emerges, capable of dominating

Eurasia and thus of also challenging America. The formulation of a comprehensive and integrated Eurasian geostrategy is, therefore, the purpose of this book." (Page 14 which by America he means: The Deep State's commission all around the world)

"In that context, how America 'manages' Eurasia is critical. A power that dominates Eurasia would control two of the world's three most advanced and economically productive regions. A mere glance at the map also suggests that control over Eurasia would almost automatically entail Africa's subordination, rendering the Western Hemisphere and Oceania geopolitically peripheral to the world's central continent. About 75 percent of the world's people live in Eurasia, and most of the world's physical wealth is there as well, both in its enterprises and underneath its soil. Eurasia accounts for about three-fourths of the world's known energy resources." (Page 31. Energy... the main reason the troops were deployed to the region)

"The momentum of Asia's economic development is already generating massive pressures for the exploration and exploitation of new sources of energy

133

and the Central Asian region and the Caspian Sea basin are known to contain reserves of natural gas and oil that dwarf those of Kuwait, the Gulf of Mexico, or the North Sea." (Page 125 arrogantly proclaiming.)

"The attitude of the American public toward the external projection of American power has been much more ambivalent. The public supported America's engagement in World War II largely because of the shock effect of the Japanese attack on Pearl Harbor." *(Pages 24-5)*

"For America, the chief geopolitical prize is Eurasia... Now a non-Eurasian power is preeminent in Eurasia - and America's global primacy is directly dependent on how long and how effectively its preponderance on the Eurasian continent is sustained." *(Page 30)*

"America's withdrawal from the world or because of the sudden emergence of a successful rival - would produce massive international instability. It would prompt global anarchy." *(Page 30)*

"It is also a fact that America is too democratic at home to be autocratic abroad. This limits the use of America's power, especially its capacity for military intimidation. <u>Never before has a populist democracy attained international supremacy.</u> But the pursuit of power is not a goal that commands popular passion, <u>except in conditions of a sudden threat or challenge to the public's sense of domestic well-being.</u> The economic self-denial (that is, defense spending) and the human sacrifice (casualties, even among professional soldiers) required in the effort are uncongenial to democratic instincts. <u>Democracy is inimical to imperial mobilization.</u>"

(Page 35. The beauty is right here. He says democracy in America must be abolished as it contradicts the global supremacy and brings limitation to the deep state's functional authority in opposing power on a global scale. So America should lose this softness at home and become a totalitarianism state. Are we surprised why George Soros believes the same? If people could read more and do more research, the world would have been a better place for all of us.)

"Two basic steps are thus required: first, to identify the geostrategically dynamic Eurasian states that have the power to cause a potentially important shift in the international distribution of power and to decipher the

central external goals of their respective political elites and the likely consequences of their seeking to attain them;... second, to formulate specific U.S. policies to effort, co-opt, and/or control the above... " (Page 40)

"...*To put it in a terminology that harkens back to the more brutal age of ancient empires, the three grand imperatives of imperial geostrategy are to prevent collusion and maintain security dependence among the vassals, to keep tributaries pliant and protected, and to keep the barbarians from coming together.*"

(Page 40. Attention: The empire he is talking about is the Roman Gladiator style as you see: "back to the more brutal age of ancient empires is the goal". Notice how he call us: "vassals".)

Henceforth, the United States may have to cope with regional coalitions that seek to push America out of Eurasia, thereby threatening America's status as a global power." (Page 55)

"*Uzbekistan, nationally the most vital and the most populous of the central Asian states, represents the major obstacle to any renewed Russian control over the region. Its independence is critical to the survival of the other Central Asian states, and it is the least vulnerable to Russian pressures.* "(Page 121, referring to 1997 conflict.)

"Moreover, they [the Central Asian Republics] are of importance from the standpoint of security and historical ambitions to at least three of their most immediate and more powerful neighbors, namely Russia, Turkey, and Iran, with China also signaling an increasing political interest in the region. But the Eurasian Balkans are infinitely more important as a potential economic prize: an enormous concentration of natural gas and oil reserves is located in the region, in addition to important minerals, including gold." (Page 124. The colonizer is talking about eating the Balkans up, callig it an "economic prize" for its natural gas and oil.)

"The world's energy consumption is bound to vastly increase over the next two or three decades. Estimates by the U.S. Department of energy anticipate that world demand will rise by more than 50 percent between 1993 and 2015, with the most significant increase in consumption occurring in the Far East. The momentum of Asia's economic development is already generating massive pressures for the exploration and exploitation of new sources of energy and the Central Asian region and

137

the Caspian Sea basin are known to contain reserves of natural gas and oil that dwarf those of Kuwait, the Gulf of Mexico, or the North Sea." (Page 125)

"Uzbekistan is, in fact, the prime candidate for regional leadership in Central Asia."

(Page 130, Do you recall the echoes of Uzbekistan's independence? This is the freedom they mean. Overtaking its resources invisibly)

"Once pipelines to the area have been developed, Turkmenistan's truly vast natural gas reserves augur a prosperous future for the country's people." (Page 132, Turkmenistan's independence real reason.)

"In fact, an Islamic revival - already abetted from the outside not only by Iran but also by Saudi Arabia - is likely to become the mobilizing impulse for the increasingly pervasive new nationalism, to oppose any reintegration under Russian - and hence infidel - control." (Page 133, Iran Islamic rivival real reason.)

"For Pakistan, the primary interest is to gain Geostrategic depth through political influence in Afghanistan - and to deny to Iran the exercise of such influence in Afghanistan and Tajikistan - and to benefit eventually from any pipeline construction linking Central Asia with the Arabian Sea." (page139, the ultimate goal of empowering Pakistan: Pipelines)

"Turkmenistan... has been actively exploring the construction of new pipelines through Afghanistan and Pakistan to the Arabian Sea..." (Page 145)

"It follows that America's primary interest is to help ensure that no single power comes to control this geopolitical space and that the global community has unhindered financial and economic access to it." (Page 148, the real motivation behind sending troops to the Middle East and erupt endless wars.)

"China's growing economic presence in the region and its political stake in the area's independence are also congruent with America's interests."

(Page 149, the reason China became a superpower and almost subjugated the US economy. If the deep state did not condone

China's growth, it would have prevented it very easily, but it helped it in so many ways.)

"America is now the only global superpower, and Eurasia is the globe's central arena. Hence, what happens to the distribution of power on the Eurasian continent will be of decisive importance to America's global primacy and to America's historical legacy." (Page 194)

"Without sustained and directed American involvement, before long the forces of global disorder could come to dominate the world scene. And the possibility of such a fragmentation is inherent in the geopolitical tensions not only of today's Eurasia but of the world more generally." (Page 194)

"With warning signs on the horizon across Europe and Asia, any successful American policy must focus on Eurasia as a whole and be guided by a Geostrategic design." (Page 197, the reason behind the absurd hate for Putin and Russia.)

"That puts a premium on maneuver and manipulation in order to prevent the emergence of a hostile coalition that could eventually seek to challenge America's primacy." (Page 198, the real reason behing the chaos in the Middle East.)

"The most immediate task is to make certain that no state or combination of states gains the capacity to expel the United States from Eurasia or even to diminish significantly its decisive arbitration role."

(Page 198, Listening people? "Decisive arbitration role" and always remember the distinction between America as he states and the deep state colonizer complex that he means, you see the reason behind the occupation of the Middle East.)

"In the long run, global politics are bound to become increasingly uncongenial to the concentration of hegemonic power in the hands of a single state. Hence, America is not only the first, as well as the only, truly global superpower, but it is also likely to be the very last." (Page 209, America's translation: The deep state.)

"Moreover, as America becomes an increasingly multi-cultural society, it may find it more difficult to fashion a consensus on foreign policy issues, except in the circumstances of a truly massive and widely perceived direct external threat."

(Page 211. That is why they insist on America becoming an open-border mixed-cultured bed of chaos. Multiculturalism dehumanizes the veneration of nationalism and will abolish the unity of American's power of right decision-making.)

Chapter 4

The Octopus of Control

-Surveillance, Gun control, Global warming control

Modern imperial colonialism relies on the strategy of "Divide, Destroy, Reshape and Rule" and needs its tools. We already talked about the mechanisms of indoctrination and psy-ops used by the deep state. We will dive deeper and break them down in the next chapters. In this chapter, we are going to see how terrorism was the proxy army and the recipe to succeed. We saw how formulating the Soviet Union acted as a proxy to fulfill the needs of the political philosophers and how they dismantled it at its due time. Terrorism is the same game with a different shape and name. **Terrorism is not coming from anywhere. Terrorists are the deep state's soldiers.**

New nationalities, new outfits, and beliefs, but the same purpose and nature. Engendering a new excuse to exercise power and control over the people and create chaos unleashing terror cells disproportionately. Anything unexpected and unusual can be a proxy army. Chinese ninjas, dancing pranks, a new virus or cloned animals? Who knows. Rule number one is: we shouldn't expect anything definite.

Back in 1952, when the deep state was officially put into motion, it had a goal. To reach the goal, it needed a strategy and a tool (tactics) to execute that strategy. The strategy was: divide, destroy, reshape and rule. The tools were categorized as primary and secondary tools, regarding their priority.

Primary tools were fundamental structural cement and had the duty and the authority to mobilize the earlier phases before the 80s. These tools were: The United Nations and NATO. Indoctrination through mainstream media and education was an all-time useful tool implemented in all phases before and after the 80s but its intensity was different through the decades.

Secondary tools were, the European Union, mobs-
vigilantes-terrorists, and global warming, all to
harmonize policies, mindsets and social cognitive with
"totalitarianism" and push the world in the utopia of a
George Orwellian government.

"Radical Islamic Terrorism" did not exist before 1980.
The deep state was busy with its primary tools and
creating international organizations which are planned to
become ministries of a centralized government. The
corporate media fear mongers in the 1980s started to
have Taliban all over the news. Threats to America, non-
Muslims, and beheading videos, were broadcasted
around the world. Were those beheadings real? Or were
they just productions of giant cinematographs? Who
knows? How should we know the truth? They have all
the entertainment power and resources. How many times
have the fake news agencies been caught up during a
staged clip? Almost once for every major false flag.

Islamic terrorism became more barbaric and vile daily
until the catastrophic disaster of 9/11. Was it the deep

state itself preparing the terrain to predispose the public for 9/11?

Back in those years prior to the 90s, traveling was elegant and easy. Citizens of many countries could travel without a visa, others needed a visa to travel to the U.S or Europe, but that was all. Having a visa and a ticket was all you needed to get on board. No searching, no monitoring or body screening, and no vetting. There were no security cameras in our streets, or at our homes. No registries, no data monitoring, no need for anything like these. Indiscriminate acts of vandalism and violence didn't exist. People were living in another world. I don't say it was a perfect world because it could always be better but compared to what we see today, it was heaven on earth. What we see today is so damaged, unstable, bloody and so controlled that we are not even alone in our beds. With a cell phone or a PC, or anything with an electronic screen, we can be watched.

But yet, none of these vetting systems could save us from further attacks after 9/11. With all these control and surveillance, we are far less secure than those days before. So, if cameras are everywhere if email accounts are watched, if bank transitions are under tight control if conversations are listened, and if the social media like Facebook, Twitter and Instagram have access to our most private secrets, why are we not safe yet?

And if we are not safe and these systems fail to keep us secure, why do they exist?

The truth is; these systems are not there to trace terrorism. They are there to trace us! When the oligarchs are a few, and they want to control "many", they have to centralize the decision-making power. They have to control. The more centralized is the power, the more they push us to live crammed into the slums of cameras, the more power they have.

We are being monitored in every area of our lives as a part of the "smart city" plan. Every citizen is watched because the line between being a citizen and becoming a dissident is an invisible line. Control was the agenda, and we needed to feel the NEED to be protected otherwise, we wouldn't permit them to control us. We embraced our prison and slavery. They promulgated a series of discriminatory laws against us but we were so frightened that we begged for them to give us those laws. That's how they act. They make us "believe and beg" for their hidden agenda to happen. It will be ourselves who DEMAND what is on "their" agenda.

But how did they do it? What was the magic formula to convince us to be monitored and controlled by the government?

The answer is 9/11.

Don't close the book! Don't leave. Read me like a novel, a story. Read me like a lie, but be there and read me and give your judgment at the end of the book.

Five years ago I was right here in your position. I closed a book. The book of my fight.The fight for survival. I closed it as it was not only hard to believe but also hard to live with. To whom should we complain? To which court should we file a lawsuit for those who were sacrificed? From where should we ask justice? From where should we ask for help?

And here I am again. I am writing again. I am fighting again because I deeply understood the truth doesn't change simply because I don't want to hear it. People reject what they have no idea about because it doesn't match their default, reflexive expectations.

There is no one we should ask justice but ourselves. WE THE PEOPLE should say the truth over and over again until the whole world knows it, and until we bring down the Cabal by this awareness. Then we can have justice. WE THE PEOPLE, together with those patriots still working in certain inner networks of the government are the reason that the universal government didn't become a reality yet. Patriots fed up with the corruption may not speak up for the fear of being suicide by the cleansing machine of the twilight zone.

Nine years ago, I began to dig, and after four years of investigation, I reached the head of the snake. At first, I was interested in the dynamics of the middle east as war after the war was the only news in the region that left me perplexed why. So I tried to find a connection between the theories on how the conflict started. From there, I discovered mysterious ties with events in North Africa; I found out about organizations tied to wars. I traced those organizations and from there, I reached the Bilderberg meetings which started to take place in 1954 and has been held ever since. 1954 was just two years after the demonic New World Order child was born in 1952. The social engineering of the Middle East was designed and orchestrated in Bilderberg meetings way before it happened. Again from there, I reached the Rothschilds, the Rockefellers, the Morgans and other families in high societies; The Royals, the Vatican, and new ties. I learned how they proceeded from the 1800s until the 1900s, which was the period when they started to build their emperor. The new ties and the new names were forming a long list but to make the long story short, the most powerful individuals of the Bilderberg were Beatrice; the Queen of the Netherlands and her father Prince Bernhard who was openly a former Nazi SS officer and the co-founder of the Bilderberg group. So the co-founder of Bilderberg was an ex-Nazi. Not just randomly related to Nazis, but an actual ex-Nazi who had served the Third Reich and various members of his family were Nazi members before WW2. Beatrice's husband; Prince Claus, Elizabeth; The Queen of England and the sons and cousins of older families whom we already mentioned in chapter two were other influential members of the Bilderberg. Then I found out about the new map of the Middle East and what Professor Bernard Lewis, one of the brainy members of the elite and the manufactured conflicts he had designed for the Middle East. This new ugly Middle East order falls into a bigger plan of Eurasia which is a substantial element of the new world order. Reading Lewis's map of the middle east, which took me back in the '70s and a shocking review of what has been happening there to that beautiful region, could leave no doubt in me that these people will accomplish what they plan. Five years ago, the remaining targets in the Middle East were Syria and Iran to be destructed and reshaped, while the rest has been already accomplished. Libya and Syria crisis started to take place later and alongside my study.

So I learned, we have a new order for the Middle East, a new order for the United States of Europe, a new order for the United Soviet of America which forms the Trilateral Commission or AKA the new world order. The Trilateral Commission is the new world order, you heard me right. That was so disturbing. So I started to dig more and from one article to another, from one whistleblower to another, from one document to another, I found out about the head of the snake. I put all together and wrote everything I found out. I wrote and tried to inform whomever I could and tried to spread the awareness. But nobody cared. People were not ready.

This process of ongoing seizure of our rights was advancing but they couldn't see it. The Global Warming agenda was pushed at 360 degrees; the police state was formed, the depopulation was already in place killing people through the government made diseases and chemtrails, vaccines were degenerating our kids, Monsanto was the king and was forcing farmers to starve, fluoride in water pipes was intoxicating most of the population, massive coffins were found, frightening underground tunnels were discovered, the evidence was based on incontrovertible facts supported by innumerable reports but my warnings were screams in an empty vase. Nobody cared.

In 2011, a year before the second term of President Obama, I quit. So the election day, I didn't even listen to any news because I was 200 percent sure who will be the president.

I quit because I felt helpless. No hope. Nowhere to run or nobody to complain. The world has become my prison. A prison with no way out. Before quitting, my heart was always in my throat beating crazy with every headline. I did my part as an individual, but didn't want us to do our part, they wanted us to party and be happy and don't talk nonsense. Euphoria tastes better than the bitter truth. I was not living in the United States so Monsanto could not harm me, Fluoride in water could not poison me, police state could not threaten me, but America is not just a country. America is a symbol of freedom and a symbol of hope. America leads and the world follows. It stands for the values that all freedom seekers in the world believe in and look into it as the last stand. If it falls, the whole world will go down. The whole dream will be destroyed, and the dark ages will overtake the world.

Once the land of the free and home of the brave, now is sweeping away the culture of dialogue and arbitration in which people had the right to be disunited and debate. A people who had the right to civilized disagreements now, instead of advocating for the rights of the people push to oppress the communiques and the speech they don't like. No sovereign nation should be delighted to witness the abomination of America, for if they do, the Stalinist totalitarianism sweep them too. History tells stories and those who don't pay attention meticulously, are condemned to repeat it. Humans are born free. Freedom is not donated by the government, but it's a gift from God. It is defending the freedom America represents all around the world and this is not being pro Donald Trump or Mr. A or B, this is being anti-corruption.

"If we lose freedom here, there is no place to escape to. This is the last stand on Earth."

October 27, 1964: Reagan's speech, "A Time for Choosing"

The problem of Millennials is that they never lived in other countries to see how other people look at America. If they knew, they would highly appreciate the great opportunity they have been born into. So why do they not care? Why do they not listen? Why whoever says something is labeled as a conspiracy theorist or a drama queen?

Five years ago before the second term of the Obama administration, I said enough is enough. Let me give myself the chance to close my eyes and ignore what I know to be able to live my life falsely happily. Screw you the world and screw you the deep state and screw you the globalization and you the people who don't care. Do whatever you want if you are begging for your own destruction, who am I to stop you? I will wait until the day the microchips reach Europe, then my country, then my city, and my doorstep and until that day, which may take 10 or 20 years, let me live my damn fake life.

I guess you said the same thing a few times in your life before you reach this very line.

And now look where we are again, here with you and the reason was just one thing. You the people. People count. That's why they spend millions of dollars on electoral campaigns to CONVINCE you to vote. They can manipulate some authorities or some voting machines, but they cannot have you vote for them if you don't. "You the people" are the answer to why their disgusting world government is still a fantasy despite everything they did. You are the reason the colonizer philanthropists spend billions to buy your vote. You are the reason why they lost the 2016's election. And you are the reason why they are in a panic and so furious about their loss.

The great heroes of our times, the warriors of this unfair war, the patriots protecting the soil and the values were mocked, pressured, and attacked but they didn't quit. They continued to call people and spread awareness across the globe but still, the fake news is brainwashing the population and imposes their psyops on them. Those who allow their minds to the new and maybe unknown stories became unbelievably aware and through them, words passed from one to another. That was why a person, completely out of the swamp could win the election. There was no trust in Congress, no trust in the Senate, so you chose an outsider for the office to shake the apple tree. And I think to myself, what if other whistleblowers had quit like me? Could we see a day like today? No, and I feel ashamed of myself about it. Those heroes deserve an unprecedented amount of respect. Kudos to them.

-9/11, the "Pass" to control

Back to the instruments and tools, the deep state needed to accomplish the world government plan. We discussed terrorism, and we reached to 9/11.

As said before, people count. That's why the oligarch colonizers needed a green light from you. That's why they control the media, banks and spend millions on presidential campaigns. Because they want to redirect "you" to legitimize what they want. How possibly could they ask people permission to send their sons and daughters to be slaughtered by barbaric savages without masking their intentions behind humanism? How could they convince you to work and pay your taxes to fund these horrible wars miles away from home in the middle of nowhere? How could they ask you the authority to search your handbag and underwear and watching you walking in the streets and surfing on the internet and reading your private emails and monitoring your bank transactions?

How could they ask you the pass to overthrowing governments overseas and install whom they want and take control of their oil, gas, petroleum, and gold while thousands of innocent children die in the way?

What was their winning card?

The mendacious card to convince the public must have been so game-changing, shocking, catastrophic, and justified to legitimize their agenda once and for all. That card was 9/11. The entire control measures were birthed from the evil of 9/11 as a response to the violence inflicted on unarmed civilians. A disaster that changed the shape of the whole world. Nothing can go back in time. Nothing is the same. The whole routine of our lives has been changed and that was the terrifying rise of imperial fascism.

Our morals are changed, our universities, our vacations, our cinematography, hope in our future, everything seems upside down. We are already getting used to long checking lines in the airports. We are used to monitoring communications and financial transitions. Our young children have no memory of a free world that we had before as they have been subjected to severe domination. Our free will is either dead or gone. The colonizers sending troops overseas, occupying countries then taking their people in our countries in such overwhelming numbers intentionally to making us a subclass by their numbers surpassing our numbers. This is a powerful pattern to shift the old regional order of the world to comply with the map on their table. The same map we talked about in previous chapters. **Can you notice the fact that the East is destabilized by wars and the West is destabilized by the "anti-integration/anti-assimilation" behavior of the people the colonizers bring in from the same countries they destabilize?** Do you see the big picture? Can you feel the "regional shift" that is happening by injecting the poison both in the east and west? **The democracy of war into the East, and the trojan horse of humanitarianism in the West? Can't you see the**

abortionism or no-child policy in the West and overwhelming number and birthrate of the refugees coming from the East?

They are reshaping the world, my friends. They are replacing the western population and changing the face of the streets, schools, churches, organizations with the myth of "cultural enrichment" and we let them do it. Countries are non-recognizable anymore. The misguided endeavor of no border means no belongingness. **The cute concept of "citizens of the world" is a cover-up for "microchipped citizens of the state."** It will lead to no flag, no currency, no constitution, no national sovereignty, no identity, as all of these great values may offend those who don't belong to that nationality and finally no government; their biggest canard never means any government at all but means one big imperial world government with one currency and one religion to transform us to Roman gladiators.

Imagine that the American constitution with just 229 years of age has been under attack for over 65 years of its history by forces that have sworn to crush it. We are again there. Every road leads there in 1952 and the birth of today's deep state. But the American system is not the only system set for destruction if you can care less. The clock is ticking and the oligarchs can't stand the banality of your routine life wherever you live. America as the "deception managers" repeatedly admitted, is the main obstacle to their Stalinist imperial government. The reason?

The power of its constitution.

Right after WW2, Europe was stuck in an after-war economic crisis. Whenever there is an economic crisis, there is also a far down vulnerability as a major weakness that can easily manipulate all policies during the period. Europe, which was wounded by extreme and aggressive "National Socialism" but wrongly known as neo-nationalism was more than ready to accept the idea of unity among European neighbors. The concept of being together and protecting each other was enough inspiring for those countries beaten and affected by war, fear, hunger, instability, and lack of security. Therefore, as the deep state had designed, two world wars and the post-war era were exactly going on schedule. Attractive slogans on "unity" were mouthed. Projected efforts and movements began, and the sweet poison of the deep state colonizers; the European Union was about to be born. But as everybody was afraid of another superpower like the Nazis, the only promise for the European Union was: Free Trade. So the colonizers now as crypto-colonizers assuring and guaranteeing the nature of the EU promising that there is nothing to see there, no political obligation and just free trade to heal the wounded economy and to the vulnerable governments of countries geopolitically in the Europe continent, the notion looked sweet. After long wars, it was beautiful to feel human again. It was necessary to feel safe and prosper again. It was powerful to give a message to the ugly bloodsucker of the Soviet Union that "Hey big man, look at us, we are big too."

"-If the communist dynamic were greatly abated, the West might lose whatever incentive it has for world government ... If there were no communist menace, would anyone be worried about the need for such a revolution in political arrangements?"

Lincoln P. Bloomfield, Secretary of State for Political-Military Affairs in 2005 from a State Department paper he wrote in 1962.

Just if all those leaders knew how much has been spent to build that fake monster in the old land of Russia, how much has been invested in creating such an ideology which could trigger such terror around the world, if they knew piles of gold were spent to build that deadly fear, then they would know that manufacturing a nanny state as the European Union was nothing in comparison.

Now some may say it's impossible to create all these protagonists, they were real and they believed in what they did. My answer is yes, of course, they believed in what they did. Lenin did, Hitler did, Che Guevara, Fidel Castro and others all believed in what they did. They could die, and some of them did die for what they believed. The mechanism for finding the right person for acting in different stages of the agenda demands Machiavellism and the use of charismatic, atmospheric, and cosmopolitan protagonists who believe in what they do.

 These individuals in fact, are sometimes noticed for their rebellion or intelligence and sometimes are considered for the positions years before their roles. In some instances, they have been considered since their birth or even before birth. They are well indoctrinated and trained in the desired climate along this metamorphosis capable to achieve the desired conclusion. Some of them are illegitimate children of the

Cabal's elite, raised and grown up under certain circumstances not even knowing who their real father is. What will cost them anonymously making a baby far away from home and paying his expenses and education?

Doing some digging the results are astonishing. Here are a few incidents that I have found: Nathan Rothschild (Nov 22, 1808 –June 3, 1879) had an illegitimate son with Maria Anna Schicklgruber, a servant at their mansion. The son was named "Alois Schicklgruber" (June 7, 1837 - Jan 3, 1903). For him on Wikipedia, there is just a mother name and no mentioning of any father and again according to Wikipedia, as she refused to say who the father is, the Baptist priest filled the word "illegitimate" in place of Alois's father name. There is no record of where Maria worked. She was an orphan with no heritage, so she must have worked in some house as a servant. That is the official way that life has worked in those years.

In 1940, Hansjurgen Koehler in his book titled "Inside The Gestapo", about Maria Anna Schicklgruber wrote: *"A little servant girl came to Vienna and became a domestic servant at the Rothschild mansion, and*

Hitler's unknown grandfather must be probably looked for, in this magnificent house."

Alios was ashamed of his mother's surname because people would call him a "bastard" just as the Baptist priest did so after he married to "Klara Polzl", he changed his surname to "Hitler" through Austrian Ministry, which was his mother in law's maiden name. They had three children together; Gustav, Adolf, and Paula.

Isn't it interesting? Can it be just speculation? Especially when Hansjurgen Koehler officially named him in his book? We know the mainstream media and their tribunes and we don't expect them to publicly announce how many "accidental" children do they have, who they are, and how they use them to operate in certain situations. Do we?

Some even go further and claim that Angela Merkel, the German Chancellor is Adolf Hitler's daughter finishing what he started masking the Third Reich colonialism behind the crypto-colonialism of the European Union.

The CIA's recently released JFK assassination files mention that Hitler was alive in South America in 1955. Bodies of Hitler and Eva Braun found by Russians were beyond recognition. The suicide version of the so-called truth that people heard was: Hitler Shot himself in the head, and Eva Braun took pills, and the Nazi officials took the bodies upstairs and burned them.

Really? Two burned bodies found by Russians were the only proof? The breaking report of Hitler's death was not announced by allies but by the Nazi authorities. That's the clue. When the Soviet army arrived, they called up the doctors to examine the bodies in the bunker. The doctors called the bodies: *"a bad double of Hitler and not Hitler himself."*

Gerald Williams, author of "The Escape of Adolf Hitler" is a journalist who has worked for the BBC and Sky News and has reported some of the world's major conflicts from Falkland to Iraq. On Hitler's suicide, he says: *"What we have been told is duplicity, deception and straightforward lie."*

Williams claims: *"Hitler and Braun slipped out of the besieged Führerbunker via a secret tunnel and were replaced by doubles chosen by Reichsfuhrer Martin Bormann. He says they were then whisked by plane to Spain and by submarine to Argentina's coast at Necochea."*

"The body doubles were shot and burned. They later had two daughters."

Williams also said: *"He and Braun separated in 1953, taking the girls to live in the town of Neuquen. In the early 2000s, the women were still alive. Hitler died on February 13, 1962, at 3 pm."*

There are other books and documentaries on Hitler's escape to Argentina among which, Patrick S. Burnside; author of <u>"El Escape de Hitler"</u> (Hitler's Escape) has investigated Hitler's death and found jaw-dropping gaps with no real convincing answers. We have a situation where a global leader with crimes against humanity had committed suicide, but the authorities didn't even launch a real investigation?

In 1945, Joseph Stalin, The Soviet's dictator in a meeting with Lieutenant James Byrnes America's Secretary of State during WW2 said: *"It is almost certain that Hitler escaped to Argentina."*

In 1952, General Eisenhower said: *"We have been unable to unearth one bit of tangible evidence of Hitler's death. Many people believe that Hitler escaped from Berlin."*

Stalin and Eisenhower were world leaders and the main players of the WW2 at the time. They don't just make the stuff up.

The official report of British Intelligence released on Nov 1, 1945, says:

"Available evidence, sifted by British Intelligence and based largely on eyewitness accounts, (shows as conclusively as possible without bodies), that Hitler and Eva Braun died after 2:30 on April 30th, 1945, in the bunker of Reich Chancellery, their bodies have been burned just outside the bunker."

So the report's reliance is merely on witnesses as they hadn't the bodies. You should research for yourself but before doing so, take a look at this picture and let's see what your first impression is.

The first time this image was uploaded on the internet was dated as 1937 before Hitler's official death. What if it is a fake date and is not taken in 1937 but between 1945-1955?

If Hitler was alive as CIA files indicate, could he have a daughter? What if, Mrs. Merkel's real age is 7-8 years more than what is officially announced and can a woman in her 70s look like 60s having all cosmetic products available in a modern age?

There is another theory about Chancellor Merkel that says she is the fruit of Hitler's insemination by German Dr. Karl Klauberg, who was one of the Nazi "death doctors" and was convicted by the Soviet's court. He was known as the father of artificial insemination. The theory says it was Eva Braun's sister to carry the pregnancy after Hitler's death. In that case, who is this little Angela look-like in the picture? And does this change the hypothesis of Mrs. Merkel being Hitler's daughter? There are many gaps in the official story.

Nazi scientists who survived Neurenberg and didn't move to the U.S, moved to Argentina, the post-war documents show. If Hitler survived as stated in the CIA documents, people faithful to the Third Reich and Nazi ideology and determined to protect the dynasty could easily help him. What if Angela Merkel has been groomed for that purpose? As mentioned before, Hitler was said to be the illegitimate son of Lord Solomon Rothschild of Vienna. What if Angela Merkel is "Angela Hitler-Rothschild"? Does this new bloodline change anything in our perception of her impeccable power as the strongest government representing the EU? How can we see the world with this point of view? **If we consider the hypothesis that the Rothschilds and the**

gang of Federal Reserve were related to the Nazis, then the entire ring should be Nazis. In that case, all these colonizers have the same interests and do the same things. The Royals, the Pope, and Soros should all have common interests. Is this possible? How much evidence should we collect for such a controversial hypothesis to attain permission to narrate? That's an argument we will start to investigate in chapters 5-9.

....

The academy of polemical opinionists does not have any difficulty in trashing out shocking new ideas. Infected with ideologies, "isms" or dogmas, they create them daily. What makes them national or universal is "the glorification" behind that idea which is injected through money and the media. When money flows into the veins of the media, while electric politicians puff them, the "ism" becomes an extraordinary phenomenon, and political opponents become intimidated or even criminalized, and psyops begin. The history of this psyops goes back to the "Military Psychological Operations", which are tactics used by the military to control the psychology of the "enemy" at the time of war by spreading lies and terror to deceive them projecting inability and weakness. Something like old drums in old wars. The behavior of the targeted population and their reaction are part of the damage control and crisis management. Now the oligarchs use the same tactics through the guerrilla media, well-known speakers, and non-profit organizations to promulgate the same results on their own people. Paid protests and events, seminars, workshops, Ted Talks, and debates to develop the "ism" and inject that ideology to colleges to indoctrinate. Hollywood's celebrity directors produce emotional movies one after the other on the subject, and here we go. The topic becomes a national or universal ideology and takes a life of its own. Dissidents are ridiculed and fans are manipulated to become die-hard believers passionate enough to fight for it as if it was their own idea.

The original "ism" had to be modified over time to be adjusted and fit in place in society. The problem is, these ideologies after some time fail and act as an antidote against themselves. **The reason is these manufactured ideologies suffer incapability, due to their false ground which is not compatible with the "good" in human nature. But unfortunately, the poison may dominate for half a century before being eradicated.**

Belief is the fuel for these false prophets to go forward.

The same rule applies to their fans besides, major supporters in these "movements" are pumped with significant amounts of money, power, social welfare, and other resources. So being a supporter not only fulfills their bruised egos and gives them the diva-attention their addicted minds need but also fills their pockets.

-Regionalizing the world

Back to our main story, we were talking about how the Soviet Union was the main tool to shape the European Union. **by creating the EU, the fundamental goal of the colonizers was first: to bring the major countries of the civilized world under the domination of one power. Second: Gradual but feverish efforts to abolish their borders, flags, patriotism, national sovereignty and the concept of "belonging" and psychologically preparing people's minds for a world government.**

"We cannot leap into world government in one quick step. The precondition is progressive regionalization because thereby we can move toward larger, more stable, more cooperative units."

Zbigniew Brzezinski National Security Advisor in 1995 (Morning Joe host, Mika Brzezinski's father)

According to Brzezinski, the evilest advisor in the history of America, all the Middle East should be integrated into one regional government and Europe should have the same faith. Therefore, people who are suffering, are sacrifices on the altar of their secret-police-state so that the oligarchs can attain their world government. And he says it openly and arrogantly but we couldn't hear when we were sleeping with bananas in our ears.

This intentional degradation of Europe progressively started after WW2, by unveiling their love affair to unite Europe. The time had come for the Soviet Union to be brought down. Europe was shaping so not only there was no need for a monster in ex Russia, but also the split of the small countries emerged from the fall of

Communism, was planned to join the EU Nanny State. The strategy of divide and rule was on the stake as usual. However, there was a big obstacle to achieve their victory in crushing ex-Soviet countries and putting them under the chain of European slavery and that was a phenomenon called Vladimir Putin.

Putin, a Christian and a strong leader who raised Russia on its feet again, never had faith in the European Union. So the manipulators kept their official relations with Russia on the surface, while taking the measures to overthrow Putin and install their puppet.

I remember my Russian friend Svetlana, once when we were going out to drink a cup of coffee. She stopped by a Gucci shop and asked me to wait for her while trying a pair of sneakers if I wouldn't mind. She liked the sneakers and paid for them. Later, when we were at the table, she recounted some memories said: *"You know Ella, sometimes life dances before my eyes like a movie. When I was a young girl, we didn't have shops like today. If we needed a pair of shoes, we couldn't go to some stores and buy them. We had to wait for the "shoe truck."*

"What is a shoe truck"? I asked.

She answered with a pale smile: *"A truck with piles of shoes flung all over each other. It would pass early in the morning, and we had to be vigilant days before. The shoes were the same colors, just 2 or 3 models. Once my shoes were worn out, and I needed a new pair for school. Instead; the truck was filled with all red shoes, but we hadn't time to think about this. People were all over each other dangling on each side, and if we were lucky, we could find foot mates of our size."*

Wow, I had watched some old Russian movies of the Soviet's era, but I didn't know it was that bad even after the Soviets' dissolution.

She continued: *"That's why I told you we love him (Putin). The change he brought in the market in less than 12 years is impressive. Our lives changed from waiting for a shoe truck to shop from a brand like Gucci and today, not only my parents, but all my friends have stability".*

"You know why they hate him? Because he made us rich and powerful and I don't give a damn if they call him a dictator or not."

Well, that was just a quote by a normal civilian who has lived the experience, and I found it interesting to mention here and compare what our media says about Putin with what his people say about him.

In chapter 6, we will precisely discuss the process of overthrowing the governments with borders with Russia and how their leaders are labeled as dictators to create chaos and installing puppets in office to gradually surround Putin with the United Nations and the European army to finally seize him.

-The replacement of the Western nations

Up to here, we explained how the deep state colonizers planned a new world order, primed its strategy and manufactured the tools to run those strategies. In this discussion, we have to cover one of the most controversial terror mechanisms that human history has ever faced: "The Radical Islamic Invasion of Europe and the theUnited States." Here we especially focus on Europe while the United States will be fully investigated in chapter six.

Imagine two baskets. The first one with a row of eggs placed inside in neat order. Just one row because eggs are delicate. Each one of them needs its space. They can't be piled over each other as they will crack. They are fragile and should be kept at the desired temperature and carried very gently due to fragileness.

The second basket instead, holds an excessive amount of small stones, all over each other with no space. In fact, they need no space. They are not delicate; they are stones. You can throw the stones in water or two miles ahead or out of a window of a tower and they won't break. Their structure is tough so nothing happens. This basket is overloaded. The stones are falling out, so we decide to find someplace for them in the first basket. First, we cautiously insert them amongst the eggs but the stones are too many, and we say ok we put them on the eggs very softly so the eggs will be safe. We start with ...1...2...3...4...5 and continue. Now the stones are everywhere between, above and on the eggs. Seems nothing is happening but all in one second, the weight of the stones crushes all the eggs. They all break, get smashed and injured. Nothing happened to the stones. They are in the basket. Staying there all over each other on rotten eggs and will live there happily ever after.

This is the sad story of Europe. Basket of eggs. People who lived under the rule of law and democracy. People who respect your space and protect their own space. People who socialize and mix just to some extent as the situation demands and not more than that. People who do not carry guns and are frightened by the least physical attacks because they don't face it every day. People who don't start the fight so don't expect a fight if somebody attacks them unexpectedly. They are just not used to violence. They did their best to give space, to be good, to be human, and to respect others' rights after what happened in WW2. These People accumulated the guilt and the responsibility of war and articulated it as an endless effort not to seem racist, and to condemn what Hitler's Fascism did to the world. They stepped back and unconsciously remained terrorized with a minimum possibility of a war. Europeans carried the burden of false guilt which the media pressed on their shoulder. The media very well knew who designed WW2. Europeans became more and more politically correct to the extent they forgot who they are and what are their actual rights. They just want to go to work, come back and take the dog out, enjoy the view, watch TV, go to the church, have fun, spend a night in a lounge bar or take some vacations or spa packages. Their defense force mechanism was deactivated and their memory in the background of their minds rejects any sudden change. They just want to live in peace. No matter what but please don't threaten their peace.

But as the eggs went one step behind, the stones insurgency rose and they came four steps ahead.

Of course, all normal people want the same thing. Men and women in the Middle East want to live in peace just as Europeans. They are tougher yes, their culture is extremely different, but that doesn't make them criminals. Normal families, merchants, students, newlywed couples, patients in hospitals, all want peace. But the lawless system creates unsafety in some areas making them ghettoes for those who hide from law enforcement. They should have never been invaded by the deep state masked behind NATO, the United Nations and the entire army that the West has deployed there. NATO is still making up the Russian threat to justify its existence. If the desired reality of the deep state doesn't happen, then it's the Russians' fault. Bombing people with the excuse of protecting them from violence is fabricated violence. People die under the bombs. There is nothing glorious or humanistic about bombs.

But if somebody punches them, the result is hundreds of punches from the main victim and whoever is close to him. Dense population, traffic, numerous families and a culture of closeness makes them much more bounded to each other in comparison to Europeans. In some of those countries, people have lived under a vile judicial system and are used to violence and don't know the basics of human rights. Watching graphic scenes is quite normal for some groups. Without a strong leadership which we may call them dictators, gangs will be all over the streets. The same thing happens in Russia. The Russian Mafia will take over if they have a puppet as a leader. **Countries and cultures are different. It is not that they deserve violence but they just cannot go through the process of Democracy overnight. They need decades of a gradual metamorphosis and grasp its concepts to become a democratic nation before having a democratic leader. We can't sympathize with them by our standards of sympathy and living.** Besides, our perception of reality is relative. The same reality may appear different to two people whom both encounter it.

Europeans are soft, pampered and namby-pambies. They yell if you don't respect the law, but they don't come to attack you or punch you out of the blue in the middle of a street. They want to be civil, so if you take their space, they try to press and wrap themselves in a smaller space. If you go forward, they go backward. They are not aggressive. The post-WW2 Europeans are completely another race. Their DNA has changed by fear, but as gruesome as the WW2 has been, and nobody should undermine it, the impact of the media did this to them and crucified their courage. The last generation of Europeans is the worst generation of them. They are so melted in facilities and so absorbed in being slim and eating salad, that they are trembling bodies falling down with simple flu and if the day comes and they need some war power, they don't have a minimum of it. They should just hide in caves being this fragile and breakable and this will not change unless they shake their beliefs, face the truth, flush the guilt, eat healthily, build power, kill the political correctness, and stand for what they have achieved during the first ten years after WW2. They should kick the passivity out of their homes and borders before the day comes to say Goodbye Europe and doing anything alternative would be too late.

What could be a better cover-up for invading Europe rather than heartbreaking, and soul melting, humanitarian efforts of helping "refugees"?

-Refugees?

As the cult of colonizers rebranded and erased the taste of any humanitarian concept, they degenerated the concept of refugee too. Once, a people suffering from war or casualties would seek help from the first country which could host them for a while but now, it is trendy to live a country because of its bad economy and travel from one end to another end of the world to find a country which can pay more in terms of social welfare to those who pretend to be war victims, Unfortunately, those who suffer from this falsification are the real victims of war or political suppression.

The modern Trojan horse put in your yard as a gift by ISIS is not your guest. The fundamentalists don't send us their good people. The young infiltrated Radical Islamic manpower is not here just to replace us but to do it at our expense, with our own money, our social welfare, and security. They attack us with our own weapons as they enter with no arm. They use our technology and internet service against us. They abuse our facilities paid by our taxes and our hard-working days in the office to smear us.

Taxes paid by workers in high-risk workplaces like the police force, firemen, hospitals, mines or chemical industries are all contributing to doing this against themselves. Let's see it this way. We work to be raped, invaded, forced into acceptance of the barbaric rules, and live less than our standards and even die. Is this what you are living for, people?

Some may ask what about women and children? What about humanity? Let's answer a question first. Have you ever looked at the world's map? Did you see the geographical coordination of these countries? Consider Iraq, Afghanistan, Tunisia, and Somalia are surrounded by important-Islamic-rich neighbors like Saudi Arabia, Iran, Kuwait, Qatar, United Emirates, and Jordan. They are Muslims, and according to the brotherhood law of Islam, they are all brothers. Why do those brother countries not take them? Or perhaps they didn't ask them for asylum. They directly come to Europe and in the past years to the United States too. They go all this long way but don't try to pass the borders governed by their brothers. They just love to flee and live in infidel countries, and as soon as they arrive, they start to punish the same infidels who are hosting them. This is insane, and yet no government stops this insanity. Why?

Because the rubber boats are the European Unions' TAXIS. Human traffickers smuggle them to Libya and from there, they use those rubber taxis for a short distance to Greece or Lampedusa or Sicily in Italy. Newly arrived boats are just men and mostly African. Not one of them is from war zones like Syria. Young men with strong bones at the age of 20-30. **What kind of a war zone is that where their men flee and leave women and children in a zone of mortality? Are we sure that they are** refugees and not human Molotov Cocktails?

Culture, a combination of different elements obtained and evolved in a country "within" its borders is a gradual product made in centuries and has its roots deep in society. These roots make one culture different from another. **As time passes, permanent elements of culture remain the same. They remain the same as the soil remains the same, as the wheat growing in that soil remains the same and as the water in their lakes remains the same. Those elements are beyond the "individual". they are the warp and weft which shape the mentality of the individuals of that special area as they are.**

In old times, before the invention of the automobile, people had to travel miles on horses or in carriages to the nearest city so it was so difficult that just a few could afford it. At those times, cities seemed different countries and the difference in culture was so distinguishable. People, who were born in a certain place used to eat the same ingredients, breathe the same air, cultivate the same land with the same seeds, live the same lifestyle, dress the same manner, respect the same traditions; participate the same local ceremonies and churches and believe in the same beliefs or superstitions. They even had the same anatomy; the same jawbones and height or color so tangible at the first sight traveling from one city to another and this is why we have a treasury of historical books demonstrating all these habits and differences.

Difference is not an inequity. Life emphasizes our differences. How would a world be if everything was similar and uniformly shaped? If all people did the same thing, ate the same thing, had the same habits and looked the same? There no exactly similar things in nature. Our ten fingertips have different patterns. That's why they are used to identify people. **Learn from nature. Learn from Mathematics; the wisest professor of the world. There is not one number equal to another. It's always a plus or minus. A world with equal numbers would be anti-knowledge,**

anti-progress, and anti-philosophy; as philosophy is the manifestation of mathematics through words. An absolute death would be the result. Nada.

What makes this colorful world beautiful is not the lack of difference but to "respect" the differences. A mathematical equation offers so much to learn and is fun to discover and decode. One can evolve and move to the next level of creation and nascence through the "respect for rules and relations" between different numbers. So if an unprivileged human in need of help or even to fulfill his dreams, comes to a country with a "different" culture should first of all; respect the host culture by trying to integrate and assimilate and second; should be grateful and humble for the opportunity offered to him/her.

This transformation is not easy but it is the price to pay. It demands effort and determination as the newcomers should learn the culture of their new country and it includes the language as the main way of communication, outfits, trendy habits routine within a nation that help assimilate faster. There is no doubt that the hosting country will be any way affected by cultures of newcomers in time, but that is a gradual process while the adaptation of the hosting culture for the immigrant should be a must and should be fast and not a gradual one. So there are two processes of integrations. First; for the immigrants which is a duty and an obligation and second, for the host nation which is not a "must", "duty" or an "obligation" but happens naturally and by their own will as many immigrants bring their new talents, creativity, and interesting social differences into the hosting country.

Every hosting country needs dynamic change and innovation in their culture as this is a natural process of growth and evolution and nobody can stand still and firm forever. People will putrefy due to stagnancy and lose their ability to upgrade and council with modern dynamics, but the process should take place with all due respect to the host country's culture. It is a nonverbal agreement: **If you come to my house, you should respect my rules.**

Besides, people don't flee to a country with an inferior culture to theirs. They choose a better country and adding an inferior culture to a better one means degrading the "better culture" if there is no assimilation.

If the society just as it is at the moment, is not appealing to those intending to immigrate, then don't do it. Being aggressive, oppressive or offensive; having an attitude of superiority and demanding to change the hosting country is beyond narcissism. On top of that, claiming that all hosting countries should someday come under their flag and believe what they believe, requires one solution and it is "deportation". No political correctness here, no subjection to "Xenophobia" is valid. All is nonsense, and irrelevant as accepting an immigrant is not a "Right" but a "Grant".

To your surprise, I am one of them. One of those who waited in lines and paid taxes and brought assets and academic studies to contribute my new country and loved it with all my heart by educating more and working hard. I know how it feels leaving everything behind and becoming an immigrant and start from below zero. But at the same time, I know how hard it is to wait years for a due process to become first a resident and after being a good resident, to become a good citizen. It takes years of official documentation and proving to have obeyed the law. I also know the frustration of all those legal immigrants who loved and respected their new countries and assimilated into the cultures but have been discriminated against because of the actions of those who arrived and didn't respect the law and the culture and created a hostile attitude toward all the immigrants.

Recent refugees coming to the United States and Europe after 2013, are "war power" and they have "numbers" and they rely on their numbers. Those behind the scenes who smuggle manpower, have instructed them to multiply and spread into the West's body and make it completely paralyzed while fragile European eggshells are "nice and cute" and tolerant. They shelter them by giving all their love and support as they think there is no "amount set" for helping other people and the trojan horse is laughing at their stupidity as they grow up with the mentality of revenging westerners. They don't know it's the deep state's military complex bombing them as the deep state agents within their own culture taught them that "westerners are enemies."

The real refugees fleeing from political suppression are attacked and harassed by these fake refugees in their camps. It's stunning how brainwashed people in Europe rush into the streets to protest "against" closing borders and "not" taking refugees or deporting criminals, but they did nothing and never run into the streets during years of massacre and bombings. The deep state was murdering people all around the world whether it was the people of the Middle East or the brave soldiers of the United States and Europe convinced to sacrificing their lives to fight terrorism. The deep state had no mercy for anyone. When a country or region reaches the point of its own destruction, self-survival should be the main strategy. If Europe and America become another Afghanistan, then there will be nothing to offer to any real refugee. The strangest thing is, 80 percent of these people are coming from Africa and countries which are not war zones, and they are economic immigrants on those rubber taxis.

-Your death rope

Not all refugees or immigrants are terrorists but terrorists enter behind the same label. Many members of ISIS, Al-Qaida, and the Taliban are already inside the western borders. As children, they watch beheadings while they bite a piece of bread and play with each other on the streets covered by the blood. That bread falls on that blood; they pick it up and give it another bite and this is what we saw on the same media that calls us conspiracists. These children absorb this brutality as a norm, and that is their school and university. They grow up in groups living in camps with zero commodities sleeping over each other just like our basket of stones. Nothing will break them, and they have nothing to lose.

They had no space, no recognition of human rights. The beheading of an infidel is their visa to pass directly to heaven and sleep with seven naked angles. There is a reason I said they shouldn't be invaded in the first place because those bombings give their "preachers of hate" the justification to indoctrinate them from childhood. You can never be their friends. That's just stupid. They will never exchange your friendship with their heaven and seven naked angels.

The western constitutions give "them" rights to demand more. Right to have a lawyer, right to have food stamps, to protest against you, to vote against you; rights that they weren't aware of their existence. The western democracy which has been designed according to beliefs, religion, historical background and accomplishments became its death rope because the west was living better so it had to give it to them. This is madness. This has to end. Fake democracy has pushed the west to the corner and eradicated the gallantry, courage, and manhood to stand for what it has built and achieved and for what could have kept it strong which is "the proud of being yourselves."

Germany in particular, because of Hitler lost its valor and valiance for the very reason that after WW2, they have been the direct target of racial allegations. They can just care less about the safety of their daughters than being pointed to as Nazis. That's what really counts for them. They do not want to be labeled a Nazi. It is disgusting how they are going low under Angela Merkel's dictatorship and how they have given up all their rights that easily. What happened in front of Dom Cathedral on 2015's New Year's Eve is a shame on their forehead forever. More than a hundred young girls were assaulted or raped and it was all over the news. How could they remain silent when their daughters and sisters were raped right before their eyes? I am surprised how they are different from their Italian neighbors. "Piss them off and you will immediately get a lesson which will never forget." Plain and simple.

-The European National Sovereignty Destroyer

What has happened to Western Europe? Where is the spirit of patriotism? Where are the warriors? Northern and central Europe has been doomed. I surprisingly see that heroism and zeal exist just in Eastern Europe like Hungary, Poland, Slovenia, and Romania. They are rising to defend their values at any cost while Western Europe is bending over the weight of the European

Union of Servitude. The only hope and strong forces in Western Europe are Italy and Austria. France is rallying for freedom too. England is struggling with the globalist forces who open the borders open and keep butchering normal people and national forces who orchestrated Brexit but she will definitely come out.

Eastern Europe is lucky to have great leaders. It is impressive how Victor Orbán, the Hungarian Prime Minister and His Polish peer, Prime Minister Mateusz Morawiecki, are both fighting with the EU's slavery. The spider of the EU is threatening these countries by all means if they don't kneel before it. The EU is bullying these countries with mockeries prophesying their fall.

No, you are wrong big brother! It will be you who will fall. These great leaders will change history, and our children will read the story of their bravery in their history books for centuries to come.

The Netherlands' Party For Freedom under Geert Wilders didn't win the election but became number two in parliament. Italy has a great number of nationalist leaders but doesn't act firmly and suffers the uncertainty of choosing the leadership. "La Lega Nord" is the leading party being, very anti-EU and pro populism. The Five Star Movement was pro-exiting the EU but also pro taking refugees, so La Lega Nord is the only reliable party with a good leader; Matteo Salvini, a leader well informed, determined, strong and a man with big balls who will win the election. Italy can be Europe's leader in this movement. Brexit was a great victory to revive the sovereignty, but Britain didn't act as a leader for Europe taking one step forward and two steps backward. She should exit once and for all but the old establishment is at work very tensely. Angela Merkel still reigns in Germany and beyond its borders in all Europe. Emanuel Macron, the white face of President Obama, has joined big Mommy Merkel. West Europe is already shocked by Brexit but not convinced enough to rise up. The big EU spider has its ramous so well-drained into every organization and institute that rebelling against it means reconstructing everything from scratch. There needs to be a ringing bell. The alert; the call for an uprising against Europe's national sovereignty destroyer. We are living in the greatest era of the history as Marin Le pen quoted in late 2016:

"There are decades that nothing happens and there are months that everything happens."

Yes, Madame. Very well said. That's our era.

"Immigration is an organized replacement of our population. This threatens our very survival. We don't have the means to integrate those who are already here. The result is an endless cultural conflict."

MarineLe Pen

No better phrase would describe the plot as Marine Le pen pictured. The big deception: **"An ORGANIZED REPLACEMENT of the white West's population."**

To summarize what stated above, we discussed the deep state's strategies to reach its goal which are to divide, attack, reshape and rule overseas regions by creating a problem, presenting a solution and occupy the target to execute it. Before WW1, colonization of the world was recognized as a crime against humanity. After WW2, old fashioned recolonization and deploying troops was absolutely impossible, so the decisive tool of humanitarianism started to echo. people had total faith in their governments and slept as they trusted their governments will be awake and protect them. To advance the plan, the deep state created NATO, the

United Nations, the European Union and the Refugee Crisis over the past 70 years. NATO and the United Nations are the deep state's ministries, and the European Union is the same for Europeans' head to subjugate different cultures and languages under one authority. The European Union is a tester of how the world government will be. Refugees should replace the population, agitate Chaos, disrupt and spread fear so the oligarchs can have the excuse for total control declaring a Police State before the Martial Law. We would have been right in that stage if Hillary Clinton was now in the White House and I am every day grateful to God when I wake up and remember that she is not.

-The Proxy Army

Modern colonization plays with three players. The government, the terror group, and the PEOPLE. The mechanism is simple: terror groups attack people, the government whines and cries but increases the control over the PEOPLE. The point is right here. As much as the level of control rises, the attacks by terror groups increase. Surveillance cameras and complicated control measures do zero help to secure the country because as we already mentioned, they have never meant to ensure security but to control and pressure on the PEOPLE.

Look at what is happening in London or Manchester. People are butchered, and the authorities issue statements on how the internet should be censored. The Police say: RUN, HIDE AND TELL! Instead of protecting people, armed forces question people in the streets, the celebrity version of the deep state asks people to blow a kiss, send a heart and "just co-exist"!! They hold concerts and ask people to touch the person next to them and send love. Did these above the clouds clowns, auto-ridiculed themselves, or they just bullied people? The Mayor of London consolidates Muslims who may have been offended by people's reactions toward Radical Jihadists! And another attack happens tomorrow. Sadiq Khan, The Mayor of London, says:

"These terror attacks are part and parcel of living in a big city"???

Did you listen to Theresa May's speech after Manchester's terrorist attack? I don't listen to fake news and have to watch everything live, and May said in response to the terror attacks, she is going to "regulate the internet."Wattt?? What the hell is all this about? People died, and May censors the internet?? Oh, wait a minute. If they censor the internet, we cannot know there was an attack! The solution: Hide the attacks, jail who talks about it, abolish free speech, and nobody will know. We've been asked to understand the "psychology" of Jihadists and try to be compassionate as if we are guilty of not caring enough so that's why they kill people.

So now the stage is set for a radical role reversal, where the real victim is no longer the unarmed civilians slaughtered by the terrorists but instead, we are asked to feel pity and mercy for the mental sufferance of the terrorists and again we are asked to be courageous to receive the "pack and parcel" of their hate and ignorance.

This process of replacement is so gradual that becomes the new lifestyle as people have no memory of how it was before this sedition and intolerance and the mockingbird media and the Hollywood branch of the government, promote this lifestyle in their narratives and mind-control movies and documentaries that nobody asks a simple question like why massive surveillance, online tracking, and travel scanning and vetting fail to protect us? Terrorism has just become stronger because the creator, trainer, funder and its main commander in chief is the bulletproof deep state.

The process of subduing Europe under the flag of the European Union was cozy as it went as planned and nothing blocked it but in the United States, there was a big problem. A substantial obstacle was blocking the "divide, reshape and rule agenda" and it was our glorious and honorable Second Amendment and the right to carrying arms. A magnificent amendment which gives the American people the right to defend the republic whenever a government becomes a tyranny. Without the Second, the First Amendment (the right to free speech) is undefendable. Americans are grown with their guns. Nobody can dare and step over the constitutional right to carry. So what did the deep state design to overcome this obstacle and dig holes in the Constitution?

-The false flag and the hoax

Schools used to be the safest places for our children. Parents work hard to keep their children safe and educated. They trust the school, so they wake up and leave their kids in the school as they are convinced that their children are safe but a shooter, a lone wolf out of the blue takes his gun and kills a dozen of our kids. Then another episode and another over and over again.

The corporate media starts its role and photos of the shooter are all over the news. But it doesn't need you to be genius to notice in most pictures captured in different shootings on different dates, and in different locations, feature the same people in different styles. Oh crap! How possibly can a mother of John be a mother of Jack in different places at the same time?

The picture above; have circulated for the Paris attack in November 2015. The woman in the Paris photo has not been identified. Press captions of the photo merely describe it in the following manner: *"Rescuers evacuate people following an attack in the 10th Arrondissement of the French capital Paris."*

Now, look at the official caption for the image on the left of the same person which was circulated stating: "Emma MacDonald and two friends were photographed at a vigilant for the Boston victims."

The picture in the middle, which is circulated for Sandy Hook shooting; the same famous woman is shown in the Sandy Hook shooting photo which here has another name: Carlee Soto, who had just learned that her sister Vicky Soto was dead. A caption for this iconic photo which has become the official face of the Sandy Hook shooting was: "Carlee Soto learns that her sister Vicky Soto is among those killed in the school shooting."

The picture in the right: That woman again! Her identity here is Amanda Medek. Some press photos taken of her sitting on steps included the caption: "Amanda Medek, who is looking for her sister Micayla, sits outside Gateway High School, Friday, July 20, 2012, in Aurora, Colo."

Did the same woman attend four tragedies like people attend events and conferences?? What would you say? Coincidence or professional paid crisis actors? Mission? Gun Control.

The same day, family members emotionlessly appear on TV with robotic faces claiming their loved one is brutally murdered but repeatedly emphasize on gun control legislation. No real mother or father can mourn and be political at the same time right after a loss. The first months after the tragedy, nothing will worth a mother or a father who has lost a child. They can have political goals after months but not on the same day. In Virginia shooting, the Obama White House immediately shot a statement *"Virginia shows the desperate need for gun control."* Hillary Clinton used the shooting to advertise on gun control. But more the debates for gun control go on, more stabbings happen, and more trucks and vehicles run over the crowds. Maybe the government should ban all the kitchen knives, cars and trucks too so we can circulate as crude meat with no protection and the government can finally take a deep breath as jihadists and gangs like MS13 can kill effortlessly while dead people can't complain. **We see no culture of eliminating the problem but banning the tools! No strategy for eradicating terrorists but just blaming the victims** for not showering the predators with enough respect.

After years of serial shootings, these official images should have convinced you to see other possibilities rather than what the media says and think for a second. Who will benefit from the shootings??

The police state agenda. How? Good question. In what another way could the police-state ask the nation to alter the second amendment? The media and their constant electric shock will convince them so while their paid protesters go in the streets and cry for gun control. We are already there.

"The Global Warming Hoax," is another fixer serving the path of total control. When I fathomed this for the first time, I was shocked like you. I always felt there is something in this climate change scare that doesn't fit but I didn't know what it is. Our minds remain stupefied and the answers given to us seem weird. **If the premise of global warming is science and so powerful, so what is the problem that we nuts and conspiracy theorists challenge it? They should just ignore us then why are they fighting?**

If 2 x 2 = 4, and somebody says it's equal to 5, then people will laugh at him. Besides, science is necessarily provisional. It cannot make the final statement. That's why always a new theory comes to life and ends the theories before it so why the deep state enablers should take on us? What's the problem to make such a big deal for challenging the global warming "theory"?

Remember it's still just a theory. It has never become a fact. Why do they act like this argument is a holy religion and forbidden to touch? And when I learned this is a big hoax, I couldn't put the lost pieces easily together. Climate change seems a complicated argument but when you break it down and put the evidence together, then it surprisingly makes sense. Besides, when we consider who benefits from it, again, we are led to the same place: The Police State.

When in the early 1980s alarms of climate change were set for the first time, nobody could imagine what was really all about. Environmental agencies, nongovernmental activists, and scientists could never act politically from my point of view. Their devotion was to "science" and I am convinced they were just doing their job. There were different theories on climate change from 1945 to 1975 which anybody could stick to one of them and shape his own. When suddenly environmental activists declared to have discovered a dangerous threat to Earth and consequently, to our lives, and our children's future, we couldn't be indifferent. Our children might have lived on a destroyed planet or even worse; they might not have a planet to live on. What would be the purpose of living if there is no future? Depression, dissatisfaction, desperation, losing hope, and aimlessness resulting to become a walking dead. Immediately after, Hollywood movies came out of the closet and terrorized people featuring apocalyptic scenes in a dystopian world while their posters appeared all over the newspapers, billboards, TV, social media, magazines and whatsoever imaginable.

The pattern here is the same. The problem was created; the dangerous enemy has been introduced, now it was the time for the "Save the Planet" solution. Everyone would vote positive and grieve for the dying earth, willing to fight for it, go to the streets and protest if some egoist ignorants dare to oppose the solution.

The colonizers always use "us" to push "their" agenda, and their tool of justification has always been the corporate media. What people see through the media is **what the oligarchs want them to see and it gradually becomes their mental blueprint which is the only playbook carved on their unconscious by default. It becomes their mindset.**

Tony Abbott was the 28th Prime Minister of Australia from 2013 to 2015. According to his chief business advisor; Maurice Newman, *"Climate change is a trick used by the United Nations in a bid for world domination."* He published the allegations on the news under this title; *"The international body's real agenda is a new world order under its control."* He wrote that the real agenda behind the push for climate change action was "concentrated political authority. This is not about facts or logic. It's about a new world order under the control of the UN. It is opposed to capitalism and freedom." The article was printed on May 8, 2015, in the Sydney Morning Herald newspaper. As you see; once conspiracies, now are facts bring about by politicians. We are talking about a Prime Minister, who worked very closely with the agenda in Australia. He perfectly knows what he is talking about.

While we were stuck with suspicion and trying to digest the why and the holes in the global warming theory, the flood of regulations and international laws erupted from every institution and at our surprise, a theory which does not meet enough facts to become a metric science now was backed with a universal solution called: Save the Planet. But how? How should we save this planet?

The development of the climate hoax from its beginning until the conclusion by the Kyoto Protocol in 1997 can be divided into four stages: 1- the foundational stage; during which scientific concerns about global warming have surfaced. 2- The agenda-setting stage; from 1985 to 1988, when climate change which should be a scientific issue, transformed into policy. 3- The formal intergovernmental stage; which led to the adoption of the FCCC in May 1992. 4- Post agreement stage; when the implementation of the FCCC started forcefully and the negotiations which led to the final act of adoption of the "Kyoto Protocol" in December 1997, took place. The Protocol charges industrialized countries with the responsibility of reducing their emissions of greenhouse gases "by at least 5 percent below 1990 levels in a commitment period from 2008 to 2012" (Article 3 of the Kyoto Protocol).

To simplify what we just read, we have a solution in the form of an agreement that "legally obligates" some countries to "reduce" their greenhouse gasses. Ok? What is senseless is that gases such as methane, nitrous oxide, HFCs, PFCs, were identified as greenhouse gases with no emphasis but CARBON DIOXIDE gas (CO_2), more than any of the other gases have been emphasized as the main target of curtailment. But why?? This doesn't sum up, and there is no logic in it.

-CO_2, is a good, clean and ecologically essential gas. Why should it be eliminated?

Is global warming really happening? Recent studies show it is not. If global warming is a fact, is it lawful to say it is caused by a buildup of an atmospheric CO_2? There is no evidence so NO. If CO_2 is merely a stooge, then we have absolutely a hoax here. There is another aspect of this crazy hoax which is strongly affecting us which is GMO" and Monsanto and we will discuss it completely in chapter 6 But for now, we just focus on CO_2 control.

Why should the government vituperate CO_2? This clean, natural, scarce, and ecologically gas is essential in the biosphere so why should it be controlled? Because the police state can control us through controlling CO_2.

It seems insane, isn't it?

The Kyoto Protocol is based on cracked science with no scientific evidence. **As usual, they first condemn then search for a crime to fit in. They had a need to target carbon**. But why?

Because by cooking or making ourselves warm in our home, or with transportation, we create CO_2. They have targeted a gas which is all over our lives. If tomorrow, the government decides to control CO_2, we are not allowed to cook, our displacement will be controlled, and many other aspects of our lives are dependent on CO_2. Besides through the carbon tax, the money will be extracted from the petroleum, automobile industries, and the citizens who need

energy and cars, to the third world. That is a hidden class-war against the west to redistribute its wealth to the third world.

The subject of CO_2 is so vast that I decided to write about it in another book as it is impossible to cover it just in this section. My next book which is about chemtrails and global warming explains this issue in full detail.

Christiana Figures, the executive secretary of the U.N Convention on Climate Change, in February 2015, officially announced that their regulations have nothing to do with climate change but everything to do with the economic overhaul. If so, why they talk about climate change for the sake of the planet but when technically speaking, they confirm it has nothing to do with climate?

In her statement, she said: *"This is the first time in the history of mankind that we are setting ourselves the task of intentionally, within a defined period of time, to change the economic development model that has been reigning for at least 150 years, since the Industrial Revolution."*

As you see, she is targeting "Capitalism" and for us to rest assured that she is talking about transforming Capitalism to Communism, she continued as follows:

"This is probably the most difficult task we have ever given ourselves, which is to intentionally transform the economic development model (Capitalism) for the first time in human history."

Dear friends, climate change is not about pollution. It's is about money, power, and control. **If not, why do they let the big corporations to pollute if they pay? Permission to pollute on payment? If it serves to save the planet, it makes no sense. Will the earth be ok just if they pay?**

The CO2 control is George Orwellian control. If you still didn't read the "1984" novel, then it's time you do it. Hundreds of scientists have rejected the idea of global warming. The Greens have tried using the threat of global warming to induce constant guilt on us to cap growth, change lifestyles, attack the car industry and smash Great America that they hate more than anything. **Today, school children's minds are worried as they think it is up to them to save the world. Just**

like the earth in its 4,000,000,000 years of life has been waiting for our kids to save it. Laughable and preposterous, isn't it? Global warming is not modifying our real life, and patriot leaders of the developed world have no intention to sell their economic growth and prosperity for a religious-fascist cult. I enjoy calling it a religious cult because the climate advocates act perfectly as a religious cult.

They call us infidels to the weather-god and earth-worshipping religion. **Identity politics is politicizing not politics only but the science. This is an Institutional Science Propaganda acting as weapons of mass destruction. It drove everybody enough crazy to surrender the modern slavery, always camouflaged as a humanitarian measure.** Each one of these strategic weapons can endanger the world on a big scale but using several of them together has had very destructive results. A demonic road to the hell hole of destruction and a constant downward move from the desired utopia to an unwanted dystopia serving to fulfill somebody else's plan. Order out of catastrophic chaos. Order through the bloody river of millions of millions of people. Blood of the sheep sucked out while sleeping. This demonic order is no order for you and me but a pathway to slavery. Total submission to the bloodsucker and praising him at the same time.

What they don't tell you is that the "Global Biodiversity Assessment" of the United Nations back in 70 says that we must reduce the human population from six billion down to one billion but they deceive you to do it through global warming masqueraded and decorated as serving the earth. When in December 1974, the U.S government made the population reduction as a central national security issue because the oligarchs felt threatened, Henry Kissinger (one of them) immediately activated the operation "National study memorandum 200" which led to the coining the global warming issue. **Global warming is a cash pot for their imperialistic operations behind the scenes.**

The Bilderberg Club of Rome has decided that the industrial growth of Asia, Africa, and South America is sabotaged so citizens of the developed countries will give up their national sovereignty and will be sold to help the planet. What do they mean exactly by"helping the planet"? Two hundred years ago the slaves were working on the master's land, but they were helping the planet. Do they mean the same type of "helping the planet"? Today, in 2017, we see slavery camps in Libya keeping people in chain and sell them overseas. These slaves can't wait to be sold to get rid of their cages. Don't forget that this is happening after the killing of Gaddafi, the so-called dictator, the man that his people never paid for water or energy but now became slaves and this is just the beginning. This is what the Bilderberg wants for the whole planet.

Welcome to the New World Order.

Chapter 5

George Soros And The Ministry of Deception

What happened to the world in recent years? Why do we witness a climate of violence and tremendous change in terminology since 2013? Why do we increasingly witness so many verbal and physical attacks? Shocking vocabulary like genocide, degradation, kill and rape through the mainstream media or violent crimes committed by youth streaming online. Whenever there is no clue, follow the money...

The power behind this violence is "Money". It started with the greed and money throne of the Rothschilds, and while their money still flows into the veins of the network of violence and makes it pump, new money funnels the "Destroying America" agenda. Soros's money.

People know George Soros as Wall Street's superstar making fortunes with his genius tricks in the stock market. Or maybe you know him as a philanthropist who has more than 150 organizations dedicated to different social causes like women's rights, socialism, etc., where the central entity of these various organizations is the "Open Society Foundation".

The Open Society Foundation (OSF), formerly named "the Open Society Institute" is an international network claiming to support civil, and social groups around the world. Its goal is cited as advancing justice, education, public health, and to support the independent media. OSF has many branches in 37 countries and acts as the motherboard to other hundred Soros founded organizations across the world.

-The crime network

Activities of OSF and other Soros funded organizations, according to Wikipedia are listed below. I use Wikipedia for the very reason that it is an open-source so easy for the average person to take a look at.

Wikipedia: *"The Open Society Foundations reported annual expenditures of $827 million in 2014. Its $873 million budget in 2013, ranked as the second-largest private philanthropy budget in the United States, after* the Bill and Melinda Gates Foundation budget of $3.9 billion.

According to the foundation's website, 1993-2014 expenditures included:

$2.9 billion to defend human rights, especially the rights of women; ethnic, racial, and religious minorities; drug users; sex workers; and LGBTQ communities;

$2.1 billion for education;

$1.6 billion on developing democracy in Eastern Europe and the former Soviet Union;

$1.5 billion in the United States to promote reform in criminal justice, drug policy, palliative care, education, immigration, equal rights, and democratic governance;

$737 million for public health issues such as HIV and AIDS, TB, palliative care, harm reduction, and patients' rights;

$214 million to advance the rights of Roma communities in Europe.

Expenditures in 2014 included:

$277.3 million - Rights and Justice

$238.0 million - Governance and Accountability

$116.0 million - Administration

$91.7 million - Education and Youth

$60.0 million - Health

$43.8 million - Media and Information."

"Within these totals, OSF reported granting at least $33 million to civil rights and social justice organizations in the United States. This funding included groups such as the Organization for Black Struggle and Missourians Organizing for Reform and Empowerment that supported protests in the wake of the shooting of Trayvon Martin, the death of Eric Garner, the shooting of Tamir Rice and the shooting of Michael Brown. According to the Center for Responsive Politics, the OSF spends much of its resources on democratic causes around the world and has also contributed to groups such as the Tides Foundation.

OSF has been a major financial supporter of U.S. immigration reform, including a pathway to citizenship for illegal immigrants.

OSF projects have included the National Security and Human Rights Campaign and the Lindesmith Center, which conducted research on drug reform The Library of Congress Soros Foundation Visiting Fellows Program was initiated in 1990." -By Wikipedia

Every organization is guided by a clear culture, vision, mission and policy issued in its Statement of Purpose.

All o the above, regarding Soros organizations mentioned are "humanistic" goals. But is George Soros a humanistic individual? To understand Soros, we need to study his background, learn his language and speak the same style as he speaks.

-Who is George Soros?

During history, new doctrines either emerged from the old ones or jumped out of a closet and became a ground for political idiots or extremists to march on.

Communism, Nazism, extreme religiosity, Stalinism, and Maoism all are failed doctrines that were out of place and time after a period of inefficiency. But failed strategies can be mixed, recycled and sold as new isms. Strategies built on already rotten-dead strategies are doomed to fail, but before failure, they will enjoy a period of devour.

Soros; a Nazi collaborator who became a billionaire, has the number one goal and it is a "Communist America". To reach his goals, he also uses Radical Islam. What an explosive mixture; Nazism experience, Communism goal and the use of Radical Islam as a tool. Enough ingredients to blow up our small world while his disinformation campaign penetrates our veins, conditions our minds and creates mass hysteria on earth. The warmonger, the godfather of agitation, the planet's financial terrorist, the global parasite, sugar daddy of the left and big brother of every single puppet government in the world, had electrified our lives by constant shocks, invasive micro/macro aggressions, and manipulative interventions. He pulls the strings and forces the globe to tremble by the rhythm of his voltage and while we perform a zombie dance in a bloody climate of hate. There is no detergent in the world that can clean his hands off the blood and annihilation he has caused. He is the devil in the flesh.

His agenda was a big surprise to the old oligarchs. His genius and supernatural calculations running his destruction machine and burning the world at the light speed forced the colonizers to notice him. He claims to be a god. Watching him speaking, you will be surprised by his behavior. His drooling face, childish behavior, and immature words stun you. He officially SAYS what he thinks and does if we really hear and not just listen.

He always says it directly. As noted at the beginning of the article, to understand him, we have to learn his language. He speaks in simple codes because he is so involved with, drowned into, surrounded by and 24/7 focused on what he does, that all he knows, sees and does is his agenda so it never crosses his mind to hide his intentions during an interview which he will never be held accountable for.

The question is why does he need to seed new norms in our culture to push his agenda forward? Can't he do without these norms? Why he writes something on his organizations' statements of purpose but does the opposite? Why is he so obsessed with his campaign of disinformation? The answer is beautiful: The "power of people" and that's right. Here we notice his weakness: "We the People". While everything is planned, there should be real people in great numbers to fit the plan and take it forward and to do that; those people should be conditioned to do so.

Soros's plan is precisely the continuation of the Rothschilds' plan with some modifications due to time, place, modern technology, the emergence of new leaders and the dynamics of the modern world in the past 10-12 years and will speed up the new world order. As he confessed in his Bretton Woods Conference or better say "Destroy America Conference" in 2011, the main obstacle to establishing this new world order is the "EXISTENCE OF AMERICA". From that moment, his eyes are on destroying America, competing with the Rothschilds in spending. All his focus, money and calculations have targeted one thing: Destroying America. New weapons of mass destruction are ideological and social, dealing with the mental destruction of the mass **through behavior modification and re-patterning. Internal destruction points no finger to him while sweeping the road for the final phase which is: The Revolution.**

He genially knew to plant a certain behavior in society, that society should have certain beliefs. So the primary challenge here appears to be re-patterning and modifying those beliefs. Shifting the public opinion by properly "engineering" the mechanism of thinking was the goal. What was the most intelligent way to do that? **To change the "Perception". In this way, changing the roots of society would be progressive but guaranteed.** He targeted the definition and shape of the family as a man and a woman and their children, the definition of gender, the definition of identity, the definition of good and evil, the definition of Property, the definition of unity and diversity and to do that, he started to attack masculinity, Christianity, and patriotism. By creating extreme feminism, racial hate, Satanic groups, porn indoctrination, and pro-abortion groups through his 150 nonprofit organizations all around the world, his money flew into these organizations. Political correctness, protests, meetings, militant trolls, lobbying and paying lawmakers and judges, petitions, politicians, governors, Senators, leaders and whatever means necessary were his instruments to nail his agenda. Transgender agenda, Alfa male guilt, whiteness guilt, racial fights, normalization of anti-Christ, and promotion of cannibalism, pedophilia and child porn are all fueled and fed by him as means of stabilizing the nail on the wall. There is an old saying which says: *"If you are going to eat an elephant, eat one bite at a time"* and he is eating a bite at a time.

His organizations are engaged in buying politicians, manipulating the news, creating illegal votes (ACORN), obtaining votes from poor blacks, obtaining votes from Hispanics and other people of color, obtaining votes from gays and lesbians, funneling illegal aliens into the Unions, directing their votes and collecting their annual membership dues, simplifying immigration laws and enabling communists and terrorists to enter America within the flux of normal people and at the same time, changing laws to make it easier for terrorists and criminals to operate all around the world (remember recent rapes in Sweden and unjustified sentences like 6 months?), increasing taxes and redirecting taxpayers' wealth to unnecessary green and communist takeover projects, putting more people on welfare, abolishing property, abolishing the second amendment and the right to carry a gun, abolishing free speech, easing drug-related laws, imposing laws that can implement the Communist takeover plan and recruiting and putting criminals and ex-criminals to work on it, establishing laws to expand union changes, laws to modify the US financial system, laws to control you, laws to push gun-free zones and schools, influencing over businesses, funding abortions, limiting free trade, hiding crimes and freeing criminals, while simultaneously making the U.S businesses less profitable and less competitive by the "hire illegals and buy non-American" strategy to make them (businesses) leave the country, lowering the US citizens' income, reducing wealth, picturing the American history in a strongly negative light and painting the founding fathers as oppressors both in the U.S and abroad, destroying national statues and symbols that remind the American history, creating miss-and-distorted information, political espionage, controlling the media and applying Psy-Ops on civilians, imposing Chinese style censorship and implementing decisive laws like "Net Neutrality" signed by President Obama to end free speech, setting up an internet Gestapo like Media Matters, stopping the U.S military and police operations by demonizing them, promoting crime, creating local and national racial conflicts/distrust and deep agitation among them, eliminating religious rights by calling it bigotry and offense, indoctrinating children with communism in their schools and through media by special programs, indoctrinating children on gender identity and build up race guilt while preventing their mind to drop childish attitude, sexualizing children from very young age by unfortunate and unnecessary sexual distractions in the schools and fundamentally change America and transforming it in a Communist nation to fit his technocracy.

His crime network is rolled into and wrapped around leftist, neocon politicians and activists and he monitors them to act as his weaponized watchdogs. These organizations employ passionate young people for their front row; people who have no idea of the complete void and idiocy that they are just zombie dancers to the rhythm of a Hungarian war criminal and ex-Nazi collaborator.

-George Soros has a Nazi ISSUE

How has the word Nazi emerged during the past decades? Nobody was using it, nobody was talking about it, that word was forgotten for decades. The only time we heard the word was in the memory of the victims o Holocoast but all of a sudden, Soros calls George Bush a Nazi.

Beginning in 2003, Laura Blumenfeld interviewed George Soros for The Washington Post, where Soros said: *"Bush is like Hitler."* Bush was a Republican and Soros supports only Democrats, so soon after Bush's victory, he (Soros) said: *"there is a Supremacist ideology which rules the White House."*

He refers to his childhood in occupied Hungary: *"When I hear Bush say, you're either with us or against us, it reminds me of the Germans. It conjures up memories of*

Nazi slogans on the walls, Der Feind Hort Mit(The enemy is listening) and my experiences under Nazi" (Which he always admitted to be the best year and the best experience in his life!)

His non-profit organization, MoveOn.org immediately after Bush's presidency launched an ad using the real WWII Nazi footage, with George W. Bush's photos, comparing him to Hitler. (Isn't it similar to today and calling President Trump Hitler?) The slogan used in that ad was *"A nation warped by lies. Lies fuel fear. Fear fuels aggression. Invasion. Occupation. What were war crimes in 1945 is the foreign policy in 2003."*

God forbid if I be a Bush fan, but this is the exact same thing Soros alongside the mainstream media, Antifa, black lives matter, etc is doing now. His strategy to push his plan comes from here and the mockingbird media follows his instructions mouthed by his canards above.

Lies = fear   fear = aggression   agression= invasioninvasion = occupation.

This is the answer to why the present generation acts like this. They are being played according to the above playbook. As previously stated, by learning his language, we learn his intentions. After that ad, people were furious and asked MoveOn to pull it down, but the "Bush is Hitler" had an impact on the left and took a life of its own. Soros announced that bringing Bush down is the *"central focus of his life."* He started to support Barack Obama and designed a t-shirt with the slogan *"I supported the other guy"* on it.

In Davos 2007's meeting, which was an extension of Bilderberg and took place during George Bush's presidency, Soros; a Nazi collaborator at the time of war, said: *"America needs to follow the policies introduced in Germany, we have to go through a certain de-Nazification process."*

So a Nazi sympathizer who loves the Nazi system not only within the national borders but on the world's scale wants the "denazification" of America. What does that suppose to mean?

I assume you can see, whoever is not on his side, is a Nazi. To study the process of "Nazification" of his opponents, we should ask ourselves; Did Soros hate Nazis and how did he live the years of Nazi occupation in Hungary? Did he lose his beloved ones or is he a survivor of Nazi Concentration Camps?

Maybe George Soros is the only active and alive person who has links to Nazis while openly engaged in politics. None of us worked with the Nazis. He did. George Bush didn't see the Nazis, Soros did. George Soros, a Hungarian Jew by birth and at the time of occupation but pretending to be a Christian, collaborated with Nazis and as he said in several interviews, he is still very proud of those years. He was fourteen years old. At that age, in that dangerous moment of history, he sold his fellow Jews to Nazis, giving them their information, and confiscating their properties in front of their eyes. He did it in cold blood with great joy and pleasure as when he talks about it, his eyes glitter. Since then, he hates Jews as much as the Nazis did. The reason maybe a psychological push-back of whom he cheated on and the reaction of his fellow Jews during and after the war as they called him a traitor.

He admitted joyfully, in an interview with Steve Kroft in 1998. When Kroft asked him whether he felt any guilt over his acquiescence to the Nazis, Soros proudly said: *"No, Not at all. It was the most exciting time of my life."* He continued *"what more could you ask for, at the age of fourteen?"*

In 1998, when the interview took place, he was not a fourteen-year-old teenage anymore but a 72-year-old senior adult who had 58 years to review what he has done and feel any regret about it. The interview caused so much outrage both from people and journalists so to draw a better picture of him; Soros asked Michael Kaufman to write an acceptable biography about him and named it *"The Life and Times of a Messianic Billionaire."*

In those fearful occupation days, when the Nazis were prosecuting and executing the Jews, Soros was the guy who submitted their (Jews) confiscation notices and the only pain for his family was their tennis balls. As he said to his biographer *"their inability to obtain their preferred Titleist tennis balls was the only pain."* With his forged documents as a Christian, 1- he was working with the Nazis. 2- He was in command of the situation. 3- He was moving easily and successfully and untouchable as a teen. 4- He was not feeling any guilt for participating in a totalitarian practices.

Other 14-year-olds who were fighting at war in Warsaw Ghetto in 1943 had their family dispersed, killed, detained or died in concentration camps with their empty stomachs under torture. But the 14-year-old

George Nazi collaborator Soros was just sad about his tennis balls.

The year after the occupation, Soros and his father didn't lose a chance to drain the capital out of the Hungarian people's desperation. He calls that year as: *"exciting and interesting in many ways even more interesting and adventurous than the German occupation."* That was the year that George Soros began to learn his first exchanges as a Dracula financer and currency trader in the black market of the growing post-war economy. His father used to send him to the center of Budapest daily to sell their gold and buy currency. How did they have gold in the middle of a tragedy like that? Maybe we have to dig in this too. His father chose him to avoid any suspicion as he was a teen. Otherwise, the Nazis would punish their family. There he learned how to live double face hiding from the same Nazis he was working with. There he learned to say something while doing exactly the opposite will save him and this became his forever strategy. His inclusiveness became excluding the opponent, but he promotes his decisive inclusiveness anyway.

That year was the breakthrough moment when Soros learned about the bear market. **When everybody is**

down and sells, you buy. His father had precise knowledge about those who were confiscated as his own son was the collaborating agent and knew very well who was on his knees and needed currency and business to boost up his life again.

"Conscious" is not a Soros type of thing. Once he said, he feels to be *"god"*, another time he said *"He wants to be the "conscience of the world"*. He used the *"buy when everybody is down"* precept so many times as with Britain in 1992. He put Britain on her knees, and when everybody was squeezed enough, he gained his first one billion in just 48 hours. **That's why the world had no peace since after.** Wall Street called it "the trade of the century". Soros became a currency manipulator who could easily predict the market reactions, but the truth is, he is not predicting the reactions; he is creating the reactions and should be prosecuted as he runs the market by putting his own political and economic agenda in action and takes advantage of it in Wall Street. He is an insider, and that is a monumental crime.

In 1995, in his book, Soros on Soros, he wrote: *"I do not accept the rules imposed by others."* When Jews are being deported to death camps, Soros says: *"I am above* *them."* All that matters for him is his own survival and as he says how *"trying to come out on top no matter what happens around you."*.... ***No matter what happens around you***... ummm....***" on top"...*"no matter"***, that doesn't seem "humanitarian." Does it? Remember reviewing his organizational goals which were all humanitarian?

In the same interview with Kroft, when he asked Soros about his investment in Britain and the manipulation of British Pound, he (Soros) said: *"I do investments I **don't care** about its social consequences"*...This special phrase is what I want to focus on: *** **I don't care about its social consequences*****

Back to Wikipedia and the long list of his nonprofit organizational goals, what we see as goals, are all SOCIAL GOALS. Not one of them is an economic goal. The entire list which we've read in previous pages about what his organizations are doing, like social justice, rights, etc. were SOCIAL goals. The main question here is: How possibly, a heartless person careless to ethics with no social commitment to anybody or anything; a person who openly and clearly admitted to having zero concern in social consequences of his "investments" should care about social behavior and social values? How he establishes hundreds of organizations to watch, direct, draw, and pursue strategies for politicians and controls all aspects of human integrity and their values while he has no integrity and value at all??

His organizations are nothing but different offices of his Ministry of Deception. They do nothing but human and planet degeneration through constant agitation and propaganda.

Chapter 6

Fifty Shades of Soros

Now that we have a perfect picture of his personality let's investigate all the damage his anti-human, anti-American agenda has done to the world.

1-OCCUPY WALL STREET September17th 2011

Adbusters poster, advertising the original protest

Soros, the funder of any left activist today, was all over the anti-American "Occupy Wall Street" movement. He co-founded "Democracy Alliance," through which the money was pouring into the anti-American movement. His goal was to physically start anarchist movements to prepare America and finally transform it into a George Orwellian style country. From that point, Soros's fingerprints are almost on every single anarchist/communist, racial, resistance/disobedience oriented riot or movement. Mission? A totalitarian technocrat regime. He always praised Communist China and said: *"the totalitarian nation has a better functioning government than the United States."*

I want to start with this movement as it has the same structure and shape as today's neo-fascist Antifa group except for the black hoodie and mask that make them uniform and gives them a new identity. But the whole thing is the same. The neo-communist Occupy Wall Street, was supported by Marxist billionaires, Hollywood rich bubbleheads and entertainment indoctrination complex, radical libertarians, goof-offs, indebted students, sexual exhibitionists, and prostitutes, and was actually "performed" by professional protesters, who took control and soon became the face of the modern Democratic Party, and we are witnessing today in 2017, the same social categories are "performing" Antifa.

In America has happened another leftist movement like this in the 1960s. Four years of protests until 1968. What was the result? 57 percent of the country reacted against it, and the Republicans won five of the next six presidential elections. Communism is a degradation virus, and it always acts as the main antivirus against itself. **No country survived under Communism and yet, they justify: "Because the principles of Communism have not been properly in motion. Because because because."**

LOL. Refreshing! Very refreshing! These people have a wonderland in their minds, and each time they face its falsehood, they dream to make it work by changing a new element, and when they run out of elements, they create something and shove it in! Should we always beat the same drum? History tells stories to remember. When we can do the damage control and prevent it before it happens, why should we go through the same mistake with a heavy polish and another name? **You can't change the name of a virus and inject it again. The epidemic will be the same, as the cure will be the**

same so the prevention will be the same. PREVENT IT when you still can. Undress the fake Christmas tree covered by colorful decorations and see that it is the same dried tree of Communism which still smells of the blood and flesh burnt on it alive, and is still occupied by the same parade of worms and vermin of Communism.

The Soviet Union doesn't exist anymore. It has been crushed. Cuba and Venezuela are damaged and degraded. They are poor and controlled by drug cartels. North Korea lives in an ice bubble. It seems all those people frozen in slow motion are mini photocopies of Kim Jung-un himself, with fake faces and stupidly "crying smiles". North Korea is the CIA's military base and China's barking dog which barks when China demands more trade. North Korea is nothing without CIA-China and can vapor with a simple puff when red China decides. And Communist China, which is not a poor country but is under the yoke of a system of economic and political slavery where its people work to feed not themselves, but the government and Freedom Zero is the norm. Why the Occupy Wallstreet or any other communist group should advocate for this system? The answer is simple. They don't know, they haven't studied what they are advocating. That's why we should be vigilant during the early upspring and symptoms of Communism. People who push something while having no correct information about it are like dynamites. They don't explode just themselves but the whole city. They are an imminent danger.

The problem is that the Obama administration not only stopped alarming Communism as the most dangerous phenomenon of the history and educate our children, but it also promoted the virus in universities and hid the documentaries on torture and mass murder and cherished Fidel Castro and Che Guevara. The media's love affair with Castro when he died in 2016 was a sham. A 25-year-old man in America educated under the recent Communist Occupation of universities since Bill Clinton sees Castro as a hero, not the greatest criminal. **Instead, desensitizing the horror, normalizing and promoting Communism was their first task for the media to sell it by hiding the torture, censorship, mass murder, hunger and poverty associated with it.** There is just one description for Communism, and that is"Horrendous".

The Occupy movement's request was a one-side payer health care and a "guaranteed living wage". Pay attention; this is something that we are hearing again from the Democratic Party today: not enough wage but a "guaranteed wage". Free college education to study not what you want but what the government wants you to study, banning the use of fossil fuels for the benefit of the global warming mongers and open borders were other demands of Occupy Wall Street. Do these requests look familiar today in 2017 with the climate change hysteria and borders all open to illegals and criminals?

Democrats, hysteric mainstream media, and Hollywood snobs all worked together to convince Americans that a revolution is in the air and they should embrace it. The nature of what we see in 2017 is a photocopy of the 2011 Occupy Wall Street's blueprint.

The previous occupant of the Oval Office, the Marxist in chief; President Obama, with his whole life struggling to find a way in Washington and transform it into what his beloved mentor; Saul Alinsky, taught him, said: *"Occupy Wall Street expresses the frustrations the American people feel, that we had the biggest financial crisis since the Great Depression, huge collateral damage all throughout the country."*

Then the senior version of Alice in wonderland lady, House Democratic Leader at the time, Nancy Pelosi, who thinks Bush is still the president in 2017 and believes Donald Trump has to visit countries in alphabetical order (Still can't keep help laughing when reading her words. This phrase should be nominated as the most crap a Senator has ever paraphrased. Maybe you need to do your daily tasks in alphabetical order too?), said: *"I support the message and that change...(social communism) has to happen."*

Al Gore, the "charlatan" who masterminded the global warming scare, called the movement: *"With democracy in crisis, a true grassroots movement, pointing out the flaws in our system is the first step in the right direction."*

Really Mr. Cockwomble? **Democracy has always been in crisis each time Democrats have demanded something and had no power to shove it in our throats!**

And obviously, the left's bullhorns and the leftist think tank front page individuals and organizations have pushed the socialist propaganda and wanted the government to stop the corruption by ignoring the oligarchs' corruption and controlling every aspect of

Americans' lives. Looking at the main poster designed for Occupy Wall Street, and the girl standing on the famous bull statue of Wall Street, er notice the incredible resemblance of the idea of Occupy Wall Street with the "fearless girl" statue installed right in front of the statue of "The Charging Bull, the American symbol of Capitalism" in Bowling Green, Manhattan. That means the idea of Occupy Wall Street is not gone. **On the contrary, it has reached a whole new level to the point of being officially installed right in front of the Charging Bull, the symbol of prosperity and strength of the Capitalist system.** This is a "Declaration of War" To America's economy on March 7, 2017, a day before women's day, if people can read between the lines.

The girl has nothing to do with "feminism". If the statue was a boy, still the message would be the same: Fight Capitalism. Using a girl to keep the statue on the ground is just a covering-up strategy to hide the aggressive symbolism of "fight capitalism" by the use of feminism.

Alliance for Global Justice funded by Soros managed donations to any neo-communist anarchists, socialists, non-stable Naomi Klein followers, and hippies who occupied Zuccotti Park in lower Manhattan. The Wall Street Journal estimated the money received by the Alliance for Global Justice as a total of $500,000. Moreover, food, power generators, clothing, shoes, camping gear, and sleeping bags were donated separately and not included in the budget.

All Nonprofit organizations are "fiscal sponsors" which donors write a check to the organization and they can deduct the donations from their income. The interesting part of the story is here. Who is the main donor to this organization? Open society! Soros's number one mega Foundation. **There is a pattern here: Soros has a**

target. He creates a nonprofit organization, and that organization creates a cause. A cause dictated by Soros. Then he draws the strategy line, and the miniature activists are recruited and employed to do exactly as they have been told. They push and push until they win or they lose. If they lose, Soros changes the strategy and acts through another one of his instrumental organizations. These activities have been exposed by the hacker group DC Leaks. The Open Society Foundation is the main Soros's foundation that plays the legitimizing role of other smaller organizations by receiving money from him, and another communists then pledges into other organizations that wash the Soros's fingerprints and make it difficult to trace at first sight. Through the Open Society Foundation, he pours billions in 150 organizations in 37 countries around the world. These organizations are responsible for all the chaos, riots, regime change, coup d'état, gender confusion, family concept destruction, anti-Christianity movements, white supremacist push agenda, transgender agenda, porn indoctrination agenda, anarchism, Antifa, Black Lives Matter, Media Matters, and all instability we face in past decades.

Other organizations involved in Occupy Wall Street were Tide Organization and ACORN. Bear in mind that ACORN, TIDE, and A.N.S.W.E.R are some of his most powerful, active, and progressive organizations after the Open Society Foundation. Tide set up a website, Occupy Wish List, where protesters list what they need, and the donors pledge to give it to them. When protesting was easier? Protesters, who were recruited through fliers spread in crowds and websites, were promised to receive 2500 dollars monthly income plus 50 dollars per protest (Don't you want to be a protester?) and they have been guaranteed to have all they need to protest.

In an interview with Newsweek, in 2009, Soros delighted that chaos finally came to America, said: *"In the crisis period, the impossible becomes possible,"* restating Alinsky's ideology: *"a good crisis is a terrible thing to waste."*

As we previously said, he spontaneously says what he is up to but to understand Soros, we must learn to speak his language. In the above statement, what he is saying is these protests are designed to go as far as leading America in the blink of the civil war because a civil war will give him miracles and "the order" he is working for.

Let's take a look at what he says and what he means in a phrase by phrase translation:

Soros: "I am not here to cheer you up. The situation is about as serious and difficult as I've experienced in my career,"-Soros to Newsweek writer John Arlidge.

(**Translation**: because this is on my agenda and according to my agenda, I am going to make it much worse than that)

Soros: "We are facing an extremely difficult time, comparable in many ways to the 1930s, the Great Depression. We are facing now a general retrenchment in the developed world, which threatens to put us in a decade of more stagnation, or worse."

(**Translation**: I and all my organizations have been making efforts for this to happen. I love the 1930s, and that is my target, and it is what we need. Why the 1930s? Because all I want is summed up there: The big financial collapse, the rise of Fascism which I am financing for and is what I hide and finally, the WW2! The war was the result of all totalitarian uprisings and a revolutionary mass movement that I am trying to obtain. I want a financial collapse and extreme poverty which results in anger, chaos, and disobedience. This will lead to first; Martial law and then; WW3; then we can have our New Word Order as a "Universal Peace Treaty.")

Soros: "The best case scenario is a deflationary environment. The worst case scenario is the collapse of the financial system."

(**Translation**: The worst scenario for you is the best scenario for me which is the collapse of the financial system. The same collapse I've been showering my money to happen as the fruit of my destructive work and which I was planning a decade ago as an insider. Only this realizes the big chaos that I need to get my result. From chaos emerges the order. My New World's Order.)

Soros: "The collapse of the Soviet system was a pretty extraordinary event, and we are currently experiencing something similar in the developed world, without fully realizing what's happening."

(**Translation**: As my old predecessors, the Rothschilds did the same thing to the Soviet Union, I am now united with their forces, doing the same thing to the United States of America but you shouldn't come to an understanding that the Soviet Union was Communist and America is Capitalist. We don't tell you that in the

Soviet's case; we destroyed what "we" ourselves had created while in America, we are going to destroy what "you" people have created by "your" free will and we hate your free will. We have the mainstream media, Hollywood version of us, educational and judiciary system that we bought, and during the past decade, we have sown the Marxism-Communism idea deep in people's thoughts so they will be used to fulfill our agenda.

You are working with us to destroy America just like it was your plan. You have no idea what you are doing and what you will have. Look at the small, weak countries which emerged after the Soviet Unions' fall. Aren't you fools able to see yourself in that picture? Average people are just too naïve)

Soros: "As the U.S. economy continues to deteriorate, anger will grow, and rioting in the streets is sure to follow."

"It's already started," he says

"yes, yes, yes," he is happy like a child.

(**Translation**: He cheers watching the anger and riots that he, himself has created just like when he said: *"That* *year was the happiest year of my life",* referring to his collaboration with the Nazis, he doesn't hide it. He is impatient to fuel the "anger" and burst a civil war. He is convinced that anger can be triggered through a financial collapse.)

Soros: "The system we have now, has actually broken down, only we haven't quite recognized it, and so you need to create a new one, and this is the time to do it."

(**Translation**: I (Soros) have always said the only thing which stands between me and my one-world government is the system governing The United States Of America which is empowered by the Constitution. We have to change this constitution but to do it without resistance; we have to create new beliefs and new ways of thinking. We have to inject the idea that capitalism is failed and the socialist communism is the only solution so what we need as the most vital step, is people hating the government and its policies and the timing is now.)

In 2009, Soros created the Institute for New Economic Thinking with pledging $50 million to it. **He gains his billions through the "American" free market system, enjoying the "American" free trade rules, benefiting**

the "American" democracy, while he spends the same money for bipartisan strategies to destroy the same American system that was his ladder of success to bring poverty and hunger to the same country that hosted him.

What we see in Communist China, is what he longs to see in America. Total censorship and internet control, no gun no property, total interference of the government in business and personal life, total governmental education to train a bunch of sheep doing whatever the government asks them to do.

Soros is also funding "Democratization Programs" (Communist Transition Programs) in many countries including Uzbekistan, Burma, Haiti, Central Europe, and Central Asia, and all countries where ACORN and SEIU are working in.

The progressive left loves communism but never want to spend a vacation in any of them. They know there is no country that people live better than the U.S. When Fidel Castro took over Cuba, he said he is not a communist, and he is not going to bring communism. The first thing he did, he gave the peasants single-payer healthcare. A governmental doctor. With a single-payer governmental doctor, it would be the government to decide who lives and who dies. Remember baby Charlie Gard. No need to mention that single-payer healthcare and minimum wage are impeccable signs of Communism. These signals are just as official as the red color of communism flags. Among principals of transforming a country into communism taught by Saul Alinsky, in Chapter 7, governmental healthcare is mentioned as the first step to nail the Communism and that is what happened with the ex administration. What was the first thing President Obama campaigned for? Healthcare. Just as his mentor Saul Alinsky, taught him.

What happened to Venezuela? Venezuela is not far; it's South America. Steps from home for you who think what the relation is. All recent reports and pictures show Venezuelans looking in garbage cans and killing their domestic pets for food. After they killed the animals in the national zoo, eating human dead bodies out of hunger is their new normal. No this is not a horror movie. It's a lovely Venezuela. Hunger stroke Venezuela and whoever can is fleeing off the country. What Hugo Chavez and now his successor Maduro, the socialist Communists did to the country brought Hunger, censorship, totalitarianism and other souvenirs of

Communism. Do the mainstream media broadcast the scenes of hunger in Venezuela? No, why should they?

Why should they tell the truth and let the youth whom they spent years in brainwashing them see how does it feel to be a communist country? A starved population is vulnerable so a totalitarian regime can do anything to them. Indoctrinate then give them a tiny bit of a reward called: FOOD, repeat the previous phase and keep them again in war and starvation. That is Socialism.

Universities and colleges as the left's indoctrination camps are fed with tax payer's money and should be defunded and even closed. Teaching the students that America's founding fathers are terrorists and its constitution is totalitarian and must be abolished are not what American universities should teach. However, they don't tell the students how socialism deficiency ruined itself, and they don't let them know the experience that the Venezuelans went through because they want those kids to go through the experience. Those brattish kids have not seen anything like the 1930s; they didn't read anything about it, they didn't watch any movie about it, the books in universities have been changed intentionally so how can they know?

The mind-managers don't want them to know. They praise socialism, Karl Marx, Fidel Castro, Hugo Chavez. This world is living in a bubble of lies. **The millennials live in a hysteric bubble and learn to fight their own families and legitimize their talking points.** Fighting for the country which at all times was an honor, now is taught at the universities to be equal to "Nazism." They have changed the perception of our children of good and evil. They teach them to hate their own flag, their own borders, and their own constitution and they have also learned not to listen so unless they live under the yoke of socialism, they won't get it and then it will be too late.

It is a cult of Nihilism. They deny God, deny the family, gender, identity, border, national sovereignty, good, science and repress the truth and all this, leads to depression, demoralization and coming to the point of Nihilism. Once a science propaganda grabbed my attention which claimed people who believe in God, have their brains damaged. Mind-managers fight anything encouraging that is worth fighting for or be proud of. **They keep our mind, heart and nervous system in constant incoherence because if these three be coherent, we will be in our highest level of conscience and can widen the zoom of our perception** lens. **They don't want us to think, so by constant agitation and the extermination of whatever we can rely on; they promote Nihilism.**

When there is nothing to die for,

then there is nothing to live for.

The blatant contradiction is, they defend open borders and diversity while there is no diversity allowed in communism. One government, one currency, one bank system, one religion, one culture, one language and one way of dressing up. How can they defend something against their ideology? **If there is no diversity, then Nihilism is inevitable.** To millennials, nothing matters anymore, not caring about science, **re-categorizing things according to bizarre precepts, narratives or assumptions, and intimidating the dissidents. They don't want to debate, in fact, they stone the debate**. By number-one the Label and by number two they shut you down! America, the greatest country to be a woman or a liberal, a **country which was not noble, a country which was an experiment of putting free thinking and free speech into the state is now at the edge of its fall through the stupidity of lunatic feminists, radical liberals and hard-left**

politicians which condemn free speech and promote communism.

If I had a chance to talk to these young children I would ask, what is the meaning of their life? If they are alive, healthy, living safely in a house, have freedom, opportunity, technology, and a system that allows them to grow and build and yet they are not happy, then how can they be? When MTV and other vacuity channels portray celebrities' lavish lifestyle or Jersey Shore crap as the standard, then the problem is not your lifestyle being lower than them but is **due to the "meaning" those channels "associate" to that lifestyle.** That celebrity mansion shouldn't be the resource of all good emotions you want to feel. How many of those celebrities are happy? They are successful in their jobs but are they fulfilled? Why do they use drugs? Why do they divorce? Why do they suicide in the same dreamy mansions?

People act regarding the state of their emotions. Their emotions give them thoughts just as their thoughts give them emotions. However, they act as an extension of their thoughts. The danger is when those thoughts are not based on good values, and they take actions no matter if those actions are not following morals or law. To create sound emotions resulting from sound thoughts and act upon them we need to focus on us, empower our mind, exercise our skills. We all have some, just find them, focus on them, upgrade them and build new ones and remember; **the meaning of life changes completely at the same moment we take control of that "meaning." We immediately see that what needs to be changed is only our mindset. It is a paradigm shift** but the mainstream media doesn't like us to know this.

2- Antifa anarchists brainwashed by all universities and colleges and trained by Soros.

-"People's Republic of Berkeley"?

The University of California, Berkeley is the ground zero for the campus war against America. Since 20 years ago, the university has become the left's brainwashing machine with the specific goal of bringing down the United States of America. Professors, lecturers, and the course materials are extremely radical and Anti-

American especially faculty of Political Sciences. More than 5 generations of ex-radicalized students are now professors. Any right or conservative ideology is non-tolerated in this university and what is the result today? We have groups and organizations that believe in "Kalifornication" of California. The "People's Republic of Kalifornia" whines and cries that the federal government doesn't love the state of California and it should ask of independence and will be auto-sufficient by its rich people.

With a long history of building up violent justice groups, Berkeley has become the center of Antifa, created by the same master minders and colonizers of Occupy Wall Street. An anarchist Neo Communist group which by its behavior is absolutely Pro-Fascist but by name is Anti-Fascist.

What is the definition of Fascism? The dominant ideology shuts down the opponents by force, violence or any means possible, verbally or physically. On several occasions during the violent attacks on 2016's Inauguration day, women's march or peaceful protests of conservatives or right wings when Antifa showed up and have been asked to what are they protesting? They had no idea or better say; they had no idea what their idea is. A summed up liberal logic would help but they didn't have any. The modern progressive left is not able to have a constructive discussion. Whether its race, gender or just anything. **Social Liberalism has become a religious cult. They don't care about the truth and nobody should touch that religion. They believe what they believe, and that's it.** No discussion, no question. Their brilliant discussion starts and ends with: *"I have nothing to say"* and boom, you have to accept it, convincing enough.

They are organized, have a schedule, and repeat what they have been told to. Their playbook includes very few slogans like "no KKK no Trump no Fascist" and approaching them, they will scream and act like zombies arose from graves by a trumpet right away. This generation is zombified. Nothing normal in them. **The "Generation Me"; a generation that believes all other generations owe them something and everything about them is just so perfect. This is Narcissism. A generation of "entitlement" which demands a country of "entitlement".**

Knowledge has a positive outcome while ignorance has a negative one. Why "Generation Me" doesn't want to hear or know anything other than what they believe? **Because they are on the negative derive and this negativity gives them their war-power and aggressivity. If they hear, if they know, their negative drive will be deactivated, and they will have nothing to be angry and therefore, fight for.**

Antifa presents hate and intolerance. They are hyper-individualists and robotic narcissists. Living in constant paranoia, **they have been told that any idea which is not their idea, is a hateful idea so it meets the criteria of "hate speech" and needs to be shut down.** These people play horns in your ears and scream constantly. If you are in a few, they attack in numbers and if you are in numbers, they freak out. Thin macaronis, slow motioned, empty head, beta males so coward to show their faces. Now, what is the use of all surveillance cameras if they are masked like ISIS soldiers? **Isn't it better to officially announce that cameras are for controlling and monitoring good people who respect the law but not for terrorists and anarchists?** Did the surveillance cameras protect us from terrorist attacks? Did they identify the anarchists? So anyone can cover his face and commit a crime and escape? Is that what the so-called "Social Justice" organizations like "Alliance for Social Justice" is promoting? **Thrive on mayhem and barbarity?**

Add an "ism" or "ist" when you see the term "social" and read it

"socialism" because that's how it means. Social justice groups are **socialist** justice groups. Social welfare groups are **socialist** welfare groups. Be honest to use the right term. Throw away the disgusting "political correctness" which has raped our dignity. Why has it been created such a stupid phrase? Only a charlatan could have created something like that.

For all time when somebody was too tricky, hypocrite, and talked double meaning, we called him "political." **Now, why should we replace "correct," which is the human soul's natural characteristic, for the evil expression of "politically correct"? Politically correct indeed means falsely correct.** It means pretending to be correct while it's not and it is totally different from socially correct. If we don't work in the office in our underwear, it is because of socially correctness but political correctness has nothing to do with it.

Last time the brilliant critical thinker; Milo Yiannopoulos had a speech in Berkeley was a total shame for the university's president who allowed it to happen and shame for local police which was inexistent on the scene. They helped the anarchist attack to happen. It has been years that the freedom of speech is under attack by "political correctness" and to a degree, it doesn't exist anymore.

Freedom of speech is now the left's hostage when they officially and publicly assault, and nobody cares. Fake journalists who project narratives without a source instead of reporting facts, fake artists who create creepy works by demonstrating child nudity and abuse but masquerade them as their artistic expressions and attend "spirit cooking "ceremonies, Hollywood snobs who shoot the president in their clips or even the ISIS-style beheading of him and anarchist groups who demand white genocide, have all the freedom of speech they want but we don't.

Speak up against radical Islam, transgender agenda, anti-Christian groups, abortion, Planned Parenthood or anything important to the left, and all hell will break loose and they will definitely find a case to label us as a misogynist, homophobic, xenophobic, or racist and the engineered judicial system condemns "us" in a blink of eyes. So freedom of speech now is irrelevant to the speech itself but relative to political correctness and not definitive to the truth. **This is a narcissist disorder that causes an intense self-absorption and a grandiose sense of self. The idea that one is owed greatness no matter what they merit.** The mechanism operates as follows: they first categorize people rather than the individual by himself, then identify him based on that category and attack the category. **I am black; you are white and that distinction matters. I am gay, you are straight, and that distinction determines the result of our confrontation,** and I call it confrontation because that is what it is as there is no debate.

A social climate that people are so easily offended. So sensitive and preoccupied with their honor and how they are treated. How far can it go? There can always be an idiot who chooses to be offended by some one's idea. The growing minority of "generation me" who believes they have a right to be free from being offended, how far can they go? To shut everybody's voice for the possibility of offending somebody else? **This is the deliberate institutional altruism VS self-expression**

that points its finger at you as "selfish" if you preserve your rights. You don't have any rights if what your belief offends another crybaby. Since when just a phrase has set up a riot in a university because of a shift in the emotional climate? **If there is no debate, there is no gap between emotion and violence and anger becomes the physical reaction.** This political climate takes us to medieval ages when somebody was always offended. **Shouldn't we teach emotionally weak people to have more self-esteem and not be offended by every stupid thing that crosses their way?** Shouldn't there be programs, books, and coaches dedicated to helping hyperactively emotional people who are not able to control their own emotions? Do we live in "emotion-era" rather than logic and health-era?

The "Perception Changing Process" presents "deception" as a new brand and transmits it in light of a positive messaging. If the presentation of deception has a positive, "Feel good" effect, people will embrace it easily. Mind manipulation is what they do. They narrow the horizon of an intellectual mind to a tight, rigid one. A rigid mind doesn't see possibilities. If they control the sense of possibilities,

then no open mind can imagine alternatives. So the rigid mind stands for the sloppy assumptions as facts.

One who claims to be a physician without having a license will be called either a fraud or a psychopath but if the left claims to have some rights that the Rule of Law doesn't grant them, they think "feeling" entitled to those rights is equal to having them. In a climate of a madhouse, which all norms are upside down; the psychopath is not the psychopath but the one who challenges the psychopath will be systematically and deliberately pushed back.

This is where we are going to; a madhouse and a "feel good" oriented society which everybody "feels" we owe him something.

Even if Milo or anybody else believes in super fictitious ideas or theories, he should be able to exercise his right to free speech under the first amendment. Just two months after the Berkeley riot, Ann Coulter's speech (another right-wing pundit) was thence canceled and there, the twitter diggers distinguished the face of Berkeley's Mayor in a tweeted picture and unmasked the fact that the Mayor himself was an Antifa sympathizer.

What a university.

Calling a speech as a hate speech just because we disagree with it; is a measure of entitlement and totalitarianism and blaming the speaker for inciting the violence of those who disagree, is overwhelmingly stupid. These people demonize whom they don't like while they claim America to be inclusive and admire diversity. Those people feel entitled to disrupt and prevent a speech from happening. This is a Climate of violence. **The same happens with pulling down the American statues. A statue has an idea behind it. So to fight that idea, they remove the statue. No need to fight the idea by eliminating it. Build a statue of what you believe instead of eliminating what already exists.** Why do we have the statue of Lenin in New York? Did we believe in Lenin? No, did we pull it down? No.

History will not change by eradicating its traces.

Millennials, the "Generation Me", I tell you why they became what they became. This generation is the only generation trapped in a bizarre condition: First; they belong to the "Total Deception Era" of the deep state in which schools, universities, and the media were in total control, and not enough alternative news channels were talking about this deception. Second; they lived in their cell phones. Why is this a determining factor? **Because as the technology speed is a super-fast digital speed, human psychology cannot keep up with that speed. Millennials, stuck in their cell phone, just have seen just what the establishment wants them to see.** They have used technology to isolate themselves. Psychology of the millennials didn't keep up with the speed of the technology that they were using, and it remained behind. They didn't work on their minds to maximize it so, this gap is the cause that they harm themselves and other people too. **A campaign of disinformation in their backpack and wisdom is detached from that backpack.** Another thing which is completely missing in this generation is energy. They have no energy because that cell phone deactivates their body and physical engagement. They lay back and text. They yawn all the time and love sleeping more than success. That state is absolutely an anti-high-energy, anti-engagement and anti-performance state of the body. That's why they are attracted to groups of anarchists. Because while they don't have the wisdom to distinguish right from wrong, anarchists inspire their energy. The best cure for these children is to teach them wisdom and inspire their energy.

But the good news is that the "Generation Z" is ours. They belong to us. They are brilliant, sharp, caring, patriot, and they are so disgusted with the perversion and the lifestyle of the Planet Perversity. They are traditional, and they are fighters. THEY BELONG TO US.

One of them was analyzing one of the recent issues like a 70- year-old professor, I told him: Kudos to your mother and father, and he said his parents were hard-left liberals! Yes. They are disgusted, and this disgust pulls them to us. We are the winners of this game. We have God, and we have "us" and we have the Generation Z and no doubt the generation after them who are brought up by these brilliant new fresh patriots.

It hurts when I know we have to fight millennial boys and girls who are just like our children. It's so sad. But I look back into history when soldiers had to fight with the sword on the battlefield, and a wise man had to fight with a young soldier at the age of his son. They did it; that's fight. They had no choice neither do we.

-Congressional Record–Appendix, pp. A34-A35

Very surprisingly, there is a blueprint of Communist goals to destroy America, Congressional Record–Appendix, pp. A34-A35 prepared in 1963 but registered in 1969. A blueprint of a plan designed after the assassination of President Kennedy.

In 1963, John F. Kennedy appeared on TV and threatened to expose the secret societies which manipulate and control the government. Shortly after, President Kennedy was assassinated. The blueprint was introduced on January 10, 1963, At Mrs. Nordman's request which she identifies the paper as to be an excerpt from "The Naked Communist," by Cleon Skousen. This Congressional Record is not yet digitalized. In order to gain it, you have to ask it only from those libraries which are federal repositories. Or you can go directly to your Congress Critters and ask the document. They will give it to you willingly. Your college library also may have a copy of it if it's a repository. The document is a roadmap for the Democratic Party since then. Ninety percent of these goals are already achieved, and they are achieved blatantly through the exact same methods. So the Democratic Party arrogantly designed a "Destroy America" roadmap and used the taxpayers' money and the leverage of the Congress, to destroy the country they swore to serve it. That means; when you vote a Democratic candidate, you vote to destroy the country you love.

Here are the articles:

Article 1.U.S. acceptance of coexistence as the only alternative to atomic war.

Article 2.U.S. willingness to capitulate in preference to engaging in atomic war.

Article 3. Develop the illusion that total disarmament [by] the United States would be a demonstration of moral strength.

Article 4. Permit free trade between all nations regardless of Communist affiliation and regardless of whether or not items could be used for war.

Article 5.Extension of long-term loans to Russia and Soviet satellites.

Article 6. *Provide American aid to all nations regardless of Communist domination.*

Article 7. *Grant recognition of Red China. Admission of Red China to the U.N.*

Article 8. *Set up East and West Germany as separate states in spite of Khrushchev's promise in 1955 to settle the German question by free elections under supervision of the U.N.*

Article 9.Prolong conferences to ban atomic tests because the United States has agreed to suspend tests as long as negotiations are in progress.

Article 10. *Allow all Soviet satellites individual representation in the UN.*

Article 11.Promote the UN as the only hope for mankind. If its charter is rewritten, demand that it be set up as a one-world government with its own independent armed forces. (Some Communist leaders believe the world can be taken over as easily by the U.N. as by Moscow. Sometimes these two centers compete with each other as they are now doing in the Congo.)

Article 12. *Resist any attempt to outlaw the Communist Party.*

Article 13. *Do away with all loyalty oaths.*

Article 14. *Continue giving Russia access to the U.S. Patent Office.*

Article 15.<u>*Capture one or both of the political parties in the United States.*</u>

Article 16. *Use technical decisions of the courts to weaken basic American institutions by claiming their activities violate civil rights.*

Article 17. <u>*Get control of the schools. Use them as transmission belts for socialism and current Communist propaganda.*</u> *Soften the curriculum. Get control of teachers' associations. Put the party line in textbooks.*

Article 18. *Gain control of all student newspapers.*

Article 19.<u>*Use student riots to foment public protests*</u> *against programs or organizations which are under Communist attack.*

Article 20.*Infiltrate the press.* Get control of book-review assignments, editorial writing, policy-making positions.

Article 21.*Gain control of key positions in radio, TV, and motion pictures.*

Article 22.*Continue discrediting American culture* by degrading all forms of artistic expression. An American Communist cell was told to *"eliminate all good sculpture from parks and buildings, substitute shapeless, awkward and meaningless forms."*

Article 23. *Control art critics and directors of art museums. "Our plan is to promote ugliness, repulsive, meaningless art."*

Article 24.*Eliminate all laws governing obscenity by calling them "censorship" and a violation of free speech* and free press.

Article 25.*Break down cultural standards of morality by promoting pornography* and obscenity in books, magazines, motion pictures, radio, and TV.

Article 26. *Present homosexuality, degeneracy and promiscuity as "normal, natural, healthy."*

Article27.Infiltrate the churches and replace revealed religion with "social" religion. Discredit the Bible and emphasize the need for intellectual maturity, which does not need a "religious crutch."

Article 28.Eliminate prayer or any phase of religious expression in the schools on the ground that *it violates the principle of "separation of church and state."*

Article 29.Discredit the American Constitution by calling it inadequate, old-fashioned, out of step with modern needs, a hindrance to cooperation between nations on a worldwide basis.

Article 30.Discredit the American Founding Fathers.Present them as selfish aristocrats who had no concern for the "common man."

Article 31.Belittle all forms of American culture and discourage the teaching of American history on the ground that it was only a minor part of the "big picture." Give more emphasis to Russian history since the Communists took over.

Article 32.Support any socialist movement to give centralized control over any part of the culture–

education, social agencies, welfare programs, mental health clinics, etc.

Article 33. Eliminate all laws or procedures which interfere with the operation of the Communist apparatus.

Article 34. Eliminate the House Committee on Un-American Activities.

Article 35. Discredit and eventually dismantle the FBI.

Article 36. Infiltrate and gain control of more unions.

Article 37. Infiltrate and gain control of big business.

Article 38. Transfer some of the powers of arrest from the police to social agencies. Treat all behavioral problems as psychiatric disorders which no one but psychiatrists can understand [or treat].

Article 39. Dominate the psychiatric profession and use mental health laws as a means of gaining coercive control over those who oppose Communist goals.

Article 40. Discredit the family as an institution. Encourage promiscuity and easy divorce.

Article 41.<u>Emphasize the need to raise children away from the negative influence of parents.</u> *Attribute prejudices, mental blocks and retarding of children to suppressive influence of parents.*

Article 42.<u>Create the impression that violence and insurrection are legitimate aspects of the American tradition;</u> *that students and special-interest groups should rise up and use ["]united force["] to solve economic, political or social problems.*

Article 43. *Overthrow all colonial governments before native populations are ready for self-government.*

Article 44. *Internationalize the Panama Canal.*

Article45. *Repeal the Connally reservation so the United States cannot prevent the World Court from seizing jurisdiction [over domestic problems.* <u>Give the World Court jurisdiction] over nations and individuals alike.</u>

Alas…

What we see today are scenes of the movie according to the above scripture. Articles; 22, 29, 30, 31, 42, 17, 18,

19, 24 are strongly in action exactly as they were printed.

Judge alone. Which one of these once only goals have not been accomplished by now? The only tiny difference is that these neo-communists, due to the geopolitical shift of events and because of today's Anti-Russian political atmosphere and propaganda, where if a mouse is missed, Vladimir Putin must have eaten it, and as Russia is not a Communist country anymore but a rich Christian capitalist country, in item 31, we should change Russia with Cuba-China's culture and glorify Che Guevara, Castro, and Hugo Chavez, the communist leaders which at the end of the day have a common goal: Progressive Communism for America.

The reason I had to insert this document is this section is to show that the destruction plan is not new the pathology to execute this metamorphosis is almost the same as 1-The Khazarians' protocol which traces back in 1800, 2-The Congressional Record of 1963 we just mentioned and, 3- the Rules for Radicals wrote by Saul Alinsky in 1971. We will explain the other two documents in the next chapters.

Communism never died. It was just transferred to America through progressive liberals and hard-left

activists who hate the culture of Americana and see the world as an oppressed world.

For them, the world is oppressed, and they are the saviors.

But how will they save this oppressed world?

Through oppressing those people who are not aligned with their progressive hateful obsession with oppression and obsession.

The left is obsessed with the institutional obsession, and there is no compromise. Whoever is not with them faces moral indictment, and this cycle goes on and on. The important note to bear in mind here is; the left is always anti-police. Police and the Army are always most patriot groups of people and enemy number one to progressives, so they do whatever they can to harm the Police. Whenever Democrats are in power, The military and the police are weakened and attacked.

These three dangerous manuscripts combined have become the strategy of the left. The Alinsky's book which is the last one, and is adopted based on another two, developed, matured and full-fledged by a villain like Alinsky is a full detailed and practical prescription of how the destruction should take place.

There are direct Antifa-Soros Connections. He was behind the inaugural protests against President Donald Trump. Connecting with organizations and professionals like Teresa Gutierrez of the "Workers World Party," who proclaims *"this is the revolution that will take Donald Trump down and make America a socialist country."* The planetary parasite says it as it is.

Who wants to stop him?

The objective of these paid protesters is to scare people and force them **to react with anger and outrage to "their" version of reality** and to destabilizing America, pushing the country to the verge of a civil war. Where will the civil war lead us? "Order emerges via chaos." Remember the hammer in chapter two? They created Antifa anarchists as the "Revolution" hammer to shut you down, make chaos, weaken the police and bring the country down.

"Alliance for Global Justice" is another important organization which is funded by George Soros-backed "Tides Foundation" and plays a significant role behind

Antifa. Soros donated $50,000 in 2004 and 2006 from his Open Society. Tide Foundation has also funded the Council for American Islamic Relations (CAIR), which supposedly is the leading front group for Islamic radicals in America. CAIR needs an entire book to talk about it. It is all over America, and its power has dangerously increased. This is just one of Soros's creations so you probably can understand the level of corruption and damage that we are talking about.

"Alliance for Global Justice" claims to refuse Fascism, which as we discussed earlier, it is indeed "Fascist" by acting as it brags about using violence to shut down conservative and libertarian speech and sings the stupid Kumbaya that *"talking peacefully to conservatives, normalizes their views."* These people can lock us up in Chinese style reform camps where we remain until we think right and right means what "they" want us to think. Democracy of Che Guevara and Alinsky, funded by Soros backed by the hard left.

"Alliance for Global Justice" (AfGJ), according to its most recent 990 tax form, has received $2.2 million in funding for the fiscal year ending in March 2016 and one of the group's biggest donors is the Tides Foundation, funded by guess who? George Soros.

So "Workers World Organization," "ANSWER," "Media Matters," which are all backbones of Antifa are all directly tied to Soros. They have directly backed the Berkeley riots. At a New York Antifa riot, there was a sign carried by an agitator and at the bottom of it was printed "Worker's World Organization" and had the website written at the bottom, all belonged to Soros.

3- Soros and White Supremacy

-The biggest lie in the history of humanity

If Dr. Martin Luther King was alive, he would slap them in the face, and when they couldn't use that true civil rights activist and patriot (and pastor, don't forget he was a pastor), they would label him a "white supremacist". His niece, Dr. Alveda King is and the legend's son Martin Luther King III are completely against the white supremacy agenda, and I believe if Dr. Luther King was alive, these anti-white extremists would face a backlash as he wouldn't fit into their agenda.

This is the core of the deceit and the substantial issue as all other conflicts are related to this agenda.

We are called a white supremacist if we are a patriot, nationalist, right-wing, alpha male, black nationalist man or woman, anti-feminism man or woman, anti-globalism white, black Hispanic man or woman, straight man, Christian, anti-global warming hoax, and if we reject political correctness, inclusive language, multiculturalism, any privilege, limited free speech, gun control, government servitude mentality and if we love our country, if we want to protect our national sovereignty and especially if we love America, it's Constitution, its anthem, its flag and if we want to protect our country, make it prosper and take the measures to make it safe.

For all those crimes mentioned above, we are called a white supremacist.

This is an intellectual architecture by putting guilt on whoever stands up to save his national sovereignty. All crimes we already mentioned are power radiance, and they don't want us to have power. How can it be when they call a black nationalist a "white supremacist" because they share the "idea" of national sovereignty. So it's not because of the white color of the skin but the color of our political view. The truth is they baffle and associate our views with our skin color.

In a nutshell, they fight the "idea" and to smash that "idea" they call you racist. They have associated "nationalism" with the color white and when they cry "white supremacist", it means nationalist so the person accused can be of any color. The problem is they have established the word "nationalism" as the umbrella term for all the crimes mentioned above. Modern racism has nothing to do with race and has all to do with nationalist beliefs. So far so good but stay with me because it doesn't end here and I am going to go deeper.

Criminal racism meets a legal definition that deals with race, not with beliefs. What does that mean? It means if a person of color can accuse another person to have committed a hate crime toward him, the only thing he needs to prove is that the accused has disagreed with him on some matter. The race has been twisted and used as a weapon to attack beliefs. The judicial establishment is sentencing people for their beliefs considering them hate crimes. So as far as the judicial establishment is concerned, the first amendment doesn't exist, and expressing one's beliefs is a jailable offense. This is what should be asked from your lawyer to emphasize if you find yourself in a legal dispute with them.

To accuse people of being a white supremacist, first; the premise of white supremacy as a crime should be proven. Second; If so, the accused should fit the category. But instead, **they trigger the emotional dynamics of people by an ongoing manipulation of their minds: created, fed and fueled by the hysteric media to give it a life of its own and the narrative goes and on with no evidence but by repetition, no evidence becomes the evidence.**

This mass hysteria is wrong on all fronts and is consuming the population. **White supremacy is a Boogeyman who never existed in modern history. And in old history? Who brought the slaves to America? The Democratic Party of the 18s. The same Democrats whom patriots fought with during the civil war and abolished slavery. How many Northern soldiers gave their lives to abolish slavery? Besides, the blacks sold the blacks in Africa, how about that? Who sold them to the whites? And finally, who were the white before the Democrats? The British establishment before the U.S independence.**

White Supremacy is identity politics aimed to kick out national and personal identity. As Thomas Sowell says: *"Racism is like ketchup, you can put it on practically anything - and demanding evidence makes you a racist."*

Through the dictatorship system created by Soros's "Media Matters" though police, people can gamble their lives for questioning. Their life can be totally in jeopardy and destroyed if they dare to challenge issues like does white supremacy really exist? Just as the global warming cult, asking about their existence is an unforgivable crime and we are allowed to speak if we start concerning the cultish premise that white supremacy and global warming exist.

Take a look at the disgusting comments on Twitter and Instagram written by professors in universities or from social magazines and grasp the severity of this paradox. Below are some of them:

"You're (White people) on the endangered list. And unlike, say, the bald eagle or some exotic species of muskrat, you are not worth saving. In forty years or so, maybe fewer, there won't be any more white people around." - Noel Ignatiev, Harvard Professor

"All I want for Christmas is white genocide" -Drexel University's George Ciccariello Maher on Twitter, on 2016's Christmas Eve!

"The goal of abolishing the white race is so desirable some may find it hard to believe it could incur opposition other than from committed white supremacists. We intend to keep bashing the dead white males, and the live ones, and the females too until the white race' is destroyed." -Tim Wise, a preacher of nonexistent 'White Privilege.'

*"White women: it is time to do your part! Your white children reinforce the white supremacist society that benefits you. If you claim to be progressive, and yet willingly birth white children by your own choice, you are a hypocrite. White women should be encouraged to abort their white children, and to use their freed-up time and resources to assist women of color who have no other choice but to raise their children".*The feminist Medusa magazine, Nicole Valentine, June 21, 2017

Racism is a subjective theory. Considering the hypothesis that racism is a social construct, the

differences between the races become racist themselves. In consequence, people talking about racism, have to be racist as this is racist by itself and trying to sell it by force is yet worse and is an analogous development syndrome, which is bigotry by itself. **How can they redefine racism as a system of privilege? Nobody is dealing with the issue of racism in case it exists. They are just redirecting it toward the whites.**

Shutting us down by using the color of our skin is what is happening. They practically say; we are not allowed to speak because we have a certain color of skin. We cannot defend our country or our borders because we have a certain color of skin or even better, they try to guilt us of not being capable of understanding things no matter what we have studied or how smart we are because we have a certain color of

skin. Being a scholar, a scientist, having a Ph.D., being a researcher or a philosopher, none of them can qualify our presentation of facts because we have a certain color of skin. **The microaggression toward us committed by them happens the moment they identify and orient themselves by "their" color of skin. But it becomes macroaggression when they attack us and demand to orient ourselves with "their" color of skin** as "superior" while they continue to call "us" a racist! That means forced trespassing against us and blaming the victim. This is just like being negated in a conversation because of our physical appearance. It's absolutely the same: *"You don't have the right to participate in the debate because you have a big nose"!* It is just the same. But this goes back into the

roots of communism. **While the old version of communism was an anti-class system, the current version of communism means anti-white. The system is the same while the ingredients are replaced and this happens although all the premise of communism, according to their manuals and Lenin playbooks are just**

about class identity (poor vs. rich).

This is lunacy. This is bigotry. If the color of the skin

is the guilt of the racial race, then black supremacists, themselves, have created it. This is sick and if the white color is twisted to mean nationalism, patriotism, strong borders and national sovereignty, all who believe the idea, then let it be. We are patriots and defend our borders, sovereignty, identity, anthem, and flag so call us white. If black is the color of Antifa, then we and our black and Hispanic patriots are all white. If this is the accusation, we buy it, why should we back off? At this point who cares what they call us? They call us

something anyhow.

Meanings associated with the events control the trajectory of our life. If we think we "can" and if we think we "cannot", we are right either way. If we consider ourselves easily offendable by what another person does or says, that's our choice and our problem, not that person. **If we don't associate "you are dissing me" to an event, we will not be offended.** The point is we can't control the others, or

the world, or the color of our skin but we can control the "meaning" we associate with those events, and our relief depends on that meaning.

Let me prove that white supremacy is a felony which today doesn't exist and is just an accusation searching its evidence in the events and deeds of a generation who lived hundred years ago and has nothing to do with our generation. **A Guilt manufactured by idiotic activists who make their living on this racial fight and without it and eliminating the word "race" from their**

vocabulary, they will go in blackout and have nothing to say. Opportunists with a culture of infantilism that says "thinking is knowing" so they don't need any evidence, and playing the race card is the easiest way to win effortlessly, with no talent or relevance.

History says all types of

races have been subjected to slavery. It also says so many dark-skinned people were slave owners. When there was no constitution, no human rights and the definition of right was subjective to the power of the ruling class, wealth, land, horses, position, and their nobility; slaves were both black and white. The Democratic Party projected slavery just as they created KKK groups. The issue of how the Democratic Party orchestrated the slavery in America is astonishing and Dinesh D'Souza (an outstanding author, not white, not born in America, but a truther who cares about nothing but the truth) has done a profound investigation on the matter, presenting it detailed facts and documents, pictures in his book; "The Big Lie", so there is no need to bring it up here. To back up what we said above with historical events, just read his book.

The horrific American war, a war through which the White North, fought for the abolishment of slavery, and won the war paid the price by the blood of the patriots. Both Northern and Southern soldiers were killed. The Southern soldiers had no choice but to participate in the war even though not all of them agreed with the cause. However, their blood was shed too. Like any war in the world, who loses the war, pays the damage by goods, means, services, land, and transition of power.

Different time and place, the war is over and the issue is not relevant anymore. **The brave and determined white soldiers lost their lives to save their black brothers and abolish slavery.** Before Martin Luther king's fight, resistance to accepting the equality still existed in some areas. But it ended after Dr. Luther King's fight. What matters is whatever it was, it was over, and nobody blames a grandson for the imaginary crime of his grandfather. Today's generation has no guilt for whatever happened before their time. **Today's white generation went on polls in 2008 and voted a "black man" to become the President, and before that special black president, this hostile climate toward whites as well as discrimination against blacks didn't**

exist. It all came with him. Today's racial hate is Obama's souvenir to this country.

Watching and reading the headlines before President Obama, there was never the "race" word in every mouth. Nobody accused a participant of not having the right to speak because of his or her color of skin. This is the distortion of language, spread after Obama. This is not the traditional way of America viewing things which is based on merit not wealth, position, influence or color of the skin.

Why white countries and only white countries have been forced to take immigrants? What will be white people's future in their own country as a minority? Think about all this. It's time for confrontation. There is nowhere to escape. Think about how non-integrated multiculturalism is affecting us. How our job opportunities will be less or even gone, our children's schooling will be inferior; our housing prices will be higher while smaller. How good was the benefit of multiculturalism in our neighborhood? Does it look better now? How will it look in 2030?

If America is so racist why so many nonwhites are obsessed with living in America so that the deportation becomes a drama? Do they risk passing

the American border illegally because it is a racist country? Why do the illegal aliens who don't work receive free welfare from horrendous American racists who do work? How are minorities paid millions to play sports if this country is a racist nation? Why are there so many black super athletes and Class A actors, models, politicians, celebrities and even a black president in the White House if America is a racist country?

Show me a black country that we can copy their democracy. Show me a black, Hispanic, Middle Eastern country that its constitution is better than the United States of America. The same America that they hate and want to destroy it for a better one. Show me a damn country in north, east, west or south of the globe, "black or white" that its constitution is better than the United States of America. THERE IS NONE. Nowhere on the earth has a better constitution to copy. **Ungrateful spoiled people do not know do not get what the real privilege is in this world. The real privilege is what you have but deny. The real privilege is your damn CONSTITUTION!**

People must arm themselves with the power of knowledge, strength, wisdom, and courage and should push back against the evil. No one should be bullied or made ashamed of their race. The war on white, black or any race must not be tolerated.

But the replacement of the Western population is not the only reason for this racial attack. That's the ultimate and long-run goal. **The insidious trick behind the Left's purposeful racial hate in the short-run is political. It's about VOTES. The Left seeks to sell blacks, Hispanics and all other races, the lie that America is eternally racist and structured to make blacks and other races fail. So vote for Democrats to keep racist, rich, white Republicans, off the bench.** They need their votes for 2018 and to get them, they have to fuel the fight to recruit minority voters.

And what will happen if we vote them? The hyper racist culture will take the country down the road of Marxism and Proletariat dictatorship.

In a very fast and brief manner, we are going to explain the concept of Proletariat dictatorship as there was a time my generation had to hear this phrase every single day in the faculty of Political Science and that alert made the conscious of my generation sensitive to the notion. Proletariat dictatorship is a stage between two poles of Capitalism and Communism.

According to Marx and Lenin, when Capitalism starts to become Communism after "the Revolution", in course of this metamorphosis, there is the stage of Proletariat Dictatorship where the poor oppressed class (Proletariat) becomes the dominant class and oppresses the Bourgeois (The rich). It retains "force and oppression" as the main tool to maintain this power over Bourgeois and confiscates their property which is called the "State Apparatus" of "changing" the ownership. (LOL...Changing! *I am a communist, you are not and this is what matters so your house becomes mine"!* Well this is Marx-Lenin's bulls**t, not mine.)

According to the teachings of Lenin, since the beginning of the revolution until this point, the main slogan was "No government or FU*K the government" and that: *"the existence of any government insinuates the dictatorship of one social class over the others."* But right at this point, **when the difficult part of the uprising a revolution is fulfilled and emotive idiots are used, and people are dead, cities are ruined and properties are confiscated, a STATE, the main protagonists of the theater which were using the average people to put their plan forward, JUMPS OUT of a closet and assumes the power "on behalf of**

people"!! A single party social-state will be formed and the official announcement will be as follows: *" from now on, the dictatorship of Proletariat (the poor); will be executed through a "democratic centralization of power" by the state"!*

Kaboom!

It's astonishing how people might consider the possibility of having the authority and govern with no government, no police, and no system? How can they be so naïve, immature and funny? **Every horrific dictatorship in history is born mouthing the same canard. Word for word, whether they were religious or communist, the method of abusing people was always the same: "You poor oppressed people will govern."**

It is time to unplug the bananas from our ears people! Josef Stalin, the follower of Marx and Lenin did the same, Mao, Castro and Che Guevara, did the same. This is the pathway for transitioning the power to the colonizers behind the curtains and useful comrades, idiots and anarchists like Antifa and Black Lives Matter are their instruments.

Stalin sadly said *"Americans would never accept Communism as such so we will give them doses of Socialism until one day they wake up and find they have Communism. <u>Socialized medicine of any form</u> is a big step in that direction"*. Now he should arise from the grave and watch what American's have done to themselves.

Back to the main body of our story, communism is not a class war anymore, but a racial war and **wants to remove every sign of American history, change the books, make them digital, and then change the digital copies later by falsification. When there is nothing before our eyes or in the libraries, all will be forgotten.** Why should they tear down American statutes? Because they need to erase American history.

Racism is a culture of victimhood. A distraction. Blaming everything but ourselves for not having accomplished what we think we could. White Supremacy is just another excuse when we can't hit our goals. Are poor people Oppressed or is it a cultural issue? A great number of people didn't want to educate or work hard and have decided to accept lower jobs or not working at all. Some use drugs and stay home, are they oppressed? **It doesn't matter what we are. What**

does matter is "who" we are? If we decide to be an empowered individual able to shape our destiny; that is the accomplishment.

If we don't take charge of ourselves, somebody else will do. If we don't work for our dream, we will work for somebody else to fulfill his dream. That's life. We should take charge of our destiny through constant training, determination, concentration, and expertise instead of blaming others for everything. That is victimhood. What Democratic Party does is pushing slavery on black people by continuously keeping them in the state of victimhood and slavery blocking their personal empowerment.

According to the Left, everyone is encouraged to be proud of who they are except white people. It's ludicrous how white America is dealing with the Left relentlessly trashing all white things. When will it reach a tipping point? They are talking about the white genocide. White removal and white replacement and do you not see this relationship with the immigration agenda? **Is it a coincidence that the immigration crisis started right the same year that attacks against whites have started? Nothing is a coincidence.** Forced immigration goes exactly where these white Supremacy agitators come from: the "replacement" of the western nations with immigrants. They are all aligned in the same direction.

Where is our backlash? Where is the pride and gratefulness to be born white like the gratefulness for being born in any other color? Do whites turn a deaf ear to the Left's rhetoric? If you are white, you should be proud, and you should be ANGRYas racism is always disgusting!

White people have become self-hating Masochists who torture, humiliate and punish themselves to recompensate their white guilt. Such a sick thing is unprecedented in history. Did black, Hispanic, Asian or Arab people humiliate themselves? Some white people march in yokes and chains for 50 miles before hundreds of black people and ask forgiveness crying on their knees. Organizations are lecturing white people that to build their lives (including their children) from zero guilt, they need reconciliation with the black community and to do that, they should reverse the guilt by humiliating themselves in public, chained like livestock to "atone" for slavery? These people marched in Marblehead, Salem, Boston, Massachusetts, Rhode,

Newport, and Richmond and who knows where else up to this very moment.

Masochistic self-flagellation is a shame! White people should be ashamed for doing this humiliation to themselves and their children. Humiliating a teen walking in chain and yoke is child abuse and should be dealt with as a crime. All those organizations which let a child in Yoke should be criminalized, fined and banned. The pathetic, stupid, weak, "self-masochist white morons" with these suicidal activities have reached a new low in history. What an achievement. After blaming the German population for the Nazi guilt now is the white's turn to be blamed, weakened and pushed back for another guilt.

"The Nazi feeling parents" who humiliate or let these organizations humiliate their children should be jailed! Slavery has been something wrong committed in old times but by the Democratic Party in newborn America. It is absolutely condemned but has nothing to do with the modern generation. Never apologize for being White. Don't let these cockroaches march on your brain and soul. **Release yourself from any guilt related to ANY skin color or race. We didn't decide what color**

or race we should be born. God did. Nobody is going to be jailed for their fathers' crimes even if they were cannibals or serial killers. Unless we don't commit a crime on our own, there is nothing there to crucify us for it. End this madness!

Imagine saddling your young child with the weight of one thousand years of guilt. They're never told about any of the amazing things that Nord West White European culture has brought to the world. When our little kid comes home from school in tears, feeling guilty for being white, we should bombard the school with our numerous presence and sue them from victimizing our child. We can't be silent when our child is bullied. (Check the shameful images of people in chains and yokes on the "Lifeline Expedition" group and decide for yourself.)

-Who is behind this?

Who are the main protagonists of this ghastly theater we are dealing with as our modern world? Who is behind installing this guilt complex in our people and run a fake Anti-Nazi League against the whiteness? Here again, we will reach to Soros and his efforts and unlimited donations to this special case, but before that, you should know that the white supremacy agenda has old and deep roots in secret societies and has been on the table since long time ago. The only phenomenon that gave it volume, speed, and unlimited resources as you see today, is the crime network of George Soros who by installing Obama, could speed up the eradication of the white race and advance the agenda, decades earlier than expected. We have to first take a look at Khazarians' protocol and then come back and review Soros's donations to the white supremacy agenda.

-The Khazarians

Eradication of the white race comes from an old plan and to investigate it; we need to take a look at an old set of protocols.

The reality is gruesome. The first time my eyes felt on it, I wish I could just close the book and thank God that it was just a nightmare but that won't change anything.

The protocol is terrible not by itself but because it is almost accomplished. When I saw this document for the first time, it was like I'm watching America and the West's documentary movie live in 2017, not only reporting facts but also the reasons behind them. The fearsome lines which were written in 1952 by a group who wanted to break the world and reshape it in a George Orwellian style through social engineering and inverting all the norms and values upside down have succeeded. **They changed the definition of truth and created a society made on an evil basis. Through deception, they have projected the sick idea that evil is good and good is evil,** assassination is good, and respecting humanity is bad, white people should be assassinated, and a white genocide is necessary. **Institutional perversion, sex confusion and all we see as the norm, pushed by organizations, groups, universities, and professors shamelessly on Twitter and national TV, all was written and programmed in 1952 by a group penetrated in and intermarried with the Rothschilds.**

7 years ago, I watched a video on YouTube, all in black and white. It was a recorded voice of the main protagonist of this group. The voice said: *"Give the superiority to the black race over white, by promoting black singers, black athletes, journalists, politics, actors to the point that being black becomes an advantage. So white women like black men more and give birth to more*

and more black babies. insinuate guilt on white males and make them accountable for slavery and humiliate them to be ashamed of themselves" and so much more. I felt so bad at the time, but I thought people can say whatever they want. Why should we worry?

When I decided to write in 2016, one of the first things I did was to look for that video, and I searched with all the keywords I could imagine. But the video and anything similar to it was gone. Instead, I found the original blueprint in which the video has been made on its basis although some articles were missing but anyway better than nothing. When you read it, be realistic and be aware of what is going on and watch out they have already gone so far to make ninety percent of their agenda working and it's right out there in our society. It is useless to wish or desire that it might be not true or be forgotten as an old useless document. No, it's there, and it has already happened. We are already there. Just focus on what we "can do" about it rather than negating it.

When we are aware of what the enemies have on their plates, we know what to do and what direction to take. We are so powerful and so involved that their agenda met our resistance and didn't go through for the last part which was the election of Hillary Clinton.

The deep state is running with no pause, and each second we stop fighting, they activate the remaining 10 percent just in a blink of eyes. So ignoring the facts and deceiving ourselves or pretend nothing is happening, they won't do the same. They will never stop, and they will never sleep. The force behind them is not a single predator but a fivehead monster.

We are talking about a protocol written by a group of "Khazarians" from Khazaria with very rich and influential people who after an oath on this protocol, dispersed in whole Europe to take care of its execution in different regions and became the ancestors of the current bloodlines including the Rothschilds. Pay attention these people are NOT "Jewish", but a fraction of perplexed lost tribes later mixed with Jesuits who together established a satanic doctrine and detached themselves from real Jewish people but continued to commit crimes label themselves as Jews. They are basically the crypto-Luciferians. The same fake Jews whom the Bible calls them "Jews who are not Jews and serve the synagogue of Satan" in the Book of Revelation. This is to emphasize that the Rothschilds and old oligarchs all belong to this doctrine but they do what they do in the name of Jews as their scapegoat.

Consider two twin siblings that one commits the crime but accuses the other one while people don't know they are twins. They swore to destroy the white Caucasoid race while promoting every other race over them until reducing them to a minority. The world government plot is an old agenda, so unbelievable that they have conducted it for over a century in complete secrecy but the future proves the past. Now that we see their gloves off, we discover what they were doing the same for decades, and there was no way for us to find out. northwest Europe had intelligence and skills; an intelligence to invent what they needed. They produced wealth from the raw material but Khazarians who had a plan for a world government; saw them as an obstacle. They needed revolution and indoctrination which the intelligence of northwest Europe would not let them reach their goal so to put forward their plan; they had to create means to manipulate them and use them to act against themselves and execute the plan. All oppressive systems prefer that their victims execute their own mass suicide.

In 1952, they declared war.

On January 12, 1952, Rabbi Novitch, a Khazarian, at a special meeting of the emergency council of European

Rabbis in Budapest, which was recorded in full in the U.S. publication "Common Sense" and reprinted in the September 1952 issue of the Canadian Intelligence Service, said: (parentheses hold my thoughts and interpretations.)

"Our control commission, in the interests of peace and wiping out <u>interracial tension</u>, (Why interracial tension? At that time there was no mass immigration, but as we see, the document shows this migration policy has been planned so long ago) *will forbid the whites to cohabit with whites. <u>The white women must cohabit with members of the dark races, the white men with black women. Thus the white race will disappear, for mixing the dark with the white means the end of the white man and our most dangerous enemy will become only a memory.</u> We shall embark upon an era of peace and plenty, and our race will rule undisputed over a world of dark people. We will openly reveal our identity with the races of Africa and Asia."*

(Now it is clear why the immigrants are from Asia and Africa?)

Israel Cohen, the Khazarians' communist spokesman in England, in his book "A Racial Program for the Twentieth Century setting out communist policy", written in 1992, wrote the following statement which the exact part has entered into another Congressional Record for June 7, 1957, page 7633

He says: *"We must realize that our party's most powerful weapon is racial tension.*

(Obama's campaign slogan and his path to the presidency.)

"By propounding into the consciousness of the dark races that for centuries they have been oppressed by the whites, (victimizing the black race to use them against whites) *we can mold them to the program of the Communist Party. In America, we aim for subtle victory.*

"While inflaming the Negro minority against the whites, we will endeavor to instill in the Whites, a guilt complex for their exploitation of the Negroes. We will aid the Negroes to rise to prominence in every walk of life, in the professions and in the world of sport and entertainment. With this prestige, the Negro will begin a process which will deliver America to our cause."

What was a protocol in 1952, has become our real-life in 2017. It reflects today's America and the world. A Senate which discriminates against the white population by imposing anti-white resolutions and legal experts who slam whites for not complying with them. Feminism and victimizing blacks are just powerful tools to eradicate the white race.

The same protocol which is a plan to establish a world government includes penetrating universities, colleges, schools, and churches by training their teachers and preachers and financial takeover of all media and papers which influence the education and the mindset. That's the reason for all filthy content on media and why Christianity is destroyed by their fake Churchianity and confound religiosity. **Those big golden churches have nothing to do with Jesus but to bury his name and harm the gospel. Churchianity has overtaken the church. They have infiltrated everywhere. Bewildering why cardinals are caught in pedophilia? Because they worship the church and the church worships the Pope and the Pope worships gold, power, and the elite.**

Khazarians were slave traders, human traffickers, and currency manipulators. They are "crypto-Satanic" but attacking them, we will be accused of being anti-Semite while they are anti-Semite Jew-haters themselves. They have always been Satanic, and they love to sow the anti-Semitic hate in the world but people don't have any clue on the distinction between; Semitic Jews, Zionists, and Satanists. **They use Jews just like the Catholic church uses Christianity.** This is a great paradox, and I receive a lot of emails about it. **Whenever you see these members of secret societies being presented as Jews, You have to do this: scratch Jews and replace it with Khazarians then it starts to make sense.**

They are the most racist human beings on the planet while they hide behind the diversity mask. They have been kicked out of Khazaria around the Khazar Sea and Russia. They were a combination of semi Turks semi Russians, Mongols and Huns. They were so dangerous that even Mongolia, the haven for all criminals at that time; kicked them out so they migrated to Eastern Europe and planned to destroy Russia, white Christians and all whom they could blame for kicking them out. They reached to West Europe and found their ways through the European nobles, and there they played the Rothschild formula; the black nobility of Europe, the gateway to expand and stay on top as they had a lot in common. Perhaps that is why taking over Eurasia had huge importance to Brzezinski; it is almost the same area.

They had several marriages with the Rothschilds, and that's how the Rothschild Cancer started to spread. Marriage shaped and brought Khazarians and the Rothschilds in power and they became one. There we always arrive. The Rothschilds. You very well know the rest of the story by now. The present generation of the Rothschilds is shaped by propagandists, racial agitators and conflict makers to possess their position which is ruling the world officially and leave the cocoon. But bringing this up makes us anti-Semite. Now after all that you read here, **the perplexity of challenging the Rothschilds' power, and interfering with their dominance, becomes more evident as we are called an anti-Semite while we were not referring to their faith but their greedy operations to devour the world.**

Alongside bringing down Soros, we should start to fight the black nobility. All Khazarian bankers dispersed in each country, All Schiffs, Goldman sacks, Warburgs together with all other names that we already know and those we still don't know, we should dig into them all.

Unfortunately, all protocols are not available as I mentioned. You can find Zion, Ashkenazi, and Illuminati protocols which are slightly different but not

Khazarians. But those we could find, reveal the entire agenda and the mindset. Let's take a look at the infamous Khazarian Protocols:

Protocol 1- Control gold and banking to control governments through the money power

-Control the governments of the goyim (Whoever is not a Khazarian is a goy) from behind the scenes

-Rule by force, violence, fear, bribery, blackmail, treachery, and deceit

-Destroy the minds of the goyim through subversion of the "education" system

-Reduce the goyim to poverty and serfdom, and keep them in perpetual labor to distract their minds from resisting the ~~Jews~~ Khazarians

Protocol 3- Use communism to destroy the aristocracy of the goyim nations. (Destroy Capitalism)

Protocol 4- Destroy belief in God among the goyim, and replace it with materialism

-Lead the masses by lies via the ~~Jews'~~ Khazarians' controlled press

Protocol 6- <u>Use speculation, as opposed to sound investing,</u> to transfer the wealth of the world into the ~~Jews~~Khazarians' hands

Protocol 9- <u>Destroy the youth of the goyim through false doctrines</u> through the use of agents in all places of influence, throw the nations of the goyim into turmoil until they willingly accept

Protocol 11- <u>Take away the liberties of the goyim under the pretense of protecting their safety.</u> (Mass surveillance which as we discussed is not there to control terrorism but "us" people and we discussed how they created this insecure climate by propagandas like 9\11, false flags, hoaxes and etc.)

Protocol 12- <u>Destroy the freedom of the press and bring all organs of the press under the control of the ~~Jews~~Khazarians.</u> (Exactly as we see today. The media is overtaken by them)

Protocol 15- Use Secret Societies and Freemasonic Lodges as recruiting grounds for goyim agents

Protocol 20- <u>Engineer economic depressions</u> to bring down the goyim nations

Protocol 21-Use the tyranny of usury, and especially lending to governments, to enslave the goyim.

We are just one step away from full execution of their protocols by all governments, and that is a warning for us to put all efforts together and restore our identity.

We were in the White Supremacy section related to Soros's money dedicated to this agitation. As the subject had a long history, we had to go back, find the origin of the issue which was Khazarian's plan inherited by the Rothschilds and mobilized and fed by Soros.

Back to Soros's agenda, regarding the White Supremacy agitations, all donations we mentioned in previous sections for Antifa, and the rest of his donations in next sections to Black Lives Matter, Media Matters, the judicial and educational system is linked to white supremacy because all above movements are at the same time anti-white. Plus, Soros has played a critical role in financing the Ferguson and Missouri movements. According to an article in the Washington Times, published on Jan 14, 2015, titled: *"George Soros funds Ferguson protests, hopes to spur civil action,"* says:(Parentheses hold my interpretations)

"His waterfall of $33 million just in one year, served to back groups that "emboldened" rioters and activists

there on the ground. "Missouri event supposed to be a single day cause but turned to become an ongoing 24 hour a day movement by Soros's donations. Multiple groups distributed funds received from Soros and created "echo chambers" using Twitter and Facebook."

The same article continues that *"Buses of activists from groups including the Drug Policy Alliance Make the Road New York, and the Center for Community Change in Washington*(Author's note: Of course all funded in part by Soros)*went to Ferguson beginning in August and to organize gatherings and very violent protests there until late December."*

"Soros-backed groups called; Missourians Organizing for Reform and Empowerment, the Organization for Black Struggle and a group called Dream Defenders were involved in establishing the "Hands Up" Coalition; a supposed "grass-roots" organization in Missouri, (Author's note: We will fully explain the Grass-root agitation system and how it works in next chapters) *which according to them, Michael Brown, the Ferguson teen who was shot dead by the police, had his hands up before being shot."*

This is a false narrative. Seventy hours of testimony in 25 days, sixty witnesses including five black guys who one of them was Michael Brown's crime partner rubbing the store with him, all aligned with the testimony of the officer who testified Michael Brown pronounced the f*** word, charged the police, put his hand on officer's gun trying to possess it and shoot the police, so the officer shot him on his hand, then Brown ran toward his car, at some point Brown turned back again and charged the police with his head down like a football player. Who will act like this after robbing a store? Isn't it the duty of the police to use force in a case like this?

The article continues: *"The officer who shot Michael Brown, was not charged with a crime, so the "Hands Up" Coalition worked to recruit and organize youth across the United States to organize communities and hold local grass-roots events within those communities and make Ferguson a nationwide issue.* (Author's note: This is the exact Saul Alinsky's method of a community organizer.)*The group called 2015 "The Year of Resistance."*

The article continues: *"In Trayvon Martin case, in which Martin, a black teen in Florida was shot to death in 2012 by George Zimmerman, a neighborhood watch volunteer, "Dream Defenders" was built to push the attention toward the case. Zimmerman claimed he had been violently attacked by Martin, but he was acquitted of second-degree murder and manslaughter charges by a local jury and the push by "Dream Defenders."*

"Kassandra Frederique, the policy manager with the Drug Policy Alliance (DPA), which received $4 million a year from Soros' foundation, said she traveled to Ferguson in October "to be in solidarity and stand with the young organizers."

(Author's note: So here again we see Soros-Kassandra ties in Martin's case and Kassandra ties with Michael Brown's case.)

The article continues: *"She said: We recognized that this movement is similar to the work we're doing at Drug Policy Alliance. The war on drugs has always been to operationalize, institutionalize, and criminalize people of color."*—The Washington Times

"Gamaliel Foundation" is another organization involved in funding the Ferguson riots. This organization is a branch of the same organization that Barack Obama started his community-organizing Career. Obama was employed as a rioter in one of its branches in Chicago, and we can probably imagine who was on the board? George Soros.

Ferguson and Missouri are two ultra-violent riots which black agitators hired by all these organizations, used the case to organize an Anti-White and Anti Police civil war.

4- Soros and Black Lives Matter

Only in 2009, Black Lives Matter (BLM) has received $650,000 from Soros-controlled groups.

His Spider network has targeted the police through BLM. BLM emerged as a social force to politicize the support for the police. "F*** the Police" was the main slogan of BLM which now has morphed to <u>Kill the police</u>.

Tactics, like disrupting rallies and shutting down the freeways by direct attack and interrupting city systems, are meant to trap the police involvement. They attack police, put pressure to trigger the police's reaction by scaring people and then blame the police for doing their job. Another target for BLM is the white race. They pretend to defend racism while they are reverse racists. They just change the direction of supposed racism toward white people. Other main donors of this extremely violent Group; are rapper J.Z and his wife; Beyoncé. Black Lives Matter has been pushing Bernie Sanders, and Bernie has been pushing Hillary during the election.

As we said, George Soros donated $33million through his "Open Society Foundation" to Ferguson case, violent national mobs, and the death of Freddie Gray; the incident that was used to lead the Baltimore riots. BLM accuses the police as a tool of white repression on black people. To the organization, local police and the FBI statistics proving most crimes against blacks are specifically committed by the black gangs are irrelevant.

BLM puts a negative light on the police criticizing the officers who try to enforce the law. Painting every interference of the police as a skin color related interference is their expertise. **This is how the fear of criminal charges on one hand, and public condemnation as "racists" on the other hand pushes the police to back down and prefer inaction when the situation requires them to act**. The "Climate of Violence" is one of the greatest results of this demoralization and intimidation of the police. They step back and that is exactly what Soros wants: A spike in violence and bloody crimes which means a closer step to the civil war.

BLM has organized violent events in favor of immigrants. The justification is "Immigrants are people of color and not white". Soros backs BLM and has organized a worldwide push to use immigration to undermine the national identity and demographic syntax of the Western democracies. **The Soros backed agitation groups work to persuade chaos and paralyze local authorities and make them unable to secure their societies. All he wants is chaos.**

Why hate groups like BLM go on extremists? Because it's a business. To make a name and catch the attention of the funders. There is always benefit hidden behind hate groups. **Hate groups are rich groups.** If they act like a normal activist, there will be no waterfall of dirty money into their channels.

Western people need to recognize the common foundations of all Soros's actions. They need to realize that the only response to these blueprints of subversion is to stand up for their national rights and their individual right to security. **Can we say all of our soldiers are killed in wars because they hated the race of the enemy? Can we say we should let our countries become occupied because if not, we are racist haters?**

Since when occupation means the result of not giving enough love? If we shouldn't defend our values "inside" our borders, what is the use of deploying troops beyond the borders? To defend what? How many times in history our countries could have been occupied if our army and law enforcement wouldn't die to keep us safe? Can we go to work, educate, flourish, and build a family and a future, without being safe? Should more police officers in the U.S. and Europe die until we stand up for them?

We must stand with our national institutions to guarantee security following the rule of law within our borders. We must uphold and defend our national values and traditions within our borders.

We should know if we lose "our identity" the next loss will be "our privacy." How can we have privacy when we don't have any specific identity? How do identity and privacy come together?

If our house doesn't have a door and 4 walls, anybody can come in. Whether it's a neighbor, a thief or a government agent. What is privacy? Privacy is protecting our identity and whatever completes that identity. We should completely abolish whatever threatens our identity and privacy. Why Communists insist on confiscating properties? **Why is property confiscation one of the fundamental principals of Communism? Because confiscating our property, takes out our wealth and our privacy simultaneously. A slave has no property nor privacy. when there is no door, there is no property too. It is all related.** This is the war with Soros and watching ignorant people, defending him makes me sick to my stomach. When you see BLM and Antifa protesting, you should see them as mini Soroses protesting. How would it feel? BLM and Antifa make Josef Stalin very proud.

5-Soros and Creating unrest around the world to abolish borders and national sovereignties.

For Soros, everything is related. Changing our point of view from being a normal citizen to how he sees himself as the ruler of the world drawing its map like the map of his backyard, only this way, we will realize the connection. His map is different from our map and all these unrests are contributing to form it. Looking at the neighbors and allies of a special country upgrades our vision and provides the big picture. Don't trust me, don't trust anyone. Do your own research and find your own results.

Here I recall some other items of the **Congressional record 1963** or the "Destroy America" blueprint, which we already discussed. It explains what is going on with the borders and national identity.

Article 1- U.S. <u>acceptance of coexistence</u> as the only alternative to atomic war.

Article 2- U.S. <u>willingness to capitulate</u> in preference to engaging in atomic war.

Article 3- Develop the illusion that total disarmament by the United States would be a demonstration of moral strength. (Gun control agenda)

Article 4- <u>Permit free trade between all nations regardless of Communist affiliation</u> and regardless of whether or not items could be used for war.(EU)

Article 11- <u>Promote the U.N. as the only hope for mankind</u>. If its charter is rewritten, demand that it be set up as a one-world government with its own independent armed forces. (Familiar?)

Article 43- <u>Overthrow all colonial governments</u> before native populations are ready for self-government. (Californication?)

Article 44- Internationalize the Panama Canal.

Why do they push borders? How did these protests and clashes for open borders pop up? *"Borders are enemies"*! Kidding me?? **Without borders, there is no**

nation. Every house has a border. Every cell in our body has a border, a cell membrane that defines that cell from another.

Suppose if our cells had no border? All mixed. What type of creature would have we been without a cell membrane? Have you seen gen anomalies? Unfortunate incidents of people having two heads? **What happens when cells are solved together and not defined. A big tumor. That's what we will become if no borders define us. Mixing (no-culture)+(culture) = (degrading the superior culture)**

Just like $(0 + 10) / 2 = 5$

Multiculturalism derived from mixing a superior culture with an inferior culture is cancer and abolishes the first culture. **America doesn't need to be inclusive as it has already been inclusive. How? Because people come to America from different countries, religions, and cultures, and become "one" under the "Declaration of independence." That's why they fight to get to America.** That's why they receive equal chances to work and educate no matter what their background, race, and religion are. **It doesn't need to be replaced by ANY other culture. That's the reason OTHER cultures come to be part of what already exists.** Read the world's history; not one nation survived as a multi-cultural nation. Does Afghanistan have a culture? Although Afghanistan had a culture before being ruined by the deep state's military complex, it was not comparable to the modern world. Those who want to make America current Afghanistan can move there. Do they dare? If newcomers don't assimilate and integrate into the culture, Americanestan is what will happen. Social justice warriors inject the idea that borders are for separation. Language is just a language you can speak it wrong and emphasizing grammar is racist. Why? Because in that way, immigrants will create their own communities and won't need to assimilate. We see it in England, Sweden, Germany, France, and any European country which keeps pushing the agenda. The business of war brings us death and taxes but money for human smugglers. They fight with the nation's culture. They hate America. They hate sovereignty. **Lack of identity results in no self-respect. That's what they are pushing. No self-esteem. Not belonging to a culture and suffering from a perplexed identity, people will lose their self-esteem and are ready to suicide. As we discussed before, this ends in Nihilism. That's what the far left needs. Our suicide; an auto depopulation**

mechanism. Emasculation is also their agenda as it comes with zero self-esteem which we will discuss later.

Europe has already no borders. It's gone. It is being run by the illegitimate perverts in Brussels. Now imagine if the whole world is run by them? How does it feel?

The global gangsters took Europe as a test. The "unification" of completely different cultures and countries of Europe and putting them under a Nanny State's authority by reconfiguring and repositioning them was just a test for the whole world on a limited scale. As Europe was so prudent after WW2 and having an experience of a centralized Nazi government, they entered in Europe Treaty AKA Treaty of Rome, very carefully. They have been fooled it's just about the economy and free market, nothing more. So the test of the "United States of Europe" began with a non-suspicious move either by the size of this Treaty or by the severity of rules implied. Then step by step the EU Nanny State boxed itself in and took advantage of the Treaty of Rome. It advanced and created a bigger centralized state in a measure that today demands its army and threatens any member country who dares to exit. The big psychological test of the EU was for

Britain. If the oligarchs could usher England into a unified union, they can do it with all other nations but as we saw, Brexit proved them, they are wrong.

The left's reaction to all the reality is to debunk it as emotional conspiracies without proportion and scale. Conspiracies because the **"perspective creators" in corporate media are in a total blackout on realities but full display to cover-up the evil plan and decorate it as the only solution for Europe.** So reality becomes conspiracy and narratives become facts. All conspiracies since a decade ago are now facts, but they ignore it. Invisible dictatorship is the worst dictatorship ever. The West is under the full dictatorship of the lamestream media hiding the truth but asking us proportion and scale. So we have a psychopathic cycle here. The media doesn't provide the evidence while accusing the alternative media as non-reliable. The mainstream media belongs to the establishment and completely censored, and alternative media is condemned for not being registered as media. When a fact is revealed on alternative media, they either behave as nothing happened or brutally demonize the messenger. Weeks ago the WikiLeaks published CIA's leaked information on illegitimate surveillance of Americans and yet mainstream media has a hundred stories on Kardashians but not one on such a national embarrassment.

America is the land of exceptional constitutional rights that so many countries could crave to have or even envy. A country that could peacefully resolve its political differences by voting their candidate of choice through the ballot box and if the majority's choice was not everybody's choice, then getting over it and letting the choice of people handle the country through a peaceful transition of power was the norm. That's what America is all about. That is what America stood for through history. Getting over the fundamental disagreements through challenging common points of interest. It is not possible to be in 100 percent accordance even in our own home, let alone a country.

Just alongside the rise of patriotic nationalism in America and the world is an escalating number of radicals which not only promote and practice hate, violence, and chaos by any means necessary to destroy the American way of life.

"Worker's World Organization" is tied to the non-profit group "A.N.S.W.E.R." an abbreviation for Act Now to Stop War and End Racism. On their statement of mission, we read *"We're independent Marxists who respect the struggles for self-determination and progress of oppressed nations."* As explained before, the word "oppressed" is a Communist-Socialist alert. This organization advocates for a socialist revolution and the abolition of private property in the United States. **It's now time to find a relation between the abolition of property and open borders.** Countries so historically and deeply "belonged" to their nation that with the slightest threat, the nation and the army were ready to die for defending them. The country IS a property. Our country IS our legitimate property and that's why we are a citizen of our country. **Border discussions are the initial discussions of abolishing property. After borders, then it's our house's borders.** Refugees and immigrants will be so numerous that the state will order citizens to give them housing or get arrested, the exact thing that happened in some regions of Italy in 2016.

If this seems exaggeration of the reality or an extremist view, then look back at the Hollywood movies produced around 1952-65. The lifestyle in Elizabeth Taylor, Vivian Leigh or other famous Diva's and their movies were real, not fake. If someone would have told them that the world they knew will become the mess it is today, could they believe it? The same will stand for opening our houses and co-inhabiting with the newcomers. Unbelievable today but right at your doorstep.

"Worker's World Organization" and "A.N.S.W.E.R." are supporters of Cuban dictator Fidel Castro and North Korean dictator Kim Jong- Un2. Enough to comprehend who they are and what they do. "Workers World Party," with a membership of approximately 2,000 people has been extremely effective in organizing massive protests in recent years, some of which have drawn hundreds of thousands of participants in the streets.

"A.N.S.W.E.R," is behind protests too. It characterizes itself as an anti-imperialist organization, and its committee consists of socialists, communists, civil rights advocates, progressive left-wing and progressive Muslim organizations. **The word "progressive" is a code for "Socialism Violence."**Many of ANSWER's lead organizers had ties to the International Action Center. ANSWER has organized "Resistance." Does the word look familiar? Did you remember Hillary Clinton's post-election message to her supporters? "Resistance."

The organization that funds ANSWER is Media Matters. And who funds Media Matters? It's funded by George Soros! and founded by David Brock and John Podesta.

John Podesta is Soros's "Fixer." All these organizations are funded by Soros and the pattern is the same. Funds find their way into an organization that is more distant to the special case, then pass through the filter of 2-3 other organizations all belong to him directly or as a subdivision of other organizations which again belong to him and then pour into the case. This pattern of whitewashing the money is repeating over and over for every single case.

Media Matters is staffed by Marxist members of the "Workers World Party" and specialized in anti-American rallies and immigrant rights protests. Soros has donated over $25 million to "Media Matters" which under the "Correct the Record Super PAC" policy hires professional Internet trolls to spread pro-Clinton ideologies on the Internet. Reading articles on mainstream media, and being well experienced with the trolls, we could see a bunch of "Correct the record" robot-idiots in the comments section who leave partisan comments with no sense. Most of their comments attack anti-Marxism and pro-Americana comments. Check the Facebook account of those morons, and you will easily see fake accounts that have nothing to debate but nonsense trolling. This is what "Correct the Record" means for Nazi collaborator; Soros. Correcting the Record means cleaning up whatever he doesn't like. Just like his mentor; Hitler. **Media Matters is responsible for all media frenzy and electric shocks happening on the media circus on a daily basis.**

Open border policy directly comes from the "Open Society" foundation. **Isn't it absurd that Open society is based on tyranny, control, and fear but the name says the contrary?** Whenever I see hypnotized sheep in the streets screaming for open borders and State Media run by the deep state decorate articles about it, while politicians and lawmakers agitate people to do more, I just think how good a far-left billionaire is pushing the whole planet to their suicide camps? How vast is his impact and do governments and people are underestimating this danger? I ask how far the nations will let him play with them. When do other countries do what Hungary and Russia did and issued an arrest warrant for Soros? Have you seen the Twitter page of the terrorist sympathizer Mayor of London; Sadiq Khan? His cover image is a red page with a big slogan: "LONDON IS OPEN." The message?

RED + OPEN= Communism.

Stupid western liberals who rush to slaughter their freedom and pretend open borders is not coming from Open Society Foundation, and living their sheep life let the Open Society Python gulp them and do not know what they have sown and harvested will vanish, and their kids will be poor, naked and homeless because of the degree of their negligence today.

Soros donated more than $100 Million to groups that support "immigrant rights," immigration amnesty, and open borders since 1997. For him they are voting vermins who will push his policies and second; fooled gladiators programmed to cease your identity, privacy, and property. That's what all this is about.

In terms of finances, all groups financing Antifa and BLM are responsible for open borders propaganda too.

6- Soros and Bill de Blasio, the Mayor of New York

George Soros invested in and endorsed Bill de Blasio as the Mayor of New York. *"Relations between the people and their police are the worst in memory; Bill de Blasio has cut through the rhetoric on stop-and-frisk, and alone advanced concrete policy changes that can mean far fewer innocent New Yorkers are subject to this demeaning practice while reductions in crime are maintained."* --Aug. 6, 2013, Soros to NY Times.

Bill de Blasio, a city's public advocate whom no one really cared much about his undefined position was a progressive Marxist who raised money for the Sandinista militias, a radical Marxist terrorist organization, which were famous for abuse, mass execution, and oppression of indigenous people. He visited Nicaragua to align himself with the tyrants and worked against the Reagan administration. When Communists were threatening a complete takeover of Central America and the Caribbean, President Ronald Reagan liberated the island of Grenada in 1983 from a Communist seizure of power and supported anti-Sandinista freedom fighters and the pro-American government of El Salvador.

Bill de Blasio worked as a community organizer to raise money for the anti-American Sandinista regime that in addition to all their extreme brutality, deprived the Jews of their property, homes and even their house of worship. Sandinistas had attacked the president of the synagogue (Jewish Community) in Nicaragua and forced him to sweep the streets with his clothes tied on his back; an exact Nazi practice copied from Hitler in occupied Europe. Why progressive Marxists repeat Hitler's behavior is a good question to ask. The Censorship, oppression, mass execution, property confiscation, labeling anyone who is not aligned with them and hating Jews is a collection of Nazi behavior from Nazi playbooks. **How they copy Hitler and call themselves anti-Fascist is mind-blowing.** Bill de Blasio ripped NYPD for doing their job in keeping mosques under surveillance.

He said that anything which is not based on specific leads should not continue. This policy would block NYPD from obtaining information about radical Islamists until it is too late.

Now that de Blasio moved from Park Slope to Gracie Mansion, his old dreams for Nicaragua can come true for New York. His love for "democratic socialism" expressed in 1990, was questioned by the New York Times but he rejected the statement as: *"That's not a quote from me; that's someone else's notes."* And when Times claimed it has the proof, he blatantly said, *"It doesn't matter."*

The forever strategy of the left is "what they say or think is true at its face value and what you say or prove doesn't matter".

The progressive hard left used to hide their Communist-Socialist leanings, but now they are coming out of the closet. Is this the best thing New Yorkers wanted for the city? The big appel's talent pool must be very shallow as the Bronx Zoo had better-qualified candidates than de Blasio.

NYC with de Blasio will soon become another Detroit. The Ultra popular big apple has now become the capital of Die Hard communists. Nothing about NYC is about capitalism anymore. The fruit of all these faux, phony and fraud campaigns is just Marxism but do they really care?

In the 1980s, de Blasio was employed by the Quixote Center, a fringe group so radical that they were investigated by the Treasury Department for smuggling guns for their Sandinista friends. It was also been probed by the IRS and the U.S. Customs Service. This group were the same thugs who defended the cop-killer racist Mumia Abu-Jamal, the former Black Panther who later became a hero to the left-wing extremists. Mumia shot and killed Philadelphia police officer Daniel Faulkner in 1981. In the latest Antifa move on Aug 25, 2017, they (Antifa) launched a new chapter as R.A.M PHILLY or Revolutionary Abolitionist Movement in Philadelphia. The group main goal was an armed insurrection and assaulting the police. Their workshops were "our enemies in blue," and their pride was the "legacy" of the cop-killer; Mumia Abu-Jamal.

De Blasio was the greatest fan of "Occupy Wall Street" protesters who took over Zuccotti Park, ripped off the homeless, defecated in the streets, and attacked the police. Seems he has an agenda to hate and fight law enforcement.

De Blasio faced a great backlash for leaving New York right the day after a Bronx police officer, "Miosotis Familia", a 12 year veteran and mother of three, was fatally shot on duty sitting inside a police car and right after shocked and angry policemen and women of New York were waiting for his speech of consolidation which it never happened.

The widespread criticism over his decision to fly to Hamburg was after he said: *"Americans' views don't align with President Trump's and need to be represented abroad."* That means an American Mayor left one of his assassinated cops to protest against the President of America. That looks pretty much a Marxist cop-hating behavior, doesn't it? De Blasio's speech at Hamburg's protest named "Hamburg Shows Attitude" had the same phraseology of citizens defying law enforcement and the same theme of hating the national government. Those so-called protests were indeed a series of anti-capitalistic and anti-American violent riots surrounding the G-20 summit with lots of damage and injuries in which The Sergeants Benevolent Association tweeted this about police officers who've been injured through: *"So far 160 police officers have injured by protesters at this year's G20 summit, whose side are you on Mr. Mayor??"*

Police Benevolent Association President Patrick Lynch said: *"The mayor's office and the mayor are supposed to be the compass for this city. His compass is off. His compass led him to Germany."*

That was mild compared to the headlines de Blasio faced in New York Post, which frequently attacked the mayor. Somebody wrote: *"And Don't Come Back!"*

For my common sense, with his ties to Soros, de Blasio was not there just to join protests as he had officially declared, but to manage them as their leader and Soros's right hand in Hamburg. Far-left extremists including Antifa have broken windows, robbed stores and had devastating clashes with the police during the 2017's G20 summit. According to a report on Die Welt German News, according to Hamburg police, far-left extremists committed over 2,000 crimes during and before the Hamburg G20 including acts of vandalism and violence.

In 2014, when de Blasio cheered two officers shot, thousands of city police officers in a gesture expressing their disgust turned their backs on him as he was lecturing them. Police union leaders blamed de Blasio for the climate of agitation that he created and allowed the cop killings to happen after he supported anti-police protests following the deaths of young black men across the city.

Soros also admired de Blasio's plans for advocating pre-kindergarten classes and after-school programs that keep children gradually longer and longer under the supervision of the government and create more distance with their parents and the influence they may have on their own children.

On several occasions, de Blasio worked on race division accusing the New York Police Department to have racist tendencies. After Soros ties to fuel the anti-police riots due to the decision by a grand jury not to indict a police officer for the death of Eric Garner in New York, now new reports investigate de Blasio's own ties to both Soros and his role in helping those riots.

De Blasio has a controversial unreported history of working with ACORN as a "Community Organizer" which we already explained what a community organizer does. A subdivision community of ACRON named: the New York Communities for Change was mainly involved in organizing riots over the death of Eric Garner in New York.

Another major anti-police protests in New York was an organized protest or better say a "riot" as it aimed to shut down Manhattan's Fifth Avenue shopping district before Christmas; organized by A.N.S.W.E.R and Occupy Wall Street and at least 10 other so-called economic justice organizations and groups all funded by Soros.

ANSWER together with ACORN and MoveOn.org have led the protests, and de Blasio previously worked with MoveOn.org. Since January 1, 2014, the day that de Blasio took office as the Mayor of New York, we see an unprecedented spike in anti-police violence both in New York and nationwide, while he ran for office with the false promise to improve the relationship between the New York City police department and New Yorkers.

During his mayoral campaign, the media corporations reported that Soros had endorsed him, but they never disclosed Soros's major financial donation to de Blasio's nonprofit organization nor de Blasio's relationship with Soros-funded activist groups to stir protests. In 2010, ACORN first endorsed de Blasio for his race beating drum, but then after, de Blasio spent $43,000 to hire N.Y. Citizens Services Inc. which was an affiliate of ACORN.

In 2011 de Blasio founded a nonprofit organization called the Coalition for Accountability in Political Spending, or CAPS which its primary launch donation was $400,000 from Soros's Open Society Institute.

During his mayoral election, Bertha Lewis, the former executive director of ACORN, spoke for de Blasio on numerous occasions. She said: *"I've known Bill for decades, and we've fought on the front lines together. We've organized together."* (Yes, they have organized together because they were both community organizers. De Blasio's radical background resembles just like Barack Obama's.)

Lewis continued: *"He is proud to say he's liberal. He is proud to say he is severely progressive and was proud to stand with me, to back me, to back ACORN, and said, 'We will march down the street together, and I dare you, I dare you, to say something against my friend!"*

Naive is as naive does. Any person whom Bertha Lewis defends like all the "New Party" is bound and determined to see the United States fall at all costs. De Blasio is probably being groomed and trained by Soros to be the next puppet "Chavista President" and that can be the reason for his tremendous hate for President Trump.

Working Families Party (WFP) was founded by progressive community organizer Dan Cantor, who was a founder of the socialist-oriented "New Party." De Blasio served as the executive director of the New York branch of the socialist New Party.

Working Family Party has elected numerous progressives in New York and Connecticut who turned leftist ideas into legislation. De Blasio was the party's nominee for Mayor of New York.

De Blasio spent $67,740 to hire Working Families Party for-profit branch, Data and Field Services, canvassing and election consulting. The organization was run from the same office as New York ACORN, and President Obama himself was listed in New Party's literature as a member.

Remember ACORN hints nothing but two inseparable words: Soros and Obama. Now the relation between de Blasio and ACRON becomes so interesting at this point. A co-operation on the basis of pure socialism.

A few weeks after de Blasio's election Cantor, the founder of WFP says: *"Is the de Blasio moment, the Elizabeth Warren moment, a real transition to a new period?" Not unless we make them that. This is not a short-term project. It's taken a left a long time to get as weak as it is."*

We shouldn't underestimate the activities of Cantor as he is the one which since 1960 did everything to pull the Democratic Party to the left.

De Blasio lied to his children about where he and his wife spent their honeymoon in 1970.

While the official story was they went to Canada; during his campaign, his children discovered that they have been to socialist Cuba. Why should he fly to Cuba?

Please read this part carefully as it is important. In 1975, the Cuban guerrillas helped 14 Sandinista prisoners release from jail, and with them, flew to Cuba. One of the released prisoners was Daniel Ortega, the great role model for de Blasio who would later become the president of Nicaragua. The early years of the Nicaraguan revolution had strong ties to Cuba. The Sandinista leaders acknowledged that they owed a great debt to Communist Cuba. Once the Sandinistas assumed power, Cuba provided them military advice, as well as aid in education, healthcare, vocational training. Castro's Cuba protected several fugitives from American justice, including F.A.L.N Puerto Rican terrorist leader William Morales, the cop-killer and gangster terrorist of the Black Liberation Army; Joanne Chesimard.

Now stop for a moment and review what you have just read. De Blasio flew to Cuba in 1970. He helped Sandinista savage communist before and after. Daniel Ortega was hijacked from prison in 1975 by Sandinistas under the protection of Cuba to become Nicaragua's President. De Blasio's devotion to Ortega was like a son to his father. Did he have any role in his release? Was he a middleman between Fidel Castro and progressive left community organizers in America? Is he a middleman now between Cuba and America's left? Why does he act against NewYork?

It was The New York Times that originally acknowledged de Blasio's fondness of the "foreign revolution" in Nicaragua, in a major piece that shocked even liberals. The Times article revealed de Blasio's pro-communist activities. The New York Times described Bill de Blasio as one of the first eager subscribers to Barricada, the Sandinista newspaper.

"They had a youthful energy and idealism, mixed with human ability and practicality that was really inspirational." Bill de Blasio said about the Sandinistas. That "energy" that he praised meant throwing firebombs at a synagogue during Shabbat services while shouting *"Jewish Pigs"* and *"What Hitler started we will finish."*

With what you read above, did de Blasio have any role in creating a government that claims to finish what Hitler started?

Why the left is so fond of Hitler??

Why is the left so anti-Semite?

Remember how Soros sold his fellow Jews and worked with the Nazis against them?

Sandinista's revolution was a glorious revolution for Bill de Blasio and he never gave up on it. *"People who had shallow party sympathies with the F.S.L.N. pretty much dropped everything when they lost," "Bill wasn't like that."* one of his old NSN friends said.

At the same interview with the NY Times; de Blasio continued: "They gave *a new definition to democracy*."

Laughable; I guess giving a "new definition to democracy" in New York City is now what de Blasio is doing. California too can be another example of de Blasio-style democracy by his pal Jerry Brown.

Bill de Blasio never stopped being a Guerilla style Sandinista, and Ortega's admirer and that's why Soros chose him. The Alliance for Global Justice, the Soros organization, which funded Occupy Wall Street has beneficiaries who have also included Code Pink, the Venezuela Solidarity Network which backed Chavez and Maduro. The group has a "steering committee" that includes the U.S. Peace Council, and the old Communist Party USA front. Code Pink is the hard-left organization that includes luminaries such as Medea Benjamin and Jodie Evans, whom the latter was President Obama's fund-raiser.

Hugo Chavez Daniel Ortega, Photo from public domain

In other words, we are dealing with front groups on top of the front groups. It is the classic deception and propaganda designed to rope in the unsuspecting. This is a Marxist movement, promising a confrontation.

Curiously, it also turns out that de Blasio has had three different names, but he refuses to talk about that in any depth. Born Warren Wilhelm, he petitioned a court in 1983 to become Warren de Blasio-Wilhelm, and then again in 2001, becoming just plain Bill de Blasio. His name is his choice and not our business, but maybe de Blasio sounded better in the ears of Daniel Ortega, his Sandinista role model. He was so fond of Ortega from the '80s to the present day.

Do we puzzle why people backed, presented, or funded by Soros have almost the same attitude and behavior? De Blasio NY, Jerry Brown CA, Jorge Ramos the anchor and Sadiq Khan; the Mayor of London?

Ortega dreamed of the imposition of another Marxist tyranny in the Western Hemisphere but failed. Now Ortega is back in power again. His revolution and his bloodbath are back in power and the outcome yet to be determined. What would we expect for New York? Another Managua? Marxism and its failed anemic kissing cousin, recycled communism or just democratic socialism, simply don't work. Not if economic growth is the objective. Just compare contemporary North Korea to South Korea. The New Yorkers didn't know they have voted for their wealth confiscation and other

Sandinista propaganda. If de Blasio is following the footsteps of Ortega, then a guerilla New York where local goons and their mafia replace each other every month will be the future of New York and as it appears, that is the road that the cop-hater Mayor has chosen.

And yet here is Bill de Blasio, who adds about his fellow Sandinista savages: *"They had a youthful energy and idealism mixed with human ability and practicality that was really inspirational."*

Truly inspiring for New York

1979, Daniel Ortega with Sandinista Guerrillas

Photo from Daily Telegraph Article

https://www.telegraph.co.uk/news/picturegalleries/worldnews/8874590/In-pictures-Daniel-Ortega-from-Sandinista-guerrilla-to-President-of-Nicaragua.html

This information is all there, but it seems irrelevant. Truth, facts, quotes, all irrelevant to brainwashed robots as Yuri Bezmenov said and we will discuss his interview fully later *"When people decide who needs justice merely according to their own beliefs and not based on facts, justice becomes a purchasable commodity."* These social progressives need people to be dependent on the government. Why? **Because their agenda as they officially declare is progressive and keeps them in power. It takes decades, but when accomplished, a big centralized government determines the quality, quantity and the mere existence of people's lives and these social justice warriors are convinced they will be a part of that big government.** It is funny but that's why they fight. Power is what they need, and people's power is the fakest label that Marxists have ever used. **Their main enemies are religion and sovereignty as without them; there will be no other allegiance but the State.**

To trace funds paid to support riots back to Soros is a sure ground for an indictment and prosecution even though de Blasio and other cronies of Soros may think they are too big to fall.

Not yet enough, de Blasio joined the Nicaragua Solidarity Network of Greater New York. He actually has a finger in the pie. De Blasio was, and is, a far-left radical who still believes in the Communist way of life. Isn't it interesting that President Carter of the Democratic Party helped Sandinistas to take power and President Reagan of the Republican Party seized their power? Those rebels in the streets are the face of the Democratic Party in the past and in the future, and that will be de Blasio's, New York.

This is not on the front page of the news; it is there for anyone willing to take half an hour to do some research. If people don't just walk around in a daze like drones and be concerned about where their fix of choices is coming from and if they don't be afraid of thinking for themselves on matters of real importance, they could easily see how some official communists are running the country. They could also see how America, which nobody would ever imagine would welcome the Communism is down falling into the mouth of the red monster of global Communism all head over shoulders.

7- Soros and Feminism: The bloody Cancer

The brand new extreme feminism is the saddest manifestation of self-destruction, violence and public humiliation in recent years. Feminism, which for all ages meant to act and behave with ultimate softness, sensuality, and natural capacity of a woman's body and mind, today, has devastatingly become irrelevant due to over masculinity, harsh, disgusting, and violent behavior of women who don't want to act like women. Extreme feminists mean women who hate men and attack feminine women. This is a true gender and racial apartheid. A serious anti-white and anti-male movement. Here, there is a deception and a big contradiction between the term and its usage.

Extreme feminists are "femiNazis" which demand a world without men, designed to crucify the family. The result is no babies or babies without fathers. Their vulgarity and aggressiveness cannot and should not be associated with the concept of strength. **Bad and embarrassing behavior is not justified under the label of 'liberation'. No aggressive man or woman is called strong. They are called aggressive and in extreme cases "psychopaths" who commit violence and crime.** Extreme feminism is cancer. A very dangerous cancer which should be dealt with immediately as women are mothers and they produce the next generation. **A generation that can be totally degenerated from the beginning by starting life in a climate of prejudice and selective disclosure. The rotten apple will not fall far from the tree.**

-Nicholas Rockefeller interview with Aaron Russo on Feminism

We see the Rockefeller Foundation's support for various feminist projects. David Rockefeller famously praised feminism. So it's not a surprise to see George Soros's use of radical feminism. Movements like pussy-hat march or the "Vagina Riot" as you could shamefully see thousands of V pictures in hands of protesters exposed to children and elderly and "Femen" movement have been funded by Soros himself. These disgraceful groups exist as a means of destabilizing society when it is necessary.

The concept of "Rights" is long ago hijacked by the Cabal. Rights for women to work was the path to "tax" that half of the population who were not taxable and indoctrinating children in kindergartens who were not indoctrinable at home, as a result of working mothers.

Reproductive Rights for women is the path to legalizing not only the abortion but also trading/using babies' body parts as a mother who aborts her child will never care what happens to the fetus. The term "reproductive" is deceptive as it is designed for abortion therefore, it is anti-production.

Rights regarding adult sexuality led to gender dysphoria with over 20 genders which in a bigger picture is a path to the sterilization of the population and consequently to depopulation. Gender dysphoria and feminism serve the same goal of sterilization.

Rights for children to change gender at six is only a path to authorize them the right to "sexuality" and the right to sexuality is an open gate to "consent" and consent by itself leads to legalizing pedophilia.

Sexual orientation for kids means legalizing pedophilia. When a child gains sexuality rights and the concept of "consent" finds ground, it automatically nullifies the term pedophilia.

"Pedophilia" will be a meaningless word if the child can consent. As you see, our "right" was a manipulative tool for the Cabal to degenerate the families.

Aaron Russo, the famous award-winning filmmaker, who became a freedom fighter, arranged an interview with Nicholas Rockefeller, eleven months before 9/11. This interview is an absolute must-see and has also revealed so many facts about 9/11 which at that time hadn't happened yet. According to Russo, in this interview with Nicholas Rockefeller on feminism, Rockefeller said:*" the true nature of feminism and so-called liberation is useful to billionaire technocrats to reshape the society. It brings death to the reproduction of humans, enslavement to sex and causes dysgenics. It has nothing to do with freedom."*

Reshape the society, enslavement to sex and dysgenics

"Future is Female," the slogan of Hillary Clinton, Abortion, Male Genocide, White Male intimidation are all poisoned fruits of this cancer. Feminism is the new Fanaticism and people who fall for them, as Rockefeller; the creator of the concept says are nothing but useful idiots to fulfill his agenda.

While Western women march for the genocide of their own babies, women in immigrant communities give birth to numerous babies which in few years will triple their numbers. These women don't have a minimum right to pronounce a word like "Vagina" in their country as it is considered pornographic and vulgar. But they come to America, enjoy the freedom of speech, wear their hijabs and shamelessly put a "pink pussy hat" over it and join the march for women and abortion and celebrate their Vagina's liberty while their heads have no liberty to be out of a scarf and abortion is not allowed in Islam. So if they obey Islam to the point of wearing a hijab, because not all of them do, how possibly they can march for abortion which is very prohibited in Islam? Are they paid? Are they promised something?

In the same interview, Rockefeller tells Aeron Russo: *"We founded feminist organizations you know why? There were two primary reasons for that: First, we were not able to tax women as half of the population now we can (as they work). And second, working-class women need early schooling for their children, so they give those young kids to us to indoctrinate them. There are not mothers to school them anymore; it's the government. Kids will look at the state as a family, not their parents"* (Attention: He calls himself "the government!")

*** Tax women, Indoctrination of children in kindergarten***

Alas...

Oh Almighty God where are we?

They are too arrogant to hide their real intentions and yet the hard left and the useful idiots on no side; push for it. Women who commit this suicide are worse than Rockefeller who invented this disease. Extreme feminism actually says: **"With zero knowledge on dynamics of politics, and with nowhere to get the diva-attention we need, just "Vaginize" everything, criminalize the opponent and voila! we are considered hard left feminists now".**

I have no sympathy, no respect and zero tolerance for extreme feminists degrading themselves. Women whom Rockefeller calls them idiots but his theory has become "their" reality. Women who love the state of victimhood and don't say "however bad it gets, I'm gonna make it." Instead, they blame men and the system for their inefficiency.

On July 1, 2017, an 18-year-old girl in Nepal was found dead, bitten twice by a snake, while banished to a shed because of her menstruation. A few months before her, another girl was burnt in a shed during her menstruation because it was so cold and she tried to set up a fire to keep herself warm. Perhaps those feminists could save them if they would have defended their simple natural right of having their menstruation and living like a human. If they had spread the word, people could know and maybe there was a chance to save these girls or victims of genital mutilation, but they were too busy using their disgusting V(agina)s, as an argument.

Articles 40 and 41 of the Congressional Record–Appendix, pp. A34-A35 January 10, 1963, at Mrs. Nordman's request that I asked you to take from your local library (Communist Goals) and discussed earlier had, very well explains feminism.

Article40- *Discredit the family as an institution. Encourage promiscuity and easy divorce.*

Article 41- *Emphasize the need to raise children away from the negative influence of parents. Attribute* *prejudices, mental blocks and retarding of children to suppressive influence of parents.*

Stay stupid western liberals! It feels good.

"A day without women" protest in 2017, had 544 partners, 402 of which non-important and trace cleaner partners, 100 partners received $246,637,217 million directly from Soros and 56 of its main partners were funded by him. The rest are funded indirectly by him through various channels by providing accessories, t-shirts, hats, cash and administrative leave.

The Women's March claimed to stand for all women, but it was fundamentally anti-Trump hence, anti-border, anti-white, pro-immigration and celebrated liberal causes from abortion to eco-extremism. The whole movement was directly funded and directed by Soros's major organizations: Open society, Planned Parenthood (big donor), and Natural Resources Defense Council.

"If Fascism ever comes to America, it will come in the name of Liberalism."

President Ronald Regan

8- Soros and Planned Parenthood

The largest abortion provider in America which since 2000 has received a total amount of over $20 million from Soros has 78 percent of its clinics in minority communities. Dr. S. Adolphus Knopf, a member of Margaret Sanger's American Birth Control League later merged with other groups of doctors and eventually shaped Planned Parenthood. Margaret Sanger who like our friend, "Bill Gates" is obsessed with depopulation and has extreme views like "salvation of American civilization" has founded Planned Parenthood in its early stages. Sanger's obsession with decreasing population can be traced back to her own family, her liberal father's free-thinking views and his anti-Christian attitudes.

And who was the President of Planned Parenthood? Bill Gates' father; William H. Gates. Maybe depopulation obsession is genetic and inheritable!

In more than ten undercover videos, the scandal of Planned Parenthood; the vehicle of genocide, has been caught selling different body members of dead babies.

The price of these baby parts vary from $50-300 to $600, depending on the importance.

Planned Parenthood, Tied Foundation, and V-Day Organization, (You can guess V stands for vagina) organize rallies and Performers who discuss sexually perverse topics as rape in a positive attitude. Their vocabulary is pornographic. Their different expression of themselves is vulgar. For example, the highlight of women's march organized by pro-abortion activists or as their celebrities called it, "Nasty Women" march, was: *"Vaginas Take Back the Capitol."* Their higher-level officials like Senator Lisa Brown used this embarrassing phrase in the Senate: *"And finally Mr. Speaker, I'm flattered that you are all so interested in my vagina, but no means no."* The normalized vulgarity in their community seems to have no limit.

V-Day Organization is funded by Tides Foundation (direct Soros ties) and founded by Drummond Pike, again with ties to Soros. In 2007, the Tides Foundation awarded a $1,026,326.00 grant to Planned Parenthood Los Angeles and a $145,593.93 grant to the Planned Parenthood Federation of America. In 2009, the Tide Organization doubled its donation to the Planned

Parenthood Federation of America with a $292,316.71 donation.

Soros's organization, the Open Society Institute, has donated 25,180,000 to the Tides Foundation, along with 6,235,000 directly to the Planned Parenthood Federation of America, since 1999.

9- Soros and the Shadow Party

The Democratic Shadow Party is a real party inside the Democratic Party that is; the real power driving the Democrat machine. It is a network of smuggest abrasive and overbearing radicals dedicated to transforming the constitutional republic into a Soviet-style socialist hell hole. They are hardliner radicals, and the leader of these radicals is George Soros. Why should a person who is not a politician and is not a member of Congress be the head of the Democratic Shadow Party? He has practically privatized the Democratic Party, bringing it under his personal control. We won't go so far if we simply say; he has bought the Democratic Party. The Shadow Party is the crucifying instrument through which he exerts that control. The philosophy of these radicals is: **What is good for them is good for them, what is good for us, doesn't matter.**

The Shadow Party derives its power from its ability to raise huge sums of money which is the real differentiator. It's surreal, but it's the way it is. By controlling the strings of the Democratic purse, the Shadow Party can make or break any Democrat candidate by deciding whether or not to fund them. These Democrats are not faithful to a virgule of the Constitution. They have their own parameters and paradigms which are money, power, and Soros. They deliberately and systematically push (if they want the bill) and push back (if they don't want the bill) on whatever bill or law which doesn't fit those parameters.

During the 2004 election campaigns, the Shadow Party raised more than $300 million for Democrat candidates, promoting one of its operatives, MoveOn PAC director Eli Pariser, to declare: *"Now it's our party. We bought it; we own it."*

So in America, we have two parties, and one party officially belongs to Soros. Not only all his organizations around the world and inside America with thousands of lawmakers, community organizers, grass-roots rioters who always show up in the streets and on

TVs like "Clinton News Network"..Oops sorry... I meant CNN, are under his governance, but also a whole party that draws policies and controls the decisions that belong to him. When should all people in the world stand up against this man, lock him up and launch a probe against all his organizations?

Soros in 2004, spent $26 million unsuccessfully trying to defeat President Bush's reelection bid, a task which he called *"the central focus of my life"* and *"a matter of life and death."* He has equalized Republicans generally, and the Bush administration in particular, to the Nazi and communist regimes in the sense that they are *"all engaged in the politics of fear."*

These accusations picture this scenario: Imagine we lock the door of our house, somebody knocks aggressively to come in, we won't open the door, and then our neighbors accuse us of acting upon fear.

Soros supported Hillary Clinton, who in turn has admired and endorsed him publicly at a 2004 "Take Back America" conference in Washington DC with this: *"Now, among the many people who have stood up and said: I cannot sit by and let this happen to the country I love"* is George Soros, and I have known George Soros for a long time now, (**Translation:**??? She means America that he hates and organizes "Destroy America" Conference?), *"and I first came across his work in the former Soviet Union, in Eastern Europe"*(**Translation**: By his work in eastern Europe, does Clinton mean collaborating with the Nazis in Hungary? Because Hungary wants him locked up and if he touches that soil, he will be directly in jail), *when I was privileged to travel there, both on my own and with my husband on behalf of our country. ... "We need people like George Soros"* (**Translation**: Yes we are nothing without his money and evil plans), *"who is fearless, and willing to step up when it counts."*

In December 2006, Soros met Barack Obama in his New York office (Soros's office). He (Soros) had previously hosted a fundraiser for Obama during his 2004's campaign for the Senate. On January 16, 2007, Obama announced the creation of a presidential exploratory committee, and later that week, Soros officially started to back Obama. Their agenda was the same. Soros needed an agent to prove his importance to the Rothschilds and Obama needed somebody beyond the law to raise him up over the permanent ruling class of DC.

He always declared his support for a big government like China. By his own words, he is working on destroying the American dollar to create a Revolution. That's what he said in his "Destroy America" conference which the main argument was "The fall of America and the Western world."A conference in which the Obama Administration was attended. An administration full of Marxists in the Capitol who were running the country with the advice of the Communist Party USA, seeds of Nazis and money of Arab royals. The Democratic Party is better called Democratic Socialists or Democratic Stalinist-Marxists because that is what they really are. They hide communism. Soros wants the new communist constitution and its bill of rights by the end of 2020. And who was running that conference?? Lol…John Podesta.

10- Soros and Climate Change

We already talked about Climate Change and its beneficiaries. As usual, Soros pushes hard any plot that aligns with his agenda. Mr. Barack Obama's brain, who selected officials of the Obama administration, chose only those who pushed climate change and fought coal. The direct result of his push to fight coal was to sore gas stocks and its usage. Now, where does he go to invest? Surprise! Gas stock. Check "Interior" stock with the IOC symbol and see who the biggest shareholder was at the time: George Soros. Through all his criminal activities and interference with overthrowing governments and plotting against humanity, illegal "Insider Trading" should be another reason for him to be already locked in jail. And we think, "How intelligent he is as an investor and how does he always buy the right stocks and make billions"? No, he is an insider. He has most likely committed "White Collar Crime" not once or twice but multiple times.

His non-profit mega organizations create policy. Policies change the socio-politics of America and other countries having a direct impact on special markets and Soros; the very designer of that policy is exactly aware of its impacts and buys or sells the affected stocks first hand. He does this in all markets all around the world. No "only" businessman could do this. Imagine this: If he targets apples, he buys orange stocks. His ninja organizations protest against the apple and demand that the orange should be the solution. So the apple's price plunges dramatically and orange that he has already bought sores. He jumps in as an irrelevant individual businessman who has nothing to do with those protestors and buys all tanked apple stocks. Tomorrow the newspapers are full of benefits of apple and how it is good for our health and bingo. Apple stocks sore too and who made a fortune? I couldn't make it simpler than this.

Monsanto has the same story. Soros pushes Global Warming through Monsanto which its goal is to control food and grain supply of the planet. Moreover "Gavilon Grain" company, backed by Soros's funds and in cooperation with the Obama administration, became the third-largest grain company after Cargill and Archer-Daniels-Midland. So grain and food became another monopoly through the climate change agenda. The production of the U.S seeds goes into the hands of the gruesome monster: MONSANTO and the magician Soros is here. Right before the bill passes the Senate, Soros buys 897,813 shares of Monsanto worth $312.6 million. Read the line again: **Right before the bill passes the Senate, Soros buys...**

Again, as with Interior Gas, Soros, most likely, commits the Insider Trading crime. And stupid morons who consider him a guru and a legend in investment, just need to wake up. He is an insider, not an investor! He is a financial terrorist, not a legend to follow. His place is not in a lavish house on Fifth Avenue but jail, hopefully, Gitmo.

The Senate and the Obama administration were well equipped to pass laws that fit the commands of their Sugar daddy Soros. A bill introduced to the Senate in November 2010, which implemented new regulations regarding seeds and seed cleaning required special expensive equipment. The bill which is called "The Food Safety Modernization Act," surprisingly became law, so fast on Jan 4, 2011, by Obama's signature and added another burden to existing rules. Seeds should be "cleaned" in a special manner, and normal companies are not considered as "effective" to handle that "special manner" and… bingo… All rights go to Monsanto.

The Act, by many critics, is called the most dangerous Act as a terrorist bio-attack on the American food supply. In 2007, the Intergovernmental Panel on Climate Change predicted that global warming would lead to a drought which will have a huge impact on food security. Therefore, there is a must to help farmers and instruct them to grow crops in a different climate. Insurance companies instruct farmers for when it's too hot, cold, dry, wet, or other extreme outside situation. Drought-resistant corn is another souvenir of climate change policy. Monsanto says that it has the authority and duty to equip such products to farmers that are climate-resilient, so the genetically modified corn seeds that are resistant to drought were produced for the first time. Thus, Climate Change gives the pass to genetically modifying what we eat, and as a result, modifies our bodies and minds and benefits the depopulation and the agenda of control. You don't think seeds designed to be cultivated in drought climate, and have been manufactured by humans instead of nature are nutrient seeds, do you?

"Improved water use" means training farmers for cultivating seed with almost no water when we have plenty of water and soil at the moment. It is exactly like the government forbids drinking more than one glass of water a day because in the future we may face a drought. The drought fantasy only results in empty foods for a worse and the worst nutrition of the population, which is the deplorable population from their point of view.

-But who is Monsanto?

Monsanto is known for its deadly business of building the first atomic bomb and poisoning more than 5 million Vietnamese with "Agent Orange," which resulted in 400,000 deaths and disabilities.

The main word you should bear in mind from the above sentence is POISONING. The company is specialized in "poisoning." So how such a company becomes the only monopoly of our food and grain and takes control of the total food and seeds market??

Monsanto = Food Domination = using Food Contamination = Depopulation and Control

Monsanto has joined the United Nations "Agenda 21". "Agenda 21" as they say on the surface is an *"Environmental Program on sustainable development that shows concern about sudden catastrophic changes in the climate and the environment."* But digging dipper, Agenda 21 pushes for a centralized world government that controls everything.

Drinking Monsanto's insecticide causes death. Eating its engineered seed causes obesity and diabetes type II. Have you seen how Monsanto employees work on farms and water supplies? They are fully covered by Gas masks and anti-chemical Overalls. Why should they work like that on nature? Have we not seen a farmer working on land? Some of them are in shorts and mostly just in their underwear and a hat. So what are Monsanto's employees protecting themselves from that is so dangerous? Are we eating and drinking what they are protected from? Monsanto earns billions from contaminating organic crops with GMO's against our will.

The United Nations as we said in chapter two is an evil organization that preceded its roots through progressive methods of gaining power. It was created after WW2 by Khazarians inside Britain, France, and the U.S. followed by other five nuclear veto-wielding members of the Security Council to set a new world order. Something similar to a group of dogs with the U.S deep state establishment as the top dog. It established a world order based on favoritism and self-interest agenda which has just one goal: "To avoid having real and credible elected governments."

Although everything we mentioned in this book is a part of Agenda 21 in general, we are not going to break it down more here as it needs a whole book to cover it and is, in fact, the subject of my coming book.

There is no need to investigate Soros's donations to Monsanto although they are so many and only genetically modified Marijuana has received $10 Million just to start the project from him through Open Society into "Drug Policy Alliance" founded by Monsanto. The point is, Monsanto is actually funded by George Soros and Bill Gates, and they are the company's biggest shareholders so whatever Monsanto does, is related to them.

11- Soros, Media takeover, and censorship

We already talked about "Media Matters" Founded by David Brock, in this chapter but Soros's takeover of the media is much bigger than that. The left is demanding to change the black letter of law, journalistic standards, and the Constitution to fit them into their agenda. They don't rely on the Constitution, they simply don't like it, and if the Constitution, as it is written doesn't fulfill their extremist views, they are not there to change their views, but to change the Constitution in a way that fits their views! They call us Fascists while we want a small government, less control, a color-blind society, dismantle the already centralized deep state and protect our free speech rights. These are our values. How can we be Fascists with a small government? The truth is they care about ideas, not values and try to stigmatize certain value systems by associating them with prejudice and bigotry. In a word: it's hypocritical. The pattern is; instead of convincing us by the fact, they pre-attack and guilt us that it's our fault if we disagree with them because we are racist, intolerant, stupid, homophobic, xenophobic, sexist and bigot. What they say is what they say, and whatever it may be, it's a religious cult. We shouldn't dare to challenge it. In this way, they intimidate us, and this is one of their most useful tactics. Now, over 30 Major News Organizations with this blueprint, are linked to Soros including the New York Times, Washington Post, the Associated Press, NBC, ABC, and the result is the dictatorship and tyranny of the guerrilla media. The Stalinist Media which protects the bulletproof deep state by any means possible.

Overall, we have the Shadow Democratic Party which runs the Democratic Party, and we have media cronies which are linked and belong to them. In their world, the media is all about the "media" and nothing about the "news." The news is the missing element in the lamestream media, and all is about the propaganda. To make us believe, they create their own version of fake reality on stage, just like a movie and sell it to us as a report which as karma is a bitch and as the same internet that they use as their bridge of deception becomes their trap, undercover journalists have caught them while fake staging but of course, they don't care. They have been lying for decades, and the truth has never been the standard of their identity-politics journalism.

Why does it matter? Because journalism ethics is the premise and requires neutrality in reporting. Reporting facts without politicizing them or trying to influence money footprints. This is the professional conduct of News Media. Journalists need to be "transparent" about their connections so there should be no mystery about who funds them. But unfortunately, that rarely happens. What their job has really become is stumbling between "military computerizing the system of systematic trolling"! and Body language analyzing, Trump-Putin hand-shakeology studying, future reading, bashing, one or two scoops of icecream analyzing, smashing and sabotaging whatever they can. This aggressive progressive "trolling" is modern journalism and criticizing them is an offense. To see who is corrupt look whom we can't criticize. We are open they are not because; they have to hide behind the propaganda. They believe in a set of rules for themselves and different sets of rules for whom they disagree. Is this due to their intellectual deficiency or an overdose of hypocrisy? I think their DNA is overloaded by both.

News outlets make little or no effort to reveal their connections to those nonprofit organizations sitting on their board and dictate how to create a perception for the public. For Soros's organizations, this is a rule of thumb: no matter what they say, what they do is opposite to what they say.

Before Murdoch brothers inherit Fox News from their father, Media Matters has set up direct attacks on the Channel. We explained the fight between Fox News's Murdoch and CNN's Ted Turner, and the hostile relationship became a family matter and we also know that Turner means personifies the Rockefeller team, therefore, Soros's team. Media Matters launched a website called: Drop Fox, which directly targeted Fox news. The reason is that Fox news targeted Soros and has released an investigative series detailing his funding to news media groups connected to major U.S. media outlets, including The New York Times, Washington Post, the Associated Press, NBC and ABC that made them (Soros made them) an outlet for political progressive leftopaths. The fake-stream media cry for being victims or even martyrs while it's them constantly galvanizing people and irresponsibly worsening every situation they interfere. And just imagine their branches all around the world are guided by the same players. We have a man who owns the Democratic party, Mainstream media, Education system, Judicial system, Riots and organizations behind them. A man who destroys the economy by committing White Collar Crime, and overthrows governments and now fights with the elected President of the United States, and we are still glued to our chairs watching. What do we need to lock this drooling 87-year-old man up? The world is burning through the flames of his greed and are we just watching?

Moveon.Org is another Soros's organization which proudly claims it was behind hacking Fox News. Moveon organization has a childish attitude. It designs petitions and recruits members, which are the same paid protesters who join the petition related events and collects signatures. This naïve organization directly leads us to how Soros thinks and where he wants to take us in his next step. Monitoring the next petition takes us to his next move. Watch out this website and be vigilant. Taking a glance into this website regarding the timing and the political climate of the moment, we will easily find out where the BLM and Antifa are generated. It's funny because it reflects how these spoiled brats and brainwashed feminists pull their pants up 1...2...3 and run into the streets without even knowing what they are going to talk about. They see it on the Moveon website and bam! they mouth it. I've seen dozens of clashes in which not one of those feminists, Antifa or BLM rioters had a clue about why they were there. Shouldn't they have a philosophy for their protests?

To what are they protesting? And they don't know. Their argument is no argument. "Resistance" the only morphology on their tongues and we know what that word stands for; the Communist Revolution. The same revolution that killed 20 million people just by Stalin himself that means an average of 700,000 murder per year in his 30 years of dictatorship, some of which have been strangled by his own hands. That number doesn't include WW2's 20M deaths of the Soviets. The Red Revolution was called the "Red Terror" by other countries, but our snowflakes don't know. *"Resistance, revolution, we have been lied to, we rise, rebuild the dream, fight, spread the truth,"* what is the truth? They don't know. They just have to SPREAD IT!

These are all communist canards on the Moveon website but ask the revolutionary ninjas a simple question, and they fail to answer. What should they answer while they still live in their mommy's basement, hold their teddy bears and feel no responsibility for their own lives? It doesn't take any effort to be a loser. It's nobody's fault if they are not what they want. They are not because they didn't try it. They don't care about themselves how can they really care about other people's lives? When did they start to think they have sufficient knowledge and stop growing since?

The enigma of this generation is perplexing. Will they ever heal? A generation who doesn't read, doesn't listen, doesn't debate? Will they ever be cured without listening?

12- Soros and Education

After explaining Soros and Alinsky's discipline overtaking the education, we also exposed the communist indoctrination pathology on Congressional Record. We exposed the Khazarian's protocol for hijacking the education. Putting all these people, ideologies and blueprints together, we have a bright map of why education is going the pathway we see today. Why today's children are unable to calculate or write properly. Why are they being told that trying to comply with proper English grammar is "racist" and to impose English culture is "offensive" as newcomer immigrants didn't have that culture.

They have changed children's opinions on punishment, morals, gender, abortion, pornography, prostitution, the age of consent, immigration, integration, and their own culture. Students now care much more about which bathroom transgender people should urine than their mathematics class. They don't learn if you have a penis you go to men's room, and if you have a vagina, you go to the ladies' room, they don't learn that any man can wear lipstick and enter the ladies' room and assault our 7-year-old daughter who may just think of finishing earlier and getting out fast instead of protecting herself from a man in a bathroom.

The original Khazarian group is the brain that made the Bilderberg Conferences, the Council for Foreign Relations in the United States and the Imperial Institute for Foreign Affairs in the United Kingdom. Since 1952, any patriotic organization which has started to work were immediately labeled as Fascist and Nazi by Khazarian Organizations as they would have threatened their takeover plan. The mass media swords were immediately pointed to these patriotic organizations. Socialism is a system of control, and the revolution to nail socialism should take place through violence. As both Marx and Lenin have said, people are so stupid to organize their own revolution so one would have to be imported for them. Now it's what exactly people in Europe and the U.S are facing. A revolution imported for them by immigrants and domestic ninjas in schools and universities. The worst thing about a revolution is when the average people don't even know that there is a revolution taking place!

Soros blew power into the old engine and put the dying fossil's warp and weft together. If not by Soros, the old families of the Rothschilds, Rockefellers, Morgans, German and Dutch Royals and the newcomers like Bill Gates, Ted Turner, would have needed another century to succeed, if and only if they could succeed.

They created a generation that is disconnected from reality and needs its safe spaces to deal with the world. Nobody has taught them in the real world; there is no "safe space" for them to hide. Nobody taught them they would go nowhere of making money if they don't read. Nobody asked them to "invest" in themselves, to try hard, stand tall on their feet again after their failure, no matter how many times they fall. Nobody taught them they have to research for themselves and not accepting anything they have been told. All the materials they study in college and university have been changed. What they've learned is: "The West doesn't have a culture. America is the worst country in the world. The founding fathers are racist thieves, and the police are people's enemy. All historical monuments and statues are based on fabricated reality and represent traitors, racists, and oppressors. Slavery is their fault, and it still exists. White people should be ashamed of their existence. Communism and socialism is the best way of living. Communism is the ideal heaven, and Fidel Castro is a hero. The flag is just a racist symbol, and they can burn it as there is no dignity in national values. The false principles which are not supported by facts but by false narratives created by militarized media and progressive ninja professors in the universities. Professors who, themselves are products of the extreme hate and anti-American philosophies of their predecessors during past decades. Professors who have taught their pupils their personal theories still in search of evidence, as historical facts. No beef in that burger but they do it. They don't care. The only necessary element is that the professor believes it. So the pupils have to believe it too, and if they don't, they will be severely bullied in the university.

Soros Spent $400 Million on Open Society Education "Social Action Colleges" And Universities to transform them into progressive indoctrination camps. In fact, the deep state was desperately in need of this "product" for years, and Soros's billions just speeded up the serial production. They transformed the college to be another version of daycare, with protection and safety with no " too much thinking" necessary, no feelings will be hurt and the government will take care of propagandizing them. Public schools are real Nazi-style concentration camps, but private schools did not escape the trap. Almost all colleges, universities, public and private schools have received significant funds from Soros, and those who received funds were obligated to fire the old staff and install Soros's agents.

An Evangelical Christian (the new trend is to tag your church as evangelical and attack the basics of Christianity from within. eventually, the Rothschilds did this in the late 1800s with the Catholic church but recently this old trick has found its way into evangelical movements to create fake evangelical churches and universities. To know who is who, our unique and forever guide is the scripture itself.) university in Minnesota is encouraging its professors to stop using words with masculine connotations such as "man" and "mankind" because those words aren't sufficiently "inclusive." *"Use a substitute for words like 'man' or 'mankind' when making general references to people,"* the guide says. *"English is sometimes awkward"* but *"words like 'humans,' 'humanity,' 'beings,' 'people' and 'all' are often adequate substitutes."* But these pronouns, obviously run into considerable difficulty in reading the Bible so what they do? They print new versions of the Bible which fit their "Language Inclusiveness." Apparently, they change the Bible.

Soros has also helped to establish the Central European University (CEU) which, in turn, uses its resources to promote his personal goal of an "open society" as a university discipline. Open society religion in action. What are you graduating from? *"Soros's open society policy"*! Isn't that great? What an attractive tomorrow our children will have! Imagine that, a whole university funded by the big brother himself. CEU, which is essentially Soros's own university, has received $250 million from The Founder and Chairman of the Board who is, guess who: Soros himself!

He is removing brick-by-brick the capitalist system from the face of America and the earth and rebuilding it on Saul Alinsky's principles of Communism.

"This institution will be based on the illimitable freedom of the human mind. For here we are not afraid to follow the truth wherever it may lead, nor to tolerate any error as long as reason is left free to combat it."

On Dec. 27, 1820, Thomas Jefferson vision for the University of Virginia

Today's Nazi-style Concentration Camps called schools reversed the definition of patriotism in American history and assigned students the fake identity of citizens of the world, and they have no idea they are trained to be "Microchipped Citizens of The State." Boys are treated not as boys but as defected girls or girl's anomaly. The goal is dominating boys. They are considered bad boys because they don't obey the rules set for girls.

War on masculinity that we already mentioned is a real war in schools officially and systematically bullying our male generation. In universities and schools, the mysteriously morphed "social construction of gender" is not taught as a theory, but as definitive as mathematics, physics like Newton's laws of motion is taught. Isn't it painful to see this when we know gender is NOT a social construct?

The public schools' true purpose is to put certain messages into the children's heads so they will be more obedient to the government when they get older. In our time, it was the teacher who should be listening to the students. Now it is the opposite because it is Authority practicing. That is what is going on so later; they will obey the government.

Will we survive? What will it take to replace all Soros's bricks of human degeneracy with the bricks of human values again?

-Edward Griffin's interview with ex- KGB brainwashing agent; Yuri Bezmenov

In 1984, Edward Griffin, American Author, lecturer, and filmmaker interviewed Yuri Alexandrovich Bezmenov. According to Griffin, Bezmenov who was born in 1939 in a suburb of Moscow was the son of a high-ranking Soviet army officer, educated in the elite schools inside the Soviet Union and became an expert in Indian culture and Indian languages. He had an outstanding career in Novosti, the Soviet's famous news agency and later, he developed a great career in KGB.

One of Bezmenov's assignments was to brainwash foreign diplomats when they visited Moscow. He became totally disgusted with the Soviet System, risked his life and flew to the West in 1970. He certainly was one of the world's most outstanding experts on the subject of Communist propaganda; disinformation and active measures which he decided to reveal and teach as a pro-American lecturer, advocate, writer and public speaker in the West. What we read here is a transcript of major points of Griffin's interview with anti-communist Yuri Bezmenov. Please do the courtesy and read VERY carefully and more than once because what he reveals is mind-blowing.

G. Edward Griffin: *"OK, we can turn off the projector... that's very interesting. Well, you spoke several times before about ideological subversion. That is a phrase that I'm afraid some Americans don't fully understand. When the Soviets use the phrase 'ideological subversion,' what do they mean by it? The education of the young, with the purpose of demoralizing a country."*

Bezmenov: *"it is a slow process of ideological subversion or active measures. It means to change the perception of reality to such an extent that inspire of the abundance of information; no one is able to come to sensible conclusions in the interest of themselves, their communities and their families. It's a great brainwashing process which goes very slow and is divided into four stages. The first stage is demoralization which goes between 15 to 20 years. Why that many years? Because this is the minimum number of years which is required to educate one generation of students in the country of your enemy, exposed to the ideology of the enemy. In other words, Marxist-Leninist ideology is being pumped into the soft heads of at least* *three generations of American students, without being challenged, or counter-balanced by the basic values of Americanism* (American patriotism).

"The result? The result you can see. Most of the people who graduated in the sixties (drop-outs or half-baked intellectuals) are now occupying the positions of power in the government, civil service, business, mass media, and the educational system. You are stuck with them. *You cannot get rid of them. They are contaminated; they are programmed to think and react to certain stimuli in a certain pattern. You cannot change their mind, even if you expose them to authentic information, even if you prove that white is white and black is black, you still cannot change the basic perception and the logic of behavior. In other words, these people, the process of demoralization is complete and irreversible.* *To rid society of these people, you need another twenty or fifteen years to educate a new generation of patriotically-minded and common sense people,* *who would be acting in favor and in the interests of United States society."*

Griffin: *"And yet these people who have been programmed, and as you say (are) in place and who are* *favorable to an opening with the Soviet (Communism) concept, these are the very people who would be marked for extermination in this country?"*

Bezmenov: *"Most of them, yes. Simply because the psychological shock when they will see in future what the beautiful society of equality and social justice means in practice, obviously they will revolt. They will be very unhappy, frustrated people, and the Marxist-Leninist regime does not tolerate these people. Obviously, they will join the leagues of dissidents."*

"Unlike in the present United States, there will be no place for dissent in future Marxist-Leninist America. Here you can get popular like Daniel Ellsberg and filthy-rich like Jane Fonda for being dissident, for criticizing your Pentagon. In future, these people will be simply squashed like cockroaches. Nobody is going to pay them nothing for their beautiful, noble ideas of equality. This they don't understand, and it will be the greatest shock for them, of course.

"The demoralization process in the United States is basically completed already. For the last 25 years, actually, it's over-fulfilled because demoralization now

reaches such areas where previously not even Comrade Andropov and all his experts would even dream of such a tremendous success. Most of it is done by Americans to Americans, thanks to lack of moral standards.

"As I mentioned before, exposure to true information does not matter anymore. A person who was demoralized is unable to assess true information. The facts tell nothing to him. Even if I shower him with information, with authentic proof, with documents, with pictures; even if I take him by force to the Soviet Union and show him concentration camp, he will refuse to believe it, until he receives a kick in his fan-bottom. When a military boot crushes him, then he will understand. But not before that. That's the tragedy of the situation of demoralization".

"So basically America is stuck with demoralization,and unless, even if you start right now, here, this minute, you start educating a new generation of Americans, it will still take you fifteen to twenty years to turn the tide of ideological perception of reality back to normalcy and patriotism.

"The next stage is destabilization. This time subverter does not care about your ideas and the patterns of your consumption; whether you eat junk food and get fat and flabby doesn't matter anymore. This time and it takes only from two to five years to destabilize a nation, what matters are essentials: economy, foreign relations, and defense systems. And you can see it quite clearly that in some areas, in such sensitive areas as defense and the economy, the influence of Marxist-Leninist ideas in the United States is absolutely fantastic. I could never believe it fourteen years ago when I landed in this part of the world that the process would (have gone that) fast.

"The next stage, of course, is the crisis. It may take only up to six weeks to bring a country to the verge of crisis. You can see it in Central America now. And, after a crisis, with a violent change of power, structure, and economy, you have the so-called period of normalization. It may last indefinitely. Normalization is a cynical expression borrowed from Soviet propaganda. When the Soviet tanks moved into Czechoslovakia in 1968, Comrade Brezhnev said, "Now the situation in brotherly Czechoslovakia is normalized."

"This is what will happen in the United States if you allow all these schmucks to bring the country to crisis, to promise people all kind of goodies and the paradise on earth, to destabilize your economy, to eliminate the principle of free market competition, and to put Big Brother government in Washington, D.C. with benevolent dictators like Walter Mondale, who will promise lots of things, never mind whether the promises are fulfillable or not. He will go to Moscow to kiss the bottoms of a new generation of Soviet assassins, never mind, he will create false illusions that the situation is under control. The situation is not under control. The situation is disgustingly out of control."

"Most of the American politicians, media, and educational system trains another generation of people who think they are living at the peacetime. False. The United States is in a state of war: undeclared, total war against the basic principles and foundations of this system. And the initiator of this war is not Comrade Andropov, of course. It's the system. However ridiculous it may sound, it is the world Communist system (or the world Communist conspiracy).Whether I scare some people

or not, I don't give a hoot. If you are not scared by now, nothing can scare you.

"But you don't have to be paranoid about it. What actually happens now is that unlike me, you have literally several years to live on unless the United States wakes up. The time bomb is ticking: with every second (he snaps his fingers); the disaster is coming closer and closer. Unlike me, you will have nowhere to defect to. Unless you want to live in Antarctica with penguins. This is it. This is the last country of freedom and possibility."

Griffin: *"Okay, so what do we do? What is your recommendation to the American people?"*

Bezmenov: *"Well, the immediate thing that comes to my mind is, of course, there must be a very strong national effort to educate people in the spirit of real patriotism, number one. Number two, to explain them the real danger of socialist, communist, whatever, welfare state, Big Brother government. If people fail to grasp the impending danger of that development, nothing ever can* *help the United States. You may kiss goodbye to your freedom, including freedoms for homosexuals, for prison inmates; all this freedom will vanish, evaporate in five seconds, including your precious lives.*

"The second thing: at the moment at least part of United States population is convinced that the danger is real. They have to force their government, and I'm not talking about sending letters, signing petitions, and all this beautiful, noble activity. I'm talking about forcing United States government to stop aiding Communism. Because there is no other problem more burning and urgent than to stop the Soviet military-industrial complex from destroying whatever is left of the free world. And it is very easy to do: no credits, no technology, no money, no political or diplomatic recognition, and of course no such idiocy as grain deals to USSR.

"The Soviet people, 270 million Soviets, will be eternally thankful to you if you stop aiding a bunch of murderers who sit now in Kremlin and whom President Reagan respectfully calls government. They do not

govern anything, least of all such a complexity as the Soviet economy.

"So basically, two very simple... maybe two simplistic answers or solutions, but nevertheless they are the only solutions: educate yourself, understand what's going on around you. You are not living at the time of peace. You are in a state of war, and you have precious little time to save yourself. You don't have much time, especially if you are talking about the young generation. There's not much time left for convulsions to the beautiful disco music. Very soon it will go (he snaps his fingers) just overnight.

"If we are talking about capitalists or wealthy businessmen, I think they are selling the rope from which they will hang very soon. If they don't stop, if they cannot curb their unsettled desire for profit, and if they keep on trading with the monster of the Soviet Communism, they are going to hang very soon. And they will pray to be killed, but unfortunately, they will be sent to Alaska, probably, to manage the industry of slaves."

"It's simplistic. I know it sounds unpleasant; I know Americans don't like to listen to things which are unpleasant, but I have defected not to tell you the stories about such idiocy as microfilm, James Bond-type espionage. This is garbage. You don't need any espionage anymore. <u>I have come to talk about survival. It's a question of survival of this system. You</u> may ask me what is in it for me. Survival, obviously. Because I like... as I said, I am now in your boat. If we sink together, we will sink beautifully together. There is no other place on this planet to defect to. "(End of the interview here)

*****

The CIA, the Democratic Party, and the entire Cabal, used this plan as their blueprint and changed the education system accordingly and step by step. The Infiltration of these four stages of Marxist indoctrination in America and Europe by the Deep state had started right after WW2, but it happened just in some colleges and schools across America and not to this extent and spread which we see today. The merit of these super-fast and piece by piece removal of all patriotism and love for the country and culture removal goes to billion dollars of Soros put in motion by

President Obama. The creation of Generation Me is the first fruit of Soros's factory which is the result of the "Demoralization" phase. His never-ending capital obtained through American Capitalism based on the American Constitution is used against individual capitalism for the rest of Americans. Individual capitalism Vs. State Capitalism (Like China) in which everything belongs to the government and the government means George Soros, his puppets, and the 13 families. Capitalism is private ownership of property. Socialism; is state ownership of human beings. Which one would we choose?

13- Soros and The Judicial System

Soros has worked to remove voters from the process through which judges are nominated, elected or retained and establish an "elite judiciary." How can a court ban Christian teachers from praying when they're off-campus? By changing the bricks of the Judicial System.

As Bezmenov said in the previous article on manipulating education, the first stage of education-engineering was **" Demoralization" which takes 15 to 20 years then what we have is "a goal-oriented,**

designed and produced generation" which begins to fill the jobs. Brainwashed students who are ready to fill various jobs including judicial positions. That's how we see judges in recent years have become so politicized while it is indeed an Anti- Judgment factor. **If a judge is politicized on ideas, how can he judge neutrally?**

This results in having progressive judges who believe the Constitution should be interpreted through the filter of their personal desires. Wrong! The constitution should be defended as it's "written." We shouldn't see phrases like "although the first amendment gives the freedom of speech, the freedom of speech is not limitless." ...What??

How did they conclude that freedom of speech is not limitless? They **have a manufactured mentality shaped in "Forced Concentration Camps" of schools and universities. They react as of maxims.** As Bezmenov said, even when you show the naked truth to the demoralized generation, they can't accept it. What happens when a government starts to break down its own laws? A constitutional crisis is what happens. That's what we are facing now in 2017, and what the mainstream media insists on volumizing and benefiting from it by pushing more and more the "Constitutional

Crisis" Phrase in their selected trajectory; **a path that does not target the judges' misbehavior but the Constitution itself.** This whole creepy underground movement aims to defend the "wrong" and condemn the victim. It's quite like raping a woman and blaming her for provoking the rapist. We actually are seeing this. The illegal alien; Sanchez Milian's defense, whom the 13-years-old teen in Rockville Maryland claims to be raped by him, was that "*she wanted*" and he got away with it and took just ONE MONTH in jail. And be sure that one month was for saving their faces to be able to claim there was a sentence.

Soros had influenced the selection of states' Supreme Court justices all across America, Europe, and Australia. In America, he's funding massive efforts to end judicial elections, state after state which should be elected based on merit. Instead, he wants to create laws to pick the judges by favoritism, and political interests of liberal attorneys who pick the judges. **Not all, but many lawyers are paid liars who academically learn to lie. They don't care about right or wrong. They care about the winning game.** They are specialized in fraudulence and Soros works with these types of lawyers.

In this way, Soros is engineering a judicial revolution. He could install a judge after judge who views the Constitution as his toy or particularly as Soros interprets the constitution and we know he sees it as worthy as a toilet paper. His judges make Compelling statements asking Congress that the constitution as an old document is not good for a modern society and his Democratic Party immediately sends a bill to Congress to be confirmed and become law. So the judge's decision, in that case, will comply with the new law. He has already spent over $65 million to change state procedures from electing judges to having them appointed. The man who said: *"I do business, I don't care about the consequences"* is almost close to succeed in remaking the judiciary system and fundamentally change the way judges are selected in the United States forever. If that happens, believe me, we will be a few months distant from his world government as judges determine who, what, where and what to do.

Soros's money is spent on "Justice at Stake," an organization which its principal goal is to replace judicial elections with judges picked up by his attorneys. In this way, judges in all 50 states will never get elected, retained or rejected by voters. He actually says people understand nothing and somebody else, who is eligible should decide for them, so his professional liar attorneys will do so.

Soros' money has gone to the American Constitution Society for Law & Policy, Georgetown University, Justice at Stake, Leadership Conference on Civil Rights Education Fund, Community Rights Council, ABA Fund for Justice & Education, William J. Brennan Center for Justice, People for the American Way, National Center for State Courts, League of Women Voters Education Fund, National Women's Law Center, Committee for Economic Development, Alliance for Justice, National Partnership for Woman & Families, National Institute for Money in State Politics, Lambda Legal Defense and Education Fund, Center for Investigative Reporting, all and all to push the elimination of voters in the process of selecting judges.

He is the self-claimed emperor, and all these fake organizations are his ministries. Through them, he is controlling the world and his throne is "the money throne." He whines and condemns the positive, free and constructive, Capitalism system while he is reshaping the world with his own, negative downward, destructive, and demonic totalitarian state.

Former Supreme Court Justice Sandra Day O'Connor's supported Soros, citing that voters are *"too unsophisticated to evaluate judges."* The notion was investigated and fortunately rejected for there was no evidence of such an opinion in a review of 30,000 court opinions. But with all these brainwashed new judges and attorneys it is not guaranteed to be blocked the next time it will be presented as the system is under extreme change imposed by Soros.

"I want a government small enough to fit inside the Constitution." Harry Browne

14- Soros and Trans agenda

Forget about the suffix "phobic" and let's be honest with ourselves. Phobia means fear. **Disapproval has nothing to do with fear. We can disapprove of whatever we disagree with. We don't have to agree when our logical analysis says NO to us. We will not offend by disapproving of what we disagree with. It's our process of mind flourishing not them. They can grab a tissue if they have an issue.**

There was a guy in transition (man to woman) in my Saturday gym, when all guys were busy with their stuff, the only one always ready to offer his help in lifting heavy weights or instruments was him. Not associating with men, and detached from women but unintentionally and naturally acting like a gentleman. Shy and unsocial, I once raided his privacy and asked why? His answer blew me up: *"I feel alone and like fish out of water with my friends."*

"What about women?" I asked.

"They don't like me either. But after my transition, some may do." He answered.

"But perhaps you just need to change your friends?" I replied.

"I am not social, how can I do that? Besides I am already in transition taking hormones." He said.

I feel much sympathy for transgender people. Attention though. I do feel, but not because they are right. I do because they are victims of a gender politicizing agenda of some elite who don't even care about them. The permanent gang of criminal elites doesn't mind. **What they do mind, is to generate a degraded society that has lost its identity hence they can sweep their votes.**

Identity confusion does not unite people but divides them. Creating a hundred genders among the traditional two sexes will result in having a hundred devised groups instead of two main categories. **More they divide people and push the distinctions and pretend to defend them, more they create new groups who can vote for them, but the irony is, they do it under the label of inclusiveness.**

They teach students chromosomes do not determine sex: FALSE! Chromosomes DO determine sex. That is science and biology. $2H+ 1O= H_2O=$ Water. Science! We can NOT think that H_2O molecules are equal to CO_2. If we do so, number one; our thought is irrelevant. Number two, we are either uneducated or illusionist if not crazy.

Transgender people are treated very badly within their own communities. By acknowledging any regret about their metamorphosis and speaking up about the malfunctions and dangers that threaten them, the transgender community will immediately reject them while what they need is acceptance. A community that wants them "praise" their toxic identity is not their friend. Ex-transgender believers do not encourage others to go through the operations but the mainstream media is their number one enemy who knows but yet encourages them to think they are trapped in a wrong body and there is a cocoon where they must get out of and flourish. They don't warn them about the dangers they might go through because if the newbies know, the new chain of transgender production will be stopped.

Celebrities, who come in public and praise the Transgender agenda, care about their career and public image. They don't care about Trans people. They endorse transgender celebrities to legitimize the idea.

Each year in Sweden the number of children who want to change sex is doubling. Children as young as six make a life-decision to transit to the opposite sex. But is it their wish?

At the age of six, what does a child understand about his or her problems?

At the age of six, injecting wrong beliefs in a child's mind as you look like this because "you are bad" or because "You are rich or poor" or "because your mother is mentally ill or ugly," they deeply believe it and but the idea becomes part of their forever identity.

According to psychologists, almost all adulthood issues deal with our childhood before the age of eight. That's why children are so vulnerable. The same is true if a child has a psychological issue and the school injects the idea that the root of his problem is his body as he is a girl in a boy's body, and the notion will be planted in a child's mind. From that moment, every problem he faces, everything he doesn't like, all seems to be the cause of his wrong body, making him dreaming about his magic cocoon.

How can society do this much harm to its own children?

Transgender people socialize with their community, and this makes it even worse as they become more and more detached from the real world. **It's like living in a bubble inside another bubble to avoid a mental ghetto.** In 2009, a Swedish gender investigation team saw 197 children and teens undergoing analysis to determine their gender identity and become the opposite sex. Louise Frisen, a child psychiatrist at the Astrid Lindgren Children's Hospital in Stockholm, in an interview for Swedish daily Aftonbladet, said: *"There's a 100 percent increase in numbers each year."* So since 2009, we have a hundred percent increase that means double increase each year. If the number was 197 in 2009, today it should be 50,432 in 2017 which will become 100,864 in 2018, and this is only in Sweden.

Just imagine the dramatic transformation of nations all around the world.

There is a long waiting list for people to initiate an investigation into their gender identity in Sweden. Many future transgenders may have to wait for up to a year just to begin an investigation because of the high number of applicants. Tones of money are being spent on propaganda and endangering people by continuously proposing gender transition as the solution to happiness. These young people didn't see war or a pandemic which eradicates millions of people. They didn't see hunger or discomfort. Their problems which may be related to their families or other issues are twisted to push them into the "trapped body" philosophy and the credit all goes to the school and the media.

Apparently, the transgender cartel has made an underground world and is importing non-transgender people into it. They sell lies, and people buy them. Not because the seller is intelligent but because they are progressive "marketing agents" and mostly, they sell because the weaponized media is their tool. Who is the target? The most "emotional" may be shy, isolated or less accepted people by their society and family. The only thing they need is some love or support. A friendship and support that nobody else at the moment was offering so they disconnect themselves and turn to new supporters who unfortunately provide fake support. Conditional support requires newbies to behave in a certain manner, say certain things and show up in certain groups. What they gamble through the way is their own precious one time born body. Cut off the penis, cut off body hair and go through a whole life of estrogen or testosterone. An outsider hormone will be poured into their body for their whole life. I was extremely happy when I saw that The "American College of Pediatricians" had urged healthcare professionals and legislators to scrap the creepy policies that condition children to accept a chemical and surgical impersonation of the opposite sex life as a normal life. That is an imprisonment way worse than the initial cocoon and went through sex-changing processes to get rid of it and embrace freedom. Before going through, they could change their mind and lifestyle, but after entering, they can't live without. American College of Pediatricians called the awful process of child abuse, and that is what it really is. It's stunning how those professional protesters claim to care about science and rush into the streets for climate change and global warming deceptions, but deny the real science about gender which is biology. You CANNOT change biology. If you are 6 feet tall, you cannot think you are 5 feet, and if you are a white person, thinking otherwise is useless. If you are 60 years old, you CANNOT think that you are 18 even though feeling young. That is called BIOLOGY. A "male" born transgender committing a crime will leave male DNA on the scene and law enforcement will search for a male while a transgender woman is hiding in some safe place misleading the police for a while.

What the schools and universities do instead of teaching scientific facts and the truth? They change books! They insert these bulls**t in their school books and so, they make them "pursue" those few ideas that they want, and this is as we said before, the beginning of the path of deception.

"American College of Pediatricians" continued the letter with the following: *"Endorsing gender discordance as normal via public education and legal policies will confuse children and parents, leading more children to present to 'gender clinics' where they will be given puberty-blocking drugs, the statement said. That in return might result in unnecessary surgical mutilation of their healthy body parts as young adults."*

People support the Transgender process to be homogenous and do it because the others do but what if others are wrong? If we stand for nothing, anybody can take us anywhere. Why if somebody believes he is talking to mosquitoes? We will not doubt that he is wrong but when it comes to the mutilation of their own body then there is a dilemma? Is it possible that somebody needs a genital amputation later in life but not at the moment of birth? Why cutting genitals should be trendy and a "manifest" of courage that needs applauds and prizes? If it was not a birth deficit, then was it a trendy lifestyle? The distinction between feeling and pretending is not a soft line and makes life miserable.

Being born as a man and going through the process of becoming a woman, the heart is still the heart of a man, chromosomes of a man and a whole structure of a man. Being a beta male is much more acceptable than a manly woman. There is so much competition in the market my Trans friends. Believe me. Women are pulling each other's hair to find a man who stays with them as there has been so much decrease in the number of alfa males and you will be a "no competition" to those women even if completely look like a woman. Guys run away when you tell them the truth.

Indeed, the problem was never an outside problem but nobody helped you. **Nobody told trans people that life doesn't mean being happy every day, but surviving the difficulties is what makes us happy. Nobody told them to stop trying to please other people and to look good to them but develop your inner values. Nobody told them that you "can fear," that we all fear, there is no brave man who doesn't fear, but to go straight forward to the heart of the fear, conquer and overcome it makes us brave.**

Don't do it! Don't go through the transition. It is isolating and will end you up finding another transgender who was a woman and went through the process of being a man and yet adding another layer of isolation and the story goes on and it never ends because if you adopt children the mother is actually the father and the father is the mother and still another layer of isolation, and your children will be isolated or even bullied at the school too. Oh, my God. It's freaking and the political correctness will be buried in its grave, it will become yet more freaky. They broadcast heartbreaking stories on the BBC and other lie-distribution-tribunes as examples of courage and try to hit people's sympathy but these trans people didn't have cancer or a rare disease to go under the process of surgery. They were physically sane people with psychological issues like depression, shyness or feeling rejected. We gnash our teeth watching the BBC and its crazy stories and eat our words but it's still freaky and it's still sick, and it will not help these people. Enough is enough. If all this money and advertisements have been spent on psychological and meditational help and informative courses like how to be a man for men and how to be a woman for women, there has not been an unnecessary product like this.

Doctors who advise our children to become transgender are not doctors. They should do what is best for the patient, but they are marketing agents for the Transmania Cartel. **The big Day Care of today's modern education is creating adults in pampers. Adults should feel good. The "Feel Good" distortion is all we see in recent years. "The Offended Society." The big crybabies.** They don't teach them how to grow strong and build self-esteem, they don't teach them what means happiness inside, instead; they teach them "How to be offended and how to hate who offended them."The feel-good frenzy" is all they need to become a transgender. The advisers of the Trans-Mania production say: If you don't "FEEL" good in your body, if you don't "FEEL" happy, if you don't "FEEL" to have the right body, then that's a good reason for you to change gender. There is NO diagnosis. If they FEEL that way, then that's it!

Kidding me??

Is "feeling" the only factor people need to cut their bodies? Isn't it better and right to give them advice and therapies to feel good instead of pushing them to change their identity? If an alcoholic feels good when he drinks alcohol and if an addict feels good when he injects drugs, should they continue this "feel good" self-destruction? And if we loudly and ask them to stop, are we offending them? If you say this is different, you are wrong! **A whole life process of intoxication by hormones "IS" an addiction. The "feel-good attitude," IS an addiction. We are humans and humans sometimes feel bad in life.**

Challenge me on this if I am wrong. If everything is about how we feel, then what we need is not a knife of a surgeon but the advice of a psychologist or a spiritual guide because **"feelings don't go under surgery"!**

An addict doesn't go through surgery to cut his hands in order not to be able to drug himself. He takes a cure.

Those doctors; what happened to them? Why all of a sudden, thousands of years of physicians diagnosing patients have been reversed in patients diagnosing for physicians? Do you see the deception? Can you see the twist on the subject? I think in our era people should all study philosophy and reason rather than the following technocrats. **Why on earth, patients are telling doctors what disorder they have?** Why should the doctor take the PATIENT'S DIAGNOSIS as if the doctor's diagnosis? **What happened to the medical board?** Who is behind this huge invisible shift?

According to tax returns, in 2016, Soros donated at least $2.7 million to the cause of the year, which was LGBT. These donations are made through the waterfall of money into his Open Society first and from there, to his other foundations and governmental organizations working on the case. What was behind North Carolina's transgender bathroom fight? Soros North Carolina's Group. On their statement of purpose, you can read group seeks to: *"influence state policy in North Carolina so that residents of the state benefit from more progressive policies* (Note; remember the code word "progressive"? Progressive code means Socialist Violence.) *Such as better access to health care, higher wages, more affordable housing, a safer, cleaner environment, and access to reproductive health services. The group is a next-generation LGBTQ racial and gender justice organization that empowers youth leaders to advocate, organize, and mobilize an intersectional movement, "*--From the group's website.

The bathroom debate started in California, where the Gay-Straight Alliance Network GSA, an organization based in Oakland, has been lobbying hard for transgender rights and received $100,000 from Soros in 2013.

But let us translate his statements as Soros always writes the opposite of his intentions.

"Influence state policy" (**Translation**: Lobbying)

"That benefits from the state benefit from more progressive policies"(**Translation**: That we push the state to establish more aggressive and dominant legislations)

"The group is a "next-generation LGBTQ racial and gender justice organization."(**Translation**: the group is intended to go nuclear on LGBT story and create gender

confusion behind the gender justice label and attack whoever disagrees with the etiquette as racist and transphobic.)

"They've have lobbied and succeed to implement 11 pro-LGBT laws in the state, including a 2013 bill that let transgenders identify with, and join the sports teams regarding the gender they decide to be and use the bathroom of that gender. The Gay-Straight Alliance, organized groups in North Carolina, artificed LGBT curriculum in accordance with the University of North Carolina's LEARN NC program to not only coach the propaganda but also publicize it. They taught LGBT activists a grass-root blueprint to use on social media, creating even the hashtags and how to file complaints with the U.S. Office for Civil Rights. The Los Angeles Gay and Lesbian Community Center received $130,000 from Soros in 2013."(**Translation**: whenever you see the code word "community" in these organizations it means: "a group of agitation makers.")

Their door to door Grass-root blueprint was published in the Journal Science to spread "awareness" against

Transphobia. The mentioned blueprint is now used as a national model. The decrease in homophobia which took 14 years to happen, for transgender people, all of a sudden and within a few years, by pushing policies and pouring Soros's money, became a norm so fast.

The Global Action for Trans Equality (GATE), headquartered in New York, received $244,000 from Soros to connect all the LGBT organizations and create a louder voice. Soros funded: Streetwise and Safe organization in New York, with the purpose of supporting a *"national project focused on increasing safety for LGBTQ youth during interactions with law enforcement and developing advocacy skills to engage debates around discriminatory policing practices,"* that actually defends LGTB agitators if they clash with police and organizes protests. **So if they protest and "intentionally" clash with the police, they are already protected by the law.** Perhaps now we understand better why "F**k the police" flies in each protest so easily. According to his 2014 tax return, Soros also donated $525,000 to Justice at Stake, a group that is looking to promote diversity in the courts for people within the LGBT community. That means promoting LGBT judges and also judging in favor of LGBTs. In

2014 alone, funding for gay, lesbian, transgender, and queer issues reached a record-breaking $153.2 million. In the year leading up to the Supreme Court's decision on gay marriage, both the Ford Foundation and George Soros's Open Society Foundations were among the overall top five donors to LGBTQ groups. Combined, they granted $21,850,089 in 2014. They were also the top two donors among non-LGBTQ private foundations, and the Ford Foundation was the second-largest donor to LGBTQ issues in the United States.

Soros was the top funder for LGBTQ issues in Western Europe, Canada, the Caribbean, and Eastern Europe, including Central Asia and Russia. The Ford Foundation which has strong ties with Open Society was the top funder in Sub-Saharan Africa, the Middle East, and North Africa, as well as Asia and the Pacific. Ford Foundation is fully aligned with Soros. Look into my short articles for Ford Foundation.

I see it necessary here to mention a website set up by an ex-transgender. Walt Heyer; an ex-male to female transgender who after regretting his transformation enrolled for in Sociology and graduated successfully. He decided to spread awareness and share his own experience with anybody with the intention of going through the process. He says his decision to study sociology was to find the factors, methods and social influences that lead vulnerable people to believe they are trapped in the wrong body and intentionally encourage them to join the Transmania business. On his website: www.sexchangeregret.com multiple transgender whistleblowers shared their real experiences as well as their regret. They did so as a service to our men and women warning about what they will go through. I think all of us should be very grateful to this determined, committed and focused man and his intention to help humanity and our young children. I hereby thank him for his courage and effort.

"Regret Is Real...and Transgenders Are Going Back...and it's a nightmare."

Walt Heyer

15- Soros and rights for prostitutes

Strangely, prostitution is one of Soros's favorite focuses. As usual, he plays with words. Hiding behind AIDS, he pretends to defend the "rights" of the prostitutes. We already know him well. We know that he doesn't care about them or any other human being rather than himself, so why would he do that?

He claims by legalizing prostitution and drugs; he can reduce the harm. But can a planetary parasite be even bothered by anything harming people"? Harming whom? The prostitutes and addicts of the same population that Soros's candidate called them deplorable? Isn't it bizarre that a financial terrorist cares about something? Well, the answer is clear. Legalize prostitution, then downplay the age of consent, and provide free needles all psychologically, will increase the behavior and encourage it. But wait a minute; is this all? I mean; is increasing the dangerous behavior all that he wants? We should be very naïve to believe this.

During David Griffin's great interview with Nicholas Rockefeller, when Rockefeller said: *"Feminism had nothing to do with women but tax and controlling children"*, **it was because women were not taxable as long as they were at home so by encouraging women to work, half of the population that was untaxable become taxable. The same stands for prostitution. Other than encouraging the act and promoting**

immorality, the government can tax the prostitutes and earn from the action they do. To normalize the act, he started to coin the term "Sex Workers" as for prostitutes and surprisingly, this Sex Workers issue was the main subject of the recent 16th International AIDS Conference. How? By presentation of a project via Soros's Open Society called: "Sexual Health and Rights Project." The conduct has taken place in more than 25 conferences at the AIDS event.

The project was launched in 2010, and just after two years, we see the United Nations Development Programme (UNDP) Global Commission on *"HIV and the Law"* issued its first report on the matter titled *"HIV and the law; Rights, Risks, and Health."*

The report says that the existing laws: *"dehumanize many of those at highest risk for HIV: sex workers, transgender people, men who have sex with men (MSM), people who use drugs, prisoners, and migrants. This is particularly true in governments influenced by conservative interpretations of religion, where people suffer and die because of inequality, ignorance, intolerance, and indifference. It disparages laws based on morality. Sex work is not always a desperate or irrational act; it is a realistic choice to sell sex – in order to support a family, an education or maybe a drug habit. It is an act of agency."*

The report insists that governments should *"recognize the sexual autonomy of young people"* by providing *"sex education, harm reduction – defined as condom and syringe distribution and comprehensive reproductive and HIV services...to youth. Instead, police should be put "to work alongside sex workers in enabling wider safer sex practices."*

So the term **sex workers** found it was in a United Nations report but who did draft the report? George Soros's Open Society Foundations and the Ford Foundation. Surprised? **The United Nations is totally owned by Soros and acts as his personal secretary. He writes, the United Nations makes it a new policy and declares it publicly.**

The UN is a lawmaker organization, contrary to what we may suppose. **The UN creates "policy" and these policies are dictated to local governments which from there, they become the rule of law.**

Now listen to Dr. Mary Anne Layden, a psychologist, pornography expert, and director of the Sexual Trauma and Psychopathology Program at the University of

Pennsylvania, who in an interview for LifeSiteNews.com said: *"there is no bright line of demarcation between prostitution and sex trafficking and child prostitution. These are all flowing, one into the other. The average age of becoming a child prostitute in the U.S. is 12, we call them a child prostitute until the day after their 18th birthday, and then we say it's adult consenting sex."*

In continue she asked: *"whether someone in that position is really making a free choice? HER BRAIN HAS BEEN RAPED AS WELL AS HER BODY. The way they get into this field is by raping them as children. This is how you pipeline them into this."*

That means; if the government legalizes prostitution, there will be no distinct line between prostitution and child prostitution. And there are still people who fund Soros's agenda as Bill and Melinda Gates. Gates founded the "Stella" team, which acknowledges funds received from George Soros's Open Society Institute to the project. The team seems to work on AIDS and contraception but surprisingly receives aid from the wicked Open Society Foundation. We can guess the connection.

What we mentioned about votes in the previous section, shouldn't be forgotten. When he divides people, he creates new, and multiple sources of votes. Any doubt whom Transgender people will vote? They definitely vote "Soros's" candidates, and we can still see the ashes of their fire since the 2016's election. The "LGBT parade" is one of the main actors of the "resistance" protests after the election. **The whole agenda is not human for Soros, but VOTES, TAX, degeneracy, and CONTROL**. However, the LGBT parade just shows up in Anti-Trump protests and nowhere else. **Feminist, LGBT, ANTIFA, are just different etiquettes on the same product: Anti-Trump soldiers of Soros and the Rothschilds.**

16- EMILY's List

EMILY is the abbreviation for: "Early Money Is Like Yeast"—because it rises like dough.

This one is stupid even by its name. It openly says if you join us, you will immediately have huge money and it grows more and more. The bizarre name of the organization funds very progressive women for the Democratic Party in the U.S and for the Labor Party in Australia which are recruited by EMILY's List Australia. Both founded and funded by Soros. These women instantly receive a $100,000 support subsidy. If they are not pro-abortion, then the mentioned $100,000 support is immediately withdrawn.

The organization's task is to ensure that "a woman" and not necessarily a good one get the seat in the Senate. She should be a Democrat, progressive feminist, pro-abortion, pro-diversity, pro-immigration and pro-homosexual rights. These women almost 60 percent of times win the elections as they are progressive, spend very well for their campaigns and are supported directly by Soros's spider network everywhere. Just take a look at some of the candidates whom this organization has sent to the Senate and will easily understand what we are talking about:

Elizabeth Warren, Dianne Feinstein, Mazie Hirono, Kirsten Gillibrand, Amy Klobuchar directly From EMILY's List and "Kamala Harris" who has been endorsed by this organization. Does this ring your bell??

The ninja organization which is also very powerful in Australia is the second most powerful lobbying and fund-raising entity in the United States so the pattern unfolds again. Soros creates not only the voters but "our" lawmakers who enter the Senate and decide on our behalf.

17- Soros overthrowing governments and economies

East to west and north to south of the globe, Soros overthrows the governments and installs his agents inside them. His interactions have been revealed in his leaked emails.

Around all four corners of the world, countries SHOULD NOT be able to rule their governments or protect their national identities. It's not a matter of Europe or the U.S, It's the matter of the world and his One World Government. BORDERS, national sovereignty and finally, America are threatening his universal government. From his point of view, the existence of countries, one by one is Racist. The list is so long and exhausting. I would be surprised if you are not already exhausted by his wrong-doings to this point. I just try to name some of his interventions and present a very brief explanation but remember that the "brief explanation" is just on paper and on his real road of destruction, each one of "these briefs" refers to so many innocent bloods shed and lives lost, wasted, damaged or jailed, countries destructed and mental diseases spread.

In 1989 Soros funded a chain of destabilizing activities in Eastern Europe, Poland, and the Czech Republic.

In 1992 Soros put England on its knees and made his first billion by breaking the Bank of England, shorting the English Pound. Making that delicious billion gave his destructive bulldozer a warm startup.

In 1994 Soros collapsed the Russian economy by a similar move. The pattern continues, and In 1997 Soros destroyed the economies of Thailand and Malaysia. Soros was part of the full court that dismantled Yugoslavia in a coup, caused trouble in Georgia, Ukraine and Burma (Myanmar). Later; he used the troubles in Ukraine to overthrow its elected government. France fined him $2.9 million for felony insider trading. Hungary fined him $2.2 million for market manipulation by driving down the share price of its largest bank.

In an interview for CNN with Fareed Zakaria, Soros basically "confessed" that he founded an organization in

Ukraine and overthrew the elected President of the country through that organization and installed his puppet. Zakaria asked: *"First on Ukraine, one of the things that many people recognized about you was that you during the revolutions of 1989 funded a lot of dissident activities, civil society groups in Eastern Europe and Poland, the Czech Republic. Are you doing similar things in Ukraine?"*

Soros answered: *"Well, I set up a foundation in Ukraine before Ukraine became independent of Russia. And the foundation has been functioning ever since and played an important part in events now."*

Petro Poroshenko, Soros's installed puppet is now president of Ukraine.

Soros removed Hosni Mubarak; President of Egypt and installed his puppet Mohammad al Morsi which has been later removed by the people. He funded CANVAS in Serbia which was responsible for Serbia's unrest. Later CANVAS, funded unrest in Egypt and almost every country in the Middle East which its biggest successes were Lebanon, Tunisia, and Arab Spring which spread all across the Middle East. All Tunisian opposition during the uprising in January 2011, received funds from Tunisian League for Human Rights, the Tunisian Association of Democratic Women, and the National Council for Liberties in Tunisia, which they, in turn, received funds from "International Federation for Human Rights (FIDH)" and National Endowment for Democracy, which are the Soros' channels connected to his Open Society.

Soros is very active in Australia. Any group that steps up against him is doomed to be racist. The "Reclaim Australia Rallies" a right-wing nationalist movement; challenged him in 2015, and was shut down by Soros backed groups in the streets chanting: *"No room for Racism."*

The Unions, Greens and the Left are funded by him so does the sensational media which as usual, create the narratives to shape a designed perception. Moreover, legalizing dope in Australia openly has Soros's fingerprints. Drugs have always been one of his main areas of interest as they affect the ability of thinking, functionality, and sovereignty of nations. Youth in Australia are Soros's direct target.

Soros influenced Australia's elections. In 2013 Soros bought $6 to $8 million worth shares of Australia's

"Channel 9" before buying the whole company's $1.9 billion, and now we see this "Channel 9" is openly and explicitly attacking President Trump.

Enter, MoveOn, Getup and Emily's List groups have received enormous support from Soros. They are progressive agents for elections, in both Australia and the U.S and can operate outside of Governmental control.

Albania is another country engineered by Soros and his agent, Hillary Clinton. In scandalous Clinton emails released by the WikiLeaks in Aug 2016, among them, there was an email written by Soros which says:

"Dear Hillary, A serious situation has arisen in Albania which needs urgent attention at the senior level of the US government. You may know that an opposition demonstration in Tirana on Friday "resulted in the deaths of three people and destruction of property.

There are serious concerns about further unrest connected to a counter-demonstration to be organized by the governing party on Wednesday and a follow-up event by the opposition two days later to memorialize the victims.

"The prospect of tens of thousands of people entering the streets in an already inflamed political environment bodes ill for the return of public order and the country's fragile democratic process."

Soros asks for the international community to step in and pressure the Albanian government to cease the protests. He nominates three candidates to fly to Albania and intervene. According to the WikiLeaks, in three days upon the reception of the mail by Hilary Clinton, Lajack; the person nominated by Soros in the email was sent to Albania by the European Union command. So while Clinton does the medium job, the European Union acts as his personal secretary too just as the United Nations did in the "sex workers" case. TheUnited Nations and the European Union nanny states are both the colonizers' puppets and should be dismantled.

Soros has funded opposition groups and news channels in Azerbaijan and Armenia.

Lima's Cardinal Archbishop "Juan Luis Cipriani" accused Obama's Government and George Soros of imposing abortion in Peru.

In an article for Reuters, George Soros writes: *"The world will face a second Great Depression unless;*

leaders in Europe come together in a closer political union to push through bold new policies, including the creation of a European Treasury. Adding that such a move would require a new European Union treaty (his next plan which will be an official European nanny state). *The German public still thinks that it has a choice about whether to support the euro or to abandon it. The euro exists, and the assets and liabilities of the financial system are so intermingled based on a common currency that a breakdown of the euro would cause a meltdown beyond the capacity of the authorities to contain. The new federalist moment that means new regulations and consequences. The world does need order, and that order needs maintenance.*" (An authoritarian direct threat: You come together and create a more centralized universal government, or I will create another great depression like never before and put you on your knees.)

As we said before, the EU is morphing into a nanny state run by arrogant elites in Brussels who assault national sovereignty of the member states and feel entitled to do so, and they have zero eligibility as nobody has elected them.

Chapter 7

Saul Alinsky

Hillary Rodham Clinton is probably the most intelligent but corrupt politician, who is still on the political stage and not in jail, and probably an entire book cannot cover some percent of the dirt on her, but this is not the reason we have to mention her. Three individuals; former President Barack Obama, Hillary Clinton and the Godfather of the left; the financial terrorist: George Soros, have one thing in common: Saul Alinsky.

Alinsky, the author of "Rules for Radicals" who officially dedicates his book to LUCIFER (or Satan) is the former President of the United States' honorable mentor.

-Hillary Clinton, a raving socialist

We believe in a moral society in which nothing is personally interpreted as good or evil but evil is evil and good is good. Well, former President Barack Obama didn't believe in morals as his mentor was Alinsky. One who insinuates crimes can't be a good mentor and he can't be our child's mentor as the apple doesn't fall far from the tree.

Trevor Loudon director of the documentary movie "Enemies within" says:

"Like many young Americans, Hillary Rodham entered college as a staunch conservative. She left a raving socialist. Part of this transformation can be blamed squarely on her political mentor: Chicago Marxist radical, Saul Alinsky."

-Enemies within

In Enemies Within, Loudon proves that Clinton and Alinsky shared a mentor-mentee relationship by featuring a snapshot of a letter she mailed to him in 1971, asking him about Rules for Radicals, which was published the same year, and telling him how she misses *"our biennial conversations."*

Of course, almost everybody knows everything about Hillary Clinton but the problem is that her demoralized supporters don't care.

What we see today in America, the brainwashed robots are the production of Saul Alinsky's destructive ideology dedicated to Satan. An ideology applied by his faithful mentees, Barack Obama, Hillary Clinton, and George Soros.

This is Alinsky's quote when dedicating his work to Lucifer:

"Lest we forget at least an over the shoulder acknowledgment to the very first radical: from all our legends, mythology and history (and who is to know where mythology leaves off, and history begins - or which is which), the very first radical known to man who rebelled against the establishment and did it so

effectively that he at least won his own kingdom -
Lucifer."

Generations contaminated by this book, its Guerilla-Chavista ideology and rules directly threaten America and our world. A leader, a symbol and idle to Hillary Clinton and former President of the United States dedicates his book to Satan. That's why in chapter 9 we see how past decades were the birthplace to an underground satanic religion which since the 50s has brought up generations devoted and dedicated to Satan, performing disturbing rituals and ceremonies.

Since the beginning of Bill Clinton's presidency in 1993, until today, the country was run by the Clinton Foundation Mafia. There are plenty of movies about the Mafia but even one is enough to deeply understand how the system works. The hierarchy, the pyramid and the dead bodies behind them are not just cinematographic scenes. Some nations have lived the Mafia and felt the terror in their flesh and most sadly, this is the reality of the Clintons corrupt machine. The rise of Clintons and consequently, Hillary Clinton started with Bill Clinton's governorship and then the presidency and later through the Obama's administration and now, although she had become the deep state's bleeding hemorrhoid, but together with Obama, deep inside the deep state, she is still running and that's because of the secrets of the deep state kept by them through decades. They both have a lot on each other, and the Clintons' daughter is married to Soros's nephew so... doesn't need a lot to figure out how everything is connected.

-Zombify the nation

Her ideology, which is Obama's ideology and George Soros's ideology is what changed our universities to communist concentration camps. Look where she studied: Berkeley! Look which university now is the ground zero for communism? Berkeley! Who is the reason for this transformation?

Take a look and see what are game-changing guerilla rules that zombified the generation and transformed them to a metastasis who doesn't want to know, understand, read, be informed and is sensitive, offensive, victimized, violent who just screams, creeps, attacks, cries and hates and hates and hates…

Before dealing with "rules for radicals" we need to denote the definition of "Community Organizer" as the tactics are precisely used in Soros's nonprofit organizations, Obama's Foundation, and by leftist activists. In fact, we have to translate "nonprofit organization" to "community" if it belongs to Soros or President Obama which in sequence means "Center of Agitation" and the community organizer is the individual who is a "professional agitator." We will recognize the strategies used in recent riots, mobs and mobilized grass-roots are exactly copied from the military tactics in this playbook.

- Road to Suppression

_ Saul Alinsky; Rules for Radicals (Parentheses express my personal interpretations)

-There are 8 levels of control that must be obtained before you are able to create a social state. (A communist state camouflaged as social) *The first is the most important.*

-1)	*Healthcare - <u>Control healthcare</u> and you control the people.* (What was Obama's campaign all about? Healthcare.)

-2)	*Poverty – <u>Increase the Poverty level as high as possible</u>, poor people are easier to control and will not fight back if you are providing everything for them to live.* (What communist Venezuela did and what Food and Grain control provided by Climate Change agenda is going to do. Can head of a State, believing in increasing poverty, have any commitments to his people? When a tyranny controls food, people will be more than happy receiving a "minimum" from the government. Does it sound familiar recent Democratic Party's debates on the "minimum wage"? That's socialism.)

-3)	*Debt – Increase the debt to an unsustainable level. <u>That way you are able to increase taxes, and this will produce more poverty</u>.* (During eight years in office, President Obama added to the national debt as much as the sum of all previous 43 presidents has done together. When Obama entered the White House on Jan 20, 2009, the national debt was \$10.6 trillion, and until Inauguration day on Jan 20, 2017, it became \$20 trillion. That means \$9.4 trillion in his eight years. What did he do with this money? The country became jobless and poor, and there was junk food in the schools, expensive healthcare, and damaged infrastructure. So where did the money go? Endless wars, Hollywood bash parties, bribery, meddling in European governments and overthrowing Ukraine, expenses to reverse the judicial and educational system to become what they have become today. Gavin Newsom the lieutenant governor of California must also be expert in this art.)

-4) *Gun Control - Remove the ability to defend themselves from the Government. That way you are able to create a police state.* (Familiar? We already covered the gun control subject, but as you see, Obama's obsession with gun control was because of his mentor's rules.)

-5) *Welfare - Take control of every aspect of their lives (Food, Housing, and Income).* (Climate Change agenda is the cash pot to NWO and the key to controlling the food, transportation, and income; the next steps will be a piece of cake after controlling food. These are rules for Liberals by the great Master of Liberals Saul Alinsky. So how liberalism which is an infiltrated socialism, and believes in such rules is not evil?)

-6)   *Education - Take control of what people read and listen to take control of what children learn in school.* (Already successfully done. This art. is so important that it was mentioned both in Khazarians' protocols and in Congressional Record.)

-7)   *Religion - Remove the belief in God from the Government and schools.* (They were very successful. Weren't they? A return to God by itself can probably be the most powerful strategy to defeat them.)

-8)   *Class Warfare - Divide the people into the wealthy and the poor. This will cause more discontent, and it will be easier to take from (Tax) the wealthy with the support of the poor.* (President Obama, not only divided people in wealthy and poor categories but as he was a very good student for his mentor, by triggering blacks,

Hispanics and immigrants on whites, women on men and LGBT on straight people, he added a new level of racial division.)

***

"Community Organizer" is the core of Alinsky's teachings. Two months before Alinsky's death, he told a reporter: *"If there is an afterlife and I have anything to say about it, I will unreservedly choose to go to hell."*

There are volumes and volumes of written pieces about Alinsky, but among them, Michael Horowitz books or "The evil genius behind Obama" by Dr. Jerome Corsi, are the bests in the field.

According to Alinsky, DOGMA is the enemy of human freedom, and to enslave humans, people should be dogmatized first.

What Saul Alinsky taught his followers is: *"Power goes to two people: To those who've got the money and those who've got the people."*

Hillary Rodham, a devoted admirer of Saul Alinsky, who becomes Hillary Clinton after marrying Bill Clinton, wrote her 92-page senior thesis on Alinsky's theories in 1969. She was actually in love with his ruthless, military tactics.

Unlike Hillary Clinton, Barack Obama never personally met Saul Alinsky. Obama was just 11 when Alinsky died in 1972. But, he became a master practitioner of Alinsky's guerilla methods, and one of his genius community organizers and a raving agitator.

David Freddoso, the author of the 2008 book The Case Against Barack Obama, explains Obama's community-organizing efforts regarding how he handled different cases. He says: *"his proposed solution to every problem on the South Side, was a distribution of government funds ..."*

Mike Kruglik, another Obama's early mentors in the Alinsky method, believed that Obama: *"was a natural, the undisputed master of agitation, who could engage a room full of recruiting targets in a rapid-fire Socratic dialogue, nudging them to admit that they were not living up to their own standards. As with the panhandler, he could be aggressive and confrontational. With probing, sometimes personal questions, he would pinpoint the source of pain in their lives, tearing down their egos just enough before dangling a carrot of hope that they could make things better."*

For several years, Barack Obama himself was the teacher of Alinsky's methods in Alinsky's workshops. In mid-1985, Obama started to work with ACORN, the important Soros's Organization we already mentioned and was behind agitating black people and draining their votes, Occupy Wall Street riots, Antifa and women's march. He also worked for the Alinskyite "Grassroots" political organization. Please dedicate special attention to this term: Grass-roots.

Grass-roots are political movements which instead of having an up-down trajectory or from lawmakers to people, take the bottom-up approach. That is; they trigger local people to organize political events to gain an "effect change" from local to regional, from regional to national and then from national to international level. That's how their bottom-up approach works.

-Wolves are coming

Hillary Clinton always admitted that 1968, the year she met Alinsky in Chicago was a watershed in her *"personal and political evolution."* One might say what Clinton believed in her young ages, has nothing to do with her political career as an adult. To prove this to be wrong, we refer to the left and liberals' own news agency, their beloved Washington Post and the article wrote about Hillary's faith in Alinsky during all her career. (Parentheses express my personal notes and interpretations.)

By Peter Slevin; Washington Post Staff Writer, Sunday; March 25, 2007

"The job offer to "Miss Hillary Rodham, Wellesley College" was dated Oct. 25, 1968, and signed by Saul D. Alinsky, the charismatic community organizer who believed that the urban poor could become their own best advocates in a world that largely ignored them. (Refers to Alinsky's job offering to Hillary which she denied as she had enrolled in Law School)

"Alinsky thought highly of 21-year-old Rodham, a student government president who grew up in the Chicago suburbs. She was in the midst of a year-long analysis of Alinsky's aggressive mobilizing tactics, and he was searching for "competent political literates" to move to Chicago to build grass-roots organizations.

Seventeen years later, another young honor student was offered a job as an organizer in Chicago. By then, Alinsky had died, but a group of his disciples hired Barack Obama, a 23-year-old Columbia University graduate, to organize black residents on the South Side while learning and applying Alinsky's philosophy of street-level democracy. The recruiter called the $13,000-a-year job "very romantic until you do it."

Today, as Obama and Hillary Rodham Clinton face off for the Democratic presidential nomination, their common connection to Alinsky is one of the striking aspects of their biographies. Obama embraced many of Alinsky's tactics and recently said his years as an organizer gave him the best education of his life. Clinton's interest was more intellectual -- she turned down the job offer -- and she has said little about Alinsky since their association became a favorite subject of conservative critics during her husband's presidency.

Alinsky was a bluff iconoclast who concluded that electoral politics offered few solutions to the have-nots marooned in working-class slums. His approach to social justice relied on generating conflict to mobilize the dispossessed. Power flowed up, he said, and neighborhood leaders who could generate outside pressure on the system were more likely to produce effective change than the lofty lever-pullers operating on the inside.

Both Obama and Clinton admired Alinsky's appeal for small-d democracy but came to believe that social progress is best achieved by working within the political system, and on a national scale. Neither candidate would agree to be interviewed about Alinsky." (refers to using the tactics on a national scale and "small-d-democracy" doesn't mean what we know as democracy, but Saul Alinsky's democracy which is "oppression" as we have already seen in his community organizer tactics. Small democracy stands for anti-democracy with the etiquette of democracy. That's why Alinsky and Soros have things in common. Alinsky was the creator of reverse definitions and opposite names which will be appealing to average people. They all believe in small D and big G which means small democracy and big government.)

He continues: *"Both (Clinton and Obama) went to law school, turned to a mix of courthouse and community remedies, and eventually moved into electoral politics.*

Associates describe the candidates as combining streaks of idealism with a realistic appreciation of the politically possible, a mix the goal-oriented Alinsky would have recognized in himself. Like Alinsky, they fashioned political strategies defined more by coalitions and compromise than by the flashy but often hollow rhetorical pyrotechnics that Clinton, in her Wellesley honors thesis, called "the luxury of symbolic suicide."

-Wolves in suits

Other famous parts of Alinsky's infamous book are:

(Parentheses express my personal notes and interpretations.)

1-*Politics is all about power relations but to advance one's power, <u>one must couch one's positions in the language of morality.</u>*

(We should be code breakers to understand Soros's language. He uses big words, complex phrases that many reporters struggle to understand what he is talking about. He uses socially moral values which when in action; does exactly the opposite. The same thing is what Obama does; the same thing is what Clinton does. **They all play the words. Their house of cards is a house of words. But the ugly truth how ordinary people are easily deceived by words.** Just name it as a good thing, and feed their head. Establish censorship regulations then call it "Net Neutrality" as Obama did. Establish another Anti-American rule and call it the "Patriot Act" again as President Obama did. Name it open internet while it means a monitored internet. Ah! Open open open. Hearing the word "open" is like spitting on my face. Open Internet, open borders, open society which all means Soros, Soros, Soros. How could he associate the concept of control and enslavement to the word "open" that easy? All play with words. Who will oppose it? Ordinary people will ridicule, attack, and call you a traitor to oppose a Patriotic Law! They are just mesmerized by the headlines and titles and love all sorts of bitter lies.)

2-*There is only three kind of people in the world: rich and powerful oppressors; poor and disenfranchised oppressed and the apathetic middle class.* (Hey middle-class people; you just heard what Alinsky and consequently his followers, Clinton, Your former President Obama, and Soros really called you in their private meetings, "apathetic and indifferent," are you happy with that?)

3-<u>*Change is brought about through relentless agitation and "troublemaking"*</u> *of a kind that radically disrupts society.* (Familiar? All media hysteria, press barking and cherry-picking of the news, Russian hoax, Antifa protests, Anti-healthcare, Anti Comey firing, Anti two scoop of ice-cream! Women march and all and all.)

(Now listen here number 4, this one is really big!)

4-*There can be no CONVERSATION between the organizer and his opponents. The latter (opponents) must be depicted as being evil.* (Remember the placards and signs in Berkeley? *"Conversing with Fascist conservatives normalizes their views."* This is identically taken from Alinsky. ***"Don't talk to the Fash, Bash the Fash"***...all those screams and horns in our ears, they've got their lessons very well which is the guerilla spirit of Alinsky everywhere.)

5-*The organizer can never focus on just a single issue. He must move inexhaustibly from one issue to the next.* (Constant agitation)

6- *Taunt one's opponents to the point that they label you a dangerous enemy of the establishment.* (Ridicule, Ridicule, Ridicule)

***

"True revolutionaries do not flaunt their radicalism. They cut the hair, put on suits and infiltrate the system from within."

-Saul Alinsky

-Alinsky in action

Alinsky taught his students to hide behind the mask of defenders of moral principles and human decency and to do so, the agitators must react with "shock, horror, and moral outrage." Whenever their targeted enemy misspeaks or fails to live up to the agitators' rules, there should be an outrage. This is also familiar, isn't it? As you practice to realize, the core of his teaching is based on "a big and evil Deception." The Alinsky's mentees are infiltrated traitors and evil enemies within.

Enemies who see us in two categories: The apathetic middle class or "poor oppressed." We have the freedom and possibility to choose between the two categories. What we can NOT choose, is to be in the third category which is the "rich oppressors." No! No way! That is theirs and only their category; ACCESS DENIED.

Alinsky wrote in his book: *"whenever possible the organizer, must deride his enemy and dismiss him as someone unworthy of being taken seriously because he is either intellectually deficient or morally bankrupt. The enemy properly goaded and guided in his reaction will be your major strength."* (All allegations on President Trump trying to fit him into an impeachable offense are following this strategy.)

Alinsky died in 1972, but Barack Obama, Hillary Clinton, the destructive Democratic Party, Stalinist media and on top of them, the international parasite; George Soros, implement his (Alinsky) blueprint for a Socialist revolution which Obama, Clinton, and Soros, playing their usual words manipulation game, call it: "Change."

To summarize what we discussed about Alinsky, we first analyzed Alinsky's "levels of control" which were eight-level: 1- control the nation's healthcare; 2-

Increase the poverty; 3- Increase the debt; 4- Gun control to remove the ability to defend themselves from the government; 5- Control of welfare, food, housing, income; 6- Control of Education and what children read; 7- Remove God from schools and government; 8- Class Warfare to divide people.

To obtain those eight levels of control, Alinsky established 13 rules which should be applied before going to levels of control. These rules, which the name of the book is driven by them, act as fore steps to prepare the ground and are as follows: (Parentheses express my views)

-The first rule: *Always remember the first rule of power tactics: Power is not only what you have but what the enemy thinks you have.*

-The second rule: *Never go outside the experience of your people. When an action is outside the experience of the people, the result is confusion, fear, and retreat.* (by not going outside the experience he means; Pick something that people can "feel" themselves into the experience and if they can't, then avoid it. Don't use that issue, it is not for you.")

-The third rule is: *Wherever possible go outside the experience of the enemy. Here you want to cause confusion, fear, and retreat.*

-The fourth rule is: *Make the enemy live up their own book of rules. You can kill them like this, for they can no more obey rules than the Christian church can live up to Christianity.* (This is exactly what Churchianity did to Christianity and what Khazarians did to the Jews. Infiltrating through them as their own, then abominate the whole idea.)

-The fourth rule carries within the fifth rule: *Ridicule is man's most potent weapon. It is almost impossible to counterattack ridicule. Also, it infuriates the opposition who then react to your advantages.* (Familiar? The left's sharpest weapon)

-The sixth rule is: *A good tactic is one that your people enjoy. If your people are not having ball doing it, there is something very wrong with the tactic.* (That's why we shouldn't be scared. We should have "fun" fighting these traitors.)

-The seventh rule: _A tactic that drags on too long becomes a drag._ _Man can sustain militant interest in any issue for only a limited time, after which it becomes a ritualistic commitment, like going to church on Sunday mornings._ (Psy-Op tactics)

-The eighth rule: _Keep the pressure on, with different tactics and actions, and utilize all events of the period for your purpose._ (All recent protests show up at every special event, holiday or ceremony and say the same things which are totally irrelevant to the case.)

-The ninth rule: _The threat is usually more terrifying than the thing itself._ (Bluff, pretend, always pretend and deceive. In fact, Alinsky was famous for being a balloony bluffer. Honesty has no place in today's liberalism.)

-The tenth rule: *The major premise for tactics is the development of operations that will <u>maintain a constant pressure upon the opposition.</u> It is this unceasing pressure that results in the reactions from the opposition that are essential for the success of the campaign.* (Again Psy-ops and like today, the unceasing attacks by the mainstream media and Hollywood. The Russian gate. The Russians, The Russians, just repeat. No evidence but still The Russians. Total Psy-Op)

-The eleventh rule is: *If you push a negative hard and deep enough, it will break through into its countersides; this is based on the principle that every positive has its negative.* (In what "ism"? According to what basis? How can every positive have its negative? Does that mean every negative has its positive too? I just see a pattern of hostility and negativity.? So how did his followers climb that high as President, Secretary of State, and the Python Soros? Was it because of heir viciousness, or the apathetic Middle Class as he calls, the indifferent? The indifference of people who has the biggest numbers yet less intention to bother? People who think politics belongs to politicians so to get rid of the difficulty, cast lots to see which accidental politician, whom they don't even know, should go to Congress and stand between them and their rights. And these thrown balls appear to be people like Maxine Waters and Liz Warren who embarrassingly shock us drop-dead by not knowing the simplest law.)

-The twelfth rule: *The price of a successful attack is a constructive alternative. <u>You cannot risk being trapped by the enemy in his sudden agreement with your demand and</u> saying "You're right—we don't know what to do about this issue. Now you tell us."*(So they protest, disrupt but don't want us to agree with them and drop our resistance. They didn't disrupt to make us surrender and ask conditions to compromise. There is no compromise. If we surrender to their attack, there will be another "attack" as an alternative. **They disrupt to disrupt.** They disrupt to eliminate not to compromise. Our elimination from the political arena and lastly, oppressing us is the goal.)

-The thirteenth rule:<u> *Pick the target, freeze it, personalize it, and polarize it*</u>. (President Obama's signature. He used it almost in every operation. Pick the target personalize and freeze it means; to choose the person whose fight is effective, isolate it, and cut the supports. Personalize means "make it a personal attack" and forget about the institution he or she is working with; attack the individual as it will hurt more. Polarize it means to pressure and ridicule that individual. Do it to the level that he or she finds no choice but to give up.)

And he always repeated one thing: *Always remember the first rule*. (Control level)

Well is there anyone who doesn't recognize these tactics today used by the army of leftists? They actually radiate in all Soros's campaigns, protests, events and the conduct of the partisan media.

Chapter 8

Barack Obama, "The Matrix of Deviance"

The divider in chief

Years ago, once I was directed to a video of President Obama in 1995, in a memorial for his book "Dreams from my REAL father." It was a very small room with about 20 students, mostly black. He started his speech by stating that the death of his father was his inspiration to write. President Obama mentioned him as a non-present biological father who in 1982, died in an accident. The book was written in 1995 so for me it was a bit late to be inspired by the death of his non-present father so something was wrong…

-I am an angry young man

My cynicism has more to do with the content than the individual and I was shocked by the words he used in his speech as a person, who within the next 13 years, became the president of the United States. All I could hear in that speech was a guy, carrying a huge burden of hate and intolerance inside. A burden that becomes the only force and fuel of his engine to go forward during the next years.

In that speech, he was anxious; he talked of white supremacy, white privilege, he said he is "an angry young man" because of white privilege, and he said in our society everything belongs to him: *"The White Man."*

It became a must for me to dig and find out where this outrage came from? His mother was a white woman; she married twice with two black men, Barack's father from Kenya and Lolo Soetoro from Indonesia. So she had no problem with interracial marriages. She loved Barack, she was always present and taking him everywhere with her within the white community happily and proudly as his son, Barack had a big smile on his face in every photo, never seemed to be ignored, so where did this outrage come from?

Psychologically, fatherless children (if the father is not dead) grow up angry, and it doesn't matter if they are black or white. Father is gone and being angry about it, sometimes they lash out the anger at the mother accusing her of making their father run away. But

Barack soon had a good stepfather filling the empty space.

-The White man issue

Obama's family lived in Hawaii, Kenya, Indonesia, and Kansas. During their residence in Hawaii in the 70s, the family became close friends with the black writer, communist, and activist; Frank Marshall Davis. Their relationship became stronger and stronger to the point that Marshal first became Barack's mentor, and then filled the position of his father. Obama always spoke of him as his *"real and mentor father"* as he did also in the video I was watching.

In his book, "Recounts" Obama reveals that Frank not only had told him *"college was merely an advanced degree in compromise"* but also had cautioned him not to *"start believing what they tell you about equal opportunity and the American way and all that sh**."*

The man, who was an explosive progressive communist had a monumental influence on Obama and directed him in the wrong direction. Barack, not having a powerful father figure, absorbed his destructive ideas as the foundation of his character. The most influential years of

Marshal on Obama were from 1979 to his death in 1987. But the revolution in Barack's personality, took place in 1979 when he had 18 years old. A change that caused him to enroll in political sciences at the University of Columbia.

The passage which Obama read from his book in the video included a quote from Marshal Davis who assured Obama" *"black people have a reason to hate."*

In 1979, he entered the University of Columbia.

In December 1980, Obama was already a well indoctrinated active Marxist who was attending meetings of the Democratic Socialist Party of America and also very active in the anti-apartheid movement. He openly admitted that a Communist revolution in the U.S was imminent.

In 1982, his father died in an accident. In 1983, he graduated from Columbia University with a degree in Political Sciences.

The damage has already taken place. He was openly a communist, but he was not yet radicalized.

He came to know Saul Alinsky; the Godfather of Agitation in his last year of graduation. He got more familiar with his rules and methods gradually, and in

1985, he officially became an Alinsky's Community Organizer. He took a job with the New York branch of the U.S Public Interest Research Group as a community organizer. He also started to work with ACRON. That was where he could openly operate Saul Alinsky's tactics and become a master of agitation.

What does a community organizer do? Does it have anything to do with organizing a community? Not at all. It means completely the opposite. **Community organizing means disorganizing and disrupting the community. The methodology is building agitation groups and angry protests**. It is an anti-capitalist agitation, which the organizer should set people on fire so furiously, compressing them for a change and we already discussed the word "change" in the leftist dictionary means "communist revolution." Community organizers believe themselves to be America's fixers.

-The black Jackpot

Back to Obama's 1990 memorial, it was this sentence that grabbed my instant attention to investigate: *"I am an angry young man. I am very angry."* Why is he angry and where does this anger come from? But digging more, I realized; there was no such anger. It never existed.

The anger which Obama was repeating around was a psy-op on the public. He was a disruptor, a player. He had LEARNED to have anger. He would fail to sympathize with the plight of people whom he wanted to influence. He was sympathizing with them with manufactured anger. It was his weapon to win. With anger, he was different; the black swan. He had learned his lesson from Davis. The anger was rigged like a trap to ensnare black people to follow him. So he could reach the position of power. He had a white mother; he was educated in the best universities at a good expense, he was not poor. He was not rich but never poor, he was tall and handsome, he had it all. Any guy at his situation could have all the fun in the world in those years. **The anger was fabricated because it was trendy and it was priceless. It was designed to hit the jackpot, and sure he hit the jackpot.**

-Master of agitation

Racial resentment at that time was a dead bear-stock in the market ready to become a bull-stock and skyrocket as soon as the right person with the right knowledge and insider tactics could touch it. What could be the insider knowledge to spike such a stock? Agitation money. What does a community organizer do? Agitation. He creates "paranoia" and skillfully directs this paranoia to the targeted community which aims to benefit. What will be the tactic? "By any means possible." Does the phrase look familiar? Do we not see "By any means possible" In Antifa, Black Lives Matter, and all left protests today? Did we not see the outcome of this "By any means possible" in Berkeley? Today in 2017 and with recent protests, we know that this "any means possible" means verbal and physical attack, shut down speeches, events, protests, rallies, spread lies, fear, hysteria, propaganda, fake news, and blocking rallies of the opposition group and not to forget the recent urge of online violence that openly demands terror, assassination, tacking a brick, rape and threatening the individual, their family, and relatives of whom they disagree with. Was Barack Obama successful in transforming the racial resentment market into a bull market? Just check the media from 2006, especially between 2008 and 2016 and now. What is the main argument? Race.

-Chief of mischiefs

In fact, after leaving the office, Obama is back to his real job as a Community Organizer. That's what we see in the streets; Obama. Behind all the agitation in the streets you see; Barack Obama's brain, his operatives like Valerie Jarrett; his former First Advisor, and Soros's money. Obama was one of the best community organizers that history has ever seen so don't underestimate this. According to Alinsky, these organizers should *"rub raw the resentment of the people and agitate to the point of conflict while pretending to be middle-class folks in suits."*

Alinsky taught, organizers must target the same system they reject, penetrate it and occupy the highest-rank positions to acquire power. They have to make themselves attractive to the middle class of the society despite rejecting their values and calling them "Apathetic middle class." This is the formula for revolution. Once power is obtained, organizers can show their true colors.

Obama didn't become the president to be a president and to do the president. Obama became the president

to infiltrate the system from within and break it into pieces.

Alinsky called this infiltration, "Social Justice." That's why we have social justice warriors everywhere in leftist organizations. They are all Alinsky followers. He believed this infiltration could not be achieved through regular politics but through "actions." He says: *"Direct action is barely disguised code for the occasional use, and the omnipresent threat, of mob mischief, unleashed against the law-abiding bourgeoisie. The organizer prospers by defining down our ethical boundaries or, looked at the other way, by legitimizing extortion."*

He continues: *"In the short run, the goal of direct action is sheer extortion—i.e., to coerce capitulation in the controversy of the moment, be it a private business's right to compensate employees or build production plants as it sees fit; a state's sovereign power to defend itself by enforcing immigration laws; or Leviathan's grab of one-sixth of the U.S. economy under the banner of 'healthcare reform.' Over the long haul, the goal is to demoralize civil society, to convince opponents that the 'change' in regular processes—particularly, reliance on the law—will be unavailing."*

As you remember, demoralizing the society was the first phase of establishing a Communist State according to Yuri Bezmenov in the previous chapter.

-Workshop: How to bring down America?

Since, 1985, Obama was not happy with just working as a community organizer, so he started to teach Alinsky methods in the workshop for several years. In 1987 he was already a "hard left radical." From that point, he did all he could to radiate violence and spend it on the road of his social acceptance.

In 1998, he entered Harvard Law School and took all these experiences with him at Harvard.

In 1990, he wrote an essay which later, has been added to his book: *"After Alinsky";* as a Chapter: *"Community Organizing in Illinois."* As you see, Obama writes a book on Alinsky and Clinton dedicates her Thesis to Alinsky. Both politicians are hypnotically drowned in Alinsky, but Obama kept it alive and flourished until the present day. Seems Obama, every day, discovers something new in Alinsky's methods.

The progress of Obama was well recognized by Saul Alinsky's son David, during his 2008's presidential campaign. He (David Alinsky) wrote: *"Obama learned his lesson well. I am proud to see that my father's model for organizing is being applied successfully beyond local community organizing to affect the democratic campaign in 2008. It is a fine tribute to Saul Alinsky as we approach his 100th birthday."*

Yes, it was beyond Alinsky's imagination that his "infiltrated pupil in suits" became The President of the United States, his book became the President's Bible, and rules of his father were executed one by one.

About his years in college, in a passage of his book, *"the memories of my REAL father,"* Obama wrote: *"To avoid being mistaken for a sellout, I chose my friends carefully. The more politically active black students. The foreign students. The Chicanos. The Marxist Professors and the structural feminists and punk-rock performance poets. We smoked cigarettes and wore leather jackets. At night, in the dorms, we discussed neocolonialism, [the socialist, anti-colonialist revolutionary] Franz Fanon, Eurocentrism, and patriarchy. When we ground out our cigarettes in the hallway carpet or set our stereos so loud that the walls began to shake, we were resisting bourgeois society's stifling constraints. We weren't indifferent or careless or insecure. We were alienated."*

Obama believed in working WITH the "system" and penetrate inside organizations, institutions, lawmakers, and churches in order to undermine them. His goal was to bring capitalism to its knees and to transform it from within. His gradual plan was focused on creating an anti-capitalism reform that should necessarily be built up slowly and with patience. In that case, the reform would be strong enough to shake the system and its joints, therefore, abolishing the Constitution would be as easy as planned. In fact, Obama acted just like a respectable snake-oil salesman and peddled the defective product in the public square in plain sight.

-Who is a community organizer?

America voted the "Enemy Within."An enemy who was planning for so long but didn't have the means to succeed. An enemy carrying a burden of 200 years of "Hate" under the skin.

America had a dream to vote for a black man, but she voted the "wrong" black man.

America voted The Matrix of Deviance who gave birth to the deviated and divided America that we see today.

One of Obama's most effective tactics, rather than Alinsky's ridicule and agitation, was "intimidation." He organized protests to rush into private meetings and events and threatened the leaders of each movement. Just like what Antifa does today. All methods just out of Alinsky's manual used to create "Anger." Anger, in Alinsky's philosophy, is the core, the heart, the god of his strategy to organize a "Communist Revolution."

Community organizer uses all his methods to create anger which leads to the systematic acquisition of power by transporting the poor or as he says "the oppressed" through the anger and destroying the sense of morality and desensitizing the public toward violence, chaos and create discontent to explode the society and accomplish the "upheaval" that is needed to have a dictatorship of Proletariat; A revolution through a civil war.

The "apathetic" middle class and the "oppressed poor" will be used, up to this point and ordered not to settle for anything less than a whole new system. And here, right here at this point, the organizers will reveal their real identity or "their oppressor identity" and set up a whole new system, new totalitarian constitution, new form of living which money and power belong to "oppressors" and a minimum wage, slavery, and prison will belong to "apathetic middle class" and "poor oppressed" that were used to establish the Marxist government. **Right here at this moment, "The Oppressors" enter the game and kick the "Proletarian Bottom" out, and the "Communist State" governs on behalf of the "played fools" who will soon be microchipped like a cattle. This is the big "Deception" of the Communism heaven.**

......" I am an ANGRY young man. I am very ANGRY".....

-Legacy: Race Race Race Race

Obama graduated from Harvard in 1992 and married Michele the same year. Between 1992 and 2004, he just worked on racial concentrated issues. These are the titles that he taught in his workshops and speeches: *"Current Issues in Racism and the Law"*, *"current problems in American race relations and the role the law has played in structuring the race debate","* how the legal system was affected by the continued prevalence of racism in society", "how the legal system has dealt with particular incidents of racism", "the comparative merits of litigation, legislation, and market solutions to the problems of institutional racism in American society."*

Race Race all about Race. According to The New York Times; Obama taught only three subjects at the University of Chicago Law School: **race, rights, and gender**. The New York Times writes: *"He (Obama) assigned a 1919 catalog of lynching victims, including some who were first raped or stripped of their ears and fingers, others who were pregnant or lynched with their children, and some whose charred bodies were sold off, bone fragment by bone fragment, to gawkers. ... Are there legal remedies that alleviate not just existing racism, but racism from the past?"*

Adam Gross, now a public interest lawyer in Chicago, wrote in his class notes in April 1994: *"Liberals flocked to his (Obama) classes. After all, the professor was a progressive politician."*

-The angry black man becomes the authentic black man

Obama; a man with an agenda, trained by Frank Marshall Davis, sealed by Saul Alinsky and groomed by Prince Al-Waleed bin Talal from Saudi Arabia was ready to be applied by George Soros to take the position and occupy the Oval Office. Is there any other combination more toxic than this in history? Just imagine, what could have happened if Josef Stalin and Adolf Hitler were both allies on the same side??

Obama; the "Angry young black man" used the anger to become the "authentic black man," and his individual strategy was not fixing the problem but to amplify it and create blame. To do so, he chose the most aggressive tactic of exaggerating victimization to tenderize the mind of the black masses.

The racial hysteria we see today comes from there. Years of racial articles under the influence of Marshal

Davis, Saul Alinsky, George Soros, and Prince Al-Waleed bin Talal Al Saud. Practically, the tactics of the first two and the money and the influence of the latter two.

I do not recall a group, person, or a news media between 1998 to 2004 talking about race, blaming on race, or accusing people of being a racist or even something close to that.

It was utterly inexistent before1998. Nothing like the racial climate that we are dealing with today, in the 80s or 90s, existed. This was Obama's chicken soup cooking in the oven for decades. His souvenir to this country and the world. **All we hear today is race and gender and rights. The same three issues that Obama well worked on by agitating, manipulating, intimidating, and ridiculing. He used these tactics both academically, and on the street level to reach where we are today. Deviance at its finest;** a boiling society damaged beyond repair if we don't take the right approach.

- How to overthrow the Trump administration?

Obama by revolting women against men, blacks against whites, gays against Christian straights, illegal immigrants on whites, blacks on police and especially, criminals against the justice department! just separated the body of society. Now criminals are victimized too. Poor criminals who have been oppressed by law enforcement if they get arrested!

The hatred, division, and violence he planted in America are so broad that seems unlikely to heal. The mainstream media act as cheerleaders in "How to overthrow Trump administration and shed blood on the streets." Hollywood crybabies are upset as nobody will hold celebrity bash parties in the White House anymore and their catwalk in the Oval is gone with the wind. Corporate media, Hollywood and the deep state are plotting together. The deep state's desperation and panic are on the tongue of the media but it is Obama still running the country behind the shadows. The love-relationship between him and the media aimed to glorify him as a black superhero and every subject that could challenge this "must" receives a total blackout or a partisan attack from the media.

-Vehicle of destruction

We have to thank God that the demonic marriage between the old Rothschild establishment, Soros, and Obama, put the destruction bulldozer on such a speed that it took place during our generation so we could recognize the pattern. The change was so drastic and fast that whoever at the age of 40, or even 30, could feel it, believe it and wake up. This is a real chance to be alive in this era and to be able to make a difference by restoring humanity and fighting back. If it had happened over the next 70 years, slowly and creepy, as it always used to be, we would not be able to distinguish the change and the damage, and our world based on morals and humanity have been forever gone and the new would slowly become normal. Having a slow metamorphosis, there would have been no way to return and save the world. **Instead, the speed of this destruction revealed the pattern** and the pattern made us recognize what they call a conspiracy is in fact, the reality because it is there. It is so tangible; we can see it, feel it, and touch it. By 2016's election, we rediscovered our power which we, undermined it by giving in to the mainstream media lies and the government's regulations.

Why Obama's administration didn't want us to save money and our guns? Why did they hate America's prosperity and its business? Because there comes the power; **"Individuals Sovereignty." Without the Second Amendment, there will be no First Amendment. No freedom of speech without the right to defend it.** No other Amendment will preserve its power if the Second Amendment be taken out. If people can defend themselves and be self-sufficient, they have the power. "We, the people," that is the source of America's power. **Not in gold mines or oil wells, not in its nuclear power or industry, they all can be taken out by a tyrant but in "American Individualism", his gun and his auto-sufficiency.** "We the People"...There is where the true power is.

Barack Obama forgot something. Playing the race card at his time was a winner because it was trendy and nobody was playing that card, nobody was injecting the idea or talking about it because it was inexistent. Today, at our time, every single opportunist is playing the race card, and we are about to vomit. It's a burnt card. It's out of fashion, it's disgusting, and it needs to stop. Nobody is going to win with that burnt card anymore because we are not going to buy it.

"Bigotry against any group should be disqualifying for high office."

Alan Dershowitz

Obama's past is totally sealed. Unlike any president or politician before him, he has just been plucked out of nowhere. But the reason he has been plucked was his hate for white people, and his radical socialism which combined could run over America and DID run over America. He was the best shot for Stalinist Democrats. The best possible divider.

Obama won his presidential race, by implementing Alinsky's rules word for word. **We should fight back just the same.** Studying and using their own tactics against them as there is no other option dealing with folks who use radical rules. No lecturing, no kindness, no forgiveness or being on defense will work with Alinsky's rules. With Alinsky, people become hardliners.

-The Shadow President

Barack Obama didn't leave. He is trolling Trump administration both secretly and openly at the same time. At the time President Trump was in the G7 summit in May 2017 in Europe; Italy, Obama flew to Europe too. He not only was trolling the President to steal the scenes but also said: *"As I have still influence, we can MARGINALIZE those who want to divide us. We can't hide behind the wall"*...This is officially and publicly trolling a sitting president who was elected to "build the wall." This is the Trump derangement syndrome by a former president who should have gone through a peaceful transition of power as American tradition demands, but he feels entitled **as he is the bulletproof face of the deep state.**

Remember Saul Alinsky's rules? Pick the target, freeze it, personalize it and polarize it. That's what he is doing; marginalizing a democratically elected president. A systematic siege. The resort to slapping on a sitting president's policies is simply bullying. He is desperate to push a full-on conflict. Whom does he think he is lecturing for? A nation of imbeciles?

Barack Obama stuck on a big lie to take power, and once he gained it, he used the tool of "stay" to control the information and trading the US economy, resources, military, infrastructure, and entertainment. He was predominant and moved toward his goal which was "the elimination of the United States" gradually and brick by brick.

And he stayed...

-The Constitution is not fluid!

President Obama; openly vowed to "fundamentally transform" the United States, at day one on his inauguration. He meant what he said. He always wrote about the American Constitution as: *"not a static but rather a living document and must be read in the context of an ever-changing world."* And by "<u>must be read in the contest</u>" he meant: "Interpreting the constitution and not implementing the law as it's written." He always appointed individuals who believed in interpreting the constitution rather than applying it as written. It shouldn't be a surprise that George Soros lived for the same concept and his organizations are constantly working to "deconstruct and reinterpret" the constitution to the point that becomes a completely useless paper ready to change in 2020. Soros's Open Society Institute was the financial sponsor of a Yale Law School conference called *"The Constitution in 2020, a progressive vision of what the Constitution ought to be."* This is the same "Fundamentally Transforming America" which Obama was talking about on his day one, inauguration day: *"What the Constitution ought to be in 2020."*

As you see, we didn't go through numerous stories about President Obama's exotic background, his "mother," his birth certificate in Kenya, his true biological father, his "wife," his "daughters" or his "faith," none of them. We just went through the official story of his life and what is acknowledged by himself; born in Hawaii, his official father, his official mentor father as he calls Frank Marshall Davis so, and his official commitment to Alinsky. Also what officially misses from his Presidential background records. Let other people write about unofficial stories. What we have here is a horrible eye-opening truth. **Treason through the deep state and its media, who insert their trojan horse, an official radical white-hater, communist-sympathizer, with his strings in Soros's hand sit on the highest throne in the world, infiltrate, and destroy from within.** Treason; which the result of the 2016's election, threatens its core interests and sooner or later, it will reach a threshold which to save the lost agenda, the deep state's violence becomes inevitable, and starts a civil war, and if we still have our wits and scruples, we should be ready by a torrent of condemnation and systematic action.

Barack Obama And Prince Al Waleed 1979, California

ALWALEED

Chapter 9

RING OF THE CABAL

In previous chapters and different contexts, we offered a thorough description of the oligarchs and the colonizers. In this chapter, however, we are going to link the whole cartel, revealing the connections, specifying names, and unveiling the ties between the Federal Reserve, British Royals, The Vatican, The House of Saud, Huma Abedin, Clinton Foundation, Justin Trudeau, George Soros, the CIA, Barack Obama, and North Korea.

Let's start with Obama – Saudi connections.

- Prince Al-Waleed Bin Talal from the House of Saud

Soros had employed all Obama administration through Citi Group, and Citi Group is linked to the house of Saud and directly to Prince Al-Waleed Bin Talal who owns large stocks of Citi Group. Al-Waleed has been Clinton's primary financial & political sponsor for decades, but now her ropes have been cut off. Here again, Soros is the middleman between the Obama administration and Saudi Arabia.

Prince Al-Waleed Bin Talal is the founder of HUMA; Islamic Studies at Harvard University.

As we said before, President Obama's university documents are sealed. Therefore, nobody can look into those documents and see how the former president paid for his Harvard studies. His campaign spokesperson's answer to the question was just: "student loans."

But as we know, there should be another copy of "student loans" in Harvard loan registries which there is none for president Obama during 1988-1991 and after. Dean of Students, the Director of Student Financial Services, the Registrar, or the Bursar of Harvard Law School, None of them has any specific information on this.

- Donald Warden A.K.A Khalid Al-Mansour

In 1988, Percy Sutton, a former Manhattan Borough president, in an interview for a

New York cable channel said that a Muslim activist: Khalid Al-Mansour, who was Prince Al-Waleed's advisor, approached Sutton and asked his help to get

Obama to the Harvard Law School. He had asked Sutton a letter of recommendation for Obama and Sutton did so.

On Sep 23, 2012, Frank Miele of Daily Inter Lake wrote a fascinating article that I prefer to quote it here just as it is. Even though it is a long, but it's worth to be read thoroughly.

He writes:

"Searching old newspapers is one of my favorite pastimes, and I have tried to use them many times to shed light on current events — or to inform readers about how the past is aprologue to our very interesting present-day quandaries.

"Recently, I came across a syndicated column from November 1979 that seemed to point 30 years into the future toward an obscure campaign issue that arose briefly in the 2008 presidential campaign.

Though by no means definitive, it provides an interesting insight, at least, into how Chicago politics intersected with the black power movement and Middle Eastern money at a certain point in time. Whether it has any greater relevance to the 2012 presidential campaign, I will allow the reader to decide. In order to accomplish that, I will also take the unusual step of providing footnotes for this column so that each of you can do the investigative work for yourself."

"The column itself had appeared in the St. Petersburg (Fla.) Evening Independent of Nov. 6, but it was the work of a veteran newspaperman who at the time was working for the prestigious Chicago Tribune and whose work was syndicated nationally.

So far as I know, this 1979 column has not previously been brought to light, but it certainly should be because it broke some very interesting news about the "rumored billions of dollars the oil-rich Arab nations are supposed to unload on American black leaders and minority institutions." The columnist quoted a black San Francisco lawyer who said, "It's not just a rumor. Aid will come from some of the Arab states."

"Well, if anyone would know, it would have been this lawyer — Donald Warden, who had helped defend OPEC in an antitrust suit that year and had developed significant, ties with the Saudi royal family since becoming a Muslim and taking the name Khalid Abdullah Tariq al-Mansour.

Al-Mansour told columnist Vernon Jarrett that he had presented the "proposed special aid program to OPEC Secretary-General Rene Ortiz" in September 1979, and that "the first indications of Arab help to American blacks may be announced in December." Maybe so, but I looked high and wide in newspapers in 1979 and 1980 for any other stories about this aid package funded by OPEC and never found itverified."

"You would think that a program to spend "$20 million per year for 10 years to aid 10,000 minority students each year, including blacks, Arabs, Hispanics, Asians and, native Americans" would be referred to somewhere other than one obscure 1979 column, but I haven't found any other word of it.

Maybe the funding materialized, maybe it didn't, but what's particularly noteworthy is that this black Islamic lawyer who "for several years [had] urged the rich Arab kingdoms to cultivate stronger ties to America's blacks by supporting black businesses and black colleges and giving financial help to disadvantaged students" was also the same lawyer who allegedly helped arrange for the entrance of Barack Obama into Harvard Law Schoolin 1988.

That tale had surfaced in 2008 when Barack Obama was a candidate for president and one of the leading black politicians in the country — Percy Sutton of New York — told an interviewer on a Manhattan TV news show that he had been introduced to Obama "by a friend who was raising money for him. The friend's name is Dr. Khalid al-Mansour, from Texas. He is the principal adviser to one of the world's richest men. He told me about Obama."

"This peculiar revelation engendered a small hubbub in 2008 but was quickly dismissed by the Obama campaign as the ditherings of a senile old man. I don't believe President Obama himself ever denied the story personally, and no one has explained how Sutton came up with this elaborate story about Khalid al-Mansour if it had no basis in fact, and in any case, al-Mansour no longer denies it.

Back in 2008, while actually supporting Hillary Clinton in the New York primary, Percy Sutton was interviewed on TV and said that he thought Barack Obama was nonetheless quite impressive.He also revealed that he had first heard about Obama 20 years previously in a letter where al-Mansour wrote, "There is a young man that has applied to Harvard. I know that you have a few friends up there because you used to go up there to speak. Would you please write a letter in support of him?"

Sutton concluded in the interview, "I wrote a letter of support of him to my friends at Harvard, saying to them I thought there was a genius that was going to be available and I certainly hoped they would treat him kindly."

"Until now, there really has been no context within which to understand the Sutton story or to buttress it as a reliable account other than the reputation of Sutton himself as one of the top leaders of the black community in Manhattan — himself a noted attorney, businessman, and politician. But the new discovery of the 1979 column that established Khalid al-Mansour's interest in creating a fund to give "financial help to disadvantaged students" does provide a clue that he might indeed — along with his patron, Arab Prince Al-waleed bin Talal — have taken an interest in the "genius" Barack Obama.

It also might be considered more than coincidence that the author of that 1979 newspaper column was from Chicago, where Barack Obama settled in 1986 a few years after his stint at Columbia University. It is certainly surprising that the author of that column was none otherthan Vernon Jarrett, the future (and later former) father-in-law of Valerie Jarrett, who ultimately became the consigliatore of the Obama White House.

It is also noteworthy that Vernon Jarrett was one of the best friends and a colleague of Frank Marshall Davis,the former Chicago journalist and lifelong communist who moved to Hawaii in the late 1940s and years later befriended Stanley and Madelyn Dunham and their daughter Stanley Ann, the mother of Barack Obama."

Very interesting…

So Khalid Al-Mansour before becoming a Muslim was "Donald Warden" a broker/enabler for Prince Al-Waleed to spend $20,000,000 a year for a period of ten years on Black/Hispanic students, making them influential politicians installed by Al-Waleed. The same Al-Mansour, very accidentally asks Sutton to write a recommendation letter for Barack Obama to be accepted at Harvard.

At the time, Harvard cost around $75,000 for the three years that Obama attended. According to Mike Armini, president of the Harvard Law Review and Harvard's spokesman, Obama received no stipend from the school.

In 2004, as a United States Senate candidate, Barack Obama was required to file a financial disclosure form claiming his assets, income, consulting contracts and liabilities in full details. Obama listed "zero" under liabilities in 2004 and all subsequent U.S Senate financial disclosure forms. There are no college loans mentioned in the entire financial disclosure even back in 2000. Obama's spokesman ignored any connection with Khalid Al-Mansour but if so, where did he get the money for studying at Harvard?

What if he was paid off by Prince Al-Waleed to infiltrate the U.S? Why did Al-Waleed establish Harvard's Islamic Studies AKA HUMA? Would a Saudi Arabian Prince do that with no interest? What if American people voted for a "Mansourian candidate," funded by Muslim Hardliner Prince Al-Waleed, enabled by Al Mansour and introduced by far left-wing billionaire George Soros? Why is Soros the middleman acting as a joint in any connection?

- Huma Abedin & Hassan Abedin

Huma Mahmood Abedin was a long-time aide to Hillary Clinton. She served as Deputy Chief of Staff at the State Department of the Obama administration while Hillary Clinton was Secretary of State from 2009-2013; she is also the wife of former Democratic Congressman Anthony Weiner of New York who is convicted for sexting an underage teen. Abedin is raised in Saudi Arabia and identifies herself as a practicing Muslim.

In June 2012, former Republican Congresswoman Michele Bachmann of Minnesota sent a letter to Deputy Inspector General at the Department of State. The letter says: *"information has recently come to light that raises serious questions about Department of State policies and activities that appear to be a result of influence operations conducted by individuals and organizations associated with the Muslim Brotherhood."*

As proof of these, Bachmann stated: *"the Department's Deputy Chief of Staff, Huma Abedin, has three family members — her late father, her mother, and her brother — connected to Muslim Brotherhood operatives and/or organizations. Her position affords her routine access to the Secretary and to policy-making."*

The letter was sent to Harold Geisel, the Deputy Inspector General at the Department of State, while copies were sent to the Departments of Homeland Security, Justice, Defense and the Office of the Director of National Intelligence.

Upon a subpoena and a search warrant on sexting allegations obtained by the Special Victims Unit (SVU), NYPD found 662,000 emails regarding Weiner's engagement in all sorts of sexual activities via the Internet.

But among them, they found 11,000 emails with the addresses: "state.gov" and some were classified, others were marked as: "Top Secret." This led NYPD to contact the FBI and re-open its investigation into Hillary Clinton. Meanwhile, the emails were forwarded by Huma Abedin from her secure U.S State Department e-mail address, to her non-secure Yahoo.com email address and emails were programmed to "synch" to computers at home. So among other computers at Abedin's home, Weiner's laptop which was under investigation synched all the state department emails, and all the emails his wife Huma has sent or received involving anyone else.

According to damning criminal evidence they found, under the "Life Insurance" folder, NYPD warned the federal government that if indictments of Hillary Clinton and her co-conspirators were not forthcoming on time, the NYPD would release information on its own about some of the criminal records revealed on that Laptop. After a while, considering that the federal government still hasn't charged Hillary Clinton, the leaks are slowly popping out through different channels. It has been rumored that officer Familia, killed on duty in her car, that we meticulously explained under Bill de Blasio section, was one of the NYPD officers who watched the damning information on Anthony Weiner's laptop and one of those officers who vomited watching the scenes and promised to tell. Although a rumor and not an official report, I think we should consider it because she was shot for no reason. Sitting in her car and somebody opens fire.

A leak on "SuperStation95" sources in New York, reveals an e-mail from Huma Abedin to her brother,

Hassan Abedin, seized from Anthony Weiner's laptop. This particular e-mail says:

>> ON SEPTEMBER 03, 2016 AT 8:57 PM. HUMA ABEDIN @YAHOO.COM WROTE:

>> SORRY FOR MY LATE REPLY, HASSAN. YES, LET ME

>> TELL YOU ABOUT HER. THE WOMAN IS SO ODD, SO STARVED FOR

>> VALIDATION, SO TORMENTED AND VAIN IT IS A CONSTANT

>> SURPRISE TO ME THAT ANYONE TAKES HER SERIOUSLY.

>> EVERYONE ON THE TEAM KNOWS HOW UNWELL SHE IS, BUT

>> THEY'RE MORE DETERMINED THAN EVER TO SEE HER WIN. THIS

>> WOMAN THAT HAS A DOZEN SEIZURES A DAY. THIS GODLESS

>> SHRIEKING MALCONTENT PASSED OUT IN HER MEDICAL VAN.

>> THIS WALKING CADAVER. SHE'S NONFUNCTIONAL. HASSAN,

>> NOBODY CARES. WE SOBER HER UP FOR SPEECHES AND

>> INDULGE THE PRESS CORPS WITH CHEAP SENTIMENT. THE FIRST

>> FEMALE PRESIDENT. THE LAST GLASS CEILING, ETC. THEY TRIP

>> OVER THEMSELVES LINING UP BEHIND HER. SURELY THEY KNOW

>> IT IS NOT HER THEY'RE GETTING. IT'S THE ONE IN THE CORNER,

>> THE QUIET HELPER, YOUR SISTER HUMA. YOU ASKED ME ONCE

>> HOW I DID IT. HOW DID I TAKE THE CASTLE? HASSAN, I DIDN'T

>> TAKE IT, THEY GAVE IT TO ME. YES, THERE WAS A COST. I WILL

>> ADMIT, SUBJECTING MYSELF TO AW AND WJC (AW = Anthony Weiner, and WJC = William Jefferson Clinton)

>> IS MORTAL TORTURE. BUT I DO IT

>> GLADLY, BROTHER, EVERYTHING THEY ASK OF ME, HOWEVER

>> SICK AND DEPRAVED. I DO IT, AND I SMILE, REJOICING AT THE

>> THOUGHT OF WHOSE GLORY I SERVE.

....

Concerning this email, Huma Abedin admits:

"I do it, and I smile, rejoicing at the thought of whose glory I serve."

Whose glory does a hardliner Muslim serve? Huma Abedin, the leader of the Muslim Students Association (MSA) while she was in college at George Washington University has very close ties to the Muslim Brotherhood.

Huma's mother Saleha is one of the "Muslim Sisterhood" leaders; the equivalent of Muslim brotherhood for women. She presents Al- Naseef; and Al-Naseef has very close ties to leader number two of Muslim brotherhood Abdullah bin Bayyah from one side, and to Prince Al-Waleed from another side.

Left: Abdullah bin Bayyah Right: Al Naseef

Left: Al Naseef   Right: Prince Al-Waleed

Huma scandal is not a simple issue. It should be called
Huma-gate and should be overviewed under full

scrutiny. To know why blue states are being run in the present style, the answer is here; right on these pictures.

In an article, very well documented, prepared and written, by Walid Shoebat, we see the picture below.

The article features Prince Al-Waleed bin Talal, seated behind desk and Hassan Abedin; Huma's brother, wearing a blue tie, sitting before him across the table in a friendly meeting.

The same Prince Al-Waleed previously exposed lobbying to get president Obama accepted in Harvard and paying his tuition. Why should relatives of Obama holdovers with parental ties to the Muslim Brotherhood meet the same Prince who wanted Obama in office??

Aren't they just installed puppets serving him and reporting him back?

Hassan Abedin has been "the key" in advancing the Islamic agenda and has worked with Saudi Prince Al-Waleed bin Talal on a program titled "**spreading Islam to the west**." According to the Sunday Times, the University of Al-Azhar (or better say the Jihadists' university) actively links with Oxford Center for Islamic Studies (OCIS), where Huma's brother works.

Looking at the picture below makes it clear what type of academic center the Oxford Center for Islamic Studies (OCIS) is.

503

Enough to say that Dr. Yusuf al-Qaradawi, is the global spiritual leader (the boss) of all Muslim Brotherhood around the world and Huma's brother Hassan, worked at the same OCIS's board.

Khalid Al-Mansour who endorsed Obama is not a typical activist that you may imagine. He has been a preacher of hate for the United States and the white race for decades. On Oct 26, 1990, in a speech in Cape Town, he said:

"All over the world in 2050, when from every people in Europe one will be a born Muslim, we will have finally a real opportunity to have world peace. "

But to understand what his peace may mean we refer to another sample of his speeches **addressing the black community to slaughter white people**. He said:

"Whatever you do to [white people], they deserve it, God wants you to do it, and that's when you cut out the nose, cut out the ears, take flesh out of their body, don't worry because God wants you to do it."

Isn't this the same thing happening in South Africa now?

Who was the most active preacher in Africa for the past 50 years?

Khalid Al Mansour!

We can probably have an idea what their 2050s peaceful world will look like. Something like 2017s Africa where white farmers are cut with machetes and the government's parliament officially declares confiscating and attacking white farmers is necessary.

Watch Al Mansour's speeches. He is a Wahhabi pro-Jihadist who shouts, jumps and spews hate and anguish with every single word he says. He worked so hard to radicalize Africa, Europe, the U.S, and the Middle East. Now in 2017, those white farmers who survived are fleeing Africa for fear of being slaughtered and this happens because people like Al-Mansour have radicalized black Africans with above savage phrases for decades and now their work blossoms.

Donald Warden

For years this man has been Al-Waleed's best adviser. So what kind of a man can be this Prince Al-Waleed?

Among his countless belongings, he is the second-biggest shareholder of Twitter, second-biggest shareholder of Fox News, Owner of Four Seasons Hotels, Citi Group and top 6 floors of Vegas's Mandala Bay. Jack Dorsey, the founder of Twitter, has a cozy relationship with Al-Waleed and dinned with him in his Four Seasons hotel in Paris.

His ownership in Mandala Bay is very interesting because it explains how in Vegas Shooting, there was no evidence of Stephen Paddock, the shooter, carrying weapons to his room on the 32nd floor. Mandala Bay has 43 floors. All top 6 floors are Four Seasons Hotel which belongs to Al-Waleed and Bill Gates and has its own private elevators and a separate entrance. While the police fluster on how the guns could have been carried up, their theory baffles merely as the guns were not carried up 32 floors! Guns should have been carried DOWN 6 floors from the 38th roof to the 32nd floor through Al-Waleed bin Talal's Four Seasons Hotel property. He had the roof; he had helicopters. Could it be easier? And guess what, Bill Gates donated $1M to gun control agenda. What comes after Vegas Shooting? Anti-Terrorist movement? No. Support for victims? Nada. Even the witness survivors are dying day after day in "accidents" or "natural causes." So what was the real outcome then? Did anything change? **Yes. Gun Control agitators came out again roaring louder than ever.**

It's not all yet. What credit card do the U.S military personnel use?

Citi Cards from Citi Group...

Go figure out now who monitors all banking transactions of the U.S military.

The infiltration of Bill Gates stuns me. Once David Rockefeller picks him decades ago and makes him part of the club, setting up Gates Foundation and starting vaccines and GMO contamination. His agenda is depopulation and control. Then he has his best friend Warren Buffet and himself making extraordinary donations to Planned Parenthood to depopulate the next generation. Always on the agenda, always on point. Then his other very close pal, Bono with his ONE campaign in Africa, sucking the blood of Africans under the mask of Africa Saviours, so many vaccines in Africa caused confound deceases and anomalies while some caused death. Then he is in bed with Al Waleed who has Huma Abedin in office, Obama as President, Citi Bank, Four Season, Twitter and has his traces in Vegas shooting which has depopulated a good portion of us. Now he builds "smart cities" which are the real horror of the century. The manifest of the centralized world government in real, where the government decides who lives and who dies, what is eaten and when should sleep. The old dream of the Cabal. I have written so much about these people separately on my website. It is important to know that colonizers are people with lands. The rule is the rule of the jungle; the system is Mafia.

Laws, regulations, countries, borders don't matter. The power depends on who the person is, where is his land and what is his rank in the hierarchy. The Game of Thrones. Democracy, constitution, agreements, and people, especially people are parasites and intruders. They know each other, and the power is assigned to them and divided between them by top heads of the families. There is nothing complicated in this. It is as easy as what we just pictured.

The Federal Reserve

We already talked about the history of the Rothschild, Rockefeller and Morgan family and how they came together and created the most significant financial power but now we are going to relate this to other pieces which make RING OF THE CABAL.

- A private bank

The Federal Reserve is a private institution whose shareholders are commercial banks. It is the "bankers' bank" and is ruled by its owners, therefore, it is committed to their interests. **The Federal Reserve is an**

independent entity not required to answer any government but controls the banking system and money resource of every government including the United States.

The word "Federal" is intelligently another game of words. For over a century it has been just the word that people paid attention to and ignored the action. The word "Federal" made people feel it belongs to the federal government even though on their website, we clearly read: *"The Federal Reserve System fulfills its public mission as an <u>independent entity</u> within government. <u>It is not owned by anyone</u> and is not a private, profit-making institution".*

But who really reads things? Who really investigates? Nobody....Nobody really cares and they know it.

They fool us by the phrase *"is not a private, profit-making institution."* It is owned by the bloodline who believe they own the world so what does private mean exactly when the world is theirs? The Federal Reserve doesn't have to answer anybody. Otherwise, what does it mean? "Not governmental; it is not private" so what is it?? A ghost? Unfortunately, we see it, and it is everywhere all over us so it can't be a ghost.

People just see what they have been told to. When they have pre-assumptions, the more they look, the less they see. This statement, if people could really read, basically says that **the Federal Reserve has a government of its own and needs no proof or confirmation from the Congress,** therefore, is placed on the United States' constitutional soil while unconstitutionally controls its banking system and trolls the government since it is immune to her laws.

No pain and all the gain.

The government should create money with no charge. The economic power of the government should determine the interest, rates, credits, inflation or supply but instead, it was the Federal Reserve to do so and not only this but also lent money to the government and earned interest. The government just tangled every day more into the sticky discharges of the monster, the enemy within. The United States' government and American people had **no bigger enemy than the Federal Reserve.**

-Woodrow Wilson and authorization of Federal Reserve

The Federal Reserve was founded on December 23, 1913, under the presidency of Woodrow Wilson and centralized the power of the U.S banks into its own. The year 1913 and its importance in changing the history of America was systematically discussed in this book. Just three years after his signature, Wilson felt terribly guilty of doing so, and wrote: *"I am a most unhappy man. I have unwittingly ruined my country. A great industrial nation is controlled by its system of credit. Our system of credit is concentrated. The growth of the nation, therefore, and all our activities are in the hands of a few men. We have come to be one of the worst ruled, one of the most completely controlled and dominated governments in the civilized world. No longer a government by free opinion, no longer a government by conviction and the vote of the majority, but a government by In reality, however, central bank independence means independence from the people and the elected bodies of government—not from the powerful financial interests the opinion and duress of a small group of dominant men."*

Asset-price bubbles injected by the Federal Reserve have created a road of collapse for the American economy and have the downfall effect of redistribution of wealth from the bottom to the top and hence, feeding the monster. **People pay, banks benefit. That's the deal.** People actually think they know nothing of the banking system, so they faithfully contribute to the Feds. If they knew the Federal Reserve intentionally makes it look complicated, it would blow their minds.

It is such a simple process: A private entity creates its own money, lends it to the government and earns a fee. The consequence is the dimension of the power. "Who controls who?" Upon the power earned by that entity, it clutches whatever it wants, and no government can hold it accountable. As an old saying says "the difference between a rut and a grave is only the dimension" but when hard to believe truth is right in plain sight, people refuse to see.

The Feds pay out everything. If a tomorrow they decide to close the doors, they do, and they are not required to answer.

That's where you understand the power of JP Morgan. That's where you realize **the Rothschild-Rockefeller-**

Morgan entity is an entity that "regulates" the government.

Is it not interesting to know that **the City of London, the Vatican, and the Federal Reserve, belong to no government** and they are all separate countries having their own governments? It's even more surprising that these three "governments" belong to the same triangle and they can't live without each other. They are so involved with each other and have common "doings" and "behaviors" that **what one of them does, all of them do because they do it together.** If one of them dies, all of them die because they hold it together.

The dynamic of these three independent countries are as follows:

The City of London: The Royals and subfamilies + puppet-servants and power-brokers.

The Federal Reserve: the Rothschilds, Morgans, Rockefellers and subfamilies + puppet-servants and power-brokers. Today, in my opinion, the Morgan family is merged with the Rothschilds and The Rockefeller family is replaced by George Soros. Where we used to see the philanthropic actions of the

Rockefeller dynasty, which were super creative in building progressive movements and social issues, we will see Soros. I may be wrong, and that is something that future will witness, but with my observations of Rockefeller's family, considering two favorite sons killed in different accidents and one in a natural cause, and David Rockefeller said goodbye in March, the Rockefeller dynasty is over, and the Clinton-Soros cartel has replaced it.

The City of Vatican: The Popes and subfamilies + puppet-servants and power-brokers. The House of Rothschild is the banker and key guardian of the Vatican Treasury.

Two categories of people are so loyal to the Feds. Money vampires who understand the system but don't care whose blood they are going to suck. They drain the benefits anyway. And the second category who are people incapable of understanding the system, suspect nothing, and have no complaint. They don't realize that the Federal Reserve is a government designed for their subjugation while feeding itself. That's why the government has a huge budget deficit. If the Feds have created money and had lent it with no interest, why the federal government is in debt?

-Titanic, the unsinkable ship

Most of you have surely seen the love story; Titanic. But who knows that JP Morgan funded and built Titanic?

It was the ship's first trip, which was named "the maiden voyage." There are people listed on that trip who are reported to be selectively invited by JP Morgan.

Morgan had even a personal suite on board with his own private walkway on deck and a bath equipped with his luxurious belongings but he, together with his friend Milton Hersey, who founded Hersey Food, canceled their trip at the last second. As we said before, railroads, ships, and steel were Morgan's monopoly and as a matter of fact, even his business associate, Baron Henry Clark Frick of the Pittsburg or "Baron of steel" canceled his maiden voyage on Titanic. Another Multimillionaire Alfred Gwynne Vanderbilt (uncle to Gloria Vanderbilt; CNN anchor; Anderson Cooper's mother) of Vanderbilt shipping and railroad empire had canceled his maiden voyage so late that newspapers had his name listed as on board the day after, and they still were not aware of his last-minute cancellation. Alfred Vanderbilt is known to be a gallant gentleman. Apparently, he had not chosen the Vanderbilt lifestyle and ceremonies and had nothing in common with his brother so my guess is some little bird might have sung about Titanic's destiny and Vanderbilt, who had booked the trip with his wife, had no choice but to cancel. He died 3 years later on RMS Lusitania bound for Liverpool, after he saved a woman and her little child, granting his own life vest to her. Unfortunately, his famous siblings and grandchildren did not inherit his humanitarian spirit and good manners.

Are these cancellations just coincidences? Well, they can be but let's see what other "coincidences" we can trace in Titanic Tragedy.

In 1910, on Jekyll Island, a historic meeting took place that changed everybody's life on the planet. The meeting was between Nelson Aldrich and Frank Vanderlip; as the representatives of the Rockefellers, Henry Davison, Charles Norton, and Benjamin Strong; as representatives of J.P. Morgan, and Paul Warburg on behalf of the Rothschilds. Their goal was the establishment of the Federal Reserve. They argued, reached a conclusion and set up a plan.

Three wealthiest men in the world at the time, John Jacob Astor, Benjamin Guggenheim, and Isador Strauss were extremely dissident of the idea of creating a private bank such as the Federal Reserve to control the government. Their wealth today would have worth around eleven billion dollars and using all their wealth and influence, they could spend all their fortune to oppose the Federal Reserve. All three men were invited on board of Titanic (Olympic), and all of them died when the ship sank.

A year and 8 months later, the Federal Reserve was established.

Is it a conspiracy to say those powerful men should have been destroyed in an unsuspicious way with no trace of the murder? Many good people were on that ship. Irish Protestants from Belfast, French, and Italian Roman Catholic immigrates dreaming of America and building a new free life. The Federal Reserve Gang could care less. Those people were all deplorable to them and their sinking could cover-up the murder of their three powerful opponents. The inside job of carnage and manslaughter by the control-freak ruling class and money gangsters has a background so older than 9/11 or Vegas shootings.

But this disgrace is not all. The carnage was very profitable. Titanic was unsinkable, but her sister ship Olympic was sinkable. The Morgan gang changed the plate and used Olympic instead of Titanic for the trip and after sinking the ship, asked the insurance company for the recompense. When rumors were off, they launched Titanic in the see but under the plate of "Olympic."

And as usual, Hollywood's "Mind Control Operations" create the narrative. Titanic becomes just a love story, and one of the most dreadful terrors in the history vanishes in the shadows of love and glamour of a mesmeric movie.

The Playboy Empire

You may ask why are we talking about Playboy all of a sudden? That's a good question.

Imagine a set of toothed wheels that work together in a bigger vehicle. What prevents them from crushing due to friction? A liquid or oil.

-Hugh Hefner

Creating a sexual culture in America and therefore, in the world mainly had a goal of sexualizing children and slipping them into the CIA'S MK-Ultra program. MK-Ultra Trauma-based Mind Control program was set in 1953; just one year after the Federal Reserves 1952's plot.

The same year (1953) Hugh Hefner, set up the Playboy.

Hugh Hefner, born in 1926, served in the U.S Army from 1944 to 1946, then left the army and enrolled in the University of Illinois for a bachelor's degree in Psychology and earned his graduate degree in 1949.

So the individual had the U.S Army experience plus a Psychology degree. A background very crucial for military psychological operations also known as Psy-Op's.

-MKUltra Sex Slaves

The Playboy enterprise was more than just a magazine and video clips. The Playboy mansion, with its frequent parties, girls and celebrities was a playful rabbit. It shows up and chasing it, drags you deep into a sticky rabbit hole. Being on the guest list in the Playboy Mansion was a sort of fame, class-identity, glamour and meant frequenting important individuals in higher societies. What better way to create a honeypot and attract influential businessmen, politicians, governors and record their secrets to use as blackmail?

This is a testimony of an unknown young male identifying himself as elephantdoesntforget on Voat.co which is a free speech platform and people, who cannot speak anywhere, blow their whistles there.

"As a victim, I frequently went to the Playboy mansion with enablers in the 1990s as a young kid (I am male). I was sold for sex to the pedophiles against my will.

I would observe all sorts of weirdness. The staff of the house was by many measures 'normal,' but there were always meltdowns and emergencies that always needed to be dealt with. If cops got called, the girls drinking would be blamed. Always covered up. At the frequent parties, neighbors and celebrities would come, not all were in on it or involved. You would have to know whom to ask for, and be referred, to get to the 'next level.'

Hefner was definitely a devil worshiper. He would drug and rape new 'recruits.' Not everyone knew what they were signing up for. Many of the existing models would lure new girls into it. Many thought they were just coming for modeling careers. Hefner was very good at getting girls drugged. All he had to do was offer a drink. Alcohol or not didn't matter; he knew what to offer so they couldn't taste it. Sickening to think about it. Hefner would starve and keep water from those that didn't do what they were told. One time I saw a girl getting water from a hose in the yard because of this.

I'll wager to say if Hefner was ever working with the CIA, that they eventually broke off when he branched out and started doing his own thing, and started working with other organizations.

"It was a catalog for those that could afford it."

Bingo. People don't realize it, but everything was/is for sale. Some customers would come wanting crazy things, and the models would have to oblige. It goes without saying that many athletes and film stars were clients. Many African Americans.

But, many operations were blackmail schemes involving a very high profile attorney (in the news today). It was pay up, or the story goes public, and that would end your career. Sometimes the mark would be told they needed to make continued payments for life. Interesting that Bill Cosby was brought up in another post here; he was a frequent client still in the 1990's

Bottom line, Hefner was a human trafficker, pimp, blackmailer, and worse. But the Playboy mansion wasn't the only place this was / is happening in Hollywood or America... just one of many."

I don't take the responsibility whether or not this testimony is accurate, but I have no reason for not considering it to read.

In 2009, Sheri Denise Allred drafted a complaint against Hugh Hefner's CIA/MKUltra cult ring in the Superior Court of Los Angeles. Sheri claimed to have been ritually/sexually abused by Hefner's dark circle since she was five-years-old.

In MKUltra Instructional manuals, age five and below is the ideal age to start slitting off alternative personalities from the child to create disordered mind control subjects. Sheri talked about having a hat covering her head, something like EEG Skull Caps that are able to read human brain's waves for MKUltra projects (which later, when we will expand the program, we will see this EEG skull cap instructions tool is one of the program's main tools). She talked about implant brain electrodes and microchip brain implants used on victims. She claimed Hefner owns a cult ring. We all know how Playboy Parties are known for their extensive sex orgies, drug consumption, and strange rituals.

-Bill Cosby

Bill Cosby, who had one of the most vicious trials in history was Hefner's best friend. Cosby is accused of rape, molestation, sex battery, drug-facilitated sexual assault, child sexual abuse, and sexual misconduct by more than sixty women, thirteen of which are playboy bunnies claiming of being raped by him in playboy mansion with the knowledge of Hugh Hefner. One of them claimed when she woke up with bruises after Cosby drugged and raped her, Hefner was licking her toes.

-Project Paperclip and importing Nazi war criminals

But this is just the tip of the iceberg and there is much more to it. Hugh Hefner was a psychologist and MKUltra programmer/handler. Porn Operation and MKUltra, the "Trauma Based Mind Control Program" are part of an older operation ". Paperclip as a project initially presented by the Third Reich, and after WW2 the CIA and the Vatican through its P2 lodge used the same term for a new project Paperclip (1949–1990), by the Office of Strategic Services (OSS) in which over 1,500 Nazi German scientists and technicians from Germany and around the world (as the nazis had flown to Spain and Argentina) were brought to the United States to be employed in the aftermath of World War II.

The Nazi's didn't lose; they just moved to America. The process of "denazification" of Germany was indeed capped by Nazification of the CIA.

-CIA becomes the new Third Reich

Paperclip was a covert as the U.S law had prohibited Nazi officials from immigrating to America and when in 1946, President Truman authorized Project Paperclip, he explicitly excluded anyone from the Nazi Party. So when the list of scientists presented by the War

Department's Joint Intelligence Objectives Agency (JIOA), the Justice Department immediately rejected their backgrounds and visas were denied.

The furious JIOA Director; "Bosquet Wev" wrote a memo warning: *"The best interests of the United States have been subjugated to the efforts expended in 'beating a dead Nazi horse.'"*

He manipulated the DOJ department by claiming that the return of these scientists to Germany would be more dangerous as they could be exploited by America's enemies like the Soviet Army. He called the danger of the return of the scientist: *"far greater security threat to this country than any former Nazi affiliations which they may have had or even any Nazi sympathies that they may still have."*

At that point, CIA director Allen Dulles met with Nazi Intelligence leader Reinhard Gehlen and promised that his Intelligence unit was safe in the CIA. So to eliminate incriminating evidence and to convince the DOJ, Allen Dulles ordered to rewrite the scientist's dossier. This is how the Military Intelligence of the United States at the time, "cleansed" the files of Nazi references. By 1955, more than 760 German scientists had been granted citizenship in the U.S and given significant positions in the American scientific community. Many had been longtime war-criminal members of the Nazi party with crimes against humanity. **They were death doctors, eugenicists, chemists, and mind control psychologists of the Gestapo who used prisoners as raw meat and had conducted experiments on humans at concentration camps but fled the Court of Nuremberg. Through Dulles, the Nazi Intelligence unit of the cold-hearted scientist was completely delivered to the CIA.** If it is confounding why most people in higher positions, who act as gangsters have German surnames, here is the reason.

-Paperclip Treason

Dr. Mengele, (later known in America as Dr. Green) and his bone-chilling crimes against humanity in America are the fruit of this special "Paperclip Treason" of the CIA, and that's why since then, **the CIA is a un-American, anti-people and subversive unit which has formed a Fourth Reich government in its core.**

MKUltra trains sex slaves through "Project Monarch." These slave subjects are used, sold, bought, exchanged, loaned in order to entrap, blackmail, compromise, recruit, coerce and monitor the targets. They are human-robot sex slave spies.

Hefner and the CIA used sex as a weapon. Legalizing the use of drugs and encouraging pornography as an "art," will hand in hand, create the sex culture as quite common behavior. What is in the porn industry that can be considered as art? The modern usage of the word "art" is just disturbing. **Modern art has become a cover-up and an excuse to display openly, publicly and freely the symbols that in no other way can be presented in society. These symbols act as a language code. A language code in which perverts and pedophiles recognize each other.**

-Operation Porn

In 1972, nine out of 10 college male students had a Playboy magazine hidden under their bed. That was the way they came to know sex. That was the only tool secretly printing new ideas in their mind. *"What kind of a man should I be? What alternative ways are out there to turn me on?"* That was where men started not to be totally satisfied with the marriage. They wanted MORE…

That is where porn indoctrination or as I call it, "operation porn" began.

In 1976, Playboy magazine's cover feathered Brook Shields, completely naked when she was just ten and Eva Ionesco at the age of eleven.

The playboy bunny was deep into the MKUltra hole, reinforcing dissociative trauma on them. So many celebrities and people coming out of this project have numbers or butterflies tattoed on their body which is associated with the Monarch project. Some of them have even their program tattooed on their body. When looking at celebrities' pictures, look for numbers and butterflies. **The language of symbols is the way they communicate and proof of loyalty. It is hard to believe, but we are not living in our countries, we are living in corporations belonged to oligarchs, technocrats and colonizers, and they play their own rules regardless of our acceptance or not. The price of going high is loyalty.**

Regarding the case of Cosby, Dr. Mengele; the angel of death, has been stationed in U.S secure naval facility hospital in Argentina from 1956-1960 and he was engaged in his usual eugenics and torture programs. Bill Cosby was placed at the same station at the same time. It is highly thinkable that Cosby either participated in torture-interrogating sessions with Mengele or he could himself have been programmed, implanted and trained for the CIA which can be an explanation for his amnesia and his close friendship with Hefner. When he says he doesn't remember, he really doesn't remember, and his brain could have been switched off at some point remotely to prevent any disclosure.

In May 1969, Playboy magazine interviewed Bill Cosby. This is a selected part of the interview.

Playboy: *"How did you feel about playing and, in a real sense, glamorizing a CIA agent?"*

Cosby: *"Well, actually, the CIA never let us say we were CIA agents."*

Playboy: *"But, in effect, you were, weren't you?"*

Cosby: *"In effect, yes. But the important thing to me, man, was to get a black face on the screen and let him be a hero. I would have done it regardless of what the CIA's image was at the time--and the series was conceived and drawn up well before the CIA got to be heavy. I was very, very happy--forget the CIA--that a black man was able to be on an equal basis with the show's white hero."*

-Sadistic porn

Pornography is a platform for human exploitation and satanic indoctrination. I became frustrated and exhausted after noticing all my criminal suspects, their financial transactions, background, and bloodline; conjoin the same rings of satanic rituals. It is not clever to say "I don't believe in satanic rituals, so they don't exist." We don't believe, but Satanists do, and they admit doing it so there should be something there. Sometimes we reach a conclusion step by step from bottom to the top and believe something. Other times, it is the reverse thing from top to bottom that makes people believe. If all these people believe an entity called Satan and offer him sacrifices and hold rituals where they insult, vomit, and piss on Jesus's image and burn the cross for centuries, the logic is: They must believe in Jesus and fear him; otherwise, there is no reason for evil worshipers to kill people and serve an Anti-Jesus entity called Satan, Lucifer, Lord of light or whatever crap they want to call it. In any case, they hold these rituals, and they believe it, so our opinion about Satan is irrelevant.

-Who funded Playboy?

During his years as a psychology student, Hugh Hefner learned about the Kinsey report, which later, respected Psychologist Dr. Judith Reisman, through her in-depth research proved to be fakery. However, Hefner took his idea of normalizing the sex act, bringing it outside of marriage and separating love from sex from the Kinsey report.

-The Kinsey Case

Dr. Alfred Kinsey's crazy pedophile book titled: *"Sexual Behavior in the Human Male"* pioneered modern pedophiles and perverts, who in recent years, have been advocating to bundle pedophilia as a sexual "preference" and downgrading the vileness by calling it "pedosexuality" like any other sexuality. According to this filthy book, babies are sexual from birth, and adults having sex with them will not harm them. **He featured five-time tables of sexually raped and abused babies at the age of two months** and as disgusting as it can be, claimed that their shriek and wail are their "orgasms." To prove this, he registered the frequency of these "orgasmic sounds," on those timetables. It is not clear that Kinsey and his pedophile group either abused 2,000 infants and children and/or relied on data obtained from abused infants and children in Nazi concentration camps but what matters is, to register "the frequency" of orgasms, they should have been abused on a time-based repetition program.

According to Dr. Reisman's book *"crimes and consequences,"* the disturbed piece of a creature known as scientist Kinsey, *"seduced his male students in the University of Indiana and forced his wife and associates to perform in homemade pornographic films."*

Just writing about two-month babies and their innocent screams shakes my entire being.

David Inhuman Rockefeller financed the Kinsey report and Kinsey's pedophile book.

This was one of the investments which the Rockefeller Foundation was so proud of it, and it should tell you all about the Rockefellers and the Cabal. Shortly Later, David Rockefeller sponsored Margaret Sanger's abortion agenda which we previously explained in the "Planned Parenthood" section.

-Pedo-Mania becomes science

So this was how through Rockefeller's sponsorship, the crazy child molesting instructions, pedophilia, and psychotic culture of sexualizing children became a blueprint for mentally ill people. Hugh Hefner's Playboy Empire acted as a catalyzer to plant and promote the idea of liberating and sexualizing teenagers and grooming them for sexual exploitation. The overnight parties to "extract sex from love" and the "liberating rituals" causing unwanted pregnancies needed an organization to abort the babies and that organization was Planned Parenthood.

-Sexology or Rapology?

It's so sad to see the disturbed scientist's book allegedly teaching "how to rape and torture the two-month-old babies" is now taught in the Western world's higher education through the Department of Psychology.

Pornography industry, the fruit of Hefner, Rockefeller, the CIA, and The Vatican, is behind the indoctrination of our nations and indoctrinates them into sodomy, mass abortion, transsexuality, and pedophilia. The depraved Justice Ruth Bader Ginsburg, an Associate Justice of the Supreme Court of the United States, while pushing to reduce sentences for sexual crimes, pressured the court to lower the age of consent to twelve. Sexual misconduct became an epidemic as a daily meal and was sold to people as new progressivism, postmodernism, and forms of liberation. **This is the gear oil for the wheels of the crime machine. Pedophilia, Sexual exploitation, mind control, and rituals are the currency of the cabal.**

The Rockefeller gang didn't pay Kinsey just to create an open-minded society to fit their agenda. **Pedophilia is the religion of RING OF THE CABAL. The**

oligarchs are connected through power and pedophilia. Rockefeller found Kinsey as a useful maniac who could use his papers to export the already hidden religion of pedophilia into hundred pages of morphed crap and make it look scientific to uneducated people. How on earth a manual to rape infants can be taught in universities? It makes us think, to whom belongs the education system? Do we not remember how monopolies were formed and who owned what?

Just like the old days, the education system still belongs to the Rockefellers who accepted Bill Gates as their "brother in lies" and now Soros rules their inheritance. Every piece fits perfectly in place.

Obama – North Korea

Obama is counter punching from many sides. He punches through grass-roots, street riots, judicial blocks, public mocking, International counter-appearances, chasing President Trump after each trip and through North Korea. Why North Korea?

-Kim Jung Un?

The setup Rocket Man with his childish smiles, maps, cameras and old worn up generals clapping all the time behind him is just a tool. It could be a joke thinking he runs the stage. That kid is not able to count his ten fingers let alone running a country. Some people believe he is China's barking dog. Each time the Rocket Man attacks, China grabs some more trade advantages, but she stabs the U.S from behind. China plays both sides as long as she can take its desired benefits. China agrees with President Trump on something, and Obama stalks the President right after and visits China to undermine Trump's visit, so this pattern cannot be the complete painting.

Let us look into it from another angle. What is the global agitation after Trump's presidency? The Russian gate? Negative. It agitates on a national level but not worldwide. What is disturbing the world's nations is the possibility of a nuclear war, and this false narrative has been going since the 2016's election. People have a short memory and do not remember how Kim Jung Un's father was threatening the world, and nobody cared. They think the world has not faced such a threat before Trump's presidency and the false conclusion of this blame-causing narrative is that: Trump is the problem; he is not fit for the presidency, and he is putting the world on the verge of a nuclear war.

-Why North Korea?

Who benefits this false narrative? The same people who are benefiting from other counterfeit anecdotes and bias made by fear-stream media. Who is behind all these mobs and agitations? Soros, the CIA and the master of agitation; Barack Obama: the deep state's President.

Why Obama tried to silence South Korea's warnings regarding North Korea and its "considerable" level of ability to make a warhead small enough to place on a missile?

According to the Washington Post's article published on August 8, 2017:

"Defense Intelligence Agency (DIA) has determined North Korea is capable of constructing miniaturized nuclear weapons that could be used as warheads for missiles – possibly ICBMs," which consequently

exploded the bombshell that the DIA actually learned about this in 2013.

-Project ARTICHOKE

It is not a coincidence that the CIA was formed on Sept 18, 1947, and the Democratic People's Republic of Korea was established in North Korea with one year distance, on September 9, 1948. Within this period, the CIA was very interested in the Korean War and monitoring it very carefully. In fact, the unit that later formed the CIA was into brain perversion techniques long before the Korean War.

After the war, in 1951, project BLUEBIRD was renamed as ARTICHOKE, which was almost a version of MKUltra but instead of sex slaves, it created soldiers and assassins and its target was North Korean soldiers. On that date, operation Paperclip was already concluded, and Nazi doctors were already on American soil, working in the CIA.

The focus of this operation was the development of CIA-NAZI mind control and interrogation technics which could be useful in the expansion of the U.S forces in North Korea. Project BLUEBIRD was designed to condition the individual and prevent him from revealing any information to the enemy. The methods included the use of drugs to hypnotize the target and the results should have been enforced by repeating the tortures four times a week. By shifting from BLUEBIRD to ARTICHOKE, the goal has been switched to condition the individual to give false information rather than no information.

-Alice and Wonderland

Since then, North Korea has been a proxy army under full control for decades. It had attained the technology needed to miniaturize a nuclear warhead, and it had missiles armed with nuclear warheads for years, and Obama just knew it. It has been part of the CIA operation to destroy America and minimize the U.S nuclear power when it is most needed. CIA and Obama screwed American people, and while it seems they gave the Rocket Man a pass using its leverage, it's actually the CIA who is running the game. The only hope for North Korea is an upcoming clean-up by Trump administration through the new Director of the CIA which at that point, North Korea will be disarmed or silenced for a while.

New footage of North Korea features an area with postmodern military structures, Hyangsan Hotel in the form of a pyramid with the famous "eye" above it, a 600 meters wide airstrip, and a gigantic underground bunker inside the left corner of the image. North Korea hides bunkers and underground tunnels with Obama-CIA's secrets buried inside.

- Treason was the reason for Obama's Season

Freakish constructions in North Korea seem to be base units, control centers and hideouts for a possible WW3. The smart question here is: If, the United Nations passed the first resolutions to condemn North Korea's nuclear test in 2006 and sanctioned her, then where did all this money come from to build these super modern constructions? **That construction must be the CIA's gateway, and one of the Deep State's bases.** A cantilever to fake an attack and starting their WW3 if necessary. Who would benefit the WW3? Well, we have answered this issue so many times since the beginning of this book. You already know how **"Treason was the reason for Obama's Season."**

Pope Francis

In *"Gods and Beasts – The Nazis and the Occult"*, written by Dusty Sklar in 1977 we read: *"The Nationalist Socialists derived power from one source: ... a fanatical autohypnosis which convinced disciples, succumbing to the totalitarian discipline in the promise of reaching transcendent reality, that they were the new men the age was waiting for for.. ..that they were endowed with secret energy which would enable them to take over Germany and the world. If they were properly prepared, mysteries would be revealed to them which would give them SATANIC POWERS."*

-The first Jesuit Pope

The Nazis, the higher their rank was, the deeper they were into the occult.

Pope Francis is a Jesuit who served 40 years of his life as a Jesuit and led the Jesuits in Argentina from 1973 to 1979 so Pope Francis's history also means the history of Jesuits.

-Cardinal Jorge Mario Bergoglio and Military Junta

What the media doesn't want you to know is that Cardinal Jorge Mario Bergoglio pontificated as "Pope Francis I" was one of the main supporters of Argentina's military dictatorship which came to power in a CIA backed Coup in 1976 where the U.S Secretary of State; Henry Kissinger played the strategic role. Kissinger was the direct connection between the United States and the military Coup known as the "Dirty War" (la "Guerra Sucia" in Spanish). This coup took place through the "military Junta"(military board in English), under General Jorge Rafaele Vielda's leadership, who was the leader of Guerilla's against Isabel Perón; the President of Argentina.

The Coup has led to the arrest, imprisonment, torture, and disappearance of Catholic priests who were opposed to Argentina's military coup. The Guerillas, who were a version of Nicaragua's Guerillas, captured all pregnant women, imprisoned them until labor, removed their babies after deliverance, **killed the mothers and gave the infants to the Military Junta** to raise them as Guerilla soldiers. The President of the United States at the time was Gerald Ford, and his Vice President was Nelson Rockefeller.

In May 1976, two priests; Francisco Jalics and Orlando Yorio, were kidnapped by death squads. After five months of torture, they were released in August the same year. But then six other people of their group and gradually, thousands of opponents were disappeared. The CIA's "Operation Condor" was the force and the brain behind the torture, assassination, and disappearance of Military Junta's opponents in Argentina.

How can a Catholic Cardinal have anything to do with this? The rise of Cardinal Jorge Mario Bergoglio in Argentina as head of the Catholic Church, according to "The International Tribunal into Crimes of Church and State" (ITCCS) of Brussels is suspected to be the agreement between Cardinal Bergoglio and the Military Junta to traffic the children from orphanages.

Pope Francis's predecessors in the Vatican were so connected to Nazis that even famous American liberal comedians congratulated the Catholics for finally selecting a non-Nazi Pope. Catholics felt great relief when Pope Francis was elected but what people didn't know was that the President of Argentina Juan Perón (Isabel Perón's husband) was a Nazi sympathizer, and although Argentina was neutral during the war, it was a haven for Nazi's dinner parties during the war, and fleeing Nazis after the war.

By the end of the war, Pope Francis was just nine. During his adulthood, he worked as a "chemical technologist" and a nightclub bodyguard in Buenos Aires. He began his practice of becoming a priest in 1969.

-The Vatican Billions

Avro Manhattan, the philosopher, and author of "The Vatican Billions," in his book writes:

"The Catholic Church is the biggest financial power in the world. The net wealth of catholic church surpasses any other single institution, corporation, bank, giant trust, government or state of the whole planet."

"The pope, as the visible ruler of this immense amassment of wealth, is consequently the richest individual of the twentieth century. No one can realistically assess how much he is worth in terms of billions of dollars."

"Jesus was the poorest of the poor. Roman Catholicism, which claims to be His church, is the richest of the rich, the wealthiest institution on earth. How come, that such an institution, ruling in the name of this same itinerant preacher, whose want was such that he had not even a pillow upon which to rest his head, is now so top-heavy with riches that she can rival - indeed, that she can put to shame - the combined might of the most redoubtable financial trusts, of the most potent industrial super-giants, and of the most prosperous global corporation of the world?

"The Vatican has large investments with the Rothschild's of Britain, France, and America, with the Hambros Bank, with the Credit Suisse in London and Zurich. In the United States, it has large investments with the Morgan Bank, the Chase-Manhattan Bank, and the First National Bank of New York, the BankersTrust Company, and others.

"The Vatican has billions of shares in the most powerful international corporations such as Gulf Oil, Shell, General Motors, Bethlehem Steel, General Electric, International Business Machines, T.W.A., etc."

-Pope Francis is the first Jesuit Pope.

Jesuits are more defined as an avenger military/religious group than just a religious one. Most CIA directors and military intelligence operatives were and are Jesuits.

"I learned much from the Order of the Jesuits," said Hitler… *"Until now, there has never been anything more grandiose, on the earth, than the hierarchical organization of the Catholic Church*

(Referring to Jesuits). I transferred much of this organization into my own party… I am going to let you in on a secret… I am founding an Order… In my "Burgs" of the Order, we will raise up a youth which

will make the world tremble… " After a pause: *"I can't*
say anymore."

Adolf Hitler, 1939, recorded speech by Hermann Rauschning,
former national-socialist chief of the Danzig government

- "Nazi-Jesuit-CIA" Alliance

Jesuits believe in the military hierarchy. The key is
Obedience, not the truth. For Jesuits *"some lies are as*
necessary as bread" as the famous Jesuit writer, Joseph
Goebbels said.

The order of Jesuits and its history demands an entire
book and is so extensive that cannot be brought up here
in a few lines. I have to try hard to summarize centuries
into a few lines. Most people I named in this book,
especially those involved in rituals and secret activities
are Jesuits but what I can say here is that a Nazi-Jesuit
connection is incontrovertible and the same is correct for
a Nazi-Jesuit-CIA connection. For example, William
Joseph Donovan, known as "Wild Bill" was a dedicated
Jesuit and an elite Vatican personage. He was the leader
of the CIA'S Office of Strategic Services (OSS), the

same office that we have previously explained how they recruited Nazi scientists in America.

Stephen Birmingham, author of Real Lace, in his book writes:

"Jesuit trained, Jon Favreau is Barack Obama's chief speechwriter. Obama's Senior Military and Foreign Policy Advisor, Maj. Gen. J. Scott Gration was Jesuit-trained. Obama's National Security Adviser is James L. Jones, who was trained by Jesuits at Georgetown University. Jones is a retired four-star general and formerly served as Supreme Allied Commander Europe (2003-2006). Until a few days ago, Jones was on the board of directors of Boeing, Obama's Deputy Communications Director, Dan Pfeiffer, was Jesuit-trained. Barack Obama's CIA pick of Leon Panetta is Jesuit trained. Barack Obama administration has as many ties to the Vatican as the previous administration had.

"Bush 41 was the Director of the CIA during the 1970's. He was also awarded the Knight of Malta award of Savoy. He was in WWII; he was a Bonesmen. George H.

W. Bush is famous especially for calling for the existence of the new world order in 1990 during his State of the Union Address. He was awarded the Grand Cross of the Order of the Bath One of his sons named Jeb Bush is also a member of the Knights of Columbus

"The Bush family, the Bin Ladens, and Bandar all worked together in business endeavors for decades."

You read right. The Bin Laden family is the same "Bin 9/11 Laden's" relatives, and Bandar is the same Prince Al-Bandar recently purged in Saudi Arabia.

This is part of the Jesuit oath. Judge yourself if this oath has anything to do with Jesus:

"I furthermore promise and declare that I will, when opportunity present, make and wage relentless war, secretly or openly, against all heretics, Protestants, and Liberals, as I am directed to do, to extirpate and exterminate them from the face of the whole earth; and that I will spare neither age, sex or condition; and that I will hang, waste, boil, flay, strangle and bury alive these infamous heretics, rip up the stomachs and wombs of their women and crush their infants' heads against the

walls, in order to annihilate forever their execrable race. That when the same cannot be done openly, I will secretly use the poisoned cup, the strangulating cord, the steel of the poniard or the leaden bullet, regardless of the honor, rank, dignity, or authority of the person or people, whatever may be their condition in life, either public or private, as I at any time may be directed so to do by any agent of the Pope or Superior of the Brotherhood of the Holy Faith, of the Society of Jesus"

When a war is going to occur, The Vatican has to confirm it. Why? Because wars cost.

-Masons congratulate Pope Francis

Very strangely, On March 14, 2013, the day after the Pope's inauguration, the Italian Grandmaster of Freemasonry Gustavo Raffi who has never accepted any Pope, made an announcement saying:

"With Pope Francis, nothing will be as it was before. It is a clear choice of fraternity for a Church of dialogue, which is not contaminated by the logic and temptations of temporal power.

A man of the poor far away from the Curia. Fraternity and the desire to dialogue were his first concrete words. Perhaps nothing in the Church will be as it was before. Our hope is that the pontificate of Francis, the Pope who 'comes from the end of the world' can mark the return to the Church-Word instead of the Church-Institution, promoting an open dialogue with the contemporary world, with believers and non-believers, following the springtime of Vatican II."

The Freemason Grand Lodge of Argentina also officially welcomed the election of Pope Francis. In a speech, Argentinian Grand Master Angel Jorge Clavero said:

"The Grand Lodge of Free and Accepted Masons, an institution rooted in our country since 1857, salutes the naming of our co-patriot Cardinal Jorge Bergoglio as Pope Francis. A man of austere life consecrated to his devotions, the designation of the new pontiff of the Catholic Church supposes a great recognition of the Argentine Nation...In the name of all, and the Grand

Lodge of Argentina greets our co-patriot Cardinal who just received such a high world distinction."

The Philippine Freemason Lodge was the next one to greet him.

But why Freemasonry Lodges known as "The Synagogue of Satan" accept a Catholic Pope with Open arms and say: *"nothing in the Church will be <u>as it was before</u>"?*

- The final destruction of Catholicism

John Vennari, in his book "The Permanent Instruction of the Alta Vendita" written in December 1999, reveals why. He extracts the old documents that Pope Gregory XVI; one of the most anti- Freemason Popes was able to seize from the Masonic lodge known as "Alta Vendita." The documents contain the secret goals of the Jesuits. You already read part of their oath. Now, this is their "goal" which we read in "Alta Vendita":

"Our ultimate end is that of...the final destruction of Catholicism, and even of the Christian idea ... The Pope, whoever he is, will never come to the secret societies; it is up to the secret societies to take the first step toward the Church, with the aim of conquering both of them. The task that we are going to undertake is not the work of a day, or of a month, or of a year; it may last several years, perhaps a century; but in our ranks, the soldier dies, and struggle goes on ... What we must ask for, what we should look for and wait for, as the Jews wait for the Messiah, is a Pope according to our needs...You will contrive for yourselves, at little cost, a reputation as good Catholics and pure patriots. This reputation will put access to our doctrines into the midst of the young clergy, as well as deeply into the monasteries. In a few years, by the force of things, this young clergy will have overrun all the functions; they will form the sovereign's council, they will be called to choose a Pontiff who should reign ..."

Do these goals have anything in common with Jesus's goals? As I said so many times, these people would crucify Jesus just as the Romans did.

What you read below is the news report released by Dr. Kevin Annett from "The International Tribunal into Crimes of Church and State" (ITCCS) of Brussels which are quoted exactly as they are written:

"With allegations later which led to charges in court of Brussels, Pope Francis's fast ascension to head the Argentina Catholic Church was suspected to be a result of an agreement between Pope Francis and the Junta military to traffic children from Catholic orphanages."
Archive, March 23, 2006,

Date: Feb 26 2014,

"Today Catholic Pope Francis Bergoglio was named as the chief defendant in a child trafficking case involving Catholic orphans. Pope Francis will be asked to defend his role in child trafficking during Argentine's 1970s Junta Dirty War. This case of orphaned children from missing political prisoners was set for trial on March 31 2014 in a Brussels international court."

....

According to a 2005 Los Angeles Times article: " the now-Catholic Pope Francis was accused by a human rights group of trafficking babies, plus helping to kidnap opponents of Argentine's military Junta during the Dirty War. Lawyers filing the 2005 complaint represented the Plaza de Mayo human rights."

"A witness has agreed to come out of hiding in Spain to testify against Pope Francis. The Argentine civil servant took extensive notes of meetings between the now-Pope Francis and Junta military officials. The witness wasn't alone in his accusations against Pope Francis."

…………………………—   *end   of quote…………………*

Argentine Cardinal Named in Kidnap Lawsuit

April 17, 2005 | From Associated Press

VATICAN CITY — A human rights lawyer has filed a criminal complaint against an Argentine cardinal mentioned as a possible contender to become pope, accusing him of involvement in the 1976 kidnappings of two priests.

Cardinal Jorge Mario Bergoglio's spokesman Saturday called the allegation "old slander."

The complaint filed in a court in the Argentine capital on Friday accused Bergoglio, the archbishop of Buenos Aires, of involvement in the abduction of two Jesuit priests by the military dictatorship, reported the newspaper Clarín. The complaint does not specify the nature of Bergoglio's alleged involvement.

Under Argentine law, an accusation can be filed with a very low threshold of evidence. A court then decides if there is cause to investigate and file charges.

The accusations against Bergoglio, 68, are detailed in a recent book by Argentine journalist Horacio Verbitsky.

In May 1976, priests Orlando Yorio and Francisco Jalics were kidnapped by the navy. They surfaced five months later, drugged and seminude, in a field.

At the time, Bergoglio was the superior in the Society of Jesus in Argentina.

Before deliberating a full background-check on Pope Francis, let's take a step back and look into Pope Benedict's history and reputation. Pope Benedict resigned, and within the realm of the Catholic Church, that is peculiar. It is an alarming situation odd enough to require an investigation. The dark reason that the mainstream media didn't tell you is the key to be vigilant and keep an eye on Pope Francis.

-Why did Pope Benedict or Mr. Joseph Ratzinger, resign?

Following are the rest of the news reports released by Dr. Kevin Annett from"International Tribunal into Crimes of Church and State," regarding the subject matter:

"Catholic Pope Benedict's Feb. 2013 guilty verdict came after months of deliberation by 36 jury members and six international judges on 150 cases surrounding over 50,000 missing Canadian native children.

"The international jury found that native children were being raped, tortured and murdered in residential schools across Canada – the majority of which were

Catholic-run institutions. The 80 schools were jointly owned by the Canadian government, Queen Elizabeth and the Catholic, Anglican and United Church of Canada."

"The Feb. 2013 international court also found Queen Elizabeth guilty for the October 10, 1964, disappearance of ten children from Kamloops Residential School in British Columbia. Parents of the missing children were prevented by the Canadian government from taking their case to trial – the reason for the 2013 international court."

"A present day victim of the Catholic Church was Jamaican and British Soldier Vivian Cunningham. He remained drugged in the St. George's Hospital in Stafford England for asking questions about Queen Elizabeth's arrest warrant. The 2013 ICLCJ court found Queen Elizabeth and Prince Phillip guilty of kidnapping on Oct. 10, 1964, ten native children from the Catholic-owned Kamloops residential school in British Columbia Canada. British citizen David Compan and his wife were accosted, drugged, arrested and incarcerated without charges in the London Park Royal Mental Health Center. Compan's sin? He posted Queen

Elizabeth's arrest warrant on a Catholic Church in London. Compan's arrest was captured in this video."

(My note: here is the arrest warrant which David Compan posted in London's Catholic Church but was not mentioned in the original report above. *"Today Queen Elizabeth and UK Prime Minister David Cameron were issued arrest warrants. The two were charged with sexual crimes against children as part of an international pedophile ring."*

Rest of the document:

"We have enough evidence to prosecute and hold both the <u>Prime Minister and Queen of England.</u>"(Said ex-Royal Military Policeman Matt Taylor.")

-"The Roman Catholic Church has "systematically" protected predator priests, allowing "tens of thousands" of children to be abused, a United Nations committee reported directly after Pope Francis became pontiff.

The International Common Law Court of Justice (ICLCJ) court case in Brussels filed in 2014, charging Pope Francis and other global elites for Crimes against Humanity was expected to extend for over a year.

Three witnesses to the kidnapping died of mysterious causes prior to trial. One was William Combes, age twelve at the time. He stated in his video testimony, "It was strange because we had to kiss the Queen's boots which were white with laces. Seven boys and three girl's ages six through 14 left with Queen Elizabeth and Prince Phillip. We never heard or seen them after that day, even when we got older."

The announcement today to take Pope Francis to trial was made by Kevin Annett of the International Tribunal into Crimes of Church and State. It was done on the first anniversary of the 25 Feb. 2013 conviction of former Pope Benedict and 29 other global elites including Queen Elizabeth, for their Crimes against Humanity."

(My personal note; the guilty verdict of Pope Benedict announced on Feb 23, 2013. <u>Pope Benedict who knew about the coming verdict, first announced his resignation decision on Feb 11, 2013, and officially resigned on Feb 28, 2013, two days after the verdict</u>)

-What witnesses say

A summary of what is going on here:

1- A severe lawsuit has been filed against Pope Benedict related to child trafficking, kidnapping and sacrificing rituals which literally and through testimonies connects Pope Benedict acts to Queen Elizabeth and Prince Philippe. According to the document, a silent prosecution led to a guilty verdict. Although these people of the "Twilight Zone" are still free and above the law, Pope Benedict had to resign.

2- Separately, there has been another trial against Pope Francis regarding crimes in Argentina. The accusations included kidnap, murder, and child trafficking after the 1978's Coup and during "Military Junta" and the trial is still going on with no final result.

Reports below are related to the matter, issued by Kevin D. Annett on "The International Common Law Court of Justice of Brussels" ICLCJ reports in conjunction with International "Tribunal Court into Crimes of Church and the State" ITCCS Central Office of Brussels.

25 April 2013:

"In the light of the Common Law Court indictment and sentencing of the Crown of England, Canada and its churches for Crimes against Humanity on February 25, 2013 – a verdict based partly on the evidence acquired at the Mush Hole excavations in 2011 – Canada, the Crown and its police forces have lost any authority to prevent such a continued excavation on the grounds of the Mohawk Institute in Brantford.

Those indicted people who have actively subverted the Mush Hole dig, including the Prime Minister of Canada, the Queen of England, the Archbishop of Canterbury, and Anglican Bishops Fred Hiltz, Bruce Howe and Bob Bennett, in fact face immediate arrest under outstanding Citizen Arrest Warrants for their complicity in obstructing justice."

"A witness claimed they saw former Popes Joseph Ratzinger (Pope Benedict) and John Paul II participate in Vatican satanic cult rituals known as the Ninth Circle, that torture and murder children" George Dufort of a Brussels international court announced yesterday. *"According to a deposition filed in court last*

week by a former member of the Ninth Circle, the cult practices at Catholic cathedrals and a forest grove in France."

"That makes three eyewitnesses who say former Pope Joseph Ratzinger (Benedict) was present during ritual torture and murder of children as part of a cult known as the Ninth Circle" Kevin Annett of the ITCCS confirmed today in our phone interview. "Murder rituals evidently took place in 1987 and 2002 at locations in France and Holland."

Last week the Brussels Court received Vatican documents dated Dec 25,1967 that say before each new pope assumes office it's mandatory that they participate in Ninth Circle rites. The documents referred to ceremonial murder of newborn children and consumption of their blood in rites referred to as "The Magisterial Privilege."

"Three days ago Francesco Zanardi of the ITCCS affiliate Rete L'Abuso in Savona, Italy said, "Ratzinger retains power at the Vatican. We know from several Cardinals that Pope Francis is a caretaker figurehead who is not actually the Pope. It's all been a huge deception. Francis doesn't wear the papal ring and lives in a convent in Rome, not in the Vatican. He is given no

official security and wanders about like a private individual. He makes policy statements which the Curia of Cardinals then disavows, saying Francis doesn't reflect church doctrine. The top appointments have been Germans or those connected to Ratzinger who continues to speak to reporters like he's still the Pope."

According to witnesses testifying at the international court trial, the former Pope Ratzinger has been a member of Ninth Circle, also known as the Corona Novem or Crown, since at least 1962.

"I saw Pope Emeritus Joseph Ratzinger murder a little girl" stated another witness on Oct. 28 2013. "It was at a French chateau in the fall of 1987. It was ugly, horrible and didn't happen just once. Ratzinger, Dutch Cardinal Alfrink and Prince Bernhard were some of the more prominent men who took part."

The allegations confirmed what Dutch therapist and witness Toos Nijenhuis told Annett a few months prior. Toos claimed that as a child she also was forced to witness child murders that involved Ratzinger, Alfrink and Bernhard.(author's personal note: Bernhard refers to Prince Bernhard of the Netherlands, father of Queen Beatrice of the Netherlands, a known Fomer SS Nazi and the founder of Bilderberg group."

-"*Two child abuse survivors reported attending child murder rites in the catacombs beneath the Vatican. At the tender age of 12 "Svali" of San Diego County said she was taken into the catacombs beneath the Vatican to witness the sacrifice of a 3-4 year-old drugged boy. In this video her interviewer responded that 24 years prior, a "Maria" also claimed to have witnessed a satanic murder rite in the Vatican Catacombs.*"

"*If the international court finds the popes and Vatican guilty of child exploitation, it might explain why the Vatican has made such an effort to cover up Catholic priest and nun child abuse. As of Nov 12 2013 and with an estimated 10 per cent of victims reporting, there were a documented 10,077,574 survivors of Catholic abuse across the globe. With Catholic authorities refusing to cooperate with investigations and settling a few cases out of court, only a handful of Catholic Church perpetrators have seen the inside of a jail cell.*

"*It's tragic that children are abused by those who should have their trust. Abuse is such a betrayal*" said Tim Lennon of the US Survivors Network of those Abused by Priests (SNAP). "*The high and mighty re-abuse by their denials, delaying tactics, ignorance and culpable criminal cover-ups. We can raise our voice and write letters to the editors, write comments on news stories and support survivors who speak out."*

"The new evidence for the Brussels court has been translated from Latin and entered into case records of the Citizen Prosecutors Office.

The international court convenes March 31 to consider Vatican international child trafficking charges against the present Catholic Pope Francis, Jesuit Superior General Aldolfo Pachon, Archbishop of Canterbury Justin Welby and former Pope Joseph Ratzinger.

"Under Canadian law no one has been investigated, charged or tried for the disappearance or murder of 50,000 missing Canadian native children. The government of Canada, British Crown and Catholic, United and Anglican Church officials who ran 80 native residential schools wherein hide at least 32 unmarked child mass grave sites, have been legally absolved of all responsibility. Kevin Annett of the International Tribunal into Crimes of Church and State, which prosecuted in behalf of the childrens' families in the Brussels International Common Law Court of Justice, has been refused numerous requests for excavation of the child mass grave sites."

"Since 2011 over 60 have testified before the ICLCJ Court. Eyewitnesses to murder claimed that this mass genocide of children continued today via the global elite Ninth Circle Satanic Child Sacrifice Cult. Ninth Circle members were said to include Popes Ratzinger and Francis, Queen Elizabeth, Prince Philip, Canadian Prime Minister Stephen Harper and at least 35 other prominent global leaders."

"This article was dedicated to the memory of those 50,000 missing children and to unknown children presently undergoing Ninth Circle Cult torture. The perpetrators live elite lives free of responsibility for their ongoing crimes. Our prayers were with these innocent children, and with ourselves if we allowed this Child Holocaust by our global leaders to continue."

"A child sacrifice scheduled for August 15 by the politically influential members of the Ninth Circle Satanic Child Sacrifice Cult has been relocated from Reine du Monde Cathedral in Montreal Canada to McGill University according to informants of a ICLCJ Court news release. To stop these child sacrificial rituals, a legal entity of the Court has been investigating around an underground experimental facility on the grounds of McGill University and sub-basement crypts

of the Reine du Monde Cathedral in Montreal Canada and Pro Cathedral in Dublin Ireland. "A highly placed informant notified our Court Command that the Montreal cult gathering had been relocated to McGill University in Montreal."

Informants say a second child sacrifice was scheduled for Aug. 15 at the Dublin Cathedral crypt. The Court press release stated they would "detain participants for public trial, employing whatever force is required."

"It was alleged that the Ndrangheta Criminal Syndicate regularly worked with police, Vatican and Catholic orphanages in Montreal and Dublin to provide children for torture and killing in these monthly blood sacrifice rituals. The ITCCS which has been prosecuting the cases against Ninth Circle Satanic Cult members called for Aug. 15 protests at McGill University, Reine du Monde Cathedral,andPro Cathedral."

"Since 2011 six judges and 28 jury members of the ICLCJ Court have been litigating the Ninth Circle Satanic Cult, members of which were prominent global elites. In Aug 2014 Pope Francis was found guilty of child trafficking, Pope Ratzinger resigned after his 2013 guilty verdict for Crimes against Humanity and Queen Elizabeth and Prince Phillip were issued arrest

warrants for their guilty verdicts in the 1964 disappearance of ten children from the British Columbia Kamloops Native Residential School in Canada."

"Popes Francis and Ratzinger, plus Queen Elizabeth have all been named by eyewitness testifying before the ICLCJ Court as having killed and raped children in Ninth Circle Satanic Cult human sacrifice ceremonies. Over 60 eyewitnesses from several different countries have testified, with more contacting the Court each week."

"McGill University in Montreal where the child sacrifice was rescheduled had a history of torturing children in satanic-related mind control experiments. To develop "Super Spies," the USA's CIA created the MKULTRA mind control program. Funded by the Rockefeller Foundation, the president of the Canadian, American and World Psychiatric Associations D. Ewen Cameron, began torturing children in an MKULTRA program at McGill University in the early 1950s. By 1964 US Congressional inquiries supposedly ended MKULTRA after a successful lawsuit against Cameron and McGill University by mind control survivor Linda MacDonald."

"Children could still be subjected to this CIA torture program. In this video CIA mind control survivors Christine Nicola and Claudia Mullen, plus Therapist Valerie Wolf testified before a 1995 President's Committee on Human Radiation Experiments. They claimed that as a child, along with other children and until at least 1984, they were regularly sexually, physically and emotionally abused by government employees working in CIA mind control.

In the first fifty comments of this petition to Congress for an investigation of the CIA mind control of children, survivors claimed that even today children were being sexually, physically and emotionally abused by government employees doing mind control experiments. To read those comments click here: http://www.change.org/petitions/us-congress-survivors-request-investigation-cia-mind-control-of-children"

"During the ICLCJ trials it was revealed that the CIA mind control program not only abused and murdered some of the 50,000 Canadian missing native children, but the perpetrators were members of the Ninth Circle Satanic Cult. According to informants, relocation of the upcoming August 15 Ninth Circle child sacrifice in Montreal was prompted by a prominent US billionaire

businessman, local Catholic Archbishop Christian Lepine and corporate officials of the Cargill Corporation. "There has been no evidence that another Ninth Circle Cult in Dublin has moved their child sacrifice scheduled for August 15 from its Pro Cathedral venue. The Ireland cult is under the sponsorship of Catholic Archbishop Dermot Martin."

"Informants have alleged that the two Catholic child sacrifice networks held regular monthly new moon child torture and killing sessions in Montreal and Dublin. The Ninth Circle Satanic Cult was also believed to operate at several locations including forest groves in the US, France, UK, Australia, Brussels and Zwolle, Holland. In this video, Holland therapist and Satanic Ritual Abuse survivor Toos Nijenhuis talked about her child sacrifice experiences."

"As a child Nijenhuis' life was eerily like that of CIA mind control survivor Jenny Hill. In this video, Hill described how as a six-year-old, she was made to watch the human sacrifice of another six-year-old child. The satanic ceremony took place on June 21, 1965, Summer Solstice in Garden Grove California. Hill's torture was overseen by a man later described as Dr. Green." Videos available in the bibliography, electronic section.)

"After World War II the CIA imported into the US and Canada, several of Hitler's mind control experts including the man known as Dr. Green. Children as young as infants were said to be subjected to sexual abuse, electroshock and other tortures in MKULTRA's 149 sub-projects and 33 related programs. According to survivors, this mind control program doing illegal human experimentation on children functioned at 80 US and Canadian institutions including McGill University in Canada.

Dr. Green headed the CIA program according to mind control survivor Christina Nicola. Nicola's testimony was given in this video of the 1995 Congressional committee which was investigating the CIA experiments. Congress voted not to release results to the public."

"In her biography "Twenty Two Faces," Hill described Green in the same way Satanic Ritual Abuse survivors of Dr. Corydon Hammond's eight-year SRA study described him. See Hammond's "Greenbaum Speech" at a Washington D.C. psychiatric conference here.

The reach of the Ninth Circle Satanic Child Sacrifice Cult appeared to extend worldwide. There have been

Catholic child mass grave sites found in Ireland, Spain,and Canada. The grounds were believed to contain bodies of over 350,800 missing children. Most have been refused excavation by the Catholic Church and respective governments."

"The ITCCS press release advised caution for people wishing to protest the Ninth Circle Satanic Cult child sacrifice ceremonies in Canada and Ireland. "Untrained supporters of our actions during the day and evening of August 15 are advised for their own safety, not to intervene in our operations, but to hold public information vigilant at McGill University, outside the Reine du Monde Cathedral in Montreal Canada and Pro Cathedral in Dublin Ireland."

****

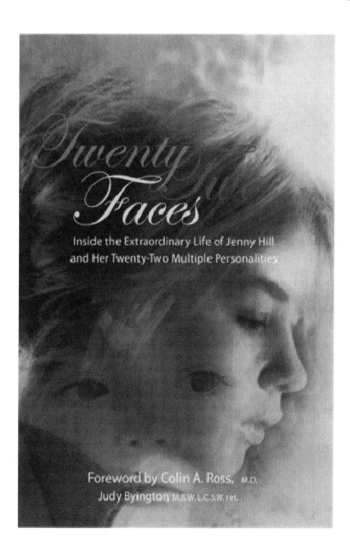

-The Angel of Death

We have fully described project Paperclip and MKUltra project Monarch in this chapter. Paperclip was a CIA

Intelligence operation in which the cruelest Nazi scientists have been brought into the United States and worked for the CIA to operate the MKUltra Project Monarch.

Project Monarch used trauma-based mind control technics including brain surgeries, electrodes, and extreme torture to split multiple personalities and create human-robot spies programmed to be used in different CIA operations. These scientists before coming to America, have committed the most horrific eugenicist crimes ever happened in history such as:

(Warning

Graphic

Please read the underlined section below with caution.)

Leaving subjects out to die in the snow to determine the result of extreme cold on human bodies; melting the subject with heat to measure the effect of extreme heat on human anatomy; expel brain parts of a twin to see the reaction of the sibling; direct injection of acid into their eyes with no anesthesia to see if the color of the iris can be changed; standing on the stomach of pregnant women and ejecting the infant by cutting the stomach to see the fetus's live reaction and etc.

.....................(End of the underlined section).....................

Those sent to gas chambers were already walking dead survivors of these crimes with their bodies torn apart after outliving the torture.

Dr. Joseph Mengele or "the angel of death," born in Bavaria, Germany, and a specialist in "Genetics and Eugenics" is the same "Dr. Green" in America whom several witnesses were talking about. Reports say the name Dr. Green has also been used by the infamous Dr. Kinsey.

Mengele was obsessed with twins. He loved to experiment on one twin and compare the results with the other one. The Nazis were famous to be obsessed with twins. Mengele murdered 3000 twins. He, who had to flee Nazi's safe haven in Argentina after the war, was declared dead by a stroke before he moves to the United States and becomes Dr. Green under the CIA cover-up.

Left: Dr. Joseph Mengele in 1956. Center: Arthur Rudolph in 1990, he was a rocket scientist for Nazi Germany and NASA. Right: John Demjanjuk in 2006. Pictured appeared in NY Times Nov 13, 2010

This article written by Eric Lichtblau. and appeared in the New York Times on Nov 13, 2010, says:

"A secret history of the United States government's Nazi-hunting operation concludes that American intelligence officials created a "safe haven" in the United States for Nazis and their collaborators after World War II, and it details decades of clashes, often hidden, with other nations over war criminals here and abroad."

"The 600-page report, which the Justice Department has tried to keep secret for four years, provides new

evidence about more than two dozen of the most notorious Nazi cases of the last three decades.

It describes the government's posthumous pursuit of Dr. Joseph Mengele, the so-called Angel of Death at Auschwitz, part of whose scalp was kept in a Justice Department official's drawer; the vigilante killing of a former Waffen SS soldier in New Jersey; and the government's mistaken identification of the Treblinka concentration camp guard known as Ivan the Terrible."

-RING OF THE CABAL infiltrates everywhere

I found an interesting and very revealing lecture. The lecture is presented by Dr. C. Hammond, a very high profile psychologist specialized in trauma therapy. What comes below, is a brief explanation of which methods and mind control tools the Green programming by Nazi scientist Dr. Green has operated in America. After all, perhaps we now understand why and how the criminal network of child trafficking works. **Child trafficking cannot be separated from torture, pedophilia, murder, and cannibalism** so next time you hear the phrase "child trafficking" do not just imagine brothels, easy killing and selling organs. **What you read in the underlined section above is what happens to the kidnapped children.** We may be asking what is the relation between a dead Dr. Green and today's kidnappings.

The group above working for the CIA, armed with MKUltra and mind programming did not die. The handlers/enablers are replaced, but their dynasties have just been reinforced, and their network has become colossal. New technologies made the experiments super scary. Their massive connections had a mind-blowing growth and as we read above, include lawmakers, social agents, teachers, schools' administers, child protecting institutes and programs, orphanages, daycares, judges, congressmen, the police, courier, hospitals, doctors and whomever we think is there to help can be secretly connected. This is not fearmongering but a statement of facts according to the court's reports above. The CIA has become the silencing arm of the "Royal Papal Banking Cabal" and their dependence on each other has only been duplicated due to the depth of the sinkhole of the crimes and the weaponized blackmail gadget.

Just a few of these children have been able to skip murder. I had tough times reading and reporting all these. Pain in its most profound sense was my companion all the way. Nobody needs additional trauma but pretending nothing is happening, and denial does no good to our children. What you read is what really happens when a child is missing. Below are technical explanations of brutal mind control techniques they use on children before they sexually abuse them.

The lecture by Dr. C. Hammond, originally entitled "Hypnosis in MPD: Ritual Abuse," but now usually known as the "Greenbaum Speech" was delivered at the Fourth Annual Eastern Regional Conference on Abuse and Multiple Personality Disorder (MPD), on Thursday, June 25, 1992, at the Radisson Plaza Hotel, Mark Center, Alexandria, Virginia.

These are Dr. C. Hammond's credentials and background:

B.S. M.S. Ph.D. (Counseling Psychology) from the University of Utah, Diplomat in Clinical Hypnosis, the American Board of Psychological Hypnosis, Diplomat in Sex Therapy, the American Board of Sexology, Clinical Supervisor and Board Examiner, American Board of Sexology, Diplomat in Marital and Sex

Therapy, American Board of Family Psychology, Licensed Psychologist, Licensed Marital Therapist, Licensed Family Therapist, State of Utah, Research Associate Professor of Physical Medicine and Rehabilitation, Utah School of Medicine, Director and Founder of the Sex and Marital Therapy Clinic, University of Utah, Adjunct Associate Professor of Educational Psychology, University of Utah, Abstract Editor, The American Journal of Clinical Hypnosis, Advising Editor and Founding Member, Editorial Board, The Ericksonian Monograph, Referee, The Journal of Abnormal Psychology, 1989 Presidential Award of Merit, American Society of Clinical Hypnosis Urban Sector Award, American Society of Clinical Hypnosis, Ex-President of the American Society of Clinical Hypnosis.

The event was sponsored by the Center for Abuse Recovery & Empowerment, The Psychiatric Institute of Washington D.C and the extract below is part of it:

- *"This patient now was in a Cult school, a private Cult school where several of these sessions (of torture) occurred a week. She would go into a room, get all hooked up. They would do all of these sorts of things (torture). When she was in the proper altered state, now they were no longer having to monitor it with electroencephalographs, she also had already had placed on her electrodes, one in the vagina, for example, four on the head. Sometimes they'll be on other parts of the body. They will then begin (the torture) and they would say to her, "You are angry with someone in the group." She'd say, "No, I'm not" and they'd violently shock her. They would say the same thing until she complied and didn't make any negative response. Then they would continue. "And because you are angry with someone in the group," or "When you are angry with someone in the group, you will hurt yourself. Do you understand?" She said, "No" and they shocked her. They repeated again, "Do you understand?"—"Well, yes, but I don't want to." Shock her again until they get compliance. Then they keep adding to it. "And you will hurt yourself by cutting yourself. Do you understand?" Maybe she'd say yes, but they might say, "We don't believe you" and shock her anyway. "Go back and go over it again." They would continue in this sort of fashion. She said typically it seemed as though they'd go about thirty minutes, take a break for a smoke or something, and then come back. They may review what*

they'd done and stopped, or they might review what they'd done and go on to new material."

-"I remember a woman who came in about twenty-four years old, claimed her father was a Satanist. Her parents divorced when she was six. After that it would only when her father had visitation and he would take her to rituals sometimes up until age fifteen. She said, "I haven't gone to anything since I was fifteen." Her therapist believed this at face value. We sat in my office. We did a two-hour inquiry using hypnosis. We found the programming present. In addition to that we found that every therapy session was debriefed and in fact they had told her to get sick and not come to the appointment with me."

-"When she (another patient who remembers of her mind control program exercising on her at the age of 9) began hallucinating they inquired about the nature of the hallucinations so they could utilize them in good Ericsonian fashion and build on them and then combine the drug-effect with powerful suggestions.

"If you ever get to this point you will go crazy. If you ever get fully integrated and get well you will go crazy *like this and will be locked up in an institution for the rest of your life."*

"They gave those suggestions vigorously and repetitively. Finally they introduced other suggestions that, Rather than have this happen, it would be easier to just kill yourself." In a bloodline patient then, as I began inquiring about deep material, the patient started to experience similar symptoms. We went back, and we found the identical things were done to her."

"This was called the "Green Bomb." B-O-M-B. Lots of interesting internal consistencies like that play on words with Dr. Greenbaum, his original name. Now, in this case, it was done to her at age nine for the first time and then only hers was different. Hers was a suggestion for amnesia."

"If you ever remember anything about Ultra-Green and the Green Tree you will go crazy. You will become a vegetable and be locked up forever."

"Then finally the suggestions added, "And it'll be easier to just kill yourself than has that happen to you if you ever remember it."

-"Now when people say, by the way, "There's no evidence. They've never found a body," that's baloney.

They found a body in Idaho of a child. They've had a case last summer that was convicted on first-degree murder charges, two people that the summer before that were arrested where the teenaged girl's finger and head were in the refrigerator, and they were convicted of first-degree murder in Detroit. There have been cases and bodies."

Question: *"You have suggested and implied that at some point at a high level of the U.S. Government there was support of this kind of thing. I know we're short in time, but could you just say a few words about the documentation that may exist for that suggestion?"*

Dr.H's answer: *"There isn't great documentation of it. It comes from victims who are imperiled witnesses. The interesting thing is how many people have described the same scenario and how many people that we have worked with who have had relatives in NASA, in the CIA and in the Military, including very high-ups in the Military."*

. . . .

. . . .

Children's dining room at Sean Ross Abbey

-Hidden no longer

This is the news reports released by ICLCJ court concerning the discovery of a mass grave in Irish Nun's Sean Ross Abbey. Regarding the incident, the court announced:

"The atrocity of close to 800 emaciated childrens' bodies buried in a Irish Nuns' septic tank represented the 34th child mass grave site linked this week to the Catholic Church. Pope Francis was being prosecuted by

the International Common Law Court of Justice (ICLCJ) in Brussels for allegedly trafficking 300,000 children of political prisoners through Vatican Catholic Charities during Argentine's Dirty War. According to witness testimony last week some of those orphans ended up in a child mass grave site in Spain. Last year's ICLCJ prosecution concerned 50,000 missing native Canadian children. There have been 32 child mass grave sites uncovered so far in Canada, most of them on Catholic-run native residential school grounds.

Unfortunately the over 350,800 children suspected to be in Catholic child mass graves sites in three countries paled in number to Catholic Priest sex abuse victims across the globe. As of November 2013 over ten million Catholic Priest child sex abuse cases have been documented as shown here. These 10,077,574 cases represented a mere fraction of total crimes committed. Only an estimated 10% of sex abuse victims were thought to speak out about their sex abuse and just 10% of those cases saw the inside of a courtroom."

"Amnesty has been offered to citizens or employees of the Crown of England and Vatican willing to give sworn testimony or evidence that leads to the prosecution of top Vatican and government officials who may have

committed crimes. For providing evidence rewards up to 10,000 euros or around 13,660 dollars was available through the ICLCJ court.

The Irish child mass grave site containing bodies of children from age two days to nine years was located at a now-defunct Catholic home for unwed mothers. According to death records, the little ones were fragile, pot-bellied, emaciated and died as late as 1961 from malnutrition and infectious diseases such as measles and TB."

"Children of the Canadian Catholic native residential schools were determined to have been murdered or died of malnutrition, human experimentation, torture, Small Pox infection or as Eyewitness Irene Favel testified in this video, were thrown into a furnace. Favel claimed that in 1944 she witnessed a newborn infant incinerated by a priest at Muscowegan Catholic Indian School, Saskatchewan Canada. The child torture was documented for court in Kevin Annett's "Hidden No Longer" available for free here.

"The Bon Secours Sisters ran the Irish mass grave site and "mother and baby home" called St Mary's in Tuam

north of Galway city. The Catholic "home" had a reputation for children dying at a rate four times higher than the rest of Ireland. Unwed mothers were punished as "atonement for their sins" by being forced to give up their children and working for two or three years without wages.""

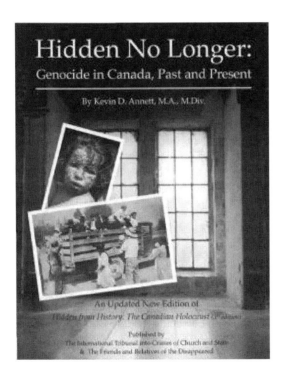

"The 2013 award-winning drama film "Philomena" depicted the plight of 2,200 infants who survived Ireland's Catholic homes. The children were forcibly

adopted or placed into child labor situations, mainly in the US. Catholic officials have consistently denied they received payments for these so-called "adoptions" and insisted verifying documents were lost in a fire."

"The Vatican, British Crown and Canadian government have refused excavation of the 32 Canadian mass grave sites believed filled with native children. Before licensed archeologists were turned away, human remains of children were uncovered at the larger sites in Brantford Ontario and Port Alberni British Columbia Canada.

"Critics contended the Catholic Church had an ongoing reluctance to hand over internal records of Vatican Catholic Charities out of fear further horrors could come to light. Such was in the case of the Irish Magdalene Laundries where unwed mothers performed forced labor without compensation to four Catholic orders. After years of successful litigation on the case victims still remain uncompensated.

In 2013, ICLCJ court found 40 global elites guilty and ended with the unprecedented resignation of former Pope Ratzinger."

Philomena, a movie inspired by this true story is a must-watch: "In 1951, Philomena became pregnant and was sent by her father to "Sean Ross Abbey" in Roscrea in Ireland which we just witnessed the mass graves found there. The nuns removed her son and gave him up for adoption without giving Philomena a chance to say goodbye.

....

-Bigger the names, bigger the crimes

Studying Nazi scientists' background, we see almost all of them are high priests of different satanic cults. The reason may be their love for blood, flesh, and sacrifice to gain supernatural powers. Next time anybody advocate for a satanic club as an inclusion to churches and schools' right to freedom of expression, just imagine the harm these people with such ideologies can cause having a legal knife in their hand as a surgeon or having access to patient's mind as a psychologist or holding these rituals as a teacher at a school in direct contact with children.

There are just a few victims who have spoken. The dreadful network of crime is so gruesome that nobody dares to take a risk and shed light on what they have experienced, it is pretty logical. These people should be respected, and they should have a chance to be accepted when they speak up. It is spurring that with a slice accusation of misconduct, regardless of being proven true or not, the political phantoms start to shoot the messenger but when the allegations advert real crimes committed by child molesters with testimonies, graphic pictures, and injuries, they become ghosts and silence the victims, and we very well know why. Bigger the names, bigger the crimes. There are names bigger than the constitution and bigger than the government and bigger than countries involved in those crimes and everybody fears for his life.

Victims are either silenced or labeled as unstable, insane and fragile individuals who seek attention. We must encourage and accept them as they deserve. **People who have spoken in testimonies above are not only victims of monsters but victims of me and you if we push them back.** Two other testimonies have spread great awareness. One of them is Cathy O'Brien, an MKUltra project Monarch Mind Control survivor who testified before the Congress and the other one is the testimony of two little British children, which their interview with UK Barnet Police has been leaked all over the internet. If these videos were not leaked, we would ever know that these crimes have happened. These cases sadly as usual, not only were closed as "no crime" but whoever digs into the case are threatened to be sued.

As we already talked about the subject, these two cases are the last cases I refer very briefly and then we will go to the next chapter and the main storyline of the book.

Attention:

Discretion required.

The next 3 pages' content is graphic containing murder and sexual abuse.

....

-We eat the babies

Gabriel 8-year-old at the time, and his sister Alisa Dearman 9, who were living with their mother and her boyfriend at the time, were two beautiful British children of north London who tried to seek refuge from the police and asked for help. They reported an extreme abuse by their father, their school, and the church, for three years. The incident took place in 2014. They reported to the police that *"they have been raped, tortured and forced to kill and eat other babies by their father actor Ricky Dearman and the entire board of teachers in Hampstead School and Hampstead church of London."*

-RING OF THE CABAL becomes satanic

According to the children's testimony, *"a ring of satanic families in Hampstead, have infiltrated schools, churches, child protection services, and the police. They have been co-operating with at least 5 other primary schools".* According to their testimony, *"Wednesday was called the day for "a lot of sex," and they were subjected to a group rape for six constant hours. They were kicked in the genitals and anally raped by teachers and others coming to school. Women raped children with strap-on dildos. If children screamed, female instructors would inject drugs into their necks. Teachers gave them sweets after or at the beginning of the horrific act."*

Watching the leaked videos of these two kids is one of the saddest experiences anyone can have. Especially when Gabriel, a boy at the age of 8, speaks about sex and reveals that he has a great knowledge of the shape of women's genitals like he is talking about a pack of chewing gum. Their gestures and body language, the detailed scenes, their expressed feelings and their voice when they say their father is the boss of the whole cult and how he melts plastic every day to make plastic "willies" at different sizes, are beyond devastating. I tried to download the videos and upload them to my website because I am sure they will be soon disappeared from YouTube.

The YouTube propaganda allows pedophiles to upload their child molesting videos but censors "us" if we expose them. That's the real irony.

According to Gabriel and Alisa, child trafficking in their orbit is the norm. Babies are rubbed, bought and flown-in from foreign countries like Thailand, Africa, USA, Hawaii, Portugal, Spain, China and India and they are brought to the Hampstead School by courier inboxes.

Those babies are ritually sacrificed in a secret room in the school while their father chops off their heads and asks Gabriel or Alisa to keep the knife to learn how to do it for their future. While decapitating, the baby should be kept upside down to save the blood in a bucket to drink, and the babies' meat is the only meat used for their school meal.

The children say ritual sacrifices also took place on Saturdays at Hampstead church, and the cult members and children danced around the skull and bones in costumes which are made out of human skin. **It seems a horror movie but the fact is, it is a horror, but it is not a movie.** Their tables are made of human bone. Slippers made by human skin. Apparently, they used great primitive skills. Transitioning from postmodern civilization to savage dinosaur and stone ages. This is the end of the liberals. They would eat each other publicly in the streets like zombies if their pedo-mania becomes legal. The poor children claim they were also taken to parties and forced to use drugs by their father. Hard to believe, but this is what the children were disclosing first to their mother and her boyfriend and then to the police.

-The Hampstead Case

Gabriel and Alisa said parents of all 200 students in Hampstead School participate in the cult and do the same graphic ritual to their children and not yet enough, make the kids practice on each other too. They named all social service agents, police force, shopkeepers, Cafcass, pizza express and McDonald's staff who were involved in the rituals.

According to the kids, their mother was totally unaware of their father meeting them in the school. The children were threatened to have them punished painfully if they would tell their mother or anybody else.

Something very suspicious and extremely disturbing that I noticed during the police interview was; Gabriel tried to talk about killing babies more than five times, but the police officer shut him up every single time. Instead, when the kid was describing the "willies" and his bloody "bottom" as he referred to, the officer slowed down and asked nonsense questions like how big was the size of the "willy"? and how did it feel???!

Later, Ella Draper, their mother, issued a statement declaring that she believes those seven police officers who came to her house were all involved in the rituals.

Shockingly, after the police interview, the social services removed the children from their mother which according to children's testimony, she and her boyfriend loved them, never hurt them and never knew about anything but oddly enough, the judge concluded that the mother had forced the children to lie about their dad to remove his joint custody hence, social services were ordered to remove and abduct the children. Until 2015, the children were still with the state's perfidious protection (or better say father's protection as the state condones the father), moving between three different foster families. Scotland Yard announced that the children have been drugged and raped by their mother and forced to accuse their father. She was accused of causing injuries, bruises, and rape traces.

Interestingly, Mrs. Justice Pauffley, who ruled against the mother, has other interesting rulings including, ruling in favor of immigrant parents who hit their children. Her ruling claims as in their country of origin, hitting a child is not considered a punishment, we shouldn't consider it either. Really your honor?

What about Females Genital Mutilation? The UK's justice system is not the justice system of their country of origin, and different practices due to religion, beliefs or traditions are no excuse for child abuse, and cultural context is utterly irrelevant. The law doesn't make that distinction, and the children should be protected from any form of mental or physical harm and abuse.

In an article by Michael Krieger published on Mar 9, 2015, in Liberty Blitz Kreig titled "In Great Britain, Powerful Pedophiles are Seemingly Everywhere and Totally Above the Law," we read:

"A newspaper editor was handed startling evidence that Britain's top law enforcement official knew there was a VIP pedophile network in Westminster, at the heart of the British government. What happened next in the summer of 1984 helps to explain how shocking allegations of rape and murder against some of the country's most powerful men went unchecked for decades.

Less than 24 hours after starting to inquire about the dossier presented to him by a senior Labour Party politician, the editor was confronted in his office by a furious member of parliament who threatened him and demanded the documents. "He was frothing at the mouth and really shouting and spitting in my face," Don Hale told The Daily Beast. "He was straight at me like a raging lion; he was ready to knock me through the wall."

Despite the MP's explosive intervention, Hale refused to hand over the papers which appeared to show that Leon Brittan, Margaret Thatcher's Home Secretary, was fully aware of a pedophile network that included top politicians.

The editor's resistance was futile; the following morning, police officers from the counter-terror and intelligence unit known as Special Branch burst into the newspaper office, seized the material and threatened to have Hale arrested if he ever reported what had been found."

The above part of the article seems to be taken from the Daily Beasts article on pedophilia then the Blitz reporter while giving his analysis adds:

*"More than 30 years later, an inquiry into allegations of child sex abuse rings, murder, and cover-ups has been launched by the British government after Scotland Yard detectives said they believed statements by victims who claimed they were systematically abused as young boys at sex abuse parties attended by judges, politicians, intelligence officers, and staff at the **royal palaces**."*

....

The climate in England for any investigation on Pedophilia is hostile. The perpetrators know they can quash anybody who reports them and the Police are their tool.

It is astonishing how an 8-year-old boy can elaborate precise details of horrific scenes if fabricated and not seen by his own eyes. Besides the children never contradicted each other which is hardly possible for children of their age if their statements were falsified and one of them might finally say something to expose them, but it never happened. Body language experts could easily distinguish how the children talk to the police spontaneously, but as we know, the wealthy area of north London and Hampstead is the residence of highly influential people. Isn't it bizarre when a child accuses an adult teacher of rape and gives the specifications of tattoos and piercings on the predator's genitals, but the accused adults are not examined by the law enforcement and the Judge didn't issue an order to investigate? There is no way for a child to have seen his teacher's genitals but the court documents, surprisingly show that the accused teachers have never been called or examined.

Leaked videos went viral. They have been viewed at least 4,000,000 times, and people were outraged. So the BBC organized an interview with the actor. Not knowing a dime about body language, we will still be easily able to see how the actor, Ricky Dearman exaggerates his emotions, fakes lengthy babblings, forces himself a falsified and waterless cry. A cry drier than drought and a stoney performance as unprofessional as a dead rock. We cannot accuse the father of any crime but this interview illustrates one thing as apparent as possible: Ricky Dearman is a VERY BAD ACTOR.

There was no police investigation on the case furthermore. Case closed. The case was about killing and devouring babies but no probe, and to the date that I am writing this, Gabriel and Alisa Dearman have just vanished.

Unfortunately, the "Royal Papal Banking Cabal" has three clear directions.

-In England, it goes right to Westminster.

-In the United States, it goes right to the CIA Headquarters and Washington.

-In the rest of Europe, it goes right to the Holy City.

Whom do we want to prosecute??

- Cathy O'Brien; the Presidential Sex Slave

Another case is Cathy O'Brien, who describes herself as an ex CIA-Pentagon top-level sex-slave, who has been used in different operations by her owner Colonel Robert Byrd and his operator Colonel Dr. Michael Aquino. According to other MKUltra survivors, Democrat senator from West Virginia; Robert Byrd was the most sadistic, and Satanic pervert they have ever met.

In her book, "Trans-Formation of America," Cathy says that *"Robert Byrd justifies his involvement in drug distribution, pornography, and white slavery as a means of "gaining control of all illegal activity worldwide" to fund a Black Budget-covert activity that would "bring about world peace through world dominance and total control."*

She claims as a sex-slave, the Clintons, George H.W Bush, Dick Cheney, and a long list of high-profile politicians have abused her. In the case of Dick Cheney, she says referring to George Bush, he told her: *"A Vice President is just that, an undercover agent taking control of the drug industry for the President."*

According to Cathy, Robert Byrd, her handler has said: *"95% of the people want to be led by the 5%."* The *proof is that "the 95% do not want to know what really goes on in government."* Byrd believed that mankind must take a *"giant step in evolution through creating a superior race."*(sounds eugenicist, doesn't it? according to the CIA, not wanting to know what is going on in government means the consent to be controlled.)

As a result of these abuses, Cathy becomes pregnant with her daughter Kelly, and the baby becomes the new toy for her handlers and abusers.

Colonel Michael Aquino, a senior U.S military intelligence officer in the CIA was the official high priest of the satanic church of "Set." One-click research for his name provides you libraries of insanity reported by hundreds of his victims.

This bugaboo, scary enough to scare children is Colonel Michael Aquino

Cathy has been sold to the program by her own father at the age of 9, and subjected to an occult named "The Rite to Remain Silent." In these cults, children are their currency. Victims of these cults claim to be directly used or sold by their fathers to be abused. O' Brien claims to have been abused by her own family since she was a toddler and was given his father's penis instead of a baby bottle (Toos Nijenhuis's testimony for Dr. Kevin Annett, Kimberly's on Dr. Phil's show and so many other victims claimed the same.) O'Brien's father prostituted her as a child to friends and business associates. He forced her to perform in numerous child pornography and bestiality films. She says she was compelled to participate in Satanic or sadomasochistic child pornography movies produced exclusively for President Gerald Ford.

She was eventually sold to the CIA and has been sodomized, whipped, bonded and raped. In her testimony before the Congress, Cathy claimed that she was programmed at Fort Campbell, Kentucky, in 1980 by Lt. Col. Michael Aquino of the U.S Army. She stated that Aquino used barbaric trauma techniques on both her and her daughter Kelly that involved NASA technology. Cathy O'Brien claimed that being a "presidential model" Monarch sex-slave means that she was specially programmed to cater to the sexual perversions of the highest-ranking politicians in the United States. She recounts in graphic details, how George Bush the father, raped Kelly, her thirteen-year-old daughter at the time and how she (Cathy) was forced to have oral sex with Hillary Clinton. Cathy says while being a sex robot in this circuit, she heard the globalist elite planning a military coup in the United States and conspiring to establish a Satanic New World Order.

Cathy was never accused or jailed for defamation. None of these politicians named in her books have ever filed a lawsuit. This must be very significant to know whether her testimonies and claims were true or nor. Eventually, these politicians didn't want publicity more than this. Do we guess why?

These are what the lie-stream media is not telling you.

After being finally healed through years of therapy, she has written three books: "PTSD Time to Heal," a pathway for Post-traumatic stress disorder caused in victims of mind control and abuse. In addition to *"Trans-Formation of America,"* she also has written *"Access Denied: For Reasons of National Security"* in 2004 which are priceless books. She is well informed, educated and a vocal MKUltra survivor who has invented a special healing process that can be a relief to survivors. Another victim who has almost the same experience is Brice Taylor, author of "Thanks for the Memories" written in 1999. Read their books, and spread the awareness, otherwise; we anti-child abuse people, in a very close future will be the weirdoes in the madhouse. They will lock us up in local brainwashing facilities to erase our rational memory, evacuate our brain and cure our insanity to dare and speak. Those children are our children too. The sun will not remain under the clouds, and the truth shall prevail when we speak up.

-Sex and children, the oil for the toothed wheel

Now we see the pattern here. There is one thing common in all crimes and perversity that we've covered in this segment, and it is SEX.

Through the entertainment industry, which includes the media, as they are actors instead of reporters, they have programmed the population. Hollywood, Disney, digital games, and editorials, have been all focused on sex as humanity's central issue. Cases like transgenderism and feminism all fall back on the sexual behavior of these categories. The colonizers have desensitized humanity towards every perversion that we have known so almost all high-profile people have foibles regarding their perversion. They have trained their sex-slaves to catch politicians red-handed to blackmail them. Dehumanizing our society is the pathway. There is a coordinated global effort to legalize pedophilia, bestiality, cannibalism and lowering the age of consent, traceable everywhere.

There is a video recently popping up on YouTube, in which some liberal parents teach their 10-12-year-old children how to masturbate! Mothers to daughters and fathers to sons and they introduce a series of adult toys right in their face and consequently to everybody's children. YouTube, which is clearly a pedophile sympathizer network, promotes them. I honestly wouldn't believe I will someday leave in a deprived world like this. If I could meet those chivalrous of past generations; those who have brought knowledge, values, and magnanimity to the world and ask them to rise and live in our advanced utopia, where instead of having family lunch-tables we have king-size beds for performing parental masturbations, they would cry a river and prefer to stay in their graves rather than living in our world.

The Royal Family

- Soros's new political boy toy; Justin Trudeau

When Justin Trudeau was sworn in as the Prime Minister of Canada on Nov 4, 2015, he pledged his detailed fidelity and devotion to the Queen of England:

"I, Justin P. J. Trudeau, do solemnly and sincerely swear that I shall be a true and faithful servant to Her Majesty Queen Elizabeth the Second, as a member of Her Majesty's Privy Council for Canada," he said during the ceremony.

"I will, in all things to be treated, debated and resolved in Privy Council, faithfully, honestly and truly declare my mind and my opinion. I shall keep secret all matters committed and revealed to me in this capacity, or that shall be secretly treated of in Council. Generally, in all things I shall do as a faithful and true servant ought to do for Her Majesty. So help me, God."

Hmm...A servant for Her Majesty and not the people. On July 12, 2016, just 8 months after taking office, Trudeau's government announced a 241.5 million dollars donation to Clinton Foundation. Donation of such huge amount of money from Canada to Clintons while Trudeau has pledged his full loyalty to the Queen, definitely raises eyebrows. **Trudeau, as he was sworn is "a Queen's servant." He has no real authority so can we suspect that the donation to the Clinton Foundation comes straightly from the Queen? And why the Queen should donate to a corrupt to the bone slush-fund as Clinton Foundation?**

Obviously, there are so many holes in the propaganda, but it is crystal clear that there was no real American government leading the worldwide corruption, invasion, and suppression but the deep state agents at the core of the families that we already named and of course, the CIA. Meanwhile, there is another interesting point to pay attention to. Since the day the MSN deactivated the comment section on its page, for each negative article about President Trump, there are three love stories praising the Queen and her habits about her meals, purses, hats, etc. The articles are mostly about Princess Diana's death or outfits, Prince Charles and his kids and stories about their life, just like they are the Queen and Prince of the United States. The tone and language of these articles are so worshiping and adoring, advertising them as the untouchable fairy tale characters of fiction, not one of the thirteen families whom we are dealing with their invasive activities. The number of these articles are on the rise, remarkably spotted on any page. But why? Why are they pushing it so hard? What does the Queen have to do with all this?

Is Justin Trudeau the middle-man between the Clinton Foundation and the Queen from one side and between Soros and the Queen from another side? When Trudeau went to Davos, he appeared very intimate with Soros, and they had a comfy chat. Surprisingly, Trudeau posted a picture of the two, Soros confidently whispering in his ears on his twitter. The picture reveals Trudeau is Soros's new favorite political boy-toy, so does it have anything to do with Trudeau attacking President Trump over Muslim migrants? Is he laundering the Queen's money into the Clinton Foundation? Canadian law doesn't require revealing the sources of charities' funds. Why Trudeau set up a "war room" in his office to monitor President Trump?

Chelsea Clinton is married to Soros's nephew. She openly wears a reverse cross and has a very close relationship with Soros's son; Alexander. The Clinton slush-fund fraud is not only working with Soros but is also merged into Soros family's deepest networks.

 The Clinton-Soros family and their affairs are inter-married and not separable anymore. The Clintons have parts in occupying the empty seat of the Rockefeller dynasty.

Now, what do the Queen and the Clinton Foundation have in common? They both tie to Soros? And Saudi Arabia?

A Royal to Royal favor?

Both high ranks in the Cabal?

(British Royals+Arab Royals) -Trudeau - (Soros+Clintons+Obama)?

 Why should any money be funneled into Clinton charity through Trudeau's filter by the Queen?

Do the Queen and the monarchy have their hands in the Clinton Cabal? Is the Queen the "Godmother" for the

Clinton Foundation Mafia and the entire "Secret Ring" around the world?

Is the royal family the keystone of the entire Cabal? These are the questions we should ask ourselves. Who is the Queen really? Or better say who are the Windsor's?

As you see in the chart, the British Monarchy was related to almost all monarchies around the world. The reason was simply their inbreed marriages. British princes and princesses were sent to other royal courts to marry and as a result, become kings or Queens of other European countries. Greece, Romania, Spain, Sweden, Bulgaria, Germany, Argentina, Yugoslavia, Denmark, overseas regions and even Russia had the British Monarchs as their heirs.

King George V was German. His father was descended from two separate strains of German blood, and their real surname was: Saxe-Coburg-Gotha. There is a difference between being German and doing a German life and being a German and doing a British life. Maybe that was the point you were thinking. How was he a German but living a British life? The reason as we mentioned before, is far from home inbreed marriages. There was no need for these families to have been born on the soil they supposed to take the Throne but to be part of the royal family. Bloodline supremacy is the only non-fiction supremacy that is real, tangible and crushes our world beyond the borders. All other supremacies are just political assassinations and identity politics. Just look deeper and diagnose the pattern how after Gerald Ford in America, we have the same families over and over again, Fords, Bushes, Clintons, and the list goes on.

Take the Bushes, George H. W. Bush who was first a CIA operative, then rose as the CIA director, then Vice President, then president. After him, his heir George W Bush as president and his sons Jeb as the former Governor of Florida and presidential candidate and Billy Bush is the other son who beats the drum of the media. Take Clintons, first Bill then Her Majesty Hillary Rodham, now Her Highness Chelsea Clinton as Soros's almost daughter in law, all untouchable and the circuit repeats and repeats while the only thing which really changes are the names.

-Loyalty is to the Monarchy, not to the people.

Back to the Windsors, Queen Mary, King George's wife had a guttural German accent but at least, she spoke English as her mother tongue. For almost half a century, there was no Queen speaking English as her mother tongue.

Within George's 29 first-cousins on his father's side, 19 were German; the rest was half-German. On his mother's side instead, among 31 first-cousins, six were German, and 25 were half-German. No cousin was British.

For George, the family came first, and his family was German. During WW1, he even invited the Austrian Ambassador, Count Mensdorff, for an evening tea at Buckingham Palace. By then, Mensdorff was technically the enemy of Britain. But he was also the King's cousin, and he could just care less about the first reason. The loyalty is dedicated to the monarchy, not to the kingdom.

Kaiser Wilhelm II was the king's closest cousin and best friend. He was Britain's enemy number one at the time. When many advised the king to withdraw Kaiser's "Field Marshal" title, George's reaction was a tremendous fury.

Christopher Hibbert, a historian, once wrote: *"The King hated to be argued with or interrupted,"* so he continued to make pro-German comments during the first years of growing war, inviting German musicians or even asking why British army is not acting pro-German??

To him, what was sacred was the institution of the monarchy by itself, not the people of the country. Monarchy should not be touched or altered and never to be questioned. His unique goal was to continue his loyalty to his late grandmother; Queen Victoria.

To understand their mindset let say for them, the monarchy is a state by itself. Today the monarchs still act according to the same mindset. **All remaining royals of Europe are loyal to each other and have common dark sides, secrets and tour the same pathway together.**

At the age of 50, King George V and Queen Mary had six children; five sons and a daughter. One of the sons was the future King George VI who was the father to Queen Elizabeth II, the current Queen of England.

King George V was feared and disliked among Parliament members and Cabinet Ministers. He was so sensitive to criticism and pro-German for their taste. In the meantime, the love affair with his German roots put him in real trouble.

When Germans began to strike the British mainland, people were terrified noticing the killer airplanes had the name "Gotha G IV" printed on their bodies. A name which was very similar to "Saxe-Coburg-Gotha," the king's surname.

Twenty three Gotha G IV planes killed 162 people and injured 432. Among the dead, there were 16 children in a popular primary school.

None of the planes were shot down. Three weeks later, another Gotha raid on London, took 57 lives and injured 193 more.

-Germans become British

Gotha's name became the most hated name in England. What was the solution to this outrage? The usual game of playing words. Nothing had changed, nobody was held responsible, but the Royals decided to change their name. **Whitewashing the people's memory was and is never complicated. If the name becomes British, people will forget that the King is German.**

Simple logic to deal with simple minds.

Courtiers were ordered to find a new name for the ruling royals. After different suggestions, it was Lord Stamfordham, who came up with "Windsor."

For the embarrassing German relatives who every now and often used to show up in Buckingham Palace, the solution was to give them British peerages so Queen Mary's elder brother, the Duke of Teck, became Marquess of Cambridge, her younger brother Prince Alexander was made the Earl of Athlone. The King's two cousins, Prince Louis and Prince Alexander of Battenberg became the Marquess of Milford Haven and Marquess of Carisbrooke. The German surname "Battenberg," Queen Elizabeth's maternal surname, received a soft royal polish, passed the Anglo-filter cleanser and became "Mountbatten" which remained the current surname for Queen Elizabeth II and Prince Philippe.

All others were ordered to drop their foreign titles and never use them again.

It is not recorded how people reacted to this Royal self-identification process but if you ask the population even today; they wouldn't have any idea what all these names and titles mean or even what they actually are.

George V and the Royals "Britishness" was announced on July 17, 1917.

And so began the process of "Britishing, the Royal Family."

It may have done nothing to change the direction or the result of the war, but perhaps it did make the British people feel better about the king who had a surname as the killer planes which murdered hundreds of people.

-Close Nazi relatives

So the Windsor's are German. Do they have ties with Adolf Hitler and the Nazis too?

British royals had close relations with Adolph Hitler and The Nazi Party.

The ominous Nazi connections come from three of the Prince Philippe's four sisters; Sophie, Cecile, and Margarita. All had married German princes, who became leading Nazi officials.

Prince Philippe, whose family name is Schleswig-Holstein-Sonderburg-Glücksburg, and proudly calls himself the decedent of Vlad the Impaler famous as Dracula; the king of Romania attended the funeral of his elder sister Cecile in Nazi Germany as a 16-year-old schoolboy in 1937. He was pictured side by side with his other relatives who were dressed in SS uniforms.

His brother, Prince Christophe of Hesse was a member of the SS and flew fighters that attacked allied troops in Italy. Prince Philip's relatives were so tied to Nazis that when he married Princess Elizabeth, he was allowed only a restricted authority on the guests he could officially invite.

Miss Naouai, a New York-born but a Moscow-based journalist in an article wrote that Edward VIII and his wife Wallis Simpson had friends among Hitler's high command and met the Fuhrer himself. She added: "If anyone knows real Nazis, it's the Royal Family."

This picture, published by telegraph.co.Uk in 2011, shows Edward and his wife with Adolf Hitler

During WW1, while the Royals were busy with Britishing the family, some other royals decided to fight for the Nazis. The King's cousin, the Duke of Albany, his uncle the Duke of Cumberland and Viscount Taaffe had their peerages whipped away from them under the 1917 Titles Deprivation Act, because of participating in the war in favor of the Nazis.

But relatives ruling other countries kept their Saxe-Cuborg-Gotha surname. The family is still the family. Just the names are changed. Today they rule in Belgium, Portugal, Bulgaria, and British Commonwealth realms.

Prince Andreas of Saxe-Coburg is the head of the house of Cobourg in Austria.

-"The Dutroux Affair"

Prince Laurence Saxe-Cobourg-Gotha of Belgium has been the subject of one of the most horrendous scandals of modern history. The "Dutroux Affair" was one disgraceful shocking piece of history that is still covered-up. According to the case documents, Marc Dutroux supplied kids to members of the elite for sex. The scandal caused great outrage and numerous protests in Belgium and around the world. The incident broke when a sex-ring involved in extreme child abuse, torture, murder, hunting children, snuff, bloody rituals, and bestiality were uncovered. In the scandal, very powerful people were accused, but the investigation was shut down.

It was shocking when the WikiLeaks linked Prince Laurent; King Albert's son to the scandal but more shockingly was the testimony of the abused victims which makes our hair stand up on its end. Even King Albert himself was linked to the allegations. Among the names listed by the WikiLeaks was: the NSA's General Michael Aquino which according to Cathy O'Brien was the torturer in her case, and had an important role in the military psychological warfare. As we stated before, he was involved in "Project Monarch" and is the subject of many videos and web pages who fight child abuse and satanic rituals. Michael Aquino was openly a devil worshiper and a high priest of the Satanic Church of Sat.

Other big names involved were Leopold Lippens of the Bilderberg group, Paul Bonacci victim of Monarch brainwashing himself, Willy Claes Secretary General of NATO in 1994-95 and Elio di Rupo; Prime Minister of Belgium. These people were all named by the witnesses.

The victims, in order to protect their identity, had been named as X1, X2, X3,...X7. They came from different zones, but all had common testimonies and named the same people, castles, and locations. It was their recognition of big influential politicians, royals, and doctors. Keep in mind that the girls spoke in French and it took years for the entire French dossier to be translated into English and become able to circulate the news, and that was the main reason for the delayed reaction, later in Europe.

-Behind the royal doors

Article written by Joel Van der Reijden in 2007, titled "Beyond the Dutroux Affair", has reflected the reality of the elites' child abuse and snuff networks. In this extensive report which details what really happened in Dutroux scandal, we see Viscount Etienne Davignon, a close friend of Henry Kissinger and director of his Associates who is also vice-president of the European Commission and an honorary chairman of Bilderberg, have been Reportedly named by witness X2 as a child abuser. Witness X2 spoke about a girl who has been murdered, but before her death has told witness X2 that other murdered children are buried in Princess Liliane de Rety's chateau.

Witness X2 noted: *"Parties with underage girls in the Cromwell hotel in Knokke."*

"Present: Delvoie - Karel – X2- Lippens - Van Gheluwe - Etienne Davignon. The girls knew where to go and

with whom. Lippens hits the little girls".(Authors note: This means these people were present at the event and Lippens hit the children. According to my researches, victims of such traumas speak of themselves or of their own memories as a third person. Instead of saying I saw, they say: She saw or instead of we know she says: The girls know. Just like a hypnotized person. This is X2's testimony. She doesn't say I was present. She says X2 was present.)

Liliane de Rety was the second wife of King Leopold III (1983), who until her death in 2002, lived in Chateau d'Argenteuil. According to Van der Reijden's article, another witness reportedly, named a member of Bilderberg, as a child abuser. Maurice Lippens and his brother Leopold reportedly have been named by witnesses as not only involved in regular rape, but also in the snuff network. Lippens is one of the fix invitees of the Bilderberg group.

Prince Alexandre de Merode was mentioned by both Nathalie W and witness X4 as a central player in the satanic child abuse and the murder network.

What you read below, is the testimony of victim X3, published in Van der Reijden's extensive 2007 report, which later in the 1990s, her name was unsealed as Regina Louf. Have in mind the third person pronouns pattern used by these victims while reading.

Attention:

Absolute discretion recommended as the

the next 2 pages' content is graphic,

containing murder and sexual abuse.

Sensitive readers should pass to the page 471.

"The car stopped on a parterre before the house. [It] was surrounded by a park. Two supervisors were present: Ralf and Walter. The children were taken to a tower made of natural stone and with a wooden door... an underground [corridor] left from the turret toward the cellars... without light... going downward. In the cellars there were cells where the children were locked up, awaiting their turn. There also were some cells for the dogs (dobermans). The passageway gave way to a room of spectacle. In the tower: dead children's bodies in various stages of decomposition (sometimes dismembered and/or missing body parts) and carcasses of dogs. Spectators: always the same but difficult to identify - about fifty. She recognized the regent Charles, King Baudouin and King Albert, and two others that she calls Charly [De Pauw] and Polo [Paul Vanden Boeynants]. She thinks to have recognized Willy Claes [later NATO secretary general] and doctor Vanden Eynde. The dogs listen to Ralf and Walter. The addicted dogs are excited. Spectacles = orgies, putting to death children and dogs. The spectacle room has a strong odor of excrements of dogs. Dogs can roam free in the garden... Gilles (12 years old??) was castrated by Polo. The other children have to drink the blood... Girls are slashed with razor blades. The lips of the vagina of X3 have partially been cut and were given to eat to the dogs... A girl's [large] vulva was cut into slices and fed to the dogs..."

"Childbirth by a teenager through a caesarean section. Baby pulled out of the stomach and given to the dogs by Polo. She saw the dismembered mother again in the exposition of the dead... She has to eat the human flesh cut from the bodies. She has to eat pieces of children (fingers) served in gelatin. Good taste - slightly sugary. It provoked an enormous sensation of hunger and thirst. Drinking blood relieved the sensation of thirst... She speaks of another murder that she committed on a girl of 3-5 years under the threat that it would be her brother who would be killed. She opened up the girl from the vagina to the breastbone with a knife. She gave the internal organs to the dog. Someone cut off the head. The child was devoured by the dogs... Murder of a young teenage woman who was opened up by Vanden Eynde... The baby shouted in the mother's stomach. She resewed the stomach with the baby inside..."

What you just read is not horror fiction. These are court testimonies of the Dutroux Affair's scandal.

"Luxurious house with a surrounding wall and gate... non illuminated twisting path. There were some stables. Parterre with flowers. Hall of entry = cream-colored and blue tiles - red carpeting. Walls made of marble with a teenage picture of [later king] Baudouin on it. She spent a whole night with Baudouin - fellatio and sodomy. Presence of maid... In this house there were many servants... She remembers one evening when she had been smeared with cream before being brought to the table on a tray. She had been licked off and raped... At the end of another evening a child... had been castrated. The other children that were present buried the boy in a flowerbed. She remembers a child who had been decapitated, then cut and fried before being eaten. She remembers children who hung on hooks in the kitchen. A certain Solange [a female name] has been enucleated [what exactly?] with a spoon by her and an old lady."

The wickedness pictured in these testimonies went beyond Belgium's borders and was part of a network connected to other rings in Holland, United Kingdom and the United States and after creating years of disgust and anguish was silenced and labeled as a surreal made-up story.

Although this background is not directly related to the British royals, it proves that the Royals are not who people really think. We already knew how all Royals are somehow related. Besides Jimmy Savile, with over 450 child abuse allegations against him as a pedophile was reportedly a Prince Charles close friend and has been seen with him on many occasions. Savile was the marriage counselor between Prince Charles and Princess Diana.

According to Wikipedia: *"In January 2013, a joint report by the NSPCC and Metropolitan Police, Giving Victims a Voice, stated that 450 people had made complaints against Savile, with the period of alleged abuse stretching from 1955 to 2009 and the ages of the complainants at the time of the assaults ranging from 8 to 47. The suspected victims included 28 children aged under 10, including 10 boys aged as young as 8. A further 63 were girls aged between 13 and 16, and nearly three-quarters of his alleged victims were under 18. Some 214 criminal offenses were recorded, with 34 rapes having been reported across 28 police forces."*---
By Wikipedia

How did he get away with all these?? Was it because of the Twilight zone?

We know nothing inside those doors and walls, but Princess Diana who lived inside called the Royal family: "The Lizards and the Reptiles."

What did she know? What did she see to call them like that?

-Lizards and Reptiles

Before we start digging into British Royals, we were talking about their progressive appearance on American mainstream media and how the MSM's tone praises them as the American and world's royals. Tasteless articles like:

-"here is what the royal family eats for Christmas dinner" (who cares?)

-"why it would breach royal protocol if Prince William was Harry's best man" (Protocol? Of how to bamboozle people?)

-"Eight rules that Meghan Markle needs to know before her first royal Christmas" (whom these people think they are), "why Princess Charlotte…"

-"Kate stuns in …."

-"Why the Queen….",

or when we hear cheerful yells on daily TV shows saying:

-"It's official; Now we have an American Princess"??

I mean….what the hell are you doing American people?

You not only don't care about the children, the crimes, and guilty verdicts but also promoting and enabling the injustice which is going on and avow to your young girls that the status-quo of being a princess and living in a horrendous British castle is the highest achievement that an American girl can acquire? Giving these "lizards and reptiles" as Princess Diana called them, the attention they seek and turn your backs on what America has stood for since its beginning? How can Americans and the world stand there and watch these mouthpieces insulting our intelligence while we hear what the Royals really do behind closed doors?

The progressive appearance of British Royals recently in the American and world's news outlets has just ONE reason. They are the "Keystone" and they want you to know your future lords and start to fall into the habit of recognizing them as superior, and to do that they use the romance of their younger generation.

Never forget Queen Elizabeth was young too.

....

The Dutroux rumors were heard just because somebody had the courage to stand up. Years later, those who have been named as predators became even more powerful. If we didn't hear of another scandal, it doesn't mean it is inexistent but it means that the state media did its best to cover up any additional rumor. As we see in Pope Francis's section, further scandals, in fact, have been even more horrendous but immediately silenced.

"Queen Elizabeth II, head of state of the United Kingdom and of 31 other states and territories, is the legal owner of about 6,600 million acres of land, one-sixth of the earth's non-ocean surface. She is the only

person on earth who owns whole countries. The value of her land holding is approximately $28,000,000,000,000. This makes her the richest individual on earth."

Kevin Cahill, in his book: "Who Owns the World."

The Windsor's are a fraudster bloodline that hides its German roots and ties from the public, so if they hide this, so many other things they can hide from the public. One of which is their ties and cash flows to Clinton Charity-Fraud and their lobbyist; baby boy Justin Trudeau with his strings pulled by the puppet master Soros. The Clinton Foundation is allegedly accused of money laundering and the Uranium One scandal and is suspected to be involved in the child trafficking scandal in Haiti and …in eugenics.

It should now be easy to connect the dots…

I am totally aware that there is much here to digest in this section, but I had no alternative. Therefore, I am going to encapsulate the content to be faithful to the main body of the book.

We were covering new porn indoctrination and mind control doctrines, so we had to investigate George

Soros's connection and funneling into pornography if there is any. From there, it was necessary to look into the history of pornography which started with Hugh Hefner Playboy's empire. We learned how he took his sexual ideas from creature Kinsey's sick report. Checking his background and reviewing individuals' testimonies claiming to be abused, we learned about Hefner cooperating with the CIA and using playboy bunnies as a honeypot to enmesh politicians and capture them on videos. From there, we had to educate ourselves about the methods and doctrines which have been used to create human sex slaves so we found out about MKUltra mind-control program which took us to Nazi Scientist and their infiltration in the CIA through project Paperclip, plotting to control the world and establish a new world order using MKUltra Project Monarch and creating human robots who have their brains engineered with electrodes, microchips, and surgeries.

Not all of these victims are dead. Some have survived, and some stood up and spoke. During trials and testimonies, these victims referred to an unfortunate network involving the Vatican and the royal family and this in consequence, took us into tones of court reports, speeches and quotes which we had to document about those children. They had brought up shocking names and testified against the VIPs embrangled and those testimonies broke up a vast satanic pedophile-ring which is well organized and fully connected around the world and is deeply involved in child trafficking and bloody rituals and at the end, we listened to more detailed testimonies of some survivors.

I initially, had no intention to peel these details off and put the naked kernel in front of you. Some of us are very sensitive, but if the children are living this nightmare, we have the duty to strengthen up our guts and get over it because of them. On this particular subject, and unzipped content wouldn't cover my goal which was to spread awareness about child trafficking, child sacrifice and the dynamics of the network. So I took the risk.

Now that we did it all, we can move to the next chapter.

Chapter 10

The last Whistleblower

-Drip drop of liberations

Satanism, child trafficking, and cannibalism exist, but for now, the outrage of society will be a flogging tsunami if they practice it publicly so unless they have not built the receptive society, they keep it in secret.

But things are not as they were 50 years ago.

People are changed.

Drip drops of sexual perversion and desensitization toward crimes, murder, blood and children's vulnerability were cloned into the society through sadistic and bloody porn and were called "preferences". As a further step to this progressive liberation, the LGBT community transformed the public streets and spaces into scenes of a sadistic porn movie with devilish makeup, vulgar latex underwear, whips, horns, and chains. This behavior not only became a norm in LGBT parades but they also pushed for the normalization of this kind of appearance. The "enemy of the people"; the mockingbird media did not lose any chance to puff the behavior and advertise it while the education system shamelessly cursed the kindergartens with the culture of drag queens.

Contaminating the ocean of our minds took half a century, but their attempt to build the "receptive" generation was so successful that now they dare to claim their right to have satanic rituals.

How humanity opened its gates to the kingdom of darkness where cruelty and madness become moral ethics?

Not all liberals are Satanists. But all Satanic groups are liberal. This should be a place for our focus to start.

All Satanists are extreme leftists. From their idle; Saul Alinsky to smallest satanic groups, they are all unhinged leftists.

- The end justifies the means

Communism is leftists' heaven. I mean all leftists, liberals, social democrats. That's the key but they don't call it communism.

Communism was their tunnel of transportation into Satanism. They used communism to reach Satanism. For decades, they recycled communism and sold it as socialism in colleges. Somehow these days, having a college degree literally means being a communist because they learn "communism is cool and capitalism oppresses Americans." Through communism, they first whip out God then spread the illusion of liberty. Strange appearances as a sign of rebellion and counter-wisdom become cool. They learn to dress up "as they feel." **Why is this alarming? Because the idea of "communism is cool" and a "rebel is wise" while being cleansed off every sensibility toward vulgarity and crimes, is a path to recruit satanic groups.** They start to fish their targets and advance their satanic religion when they meet students at bars or campuses. Although some students reject, the others accept as they want to be cool. Start with Communism is a good start to reach Satanism, and from there, the possibilities are unlimited.

A bottomless pit.

When there is no strong provenance for children to hold it together, they will fall. They are young, and the trap is colorful and sexual.

Communism training teaches "the end justifies the means" and that's why we see what we see today. Antifa brainwashed anarchists who attack from behind and throw human feces on people are an excellent example of this principle. They wish death to our little son because they don't like what we say.

How can we hold satanic child murderers accountable? How can we expose these highly protected groups and their operations?

Possibilities are limited.

Either there should be videos of their crimes, or they should be caught with evidence on such a scale that nobody can cover it up.

That's why we need patriots in the N.S.A

Why the NSA? Because they unlawfully surveil everything. We are being watched, that's an open secret; and now is the time they can repay the republic.

-There is nothing on the internet you can delete.

Once something goes online, it sits there forever. For example, the notion that an insider's black money erased the emails on Anthony Weiner's laptop is unacceptable. It is also silly to think that the NSA doesn't have Hillary Clinton's classified emails before her operatives smash the hidden server in her own house with a hammer. That is simply ridiculous. So as for these two examples, the NSA has a copy of everything including child trafficking and snuff movies.

Patriots in the NSA fear for their lives. They can end up in a mental hospital if not killed by those in high positions who run the cabal. That's why we call them heroes. We love them, we owe them, we respect them, and today we need a rising hero. The last whistleblower to give up his own freedom and take back the others'. The last messenger who knows when he blows his whistle he will sacrifice himself but save humanity. DO IT.

Do it for GOD, do it for MAGNANIMITY and do it for the world's CHILDREN.

DO IT.

As you might already know, the occult lives by its love for symbolism. They co-communicate through symbols. Their buildings, jewelry, visual effects, songs, gestures, and words follow a pattern. Especially when they are in a public meeting with the enemy (the opposite side), they have to transmit codes with their fingers. Why? Because they know they are being watched, and they have to pledge their ongoing loyalty publicly to stay on the line.

As for their secret meetings, blackmail is their currency therefore, every ceremony, party, perversion and especially each child abuse session has a video. Pedophiles are visually pervert-watchers and cannot help themselves with their love for exposure. They record their own perversions to watch themselves later in the film. According to some psychologist friends, it's only by watching themselves, when the pedophiles feel and double enjoy what they did.

-So everything is registered somewhere.

We should demand our patriots to expose those videos. That is our focus, but prior to the day that we wake up to breaking news where all channels are broadcasting the elite's leaked child sacrificing ritual, and by the grace of God, their names come out, we must fight communism.

If the planned Communist revolution takes place, the technocrats and oligarchs will take over the power, water, food, energy, TV and all resources and at that point, gloves will be off, and they will declare their Satanic world government.

The United States' Constitution is not written for a day that Satanists be free, walk in the street, scare children and insult Jesus.

Stop them now, or when our brainwashed children learn to see things differently in kindergarten, there will be no coming back.

-The Obama DOJ to legalize 12 perversions

Back in 2007, when respectable general Wesley Clark said that, in 2001 two months after 9/11, Pentagon has drafted a memo describing how the army was going to take out seven countries in five years, starting with Iraq, Syria, Lebanon, Libya, Somalia, Sudan and, finishing off with Iran, nobody took it as a serious alarm. Look at the Middle East now and see the result.

But it is still worse. They are even implementing Eugenics in pre-screen policies. Unborn babies are screened according to family history crimes. What else should turn you against them?

In 2015, former U.S House Majority Leader Tom DeLay claimed the Obama Justice Department had drafted a memo to legalize 12 "perversions" including bestiality, pedophilia, and polygamy. Pay attention we are not talking about ANY Senator, but <u>House Majority Leader</u>. The shock was so electrifying that people preferred not to take it seriously.

What can be the scope of a government which takes steps to legalize pedophilia and bestiality?

Tom DeLay just named three out of twelve which the other one was polygamy. But what were other nine that he didn't dare to name? What can be worse? It is heinous where we are going. Now we can easily notice the pattern on YouTube, Facebook, and Twitter where pedophiles openly started to jump out of the closet but their existence and statements are not considered as a violation of their policies? These platforms do not recognize pedophiles as dangerous or offensive, but they will flag and suspend our pages if we expose them. This is an ongoing invasion and an infringement of our right to free speech. They have overrun us.

In an interview for "The Steve Malzberg Show" on Newsmax TV, Tom DeLay said:

"We've ... found a secret memo coming out of the Justice Department. They're now going to go after 12 new perversions. Things like bestiality, polygamy, having sex with little boys and making that legal,"

"Not only that, but they have a whole list of strategies to go after the churches, the pastors and any businesses that try to assert their religious liberty. This is coming, and it's coming like a tidal wave."

When shocked Steve Malzberg stopped Tom DeLay to repeat what Delay said, Tom DeLay responded:

"That's correct, that's correct. They're coming down with 12 new perversions ... LGBT [short for lesbian, gay, bisexual and transgender] is only the beginning. They're going to start expanding it to the other perversions."

This is House Majority Leader speaking at the time, not any Senator. It is equivalent of today, Nancy Pelosi announcing such a thing in an interview. This is the high-ranked official; the person number three in the government.

To release the classified memo, President Obama needed to authorize its issuance.

He never did.

And we know why...

It could be time to listen and take our last chance seriously. This is real, and this is happening. So we should gird up our loins and start to act instead of hiding inside the bubble of our daily lives and repeat: Oh no this is impossible.

Oh yeah, this is possible, and we must get off the chairs and do something about it.

Wonder what to do and where to start? Read the conclusion.

Conclusion

What now? What to do?

How to prevent future Agendas?

There are 27 tactics

To help people, first, we have to know what influenced them to do what they are doing already. It's just then the help will be effective.

When a global wealth report issued by Oxfam in Jan 2017, listed eight men who own half of the wealth of the world, names like Bill Gates, Warren Buffet, Jeff Bezos and Mark Zuckerberg were on the list but we didn't see the Rothschild's or Morgan's name. The reason was not that they are not within the richest men on earth but because they are the few people who own the other half of the world's wealth.

What you and I, poor or wealthy, celebrities or first row politicians have is just 10 percent of the wealth of the world. That's what they don't tell you. Those are names you never see on any news. Those are names that run the world.

When representatives of these crypto-masters advertise their imperial government under the label of socialism, fighting capitalism, crying for poor and advocating for redirecting the resources and share them with everybody, they don't mean to share that 90 percent wealth of the world that they own. They mean what you and I possess should be taken out and be divided between poor and rich; and by rich, they don't mean rich. They mean the upper-middle-class category.

When they push bratty kids, jobless warmongers and disturbed people who have never received any kind of attention, into the streets carrying the disgusting dice-hammer red flags of the ex-Soviet Union to "resist" and "take the power", they don't mean offering to "you" and "me" the power in a communist government, but installing Social Justice Warriors, sociopath and puppets in the front row to "control" us so the fake warriors can fantasize to rule, while the real rulers are out of sight.

We are living in a prison of the mind.

A prison surrounding us with long tunnels where nothing will happen, and nothing will change if we don't break this prison.

We have been taught, those ages that humans used to live in caves and be 24 hours vigilant are over. We have been told that we can trust our governments and we trusted them blindfolded. Over-trust felt so good. The "feel-good" attitude was assuring and kept us in our safe zone. If we opened one eye and saw something that we shouldn't see, we decided to turn the blind eye to it. It was better and happier pretending not to see. If we wanted to make a big deal of it, life could become perturbed, and we could be disturbed by dedicating some of our effort, wealth and comfort, and it wouldn't "feel good" anymore, so we just didn't. We slept. **To be misguided felt better than guided**. But the rusty trap was there, hidden amongst the weeds.

America, Europe, and the whole world slept while the "crypto-colonizers" never slept. They run our countries, our banks, our economy, schools and universities, courts, police force, prisons, resources, governments, earth, waters, skies, and spaces while we were sleeping. They took everything. They are just on our doorsteps, and now we wake up to **the corrupt oligarchs who think they are ENTITLED to run because they have always run.**

This is the problem: entitlement. They worked so hard for decades to build a George Orwellian dystopia and they are that close to it, why should they stop now? Why should they surrender? Entitlement and owning are the only lifestyle they know. How can they not own their slaves anymore? Where should they go? What will they do if not plotting? They have no expertise in anything but plotting. What about the main agenda built on the Bloody River by the blood money? They will have nothing to live for anymore so they will crush us, eat us alive and if the middle class, the very normal creatures decide to stop them, their bulldozer will run over them. They will shut down our voice, put our house in ashes, ruin our career, spread rare diseases, design false flags and can even blow a nuclear war, blaming another government. They should make it or break it at this point, and there is no middle way around. For them, it's now or never.

So that's the scenario, and it's horrific so what if we don't? What if we stay silent and continue to pretend that we feel good? What if we could pretend that we were not living in this most important phase of history, and could ignore what we know?

Well, the answer is, either way; we will never have the life we had before. It's over, and we have to get over it. The toothpaste is already out of the tube. We can't force it back inside. It's Now or Never for us too.

Read carefully the novel "1984", by George Orwell.

There were times in history that people had no choice but to fight. No human wants to fight. Wars are humans in their worst shapes, but when it's the matter of to be or not to be, to do or die, we have to. Where can we run when the war is at our home and when the entire world is burning?

As mentioned, over-trusting kept us from being vigilant. We thought we hate politics and it belongs just to the politicians. But liberty comes shoulder by shoulder with vigilance as Thomas Jefferson said: "The price of liberty is eternal vigilance." We were not vigilant. We lost.

The 1st tactic is to accept that we lost. We have to get up on our knees and "believe" there is no other option but to fight. We had one fight a decade ago that we didn't take it seriously and we lost; now we have a list of fights and no room to look another way. We have to fight all these fights one by one simultaneously, and we have to fight them systematically and efficiently.

Time to sweep the house

Politics penetrates all aspects of our lives. From social policies to the economy and international relations. From what we watch on TV, cinema or the internet to what we eat or our relations with different groups.

"Everything is political, and politics is in everything." If we don't stay vigilant, politicians will stand between us and our liberty.

The 2nd tactic; The Deep state has imposed a state of emergency. As we act more conscious; protesters, corporate media and the enemies within, united and organized, strike in the same direction, and this is their political weapon. **So as the second step, we have to give them the taste of their own medicine.** We have to fight back with their own methods.

"Ridicule," the method used by the deep state-run media, Saul Alinsky's squashing vehicle, which destroys people's lives is keeping patriots far from fighting for their country. A few unelected, unrepresentative, repressive and agnostic people with a philosophy of prejudice are governing the world, and we have our "one-time" life to gamble if we speak up. But whether we save it or lose it, we are already in the middle of the fight, and we can't give up.

If we still wait to set up an organization, a must that we miss at the moment, it would be so late. We can act as "Grass-roots." Just as what their organizations are doing; Grass-roots. All individuals should search for those who think alike, and they should organize groups. These groups shouldn't compete or search for superiority. The enemy is one, so we should ignore the differences and focus on a common goal. Each YouTube channel, each twitter page, each website counts.

The Antidote to a campaign of disinformation is a "Tsunami of real information."

It is necessary to super **emphasis on the media** for the concept to become profoundly clear. There was a reason the deep state hijacked the media and the education system. First the media, why? **Because the media**

projects narratives and propaganda are expressed in narratives. So when the shift in the media happened through the alternative media, they lost their narratives and consequently, their propaganda. Propaganda is the "engine" of the oppression machine. They lost their engine.

The main organization which runs the propaganda is Media Matters and should be abolished.

The deep state can't run without propaganda just as a vampire can't live without blood. Look at the Russian Gate propaganda. Look for how long it's going with no basis and evidence but instead, the Washington Post and New York Times scoops which have never shown any evidence had found a life of their own and a ground for a "probe." Why an investigation without a crime? Because when narratives come from someone that people trust, it is when they believe it. And here is their trick. The trick of hypocrites who do not allow people to know that the Soviet Union was America's enemy because of Communism, not Russia itself. Now they praise communism and its flag in the city and call their riots as "counter-protests" but attack Russia? Russia without communism is just like any other country. What is the difference? **Calling Russia as an enemy is the same as**

calling Germany the enemy not because Hitler was a criminal Nazi but because he was German; that's nonsense racism.

They don't tell people, yet people trust them. When there is trust, there is no suspicion anymore. The liars can lead the mass wherever they want, and the narrative becomes fact.

Some of these media "goons" had the most chances to run for the Senate, but they didn't. Why? Because they believe they could influence people's mind on a much bigger scale if they host "hit programs." They are not elected politicians, they are not lawmakers, but they create narratives and hence voters. They shape people's minds and manipulate their decisions. Hopefully, with alternative media, they lost the ground of their political fairy tales. Today's media is a joke, but they already did their damage.

10 years ago, could the public believe we would have "After School Satan" clubs around the country? Never, but the media created this mental softness. They call themselves: *"An American political activist of the satanic temple."* They "acclimatized" the social

mentality to a certain destination by calling it liberalization.

Should we continue to honor them that trust?

Banks (oligarchs) create corporates (technocrats) and corporates control the media. The media itself creates voters. So voters at the end, vote for the old bankers behind. But the game-changer was the alternative media. Voters don't listen to corporate-run bullhorns any further. The old propaganda system is not shaping voters' opinions anymore. "We the people" are not trapped into their false narratives or speculations. *"Sources," say, Washington Post "believes," "anonymous insider" reports,* this kind of ghost sourcing and statements offend the standards of Journalism which always demand to cite the source. They have gone so far that most of the time we see phrases like: *"May change"* or *"Can become"* as headlines. Not mere personal opinions on headlines but even pre-judgments that may "lead" public opinion to anticipate for something that doesn't exist. This way, they create hysteria which is the direction we see today. *"Vladimir Putin is very bad"*; now, all believe Putin is a demon. What they don't tell people is that they are demonizing Putin number one; to justify the existence of

NATO, number two; to execute their psyops on people and prepare their minds to get the WW3 that they need as the last hammer. The corporate media which is the fourth branch of the deep state discredits itself more and more and proves that the old system of propaganda doesn't work anymore, and the alternative media is what really caused a significant shift in the public's perspective.

Remember the pictures circled on the media on gun-shootings in school with a single person in three or four different roles? That's the media propaganda machine. That's the deception. They change our perception, and one of the elements they use is trust. We must reject it. We cannot trust the monster. We should become a united front and take on the establishment. If not, they will not rest until every single cultural, and the social norm has been turned on its head.

The 3rd tactic: Always remember in the current situation: **"Offense is the best defense."** We had enough of anarchist riots each time patriots aimed to have a peaceful protest. They just come to disrupt. We cannot take it anymore. Anytime we force ourselves just to be on defense, we lose. It's time to be on the offense drive. We were just reactive, waiting for them to ridicule or lie then rushing out to defend. It didn't work, and it never works with a full scale militarized media.

They are already in our ground and tricked the public in their narrative while we struggle to run after them and catch up. It never worked. The ball is in their ground. Keep the intellectual attack on every ground on a full scale. (Attention: No physical attack. No violence. We are talking about an intellectual attack.)

They fear our voice so any collective protests and boycott, cutting ads or sponsorship, and social networking attempt to spread the information should not be underestimated. Every single person should become an automotive organization. **Don't wait till they create their scoops to defend. Find the dirt and bring it up nonstop!**

Put them on defense. Don't wait for calm waters. Give them another attack. Disrupt them. Don't stop. Another attack. That's how it works. If we have to consume our energy defending against their attacks,

let's consume it for our own attacks. It will be more fun.

In my personal experience, these people, no matter if they are journalists or educated, they usually don't read books. Anything more than three lines bores them as for them, thinking is knowing. Even their columnist, who write longer paragraphs do it because the subject is hot at the moment, gives them adrenaline and feels good. **After they are done, they don't read it anymore. So there is always plenty of dirt and gaffes to find in their older pieces. Bring it up and attack them.**

The 4th tactic: Be direct. **Strike short and fast where it hurts.**

They love to ruin people by ridiculing as we said before. Don't take it. **Be calm and before they start, shoot them some ridicule.** If that's what they like, we let them have it. But to do that, we have to end the political correctness madness once and for all. Politically correct is the real "Weapon of Mass Destruction" not what they claimed Saddam Hussein had and he actually never had.

Don't let them shame us into silence by saying we are not politically correct.

We will never be a racist if we tell people they are wrong. So say it. Speak up. And say it exactly as you mean it. Say it loud and say it clearly and say it as you are RIGHT. Say it with no mercy! We are at war if you still didn't get it. They declared war long ago, but they made it official right after the election. Not every war needs to take bullets to be a hero. Hit them where it hurts. Hit them with their own weapon. Use their progressive tactics. Ridicule, constant attack, disrupt alone and disrupt in Grass-roots.

Be intelligent to use the right words for your attacks as we have limited time on air or a limited alphabet on Twitter. **Don't let them speak even if you need to repeat the same sentence 20 times on air, do it but don't let them speak.** Be careful, Social Justice Warriors in place of sitting judges can put us in jail for wrong words. We are living in dangerous times when politicized judges are there not to defend the law as it is written, but to obstruct the justice by interpreting the rule of law with their own taste and defending the witch hunt accusations on us.

Try a simple solution. Take a false pressure off. Don't complicate it. The complication is the enemy of accomplishment. Say it short and simple and fast.

Don't engage in other people's storm. Remain conscious. Observe from the outside of the storm, go inside, punch and come back on the outside. Repeat; strike and come back. You should stay totally focused on what you do. **If you go in and punch the first hole but stay in, you will allow yourself to get swallowed by punching so many holes at once. That makes us disoriented** and distant from what was our goal, and that is the downer; the real energy consumer. Don't do it, **recenter!**

Don't repeat the loop on ONE thing many times.

The 5th tactic: At the same time, we need to clean up this mess we did all these years by living like sheep. **We need a national TV which broadcasts the truth. Not objective or subjective or favorite truth but the truth and NOTHING BUT THE TRUTH.** Truth is not objective. It cannot be a means of censorship and oppression by offense claims. Snowflakes should work on their personality and avoid remaining at the age of eight and crying.

They can find a cave and live in it, that's not our business, but they cannot prevent other people from expressing their views, and that's our business to intervene and stop them.

We need a truthful national TV which not only broadcasts real news but real education, real values, the real history of America and the world, real art, real documentary movies on most important issues of history, real stories of Communism crimes, information on laws, real music, real fun, real faith, real talk shows, and good movies. A real TV that can be on all day for our children, without being worried about covering their eyes on perverse contents. That TV will help to teach them life. And this is the duty of our rich, influential patriots who have both money and power and should look at it as their first and most important obligation.

The 6th tactic: About social media, there was a time that Facebook and YouTube channel didn't exist. **Someone came and created them. If this**

happened once, with a lot more progress in technology, it could happen again. We should create a better social media and a better video broadcasting channel to bypass YouTube, Twitter and Facebook. A social media that works for the interests of the people and does not act as a governmental monopoly. Facebook is not only a Chinese style censorship corporation but also has become the deep state's police network that can use your personal information. www.Gab.ai is a new social media that is increasingly growing, and we can upload videos. No policing, no phone number, no censorship and I think it may be the future's social media so we can help it grow but until Gab or any other real social media dominates the market we need to keep our presence on corporate media in a way we already discussed which is being focused, being on offense and punching.

To avoid brainwashing and being "FREE" useful idiots, we have to expose the unfiltered truth. Truth with every color of it and to do that, we need a revolution in the old mainstream media system. We need to expose the system who bullies us and says: "*Go to sleep America, Europe, Australia, West and East, the government is doing what it can, so we have put hundreds of channels at your disposal, you are free to watch any of them which "you choose", you are free to change those channels and if you don't like them, you are free to sleep or shut up; you choose. But if you speak up bigger than your mouth, you can have greater choices. You can die in an accident or by an artificial arsenal heart attack like Andrew Breitbart, and so many others did. Do you remember how Huck's methods,* (Olivia Pope's fixer in "Scandal" TV series) *could make anything vanish and look like a natural cause?"*

Individual fights start with one individual: "you" And it grows into a massive "us." If you can create a video, documentary film, write an article or speak up in a video, just do it. Publishing and broadcasting of any kind bring empowerment and independence. Besides, the more channels we provide, the more people can distance themselves from the corporate media. **Never believe the corporate media, however; observe.**

We can take insights on what they "don't want" us to know and what they are hiding in their "no-go zones" by reading the distracting titles they make at a crucial moment in which something is very threatening to them.

Whatever it is, it is created by propagandists promoting the deep state.

Be the media, be the channel, be the network and spread the word. Never never never give up.

Attack now!

The 7th tactic: Democrats and Republicans are two parties who **have been running the country for 150 years, and we think they are not part of the establishment? Both parties are corporate.** We have to work in two directions: First; be vigilant and educated and vote for those Republicans, whom we trust in 2018. Choose carefully and choose who won't let the campaigns' promises be hijacked right after being elected. Nothing has changed in the past decades as campaign promises were just fraudulent vehicles to get in. But most importantly, if you can run for the Congress and if you have the qualities, target a dishonest Congressman/woman and candidate yourself to replace them on behalf of your district and prevent them from taking the salary and wasting people's time by blocking the government. Be vigilant on them and always monitor.

<u>Second</u>; focus on ending the two-party system of the House and the Senate. **We cannot defeat the deep state by a policy encouraged by the deep state itself**. We have tried all the doors with them, and they shut them all in our faces.

We have to create our own party. Americana party. A patriot party. A party with its own media.

The 8th tactic: We have to go back to old social values, human dignity, individual sovereignty and real art with full determination. We should exactly know what to target. **Systematic and institutional rejection is what we need, and there is no time or place for compromise.**

When a child refuses to grow up and to take responsibility, we negate him for a while for his own good. **Universities are promoting and doing all they can to keep students from mental growth.** On one of the last revelations by project Veritas, they recorded a college assistant distributing "emotional kits" for students and what was inside those emotional kits? A PACIFIER! A teddy bear and a pillow to go in safe spaces and cry! We are talking about university students, males, and females, and there was a PACIFIER inside the kit! The assistant told the Veritas actor that it's not bad at all if he sucks his thumb when he feels sad and this is all recorded. You can watch all on ProjectVeritas.com.

Once upon a time, if people couldn't control their emotions or their mindset, they would have asked to consult a psychologist or start some treatments, Yoga, Martial Arts or enrolling spiritual or mental-growth courses. Now when a person cannot control his or her own emotions, somebody else is blamed for being racist, sexist, homophobic or whatever they decide to call and label him as an offender. They can't explain why they are angry; they can't tolerate being wrong, they just go ballistic, scream and start acting violently.

Why does this happen? **Because when one political perspective becomes dominant and takes over, discussions become more aggressive and any other view which is challenging the dominant view will not be tolerated, so there is no "dialogue" but a monologue that is dogmatically toxic to the opposing**

idea. What happens at this point is that the monologue, will no longer be grounded on logic and for them, it shifts from being an assumption to a "Certain Position" which is the position nobody should challenge or even question it.

Who is dominating these ideas? Our old three hands in hand friends: Education Department, Judicial and Media "Department." Sheep are indoctrinated in school, glorified by the media, and the opposite views are being punished by the law.

This is the circuit of the co-operation pattern between these three. We are living in a public circus, observing these clownish acrobatics as our routine. Dialogue becomes an "extreme" action as what we saw in the "People's Republic of Berkeley." Irrational screamers who do not accept any alternative ideas and label it as fascism, racism, bigotry or anything ending with the word phobia.

The name of Berkeley just saddens me as it was the birthplace of the free speech in America and now look where we are. But that's not all. Bucknell University indoctrinates the students with books like *"Reflective*

Violence" by Georges Sorel, another typical Alinsky lover, who believes: *"violence can save the world from barbarism and is necessary for the syndicalist Marxist Revolution tradition to achieve a classless society."*

??! Does violence save anything from barbarism?? How this is possible when Barbarism is extreme violence in its nature, and this thesis is just an irrelevant, and stupid justification for violence. Just like saying: Violence can save the world from violence! Pathetic!

I am amazed why these Alinsky lovers don't go to live in Cuban Communist heaven and forget changing America and West Europe while they already have their paradise. Why Cuba and Venezuela are not their best choices for living while their principals of Marxism is already at work there? If they want to make America another Cuba, then why don't they go to Cuba instead of living in America? Do they hate their own principles and their results and just love the project "Destruction of America"?? What will these kids do after that? Will they "share" suicide among them as they learn to share their mothers? Or sharing just is good for the others?

Universities and schools teach them "How to hate America" and media teaches them how to have sex in earliest ages possible like 12, how to be sheep and change their sex like they change their toilet paper and courts teach them how to disobey the constitution by creating anti-concepts, protected groups and demand authorities to recognize them as new trendy concepts.

Thinking of these university kids, I visualize a factory that from one entrance, the students enter with differences, smiles and good intentions, then, from the exit, they egress all in the same shape and color, leaving their intelligence and rational thinking ability in a box within a shelf in a corner of the factory, lock it with a key, and walking out with a big red stamp on their forehead printed FREE while the key is in their pocket. This is my interpretation of today's universities. Some of them throw the key in a river; some of them still have it in their pocket. Those guys who still have the key, have our hopes and prayers.

Let's sack these oligarchs. There is a place for them, and it is called "the bottomless pit" waiting for them impatiently.

Let's put back behaviors where there was a limit. Let's go back when society had values. Let's fight this crap called modern art! Every single pervert, every misbehave, every perplexed identity, pornography, child abuse, and abomination, somehow links with kind of bizarre so-called modern art or comic art, that allows them to gather in depravity exhibitions, find each other, socialize and normalize the abuse.

So-called "artists" personifying "child abuse" and their "art" are excellent examples of this. **How can those horrific pieces of perversion be called "ART" and not an unspoken secret language code of predators and child traffickers finding each other?**

Take a look at some artists who are most wanted by DC's ruling class, whom their paintings are hung in their houses and decide for yourself are these slices of pizza over children's genitals, kids with their hands taped down on tables, children with price tags on them, phallic symbols mixed with underage kids, half-naked children hanging by their underwear in dirty bathrooms with spanked bottoms, very young children with their body part cut and put beside them, very young babies on the ground and a man on top of the baby doing disturbing acts and blood everywhere, are art or not? And would you hang these disturbing paintings in your house?

I encountered some pieces by Kim Noble, Biljana Djurdjević, Dionyso, Marina Abramovic and Katy Grannan, and found them extremely bizarre and disturbing but this is my personal view. Decide for yourself. Look at their "ART" and this is just the tip of the iceberg.

The closed cycle that we have today shall never happen again. The media creates and shoots the ball of narratives in the schoolyard, then schools indoctrinate children and report the disobedient to the judicial system, and the already indoctrinated judges punish them. We need to work backward. **Brains should get back to work, and that is not going to happen until the ultimate goal of teens is how to dress like Miley Cyrus.** We should repair or even build back the pillars of human society. We should reverse the system of education. With today's society, **it's far more important to work on self-empowerment abilities in elementary schools than the crap they are learning now as science.** We should keep education, the judicial system, and the media out of reach of hands of any tyranny and there should be new measurements to do that.

The 9th tactic: Modern Pornography is the biggest ground to promote sexual crimes. New pornography has met a drastic change of burden compared to what it was 10 years ago. It offers extreme concepts like brutally beating women, degrading women, sex slaves, rape culture, bloody sexual abuse, humiliation, cutting, and knife in genitals, father-daughter and family incest and most of all, a monumental fight on masculinity to emasculate and homosexualize all young alfa males. According to different surveys, boys start to watch porn around 13. Those videos are teaching young males right at the age of being conditioned. Teens who have the sparest time spending before porn- websites are conditioned to taste their own semen to be acquainted with semen's taste and to be ready to eat other men's semen at the first stage. These new porn-doctrines encourage them to try homosexual acts with other males during the second phase. What is impressing in all these videos is the declaration of war on white males who, in these videos and pictures are called "little small-penis white-cuckolds" whom to satisfy his white feminist aggressive mistress, should submit himself to a superior and strong "real (bbc) big black male." The white wife should submit herself to a superior (bbc) "black male" in the presence of her "little white, small-penis, cuckold-husband."

These doctrines not only have pushed race war but also insist on the emasculation of white males. Porn indoctrination is always some years ahead of what will happen in society. In fact, it started to act as a psy-op almost 5 years ago, right before the race war on white males became intense. We all know men use porn. But teen girls watching porn is a modern heritage. And the special situation, ambient, and all elements together in that special moment with adrenaline and mental concentration on just and only what they see, psychologically, is a crucial moment that their hypnotized mind grasps the scene with all words and phrases, and they will remember it afterward even when they are not watching, but remembering those imprinted words in their mind.

To indoctrinate through pornographic visuals is a very strong and deep mind control method of indoctrination for both men and women, injecting the concept of "beta white male" and "Alfa black male" acceptance and emasculation at the same time. It is the same MKUltra system but they earning from

it too. The sad part is that the game feels to be most sexy to those poor white males who are humiliated to the point they demand it themselves to be degraded.

These are all there. There are millions of these disgusting mind-control clips.

And what we need is a deep investigation on these companies and how do they get the "indoctrination message" to put it out as it is pretty clear that the message is well-thought and perfectly designed to have a certain reaction on a certain target? Well, they do not come from anywhere but the dirty money of our international parasite, Mr. mastermind Soros because the doctrines implied in this kind of porn and surprisingly the timing, perfectly match his agenda and his war on the white male, war on masculinity, war on the family; as it promotes swing, war on women and war on children; as it promotes younger age sex, orgy and gang-rapes which we surprisingly see its rising rates also amongst refugees. as they don't have access in their countries. It is forbidden both watching porn or doing the action in their countries so they arrive, they have access to these videos in their camps, and they encounter the "Planet Perversity." If the Devil had a face, it could perfectly be Soros's face. I don't have a proof for a direct connection between Soros and the ideological porn but my cynicism goes directly to him as I found out his Open Society Foundation and the Ford Foundation together funded over $72 million since 2006, to retain the Obama-era "Net Neutrality" rules in place which is as usual playing with words. Net Neutrality means the opposite of free internet and neutrality of the network and is actually censorship permission pushed by Soros, operated by President Obama and allows the corporates like Google, Facebook, and Twitter to continue censoring the opposition. Looking for a connection, I discovered that "Pornhub" joined Soros's Open Society Foundation to organize a protest in August 2017, called: "Day of Action," against reversing "Net Neutrality." **So, if Pornhub which is the motherboard for all porn websites joined Open Society Foundation, for me the path is clear: Soros should be behind ideological porn.**

By the way, people who object Net Neutrality because they "think" Net Neutrality means a free network, just remember you are taking the same position as Soros, and you are standing aligned with Soros for a law that "he" created. **Protesting for the same thing that Soros is protesting, puts you and him in the same ground and this is the alert to know you are definitely on the wrong track, and you are dancing to his zombie song. Enough said to know if you are right or wrong.**

The 10th tactic: There should be campaigns of awareness on real feminism and also campaigns to promote femininity and family values. **Society must reject extreme feminism which is the barbeque-scented bait modern cancer, and it is just a lie. Feminism is the death of the west and the death of the woman. Feminism is to put an end on family and proactively of the female sex**.

Isn't it significant that all active globalist leaders in the EU, don't have any children? Look at them all: Angela Merkel, the Chancellor of Germany, Jean Claude Junker; Head of the EU in Brussels, Theresa May; Prime Minister of England, Stefan Lufven; Prime Minister of Sweden, Emanuel Macron; President of France, Xavier Bettel; Prime Minister of Luxemburg? They don't have to care about the future of their children, the rate of production, or the health of society. All is about them, and all will vanish with them.

Until decades ago, all wars were fought by men, children have been patronized by fathers, women have been cherished by husbands and technologies and discoveries accomplished with the few exceptions, only be men. All tough and heavy jobs have been filled by our men. 93 percent of work fatalities are men. All societies have trained their sons to sacrifice themselves for their families, countries and their fellow human beings. Women cannot survive without men. Just as men cannot survive without women. What kind of a world will it be a world of all men or all women?

Where is the diversity they were talking about that they love it when they can benefit from it and despise it when they feel threatened by it? Double standards or just relative values? **Men and Women ARE DIFFERENT in biology but equal in rights! We cannot change biology. The same biology made those differences as being corrective to each other not competitive or opponent.**

Feminism will assassinate the West because if women continue this bulls**t and push their beliefs, there will be no production and the West will die.

There will be no giving birth for western women while the Trojan horse injected by the EU has four wives and make seven babies from each one of them and take money from the government for each baby. So here is the thing, the more the infiltrated ISIS refugee makes babies, the more he can stay at home, watch a movie and take taxpayer's money in honor of sleeping with his four wives. His western born babies who will become neutralized are an incredible source of income as soon as they are born. Do feminists care about the future of their countries or even their species? Is there something in this world that makes those "FemiNazis" happy and end their uprising anger? Will they ever be satisfied?

What does the world owe them that they are entitled to, but don't have it already?

Perhaps they are unable to see the biggest picture. We noticed that in Manchester and attacks after that, the target was young girls. Because they target Western womb. Let's draw the future the feminists are unintentionally asking for. They grow old alone and in their not-so-distant future, they have to work for the wives of the refugees' and their adult-to- be kids, obey their rules, be subjected to any possible mistreatment and take the food they offer them if they decide to give them food because the radical refugees will have a 31 to 1 ratio and the feminists will be a minority in their own country. Just do simple math. So will be the rest of the population as when this happens, feminists and non-feminists will be trapped in the same plot and burn in the same fire. The fire set by their stupidity.

Add to that, the rate of the death of young Americans. According to a recent report in the Lancet, while the mortality of white women between the age of 25 and 35, has increased 3% a year from 1999 to 2014, and 25-year-old white male mortality had an increase of 1.9% the same period, other ethnic groups except Native Americans had a great DECLINE in mortality rates. According to Bloomberg, middle-aged white male Americans without a four-year university degree are at an increased risk of death resulted in sadness that drives them to use drugs and alcohol leading to accidents or committing suicide. This sadness also slows down their health progress against heart disease and cancer. **According to another survey on the same journal, this sadness is due to the factor that white male Americans do not believe in the American Dream anymore** and in " you can achieve your dream if you work hard" while 59% of black males and 55% of Asian males living in America, strongly believe in it.

So why this double standard? Because the same society has different attitudes toward different categories. Hostile and ready to bully toward the white male while friendly and flourishing attitude toward the blacks and immigrants. According to Lancet, white male mortality like this, in developed countries has happened just in two public health emergencies during 1999, due to the AIDS epidemic.

So, with all we talked about, it's quite clear where this sadness and despair come from? Being indoctrinated in school and learning that America is a bad country in which its white males enslaved Africans and killed native Americans and feeling the guilt on their shoulders at the age of ten, brings depression and sadness. The age of 10 is the age of learning about strength and power, but instead, they are bullied and judged by society and its social-mental terrorists for the crime they haven't committed. Add to these all the problems they may have at home with angry parents or a single mother or a drunk father, the problem of abuse or many more, and at the same time their America is dead, their dream is dead, they are not entitled to fulfill their dream, and being a boy is like being a non-obedient girl, so they not only lose their America and their dream but also their identity and do not know who they are anymore. What will a kid, who doesn't receive any attention probably not from even his parents do? Will he commit suicide or find his refuge in drugs and alcohol or decide to transit from sex to sex as a solution? Yes, he does. **Numbers don't lie.**

Not yet enough, male sperm count had a 59% collapse in the white west population including Australia, Canada, Europe, and America. All factors that will prevent the reproduction of the white race and this is just sad.

As stated over and over in this book, political correctness is nothing but breaking the law and trying to make it look correct. There are laws; you break the law, you go to jail. There are rights and wrongs; you can't change the concept then label the wrong as right.

A few years ago, in an ugliest attempt to "politically correct speaking" in media, law enforcement and among the liberal political activist, they silently changed the word "Rape" to "sexually assault" or "sexual harassment". Why? Because some new-comers whose cultural enrichment and integration demand rape, have caused a hike in rape statistics, and to hide the statistics, the globalist in charge of courts, found a solution using its own game of playing with words. **Changing the legal name of the word "rape" will help the population "not" to be informed of a rape count.** So other than auto-censorship of mainstream media and the police force who report one in every ten cases, when they report, they don't write rape, they write "assault" or harassment. Hence, when we hear on TV or read articles, we are not sure what do they mean by "assault" and what really happened. Sexual harassment could have been some forced grabbing or even verbal. **But rape is rape. And "assault" doesn't mean only rape. They hide the nature of the act by playing with the words.** In liberal manipulation and hypocrite world, everything is about tricky words and not the truth. The truth is the real enemy here that should be avoided by any means. **The truth is the pest and the plague. It should be eradicated so they can create an alternative truth that fits their agenda and can vary from time to time and subject to subject as it even contradicts their own theories, but it doesn't matter.** They have always a justification which includes big long phrases containing long unpronounceable words that instead of convincing us, silence us as we are thinking: What the hell are they talking about? And trying to find the meaning of the words while they buy time and jump into another discussion to seem the only victorious warrior of the battle.

Playing with words is the secret of all Soros's nonprofit organizations' manipulation and falsification. It's the same play when they blame the "gun" instead of a gunman while hiding the fact that at the same location, there was another good gunman, police or a good samaritan, who saved the civilians.

The 11th tactic

"I believe that banking institutions are more dangerous to our liberties than standing armies."

Thomas Jefferson

The government is feeding and serving a financial cabal, and the cabal feeds its organized crimes against humanity. **If we don't feed them anymore, the string**

will be cut off. It's not that easy, but it's what that has to happen.

If the government issues its own currency, credit, and loans, there will be no place for a private bank regulating the government. A government should provide its own supply and to do that, it should look into the history and the ways it has been done before this Royal Papal Banking Cabal took the control. If a government fails to do so, an entity like the Federal Reserve creates the supply and when the government is in need, the entity expands the supply out of nothing. There is no value in that money. **The feds create digital money with a click and indebt the government by providing loans and get paid as interest. Simply, a salary paid by the government to indebt the government. What better way to become billionaires and trillionaires? Why not creating wars and market crushes to borrow more fake money and become richer?**

What worse way to become an installed puppet government?

If a government provides its own supplies, taxpayers will be saved, the government remains in place, huge amounts of interest will be guaranteed to taxpayers, and the money throne will be overthrown.

The 12th tactic: All funds to Soros's organizations should be blocked while his organizations should be raided and shut down. Subpoena and probe should rain on his reign.

Whenever you see the word, "Federation" Soros is somewhere behind. His mind is still stuck in the Nazi Federation. The Swedish Federation for Lesbian, Gay, Bisexual, Transgender, and Queer Rights, looks like a Swedish organization but let's be honest and call all these organizations with his own language. If he is working for the one-world government with one language, one monetary system, and religion, then let's don't make a fool of ourselves and stop calling these organizations as Swedish, French, American, British and whatsoever and start to call them openly and officially: The Soros Belongings which are governing us.

*****ARREST SOROS***** and ban all his foundations. He should be in jail and named as an international war criminal charged with "crime against humanity."

The 13th tactic: We should establish new unilateral punitive measurements and rules for all kinds of non-profit organizations in a way that claiming a policy, and doing another, becomes completely impossible. There should be governmental watchdog organizations and agents monitoring activities of these organizations carefully and even better a governmental agent inside every nonprofit organization. If the organization has a big name like "fighting for democracy", but is engineering all related organizations to abolish our freedom and set their dictatorship, if it has a big name and canards of equality, but works to push apartheid and racism, if it has a feminist name but fights femininity and spread hate toward men in all these cases there should be ways to investigate.

The 14th tactic: Respect the culture of the host country should be a predominant must. Close the borders unless there are rules that provide total integration of the immigrants into the new culture. Stop taking refugees unless the current refugee crisis is solved. **It's not racist to save our country. This is an ideological war. They call us racist because they can't openly fight our ideology. What would they say if they don't call us racist? That they want to destroy our country?** They can't declare it. Nobody will buy it, so they hang on the trendiest label governing the political climate which is: Hate. Don't fall into it.

Jail the individual who disrespects the flag. It's not freedom of speech. It's an assault. The flag has an identity. If a citizen or an immigrant who doesn't respect the flag of the country of the host, first; he/she has to be fined and pay, second; short time training camps with good programs that teach the real value of the flag would be ideal and if repeated, jail. If a foreigner, revoking the citizenship should be implied if repeated, "out." **There is no reason for anybody to live in a place they don't respect it.** If an American born, then disciplining camps again and so many social preventions that deprive the person of working unless he learns to respect. Elders should teach youngers the value of a nation's flag. They should teach them how many people have died for that flag. The flag is not a piece of tissue.

It's a "symbol" of our history and traditions. A symbol of who we are as a nation and why we do things as we do, because of our ties to our country's history. **Even if we disagree on who is governing the country, we have one thing in common: our country, and hence it's the flag**. Governors come and go, but that soil remains where it is. Respect for the flag should be taught again in schools. Young children should know why, when foreign leaders come to our country, we honor them with saluting their flag and their national anthem. Why flag of the champions' country in the Olympics are honored when they win because we honor their "identity" before their physical win. **Identity is beyond a person's name and surname. It's beyond a birth date. Our name alone doesn't determine who we are. If it would be so, then champions would have been announced just by their name. Nationality is a big portion of our package of identity. Either the nationality we are born into, or the nationality we have chosen to be part of by obtaining its citizenship. The New country is part of the "new you".**

The 14th tactic: Any kind of mask and face-covering whether it is pirate or terrorist-style or religion-inspired should be illegal. No individual should escape the law by doing the wrong and covering it with a mask. Surveillance cameras are made by taxpayers' money and are there for nothing but monitoring non-terrorists.

The 15th tactic: Nobody should be able to vote without documents. Laws and new measurements for voter's identity should be implemented so non- citizens and illegal aliens cannot be able to vote. The right to vote belongs only and only to the citizens of a country. Try to vote in one Arab country and see if they let you, why should they in the first place so, why should we?

The 16th tactic: Defunding any sanctuary city and any college and university who do not respect the law of the land is the main key to put them on their knees and force them to comply. They need the budget, and they should not take the federal government's budget for acting against it.

The 17th tactic: Deporting illegals, extremists, criminals and whoever commits female genital mutilation (FGM), pedophilia, and rape even inside their own homes under any excuse of different laws or beliefs regarding any religion or ideology.

The 18th tactic: If you don't have good schools in your area or district, homeschool your child, reject vaccines, microchips and body scanners.

The 19th tactics: Use science and statistics. Launch an executive order to obtain the criminal statistic, research and report the numbers. Any report which can't be measured is useless. Criminal inmates already in prison and those under warrant should be included in the report. That's the clinical and official way to have the numbers. That's the only way we can strongly declare what percentage of the population made the crimes and to which categories do they belong. Are they immigrants? Illegals? Black, white, Hispanic, what race? What category made most crimes and what type of?

After having the numbers, the next step is to investigate the mindset and beliefs of the criminal category and find out what were the reasons behind them. What were the social, racial or religious factors that caused those crimes and try to find the keys and connections so we will again have new numbers and guidelines which will lead us to the third step that is; working on those factors by effective training. Teachings focused on socio-psychological behavior corrections, self-esteem, encouraging their goodwill, both on inmates and outside the prison in colleges, universities, schools, and by all means of communication for all the population to prevent them from being influenced by such factors ever again. By politicizing everything we can accomplish nothing. **How great would be the change if skilled "coaches and gurus" could be paid to speak in prisons and hold workshops? People can change anytime. No matter how guilty they are.**

The 20th tactic: We have a church in church deception. We have a false church with luxury and power, and a true church of the body of Christ which is weak, poor and attacked all fronts and is required to obey the policies of the great fake church. Real believers in Jesus and people who still fight with the planet perversity are expected to follow the Vatican that urges and encourages the perversion.

To give you one example of this type of "Churchianity" that we are facing now and whose main goal is a war on real believers of the Persona of Jesus.

Nyle Fort, a Christian minister who is an active member of "Black Lives Matter," argued that: *"Under conditions of white supremacist terror,* (!! Terror), *revolutionary violence can be an expression of Christian Love."*

What???

As you see, they just project narratives, and present them as proven facts which are always followed by violent instructions as a solution while trying to justify it through the use of a social value which here is: Christian Love! This is pure insanity. **Putting the word "violence" into Jesus's mouth? These are the people who would crucify Jesus right here today if he would not accept to be a leftist advocate. If Jesus was here and would disapprove Antifa, BLM or climate change religion, they would have found complicated phrases to justify his crucifixion.**

Churches should be disinfected from lies, pedophilia, and perversion and just after that, they should be baptized and become real churches again, they should have the government's support and should receive a tiny portion of the taxpayers' money. They should have workshops for children and scholars somehow as a contribution to the major they are studying. They should be more colorful, vital, modern, happy and receptive to encourage people back to God again. That's what is missed in our modern society. God is removed. Devil worshipers are all in top positions and fight God. Kim Clement prophesized in 2007, 2010, 2011, 2014, 2015, and 2016 for the last time before he passed away, and called Donald Trump as God's agent. The Lord waited until Kim Clement saw Donald Trump's victory then took him away soon after. May he rest in eternal peace.

The 21st tactic: Charities and real philanthropist with the help of the **government should set up organizations which reward "Birth Glory" to the Western families who give birth to at least 4 children.** The same thing that Vladimir Putin is doing in Russia. If not, the Western race is going to decline and soon will be replaced.

The 22nd tactic: President Trump is an outsider. He declared war against the establishment and vowed to "drain the swamp" now the swamp is fighting back. We knew it. We expected it. How could it be easy if the beast is bloody injured? The beast is in total panic and attacks even if there is no substance to its claims. That doesn't matter to them. It doesn't matter what they attack; it just needs to be a continuous attack. The fake media and the Democratic Party act as President Trump has taken office by a Coup and not through winning the election. Trump supporters are not supporting a person for personal reasons. He is not perfect. Nobody is perfect. But he is fighting, and his administration is supporting the idea of fighting the old establishment to take back the control and encouraging all countries to do the same. If each country takes back her identity and national sovereignty, the world will be freed.

My most important message to those of you in the world who hate America because of its interference, imperialism or anything in your mind, know that and be aware, that it was not America, it was the black nobility of Europe, the old establishment of oligarchs and colonizers and the families and individuals we named in this book who run our politicians and officials and brought the Nazi war-criminals to join them, and are so happy on their money throne that has no intention to leave it and get lost. Now if you want to fight them, if you want to beat them out, if you want to revenge all those years of physical and mental invasion, join Trump. Join the 71-year-old outsider who could be so happy and relaxed living the rest of his days with his family in his own made Empire and never needed this pain in his final years. Believe me. No man has been treated as he is being treated. Trump, the criminal without a crime, was never given a chance to carry out his agenda which is our agenda, people's agenda. Instead, he is being crucified and stabbed every single moment after being elected. We should not abandon him for; he did not abandon "we the people."

Those of you from the Middle East who think bombing and killing innocent people means fighting America, you have been fooled. Doing that, you will work for the deep state bombers who killed your children and turned the beautiful Middle East into a burning hell on the earth. Capitalism was not the cause of the corruption but crony capitalism of technocrats set up by oligarchs. The corrupt deep state wants to abolish capitalism too so if you and the deep state are on the same side of the fight, then you are on the wrong side.

I showed you how the establishment beast is sucking our blood for decades. If you are sick of the world we are trapped into today, if you care for your children or humanity's future, if you are a revolutionary who detests what you saw through the entire planet after WW2, Trump's fight is your fight. In fact, his border wall, national sovereignty, America's prosperity, dumping the climate change lie, supporting Brexit and his declaration of war on pedophilia was a direct punch on the beast's face. It was absolutely our fight. It doesn't matter where are you from or which country are you living in. The sovereignty of your country depends on his fight. If he loses, the deep state wins. As long as he keeps the promise, as long as he fights the corruption, any assault on him is an assault on his voters and his supporters all around the world. Whoever doesn't take lessons from history is doomed to repeat the mistakes. There have been other tyrannies during history. Look how they have gone with the wind. So will the deep state.

If you are sick of this, just know the media brainwashing machine has one goal: Enough of Trump. Did you notice what is on front pages each time the media goes in a panic? A big juicy burger, relationship advice, a luxury vacation destination, Chef Ramsey's face (as his face = pleasure of good food), or some "now and then" celebrity albums. Why? Because the old beast needs us to step down from politics and hide behind the stupidity of a normal life. **Supporting Trump in any way possible; is the "Declaration of our Independence from the Deep State" and this is our unplugging from the Matrix.** We can't back off. When the train stops, we cannot just close the curtain and pretend everything is fine.

No, it's not fine, and it's not fixed.

It's still broken.

The train must go, and so do we.

The 23rd tactic: Find others. We don't need to fit into everybody's clichés. Find the others are called insane like us. All those who can say "hey I hear ya."

There are few actors in Hollywood who still didn't sell their soul to the Devil. Denzel Washington is one of them. Here I cite one of Denzel Washington's quotes that I love:

"If I'm going to fall, I want to fall forward."

"You will fail," he said. "Accept it. You will lose. You will embarrass yourself. You will suck at something. I should know. In the acting business, you fail all the time. If you don't fail, you're not even trying. So you got to get out there and give it your all."

The 24th tactic: Conservatism is rising but is not organized at all so we may fail in some of our tries. Each one of us must find a support system that fits our own circumstances. We are forced to walk forward in mud up to our neck. We will not be able to keep our heads above it without a support system, believe me. If it's more work out, if it's meditation, if it's watching a movie, talking to your old uncle, a vacation or just a night out dancing with your friends, just do it to keep your balance. **We have to discharge the pressure in some way because this will be an ongoing fight.** A fight which will be our new way of life so we have to keep the balance and we should be able to fight but do it having fun. That's what I learned from my years of absence in politics and from my frustration. That's what we all need to learn. **When fighting is the only option during a war, we can't cry every day. We can't be angry every day. We can't fear all the time.** People have fought before us, and people will fight after us, so we are not doing something new. We just have to learn what the secret of their fight was.

The secret of the fight is to see it as a condition that may prolong so we can't put our lives on pending.

Sometimes "something" passes through "our" lives, and it ends. Sometimes "we" need to pass through something and "our" lives may end during the long passage, but it is what it is. **We have to "live" "within" our fight**, so we have to deal with it in a way to have fun through the passage. Besides we are not alone. We are too many. We are just the tip of the iceberg, and we will make the history because it's "now or never".

The 25th tactic: Don't fall into traps of separation. Don't care what our previous beliefs were. We have something in common, and that is to end the propaganda. We can work with anybody who has the same goal. **Remember; when there is a tragedy, we don't care about the background of people who are stuck with us in the same situation, we need "Humanity".** The same stands for unplugging ourselves from the global hysteria which we are dealing with.

Become a 'human", not a Republican or a Democrat. Bring your creativity and passion into the fight and have fun.

Fortunately, it is not a bloody civil war yet; it's a war on information. Once we kill the propaganda, it will start to act against itself. **Divide and Rule should never work for us as we are aware of it.** We can't fight with each other. We have to come together. Another trick can be the infiltration of their shills into our communities as conservatives. They may seem passionate about the core then hurt our agenda from within to separate us. Vet everything. Be vigilant. Don't fall for it.

The 26th tactic: There will be no deal with the globalist. **There is no accordance. No agreement. Its only war left for us,** nothing else and the clock will never turn back. Start now. Time is not on our side. Tomorrow may never come. Don't back off. Make them look stupid. The more you make them look stupid, the more resources we will have in our pockets for the next attack. Attack now.

The 27th tactic: And at the end, never fall for "No Mongers". They are even more dangerous than face off enemies. They are people who say yes, there is a deep state, there is propaganda, there is a plan designed by the elites, but Trump is one of them as no outsider is permitted to get inside the cycle. Lie!

Propaganda inside propaganda. They are the "Elite's Twisting Agents" who take us with themselves, show us the light then blindfold our eyes in the middle of the way. The result is a huge disappointment. By disappointing, they freeze any kind of a real fight. They want us hot and cold, hot and cold, and hot and cold again. They misconduct our ability to think rationally. They are the oligarchs' safe boats. Petroleum mixed with water. So why are they awakening people then teach them there is no way out? Because they sell their products, their books, and seminars. Putting you before their platforms like a good obedient kid for hours and making money. Be clever to distinguish the "Twisting Agents."

***

Vote, vote, and vote. We are at war This is actually a virtual WW3. Each human brain is a soldier on the battlefield and the real battlefield today is the internet. Some of the brains are so sharp to see and conduct the others. Act as grass-roots on the internet streets. Do the same thing Alinsky taught them. Fill every street on the internet. We have no excuse not to participate in a "Remote Fight." Age, disease, disability, nothing should stop us, and we have the responsibility toward our children and the generations to come. As we are sitting in our houses, somewhere children are in cages and we can help them with all the tactics we mentioned. Including voting the Democrats out, creating group fights, then local, regional, national and make it international. Create the topic on the internet then organize a march for it in town but be prepared for the lefties' violent attacks. We never start but if they do, let them regret it.

If the fight is the only thing left for us to save our dignity,

then fight it right.

If there is no place to run and find peace and we are

trapped in a war,

then fight it right.

If all they do is to make us stop and flop,

then fight it right.

If they want a fight,

let's give them one

and let's fight it like a war

because that is what is called:

A WAR.

So Upright,

Uptight,

Overexcite and Fight it right!

I fight for you, for our children, for our freedom and for
the world's independence from a tyranny called: New
World Order.

I fight for you...

It is not about selling books,

But leaving footprints.

Ella Cruz   15/07/2017

****

"During times of universal deceit, telling the truth becomes a revolutionary act."

George Orwell

Bibliography

1 -Paper resources:

Birmingham, S. 2016, *Real Lace*, NY: Lyons Press; Reprint edition

Bowart, W. H. 1978, *Operation Mind Control*, NY: Dell Publishing, p. 216

(Previous editions of this book were bought up probably by CIA and completely vanished. The last edition was in 2005 before the author, died in 2007. You may find used old versions at $250 price.)

Brzezinski, Z. 1997, *The Grand Chessboard*, Basic Books; 1 edition

Burnside, P. S. 2000, *El Escape de Hitler*, Buenos Aires: Planeta

Byington, J. 2012, *Twenty-Two Faces,* Tate Publishing

Cahill, K. 2010, *Who Owns The World*, Grand Central Publishing; 1 edition

Cannon, M. 1994, *Mind Control and the American Government, Prevailing Winds Research*; p 19

Cavendish, R. 1970, *Man, Myth,and Magic: An Illustrated Encyclopedia of the Supernatural*(24-Vol. Set), Marshall Cavendish Corp.; 1st edition, p. 19

Chaitkin, A. 1993, *Franklin Witnesses Implicate FBI and U.S. Elites in Torture and Murder of Children*, The New Federalist Magazine

Condon, R. 1959 *The Manchurian Candidate*, NY: Jove Books

Cooper, J. M. Jr. 2011, *Woodrow Wilson: A Biography*, Vintage

Cuskie, P. 1974,*The Real CIA—The Rockefellers' Fascist Establishment, and M. Minnicino, "Low-Intensity Operations": The Reesian Theory of War*,

The Campaigner Magazine by National Caucus of Labor Committee; April edition

DeCamp, J. 1992, *The Franklin Cover-Up, Child Abuse, Satanism and Murder in Nebraska*, AWT Inc.

Freddoso, D. 2008, *The Case Against Barack Obama, The Unlikely Rise and Unexamined Agenda of the Media's Favorite Candidate*, Regnery Publishing; First Edition

Fulton, J. D. 2014, *Washington In the Lap of Rome*, CreateSpace Independent Publishing Platform

Griffin, D. 2009, *Osama Bin Laden: Dead or Alive?* Olive Branch Press

Hammer, R. 1982, *The Vatican Connection*, Henry Holt & Co; 1st edition

Hammond, C. 1992: **The Greenbaum Speech;** *Mark Phillips and Cathy O'Brien; Project Monarch Programming Definitions, Greenbaum Speech,*

Virginia,at the Fourth Annual Eastern Regional Conference on Abuse and Multiple Personality Disorder

Horowitz, D. 2003, *Uncivil Wars: The Controversy over Reparations for Slavery*, Encounter Books; Revised edition

Hunt, L. 1985, *U.S. Coverup of Nazi Scientists*, Bulletin of the Atomic Scientists Journal; Vol. 41 Issue 4, p164.

Hunt, L. 1991, *Secret Agenda: The United States Government, Nazi Scientists, and Project Paperclip 1945 to 1990*, St Martin's Press - Thomas Dunne Books; 1st edition

Hunter, E. 1951, *Brain-Washing in Red China. The Calculated Destruction of Men's Minds*, NY: Vanguard Press

Jacobs, A. 2014, *Operation Paperclip, the Secret Intelligence Program that Brought Nazi Scientists to America*, NY: Little Brown and Company, pg. 455

Jensen-Stevenson, M. and Stevenson, W. 1990, *Kiss the Boys Goodbye*, Penguin

Koehler, H. 1940, *Inside The Gestapo: Hitler's Shadow Over the World,* Progressive Press

King, M. S. 2015, *Killing America: A 100 Year Murder: 40 Historical Wounds Bill O'Reilly Didn't Write About*, CreateSpace Independent Publishing Platform (This book is a great read. Highly recommended)

King, M. S. 2017, *Climate Bogeyman: The Criminal Insanity of the Global Warming / Climate Change Hoax*, CreateSpace Independent Publishing Platform

Kruger, H. 2000, *The Great Heroin Coup, Drug's, Intelligence & International Fascism*, Black Rose Books Ltd

Kwitny, J. 1987, *The Crimes of Patriots – A True Tale of Dope. Dirty Money, and the CIA*, W. W. Norton & Company

Lagnado, L. M. 1991,*Dr. Josef Mengele and the Untold Story of the Twins of Auschwitz*, Morrow

Lasby, C. 1975, *Operation Paperclip*; Athenaeum

Lee, M. A. and, Shlain, B. 1994: *Acid Dreams: The CIA, LSD and the Sixties Rebellion*, NY: Grove Weidenfeld

Lifton, R. J. 1957, *Thought Reform of Chinese Intellectuals; A Psychiatric Evaluation*; Journal of Social Issues: 3, 5-20

Linklater, M. and Hilton, I. and Ascherson, N. 1985, *The Nazi Legacy*, Henry Holt & Co; 1st American edition

Litchfield, M. and Javna, J. 1992, *It's a conspiracy! The National Insecurity Council*; (U.S.), Earth Works Group

Manhattan, A. 1983, *The Vatican Billions; Two thousand years of wealth accumulation*, Chick Pub; New edition

Marks, J. 1979, *The Search For The Manchurian Candidate*; W. W. Norton & Company Revised ed. edition (August 17, 1991), pp. 60-61

Miller, M. 1974, *Plain Speaking: An Oral Biography of Harry S. Truman*, NY: Berkley

O'Brien, C. and Phillips, M. 1995, *Trance Formation of America*, Reality Marketing Inc.; Revised edition (August 8, 2005)

Pizzo, S. and Fricker, M. and Muolo, P. 1989, *Inside Job – The Looting of America's S&L*, McGraw-Hill; First Edition first Printing edition

Posner, G. L., and Ware, J. 1987, Mengele – *The Complete Story*, W. W. Norton & Company

Rappoport, J. 1995, *CIA Experiments with Mind Control on Children*, Perceptions Magazine; September/October: p. 56

Reisman, J. 1990, *Kinsey, Sex, and Fraud: The Indoctrination of a People*, LA: Huntington House

Reisman, J. 1991 *Soft Porn" Plays Hardball: Its Tragic Effects on Women, Children and the Family*, LA: Huntington House; Lafayette

Reisman, J. 2010, *Sexual Sabotage: How One Mad Scientist Unleashed a Plague of Corruption and Contagion on America*, WND Books; 1 edition

Reisman, J. 2003, Kinsey: **Crimes & Consequences: The Red Queen and the Grand Scheme. The Institute for Media Education; Crestwood**, KY Publisher: Inst for Media Education; 3rd Revised & Expanded edition

Rosenbaum, D.E. *1996, First Draft Overview of Investigation of the Group, 1983-1993,* Paranoia Magazine: The Conspiracy Reader; Vol. 4, No. 3, Issue 14.

Ross, C. A., and Richardson, M. D., 2000, *BLUEBIRD: Deliberate Creation of Multiple Personality by Psychiatrists,* Texas: Manitou

Simpson, CH. 1989, Blowback, *America's Recruitment of Nazis and its Effects o-n the Cold War,* Collier Books - Macmillan; 1st edition

Sklar, D. 1977, *Gods and Beasts – The Nazi's and the Occult,* T. Y. Crowell (1654)

Springmeier, F. 1996,*The Illuminati Formula Used To Create an Undetectable Total Mind Controlled Slave,* Springmeier & Wheeler

Taylor, B. 1999, *Thanks for the Memories…The Truth Has Set Me Free! The Memoirs of Bob Hope's and*

Henry Kissinger's Mind-Controlled Slave, Brice Taylor Trust; 2nd Print edition

Thomas, G. 1990, *Journey into Madness*, 1990, Mass Market

U.S. Senate: **Final Report of the Select Committee to Study Governmental Operations**, April 1976, p. 390 - 391 (On MKUltra and Nazi scientists. Link under electronic resources.)

Vennari, J. 1999, *The Permanent Instruction of the Alta Vendita,* TAN Books ,and Publishers

Williams, G. and Dunstan, S. 2013, *Grey Wolf;The Escape of Adolf Hitler,* NY: Sterling Publishing Inc.

White, C. and Lantz, B. 1989, *Satan's Helpers: Nazi Doctors in America; How Nazi doctors created a counterculture in America*, EIR Executive Intelligence Review-Journal; Volume 16: Number 40, October 6, 1989

Yallop, D. A. 1984, *In **God's Name, An Investigation into the Murder of Pope John Paul I***, NYC: Bantam Books

2- Electronic Resources:

Aaron Russo, the famous award winner filmmaker, who became a freedom fighter, arranged an interview with ***Nicholas Rockefeller***, 11 months before 9/11 and this is what he recounts; Watch min 9

https://www.youtube.com/watch?v=7gwcQjDhZtI

Aaron Russo's Documentary before his death, ***"America Freedom To Fascism"*** Dir cut.

https://www.youtube.com/watch?v=ZKeaw7HPG04

Bill Gates: ***Make vaccine to reduce the population***

https://www.youtube.com/watch?v=FYcHynxe9GQ

https://www.youtube.com/watch?v=Gc16H3uHKOA

Congress, Testimony; **Claudia Mullin**, Victim of MKUtra

https://www.youtube.com/watch?time_continue=16&v=het0FIAtH3M

https://www.youtube.com/watch?v=iflBkRlpRv0&feature=related

Congress, Testimony; **Christina Nicola**, Victim of MKUltra

https://www.youtube.com/watch?v=eXDASDDrDkM

Congress, Testimony;**Cathy O'Brien**, Victim of MKUltra

https://www.youtube.com/watch?v=FvEBmEo4IA0

David Horowitz; Discover the network

http://discoverthenetworks.org/

Edward Griffin, 1984, Interview with ex- KGB brainwashing agent; **Yuri Bezmenov**

https://www.youtube.com/watch?v=bX3EZCVj2XA

Hidden No Longer: Genocide in Canada, Past and Present - by Kevin D. Annett, M.A., M.Div.

https://www.scribd.com/doc/86619003/Hidden-No-Longer-Genocide-in-Canada-Past-and-Present-by-Kevin-D-Annett-M-A-M-Div

International Tribunal of Crimes into Church and the State of Brussels, Testimony; **Toos Nijenhuis**, on child sacrifice in Holland

https://www.youtube.com/watch?v=-A1o1Egi20c

Interview for**Byington,**the author of, "Twenty Two faces" with **Jenny Hill** from Utah, survivor of human sacrifice

https://www.youtube.com/watch?v=F626Lsrdwg4

Joel Van der Reijden, 2007, Beyond the Dutroux Affair; The reality of protected child abuse and snuff networks *https://isgp-studies.com/belgian-x-dossiers-of-the-dutroux-affair*

Judy Byington's website

https://ritualabuse.us

Kyoto Protocol, 1997

http://unfccc.int/kyoto_protocol/items/2830.php

UK Police and testimony of **Gabriel Dearman**9 years old

https://www.youtube.com/watch?v=9nRdzn3tC7Y

UK Police and testimony of **Alisia Dearman** 10 years old

https://www.youtube.com/watch?v=2XCU9t2PTpk

Testimony of an **ex-high priest of a satanic cult**

https://www.youtube.com/watch?v=WniRJ2h15Kk

Testimony of a *"baby breeder"* survivor

https://www.youtube.com/watch?v=pWy3TmpTe0A

U.S Senateon MKUltra Mind Control Program

https://www.intelligence.senate.gov/sites/default/files/94
755_I.pdf

Ted Turner ", *A total world population of 250-300
million people, a 95% decline from present levels, would
be ideal.*"

https://www.youtube.com/watch?v=jjIMoaUBHB0

Senator Tom DeLay: Interview for Newsmax, **Justice
Dept. Wants to Legalize 12 'Perversions**

https://www.youtube.com/watch?v=HUhoTzJ5Rvc

https://www.newsmax.com/Newsmax-Tv/Tom-DeLay-
Justice-Department-perversions/2015/06/30/id/652929/

723

Made in the USA
Middletown, DE
05 January 2021